Images of Anarchy

Hobbes's concept of the natural condition of mankind became an inescapable point of reference for subsequent political thought, shaping the theories of emulators and critics alike, and has had a profound impact on our understanding of human nature, anarchy, and international relations. Yet, despite Hobbes's insistence on precision, the state of nature is an elusive concept. Has it ever existed and, if so, for whom? Hobbes offered several answers to these questions, which taken together reveal a consistent strategy aimed at providing his readers with a possible, probable, and memorable account of the consequences of disobedience. This book examines the development of this powerful image throughout Hobbes's works and traces its origins in his sources of inspiration. The resulting trajectory of the state of nature illuminates the ways in which Hobbes employed a rhetoric of science and a science of rhetoric in his relentless pursuit of peace.

Ioannis D. Evrigenis is Associate Professor of Political Science, with a secondary appointment in Classics, at Tufts University, where he directs the Bodin Project. He is the author of *Fear of Enemies and Collective Action*, which received the Delba Winthrop Award for Excellence in Political Science, and coeditor of Herder's *Another Philosophy of History and Selected Political Writings*.

VAIN GLORY ... is exemplified in the fable of the fly sitting on the axletree, and saying to himself, What a dust do I raise!
– Hobbes, *The Elements of Law*

To Chrysoula

Images of Anarchy

The Rhetoric and Science in Hobbes's State of Nature

IOANNIS D. EVRIGENIS

Tufts University

CAMBRIDGE
UNIVERSITY PRESS

CAMBRIDGE
UNIVERSITY PRESS

32 Avenue of the Americas, New York, NY 10013-2473, USA

Cambridge University Press is part of the University of Cambridge.

It furthers the University's mission by disseminating knowledge in the pursuit of
education, learning, and research at the highest international levels of excellence.

www.cambridge.org
Information on this title: www.cambridge.org/9780521513722

First published 2014

Printed in the United States of America

A catalog record for this publication is available from the British Library.

Library of Congress Cataloging in Publication data
Evrigenis, Ioannis D., 1971–
Images of anarchy : the rhetoric and science in Hobbes's state of
nature / Ioannis D. Evrigenis.
pages cm
Includes bibliographical references and index.
ISBN 978-0-521-51372-2 (hardback)
1. Hobbes, Thomas, 1588–1679. 2. Natural law. 3. Fall of man.
4. Nature and civilization. I. Title.
JC153.H66E87 2014
320.1–dc23 2014002044

ISBN 978-0-521-51372-2 Hardback

Contents

Acknowledgments

During the composition of this book, I have had the good fortune to have been surrounded by individuals and institutions that have encouraged and supported me in more ways than I can list. I am humbled by their attention and grateful for the opportunity to acknowledge their help and thank them.

Research of this kind relies heavily on libraries and archives, so it is my pleasure to acknowledge the assistance I have received over the years from the staff at the Tisch Library at Tufts – in particular, Martha Kellehan and Chris Barbour – and the staff of the Huntington Library; the staff of the rare books reading room at the British Library; the staff of the King's College Library, Cambridge; and the staff of the Houghton Library at Harvard University. Susan Halpert at Houghton, John Minichiello and Leslie Tobias-Olsen at the John Carter Brown Library at Brown, Anna Cook at the King's College Library, and Adrian James at the Society of Antiquaries of London helped me obtain some of the images contained herein and the permissions to use them. I am very grateful to His Grace the Duke of Devonshire and the Chatsworth House Trust for granting me access to the Hobbes manuscripts in their archives, and to James Towe for his valuable help there.

A Franklin Research Grant from the American Philosophical Society and a summer stipend from the National Endowment for the Humanities facilitated the initial research for this book. A Colcord grant from the Department of Political Science at Tufts University, arranged by Rob Devigne, funded a workshop that allowed me to complete it. At that workshop, Kinch Hoekstra, Cary Nederman, Mark Somos, and Tom Sorell provided invaluable feedback that helped me improve the argument beyond measure. In between, I was privileged to spend the 2008–09 academic year as a Laurance S. Rockefeller Visiting Fellow at Princeton's University Center for Human Values. I am grateful to Stephen Macedo and the center's faculty and staff for their hospitality, and to the many individuals who discussed Hobbes's method and the state of nature with me during my stay. I was also fortunate to be part of a

National Endowment for the Humanities Summer Institute entitled "English Encounters with the Americas, 1550–1610," superbly orchestrated by Mary Fuller at the Massachusetts Institute of Technology, in 2011. During the 2011–12 academic year, I used the time provided by a fellowship from the Faculty Research Awards Committee and the Dean of Arts and Sciences at Tufts University to put together the main body of the book.

I presented parts of the argument at Princeton University; the New School for Social Research political theory seminar; the Saint Andrews Reformation Studies Institute seminar; as well as the New England and Southern Political Science Association meetings; the "Wrestling with Machiavelli" conference held in Cambridge, Massachusetts; a conference on absolutism, monarchism, and despotism organized by Cesare Cuttica at the University of Sussex; the European Association for Biblical Studies meeting; a conference on the passions and subjectivity in Early Modern culture organized by Freya Sierhuis at the Center for Advanced Studies of the Ludwig-Maximilians-Universität München; and the European Early American Studies Association conference in Bayreuth. The questions and comments I received on every one of those occasions pushed me to think about ways to improve the argument, so I am grateful to those who raised them.

An earlier version of part of Chapter 1 appeared in "Hobbes's Thucydides," in "Thucydides and Civil War," ed. Gregory M. Reichberg and Henrik Syse, special issue, *Journal of Military Ethics* 5, no. 4 (2006): 303–16, and is reproduced here by permission of Taylor and Francis. A section of Chapter 3 was published in "'Not Truth but Image Maketh Passion': Hobbes on Instigation and Appeasing," in *Passions and Subjectivity in Early Modern Culture*, edited by Brian Cummings and Freya Sierhuis (Farnham: Ashgate, 2013), 165–80.

Beyond the confines of conferences and seminars, David Art, Marie-Claire Beaulieu, Hans Blom, Janet Coleman, Alan Cromartie, Kevin Dunn, Eric Eben, Mary Fuller, Angus Gowland, Anthony Grafton, Felicity Green, Kelly Greenhill, Michael Hawley, Bruce Hitchner, Seth Holm, the late Istvan Hont, Victoria Kahn, Marketa Klicova, Petter Korkman, Gerald V. Lalonde, Scott Lyons, Daniel Margócsy, John McCormick, Russ Muirhead, Cary Nederman, Amit Paz, Daniel Pellerin, Philip Pettit, Edward Phillips, Paul Rahe, Rahul Sagar, Paul E. Sigmund, Johann Sommerville, Tom Sorell, Vickie Sullivan, Vasileios Syros, Richard Tuck, Catherine Wilson, and the late Robert Wokler assisted me by discussing the argument with me, reading drafts, answering my questions, or pointing me to useful sources. I am grateful to them, as well as to my editor, Lew Bateman, and to Shaun Vigil at Cambridge University Press, for their eagerness to help me and their patience. I must single out Kinch Hoekstra, who fielded countless questions with exemplary good humor and saved me from several blunders. Once again, Mark Somos read and commented on successive drafts, discussed every conceivable aspect of the argument with me, and made suggestions that have improved the book vastly. I am indebted to him for his help and grateful for his friendship.

In a variety of ways, Socrates Antsos, Vangelis Himonides, Theodoros N. Ikonomou, Dimitris Kastritsis, Yianos Kontopoulos, Antonis Kouidis, Alex Vratskides, and Steryios Yannoulis have proven to be the kinds of friends of whom one dare only dream. I owe the most to Tra Evrigenis. Skillfully assisted by Georgia, Olive, Daphne, and Thomas, she has remained an unceasing source of inspiration, encouragement, and support.

Over the years, I have accumulated an incalculable debt to Chrysoula Evrigenis. I dedicate this book to her as a very small token of my gratitude.

[T]he narration itself doth secretly instruct the reader, and more effectually than can possibly be done by precept.
  – Hobbes, "Of the Life and History of Thucydides"

Abbreviations

Unless otherwise indicated, references to Hobbes's works are to the following editions:

The Correspondence of Thomas Hobbes	Noel Malcolm, ed., *The Correspondence of Thomas Hobbes*, 2 volumes (Oxford: The Clarendon Press, 1994).
De Cive	Thomas Hobbes, *De Cive, The Latin Version*, edited by Howard Warrender (Oxford: The Clarendon Press, 1983). I quote mainly from Warrender's edition of the English, though on occasion I have opted for Silverthorne's translation or provided my own.
The Elements of Law	Thomas Hobbes, *The Elements of Law, Natural and Politic*, edited by Ferdinand Tönnies, Second edition, with an introduction by M. M. Goldsmith (London: Frank Cass and Co., 1969).
EW	Thomas Hobbes, *The English Works of Thomas Hobbes*, edited by William Molesworth, 11 volumes (London: John Bohn, 1839–45).
Leviathan	Thomas Hobbes, *Leviathan, or the Matter, Forme, and Power of a Commonwealth Ecclesiasticall and Civill* (London: printed for Andrew Crooke, 1651).
OL	Thomas Hobbes, *Thomæ Hobbes Malmesburiensis Opera Philosophica quæ Latine Scripsit Omnia in Unum Corpus Nunc Primum Collecta*, edited by William Molesworth, 5 volumes (London: John Bohn, 1839–45).

Prologue

No part of Hobbes's legacy is as well known as his account of the natural condition of mankind – his "state of nature." Hobbes did not coin the term. Christians had known it for centuries as one of the designations for the condition of man in the opening chapters of Genesis, sometimes referring to the age before the Fall, but occasionally assigned to antediluvian human beings as well.[1] Before them, Greeks and Romans had used one or another variant of it to describe the condition of men prior to the establishment of societies that formed the starting point of their anthropologies. The political undercurrents in these uses are evident, and others had explored them before Hobbes. As the young Hobbes went about the business of the Cavendishes, for instance, Grotius described the state of nature, in the context of a discussion of succession, as a condition in which there was no jurisdiction.[2] Yet, as a result of what Hobbes did with this term between 1640 and 1651, the state of nature became not simply a mandatory point of reference for emulators and critics alike, but also an element of basic political calculus familiar far beyond the confines of philosophical debates regarding obedience. Many of those to whom the details of the social contract and the minutiae of the law of nature mean nothing nevertheless recall having come across the description of a life that is "solitary, poore, nasty, brutish, and short."

The stark contrast between the misery that accompanies anarchy and the peace that comes from government, however imperfect, seems enough to explain the appeal of the image of the state of nature. Here is a powerful and succinct account of a condition sufficiently undesirable to cause one to reconsider one's plans for rebellion. Hobbes's description of the state of

---

[1] See, e.g., William of Ockham, *Dialogue*, III.ii.III.6; cf. Offler, "The Three Modes of Natural Law in Ockham."

[2] Grotius, *De Jure Belli ac Pacis*, II.vii.xxvii. This book, along with other works of Grotius's, was available in the Hardwick library, according to a catalog in Hobbes's hand, dating from the late 1620s (Devonshire Mss., Chatsworth HS/E/1A).

nature, however, is puzzling. If it is the most memorable element of his political thought, it is also the one that violates, in the most blatant ways, the principles that he considered necessary for civil philosophy. Hobbes locates the source of conflict in disagreement, and declares his intention to begin from the right foundations. His works are thus riddled with definitions of everything from the most mundane details of human nature and behavior to the fundamentals of the body politic. Yet, despite his insistence on the need for precision, he composed a different account of the state of nature in each of his several political treatises. To make matters more frustrating, within the confines of any single treatise, he describes the state of nature in ways that confuse, rather than clarify.

A reasonable reader might wonder whether such a condition existed and, if so, where, when, and for whom. Alas, Hobbes's answers range from the Amazons, Cacus, and Polyphemus, to the Indians and the ancient Germans; include thought experiments in which one is invited to consider men as though they had sprung from the earth fully formed, like mushrooms; suggest that the state of nature is an inference made from the passions; and liken it to civil war and, with an important qualification, to the relations between sovereigns. Hobbes's explicit claims regarding the state of nature, coupled with the numerous associations that the use of this term and its imagery would have evoked in the minds of his readers, make for an image so hard to pin down as to sometimes defy even that simple juxtaposition with civil society. It would seem that the other side of that contrast promises a condition of complete peace, but can one ever escape this manifold state of nature completely?

Although these questions are by no means confined to the state of nature, the evolution of that concept exemplifies the difficulties involved in making sense of Hobbes's several, unusually rich, and challenging political treatises, and provides a unique vantage point from which to address the issues surrounding the interpretation of Hobbes's works. Over the years, commentators have struggled to reconcile those treatises with one another and to situate Hobbes both in his time and in the traditions that shaped him and his interlocutors. To do so, they have invoked paradigm shifts, life-changing discoveries, political and legal disputes, and even unusual work habits. These explanations contain a certain degree of truth, but for the most part, the interpretations that they have yielded are unsatisfactory, either because they do not accord with Hobbes's own assessment of what he was up to, or because they emphasize only certain aspects of his thought or disregard key evidence.

In addition to several versions of a comprehensive political treatise, Hobbes also left us several assessments of his own work. These are often dismissed as self-serving or revisionist, yet Hobbes was remarkably consistent in those assessments, and insisted that he was devoted to persuading his readers of the benefits of peace. We also have substantial evidence which suggests that Hobbes disseminated drafts of his work to various readers and was very much interested in revising them according to their feedback. This method is in keeping with Hobbes's avowed aim, and returns the focus of an inquiry into the meaning of his political thought where it belongs: on the role of persuasion toward peace. There is no better prism for such an inquiry than Hobbes's most effective, elusive, and unlikely image: the state of nature.

Although he praised modesty as the utmost political virtue, Thomas Hobbes was a man with immodest goals. He proclaimed civil philosophy no older than his book *De Cive*, and saw himself as engaged in a persistent attempt to change the political behavior of those around him, so as to put an end to conflict. In the Epistle Dedicatory of his earliest political treatise, for instance, Hobbes declares, "it would be an incomparable benefit to commonwealth, if *every man* held the opinions concerning law and policy here delivered."[3] In *De Cive*, he expresses the hope that he will convince readers to bear a certain amount of inconvenience in their private affairs, "*because humane affairs cannot possibly be without some*," by persuading them to consider their best interests for themselves, rather than allowing "*ambitious men through the streames of your blood to wade to their owne power*."[4] In *Leviathan*, Hobbes addresses the reader only rarely and usually indirectly, but he opens the book by announcing that he has done most of the work, leaving the reader the simple task of comparing Hobbes's findings to himself and his own experience.[5] In the main body of that treatise, Hobbes urges the sovereign who has been persuaded by his teaching to adopt it and spread it to his subjects.[6] A handful of years after the publication of *Leviathan*, he judged that his book had "framed the minds of a thousand gentlemen to a conscientious obedience to present government, which otherwise would have wavered in that point."[7]

It is not uncommon for a writer to think that everyone else who has written on his subject matter was wrong, and that he has uncovered the truth where others have failed. Even so, Hobbes's claim was unusually immodest. Proposing to guide not only one's sophisticated interlocutors, but everyone, to the same conclusion is an extraordinarily tall order, and doing so by inviting

---

[3] *The Elements of Law*, xvi, emphasis added.
[4] *De Cive*, Pref., § 20.
[5] *Leviathan*, Introduction: 2.
[6] *Leviathan*, Review and Conclusion: 395; cf. XXX: 179; *EW*, VII: 335. In his prose autobiography, Hobbes describes *Leviathan* as a work that, he hoped, would be acceptable to his fellow countrymen (*OL*, I: xvi).
[7] *Six Lessons to the Professors of the Mathematics* (*EW*, VII: 335–36). Cf. *The Elements of Law*, Ep. Ded.; I.1.1; *De Cive*, Ep. Ded., §§ 4–10; *Leviathan*, XXXI: 193. Hobbes's intention was not lost on his contemporaries (see, for example, Ward 1654: 51–61). On Hobbes's attempt to persuade his readers, see Farr, "Atomes of Scripture," esp. 184–88.

readers to participate in the process, a risky proposition. Yet, this is precisely what Hobbes promised to do in presenting his successive treatises on politics, and this is why he insisted that his method amounted to a civil science.[8]

It is widely believed that the model for this science was geometry. The founding myth behind this belief is a famous anecdote from Aubrey's brief life of Hobbes. It tells of a moment, during a trip to the continent, when Hobbes "discovered" Euclid:

> He was (vide his life) 40 yeares old before he looked on geometry; which happened accidentally. Being in a gentleman's library in ..., Euclid's Elements lay open, and 'twas the 47 El. libri I. He read the proposition. "By G –," sayd he, "this is impossible!" So he reads the demonstration of it, which referred him back to such a proposition; which proposition he read. That referred him back to another, which he also read. Et sic deinceps, that at last he was demonstratively convinced of that trueth. This made him in love with geometry.[9]

This episode has been given a pivotal role in attempts to make sense of Hobbes's thought, which presents some singular challenges, as it is rare for a theorist of his stature to have left us with five attempts at a comprehensive political theory, four of which were composed and circulated over a little more than eleven years. The first of these came in 1640, when he wrote a two-part treatise in English, entitled "The Elements of Law, Natural and Politic" and distributed it to a few friends and acquaintances.[10] Two years later, while in exile, in Paris, he printed a Latin treatise entitled *Elementorum Philosophiæ Sectio Tertia De Cive*, which also circulated privately. In 1647, Elzevir published a revised version of that treatise, this time entitled *Elementa Philosophica De Cive*, and bearing some important additions. These works were followed by the English *Leviathan*, in 1651, which was in turn published in a Latin translation, with certain significant changes, in 1668.

---

[8] *Leviathan*, XVIII: 94, although it should be noted that Hobbes usually refers to "civil philosophy." See, for example, Hobbes's repeated invitations to the reader to consider his contemporaries' misunderstanding of *nosce teipsum* and correct it (*EL*, I.5.14; *Leviathan*, Introduction: 2). In *De Cive*, Hobbes notes that one who wishes to introduce a sound doctrine should begin with the Universities [ab Academiis], whence young men "imbued with its foundations, can instruct the common people in private and in public." Such instruction, argues Hobbes, would allow men to "entertain true doctrines suitable to their own understandings, and the nature of things" (XIII.9).

[9] Aubrey, '*Brief Lives*,' I: 332. According to Malcolm, "Aubrey's manuscript gives the name of the city as '... a'" (*Aspects of Hobbes*, 9, note 34), which suggests that the incident took place in Geneva. Cf. *The Correspondence of Thomas Hobbes*, I: 10, n. 23. In his own account of this incident, Hobbes also notes that he was struck less by the theorems themselves and more by Euclid's method of reasoning. He writes of his trip to France and Switzerland: "In peregrinatione illa inspicere coepit in elementa Euclidis; et delectatus methodo illius non tam ob theoremata illa quam ob artem rationandi diligentissime perlegit" (*T. Hobbes Malmesburiensis Vita, OL*, I: xiv).

[10] Three copies of this work survive at Chatsworth (Devonshire Mss., Chatsworth HS/A/2A; HS/A/2B; HS/A/2C), and four in the British Library (Egerton 2005; Harl. 1325; Harl. 4235; Harl. 4236), which also has a copy of the first thirteen chapters of the first part, "Humane nature" (Harl. 6858).

This unusually rich set of primary sources has given rise to certain well-entrenched orthodoxies that enjoy widespread support despite obvious evidentiary problems. In one way or another, these revolve around Hobbes's Euclidean moment. Two are old and venerable, because they claim their origins in Hobbes's writings. According to the first of these, Hobbes was a rabid anti-Aristotelian whose conversion to science provided him with new means to challenge the authority of the schools.[11] The second holds that he believed it possible to construct a civil science, the truth of which would be evident to reasonable individuals in the same way that the truth of geometrical theorems is.[12] More recent ones consider Hobbes a humanist who, once converted to science, pit his civil philosophy against rhetoric and tried to base it exclusively on reason, only to discover eventually that the complete separation of reason and eloquence is not possible.[13] According to this last story, *The Elements of Law* and *De Cive* belong to Hobbes's "scientific" phase, and *Leviathan* marks his begrudging acceptance of the fact that reason unaided by "powerfull Eloquence" will not suffice.[14] On the basis of these views, it is not unusual to see Hobbes's intellectual development described as a series of "turns," the most important of which was from humanism to science, the very turn that is encapsulated in Hobbes's Euclidean moment.[15] None of these stories is unfounded. Indeed, they rest on apparently strong evidence, some of it from Hobbes's works and some from his biography.

[11] See, for example, *Leviathan*, XII: 59; XV: 76–77; XVII: 86; cf. Aubrey, 'Brief Lives,' I: 357; Harwood's introduction to *A Briefe of the Art of Rhetorique*, 11; Robertson, *Hobbes*, 9; Strauss, *The Political Philosophy of Hobbes*, 35; Peters, *Hobbes*, 16; Leijenhorst, *The Mechanisation of Aristotelianism*, 1–4, 219–22; Leijenhorst, "Insignificant Speech"; Sorell, "Hobbes and Aristotle"; Sorell, "Hobbes's UnAristotelian Political Rhetoric."

[12] See, for example, *The Elements of Law*, Ep. Ded.; *De Cive*, Ep. Ded. and Pref.; *Leviathan*, Introduction. Cf. Goldsmith, *Hobbes's Science of Politics*. According to Skinner, "Hobbes's conception of civil science in *The Elements of Law* and *De Cive* is founded on the belief that scientific reasoning possesses an inherent power to persuade us of the truths it finds out" (*Reason and Rhetoric in the Philosophy of Hobbes*, 426).

[13] Compare, in particular, *The Elements of Law*, Ep. Ded. with *Leviathan*, A Review and Conclusion. The broad consensus that Hobbes was a humanist conceals the considerable disagreement about what that means. See, for example, Reik, *The Golden Lands of Thomas Hobbes*, 25–34; Tuck, *Hobbes*, 1–11; Skinner, *Reason and Rhetoric in the Philosophy of Hobbes*, Chapter 6; Martinich, *Hobbes: A Biography*, the title of Chapter 3. Strauss also uses the term (*The Political Philosophy of Hobbes*, 44), but with an important qualification that we will discuss in Chapter 2. On the shift from outright hostility to rhetoric toward a more conciliatory position, see Johnston, *The Rhetoric of Leviathan*; Martinich, *Hobbes: A Biography*, 97. Skinner claims that *Leviathan* "reflects a remarkable change of mind on Hobbes's part about the proper relations between *ratio* and *oratio*" (*Reason and Rhetoric in the Philosophy of Hobbes*, 334).

[14] *Leviathan*, A Review and Conclusion: 389. See, for example, Skinner, *Reason and Rhetoric in the Philosophy of Hobbes*.

[15] However, not everyone accepts the separation of the two. Tuck, for instance, sees scientific pursuits as part and parcel of humanism (*Hobbes*, 12–13; *Philosophy and Government*, 283–84).

Faced with this body of work, and erring on the side of context, certain commentators have challenged the general notion that anything like
Hobbes's "political theory" could exist. If authors respond to their historical
settings, then closer attention to those settings should yield greater detail
about the stimuli and motives behind the composition of any particular text.
This closer focus seems especially apt in the case of Hobbes since it provides
a prima facie explanation for his many variations on the theme of civil philosophy; it must be that the differences between his political works are the
result of Hobbes's response to changing circumstances, and the period that
encompasses these works was sufficiently eventful to justify the publication of several different treatises in a relatively short period of time. Thus,
beyond the obvious differences between them – such as their titles, size, and
scope – *The Elements of Law*, *De Cive*, and *Leviathan* must also be different
works insofar as they were occasioned by different motives, rendering the
search for a consistent Hobbes tantamount to a quest for the Holy Grail.[16]

Yet, despite having been adopted enthusiastically by contextualist historians of political thought, the view that Hobbes's intellectual development
consisted of a series of turns had a very different point of departure. Its most
forceful and influential proponent, Strauss, argued first that Hobbes's moral
attitude constituted a break with tradition, in particular with Aristotelianism,
and second, that it predated his turn to science, which only served as window
dressing for that moral attitude in Hobbes's subsequent political treatises.[17]
Strauss's account also made the earliest case for the significance of rhetoric in
Hobbes's thought, an argument that has also become central to some of the
more influential recent interpretations.[18] Thus, interestingly, those commentators who see Hobbes as largely consistent and those who see the search for
consistency as quixotic have come to share a lot of common ground.[19]

That there are important differences on the way from the *Elements* to
the Latin *Leviathan* is indisputable. The question is, what do those differences say about Hobbes's aims and method? Some of the answers offered
by the aforementioned interpretations are unsatisfactory. For instance, interested readers are asked to believe that Hobbes went through a phase during which he thought it possible to persuade others without recourse to
rhetoric. Or that his admiration for geometry was such that he thought it
possible to simply transfer its methods to politics. If one were to object that

---

[16] The metaphor is Baumgold's ("UnParadoxical Hobbes," 689); cf. McNeilly, "Egoism in
Hobbes." The manifesto of this approach is Skinner, "Meaning and Understanding in the
History of Ideas."

[17] See Strauss, *The Political Philosophy of Hobbes*, but cf. Oakeshott, *Hobbes on Civil
Association*, 141–58.

[18] The most notable examples here are Johnston, *The Rhetoric of Leviathan* and Skinner,
Reason and Rhetoric in the Philosophy of Hobbes.

[19] Dienstag captures Skinner's gradual shift toward Strauss nicely in his review of *Hobbes and
Republican Liberty* ("Man of Peace," 703).

the Hobbes who emerges from these accounts is hopelessly naive, their proponents might defend themselves by pointing to the fact that he was, after all, the same person who insisted that he had squared the circle.[20] The main difficulty with these propositions, however, is not that they sound implausible, but that they overlook crucial evidence.

Hobbes identifies the inconstant signification of terms as the source of conflict and devotes a significant portion of his political treatises to definitions, including the proper definitions of fundamental concepts and methods. A program of this sort can have far-reaching consequences since it calls into question the meanings of terms that are considered familiar and used with abandon. Yet, having declared his intention to establish an entire system, Hobbes does not hesitate to redraw the map of knowledge and redefine what constitutes the appropriate method for each realm of inquiry, as well as what sort of expectations one ought to have from each field. While it is clear, given his interest in precision, that these classifications should be taken seriously, it is also possible to take them too far.[21]

The problems involved in the application of these divisions to Hobbes's own enterprise are numerous and significant. For instance, given Hobbes's apparent embracing of the notorious distinction between philosophy and history, according to which the former yields certainty whereas the latter only prudence, and his observation that "experience concludeth nothing universally," why does he commend history for its practical utility in his edition of Thucydides, and why does he invite the reader to test his propositions against his own experiences in *Leviathan*?[22] One might be tempted to respond that the former work belongs to his "humanist" phase, during which he still took history seriously, and the latter to his reconciliation with the inescapability of rhetoric.[23] And yet, it is in the *Elements*, the first political treatise of his allegedly scientific period, that Hobbes describes the science "from which proceed the true and evident conclusions of what is right

[20] See, for example, Hobbes, *Quadratura Circuli*; *T. Hobbes Malmesburiensis Vita* (OL, I: xix). Cf. Jesseph, *Squaring the Circle*, 3.

[21] We will see in Chapter 5, for instance, that Hobbes's assessment of the power and workings of poetry blurs the line between it and philosophy considerably. See Lemetti's discussion of the relationship of the mind to science as a continuum, along which one may encounter wisdom and "semi-scientific thinking" ("The Most Natural and the Most Artificial," 62–63). Weinberger argues that for Hobbes "[a]ll 'philosophy' is reason, but not all reason is 'philosophy'" ("Hobbes's Doctrine of Method," 1342). Cf. Kahn, *Rhetoric, Prudence, and Skepticism in the Renaissance*, 181; Strong, "How to Write Scripture," 143; Struever, "Dilthey's Hobbes and Cicero's Rhetoric," 243–44; Vickers, "'Tis the Goddesse of Rhetorick," 27; Biletzki, "Thomas Hobbes," 61.

[22] See, for example, *De Corpore*, I.1.2–8; *The Elements of Law*, I.4.10; *Leviathan*, III: 11.

[23] Strauss makes the former argument (*The Political Philosophy of Hobbes*, 79–107), although a version of it is implicit in Skinner's description of Hobbes's view of Thucydides (*Hobbes and Republican Liberty*, 13). For the latter argument, see Skinner, *Reason and Rhetoric in the Philosophy of Hobbes*, esp. 426–37.

and wrong, and what is good and hurtful to the being and well-being of mankind [as what] the Latins call *sapientia*, and we by the general name of wisdom," and adds that "generally, not he that hath skill in geometry, or any other science speculative, but only he that understandeth what conduceth to the good and government of the people, is called a wise man."²⁴ Nor is this an aberration. In *De Homine*, the last part of his tripartite system to be published, Hobbes notes the utility of wisdom for its ability to provide some protection, and the crucial role that natural histories and civil histories play in providing "the evidence on which rests the science of causes" in physics and civil and moral science, respectively.²⁵

The other antithesis, between reason and rhetoric, is equally questionable, for it rests on the assumption that Hobbes's persistent and vehement attacks on rhetoric in the *Elements* and *De Cive* should be taken simply at face value. Assuming, for a moment, that such a thing as communication without rhetoric were possible, one would then have to wonder what to make of an author's various propositions whose literal meaning is either puzzling or contravenes other statements he has made. For instance, in the opening lines of the *Elements*, Hobbes describes the contents of that work as "opinions," hardly a designation that inspires confidence in scientific certainty.²⁶ In that same work, he claims that the difference between rhetoric and teaching is that there is controversy in the former, but absolutely no controversy in the latter – a criterion that precludes the very possibility of teaching.²⁷

"Rhetoric," however, does not refer simply to a humanistic discipline or to a very particular practice. It is also a designation invoked to signal disapprobation of someone's views and intentions, in an attempt to delegitimize his authority and message.²⁸ This was no less true in Hobbes's day than it is today, and it is hardly surprising that a comprehensive attack on well-established doctrinal traditions would include an attempt to challenge their authority by accusing them of self-interested, insincere, manipulative, or even nonsensical language.²⁹ Even those who recognize that Hobbes often

²⁴ *The Elements of Law*, II.8.13. Aubrey notes that

> [a]fter [Hobbes] began to reflect on the interest of the king of England as touching his affaires between him and the parliament, for ten yeares together his thoughts were much, or almost altogether, unhinged from the mathematiques; but chiefly intent on his *De Cive*, and after that on his *Leviathan*: which was a great puttback to his mathematicall improvement ('*Brief Lives*,' I: 333).

²⁵ *De Homine*, XI.8, 10.
²⁶ *The Elements of Law*, xvi. Cf. Weinberger, "Hobbes's Doctrine of Method," 1339.
²⁷ *The Elements of Law*, I.13.3.
²⁸ See, for instance, Hobbes's highly rhetorical autobiography, in which he claims that he wrote not for scholars, but for those of sound judgment, in language "pure and clear, and not rhetorical" (*T. Hobbes Malmesburiensis Vita, OL*, I: xvii).
²⁹ See, for example, meaning 2c of "rhetoric, n.1" and meaning 1a of "rhetorical, adj," in OED Online (September 2012), Oxford University Press, http://www.oed.com/view/Entry/165178; http://www.oed.com/view/Entry/165181 (accessed August 3, 2013).

uses the term "rhetoric" in this sense, however, tend to focus on *Leviathan* and more or less accept the earlier works as earnest attempts to steer clear of rhetorical practices. I wish to suggest here that doing so is a mistake, for it causes us to lose sight of certain important features of these works and their role in Hobbes's project. As Tuck has observed, even though Hobbes's approach in the *Elements* and *De Cive* is in many ways different from the one he chose in *Leviathan*, the earlier treatises are every bit as rhetorical.[30]

This contention might strike one as problematic. After all, Hobbes himself has billed his treatises as scientific and has placed them in explicit opposition to rhetoric. The first thing to note, therefore, is that we will be using the term "rhetoric" not in the way that Skinner defines it, namely as "a distinctive set of linguistic techniques … derived from the rhetorical doctrines of *inventio, dispositio* and *elocutio*, the three principal *elementa* in classical and Renaissance theories of written eloquence," but rather in the way that Hobbes himself defines it, namely as "that Faculty, by which wee understand what will serve our turne, concerning any subject, to winne beliefe in the hearer."[31] The latter understanding may, of course, include some of those distinctive techniques, either consciously or unconsciously, but it is clearly broader than, and in no way constrained by, the former. It takes account of the fact that "science" and "reason" are terms of approbation much in the way that "rhetoric" is a term of disapprobation.[32] More importantly, it encompasses all those techniques that even a scientist committed to scientific inquiry in earnest would have to use in order to persuade his audience of his discoveries.[33] As Bacon put it in *Of the Wisdom of the Ancients*, fables are "of prime use to the sciences, and sometimes indispensable: I mean the employment of parables as a method of teaching, whereby inventions that are new and abstruse and remote from vulgar opinions may find an easier passage to the understanding."[34]

That Hobbes drew a sharp distinction between rhetoric and science in order to buttress his claims does not mean that we must accept that distinction as an absolute and unquestionable fact.[35] Neither, however, does it mean that Hobbes's interest in and talk of science was just a façade, for if he had discovered what he took to be universal principles of human behavior and universal reactions to rhetorical appeals, then his method for dealing with them would constitute a science of the sort that from the nineteenth century

---

[30] See the introduction to his edition of *Leviathan* (xxxviii, n. 52). Cf. Johnston, *The Rhetoric of Leviathan*, 23; Slomp, *Thomas Hobbes and the Political Philosophy of Glory*, 1–3; Nauta, "Hobbes the Pessimist?"

[31] Skinner, *Reason and Rhetoric in the Philosophy of Hobbes*, 6; *A Briefe of the Art of Rhetorique*, I.2. Cf. *The Elements of Law*, II.8.14.

[32] See, for instance, *Decameron Physiologicum*, *EW*, VII: 73. Cf. Weinberger, "Hobbes's Doctrine of Method"; Keller, "In the Service of 'Truth' and 'Victory.'"

[33] See Biletzki, "Thomas Hobbes," 64.

[34] *The Works of Francis Bacon*, VI: 698; cf. Cicero, *De inventione*, I.ii.2.

[35] Tuck, for instance, finds Hobbes's science "of an extremely exiguous kind" (*Hobbes*, 114).

onward has been described as psychology.[36] This understanding of science may be at odds with the way in which Hobbes defines natural philosophy, but it is consistent with the way in which he understands civil philosophy, or what in the *Elements* he refers to as the science of right and wrong.[37] Strauss wonders whether "Hobbes's earliest scientific ambition was perhaps to write an analysis of the passions, in the style, i.e., according to the method of the *Rhetoric*."[38] In fact, in a letter to his patron in 1635, Hobbes expresses his hope that Robert Payne could give "good reasons for yᵉ facultyes & passions of yᵉ soule, such as may be expressed in playne English," noting that if Payne could do so, he would be the first, but adding that "if he can not I hope to be yᵉ first."[39] Hobbes offered a sketch of his theory of the faculties and passions of the soul in the *Elements* not long thereafter, but he continued to add to it in his subsequent political treatises.

It is not only Hobbes's alleged turn to science, however, that poses problems for those who see his development as consisting in a series of phases marked by turns. Equally debatable is the widespread agreement in characterizing his early phase as "humanist."[40] On the surface, the term might appear to have a consistent meaning, and its application to Hobbes might strike one as fitting, in light of his education and strong interest in ancient authors. Yet, the degree to which this term is problematic becomes apparent as soon as one observes the meanings that commentators attach to it. Some, for example, consider it an appropriate description of Hobbes's education in the "Renaissance curriculum of a sixteenth-century grammar school with its emphasis on a fluent and stylish grasp of Latin and, *though to a lesser extent*, Greek."[41] As we will see, this emphasis on Latin is problematic in general when it comes to Hobbes's environment. It is especially misleading, however, when it comes to Hobbes himself, who was primarily interested in Greek rather than Roman authors and texts. There is abundant evidence of this preference, but suffice it to note that if Hobbes's literary output were to be placed on a shelf in chronological order, on the one end we would find his translation of Thucydides' history, and on the other his translations of Homer's *Odyssey* and *Iliad*, with nothing Roman in between. Hobbes

---

[36] Cf. Struever, "Dilthey's Hobbes and Cicero's Rhetoric," 233–34, 244.

[37] See, for example, the chart that accompanies *Leviathan*, IX; cf. *The Elements of Law*, II.8.13.

[38] Strauss, *The Political Philosophy of Hobbes*, 131.

[39] Hobbes to William Cavendish, Paris, August 15/25, 1635 (*The Correspondence of Thomas Hobbes*, I: 29).

[40] Once again, agreement extends from Strauss to Skinner, although the former notes that Hobbes's humanism was "peculiar" because of Hobbes's interest in history (*The Political Philosophy of Hobbes*, 44). Skinner, on the other hand, finds that interest in keeping with humanism (see, for example, *Reason and Rhetoric in the Philosophy of Hobbes*, 231).

[41] Tuck, *Hobbes*, 2, emphasis added. Skinner presents a more detailed argument along similar lines (*Reason and Rhetoric in the Philosophy of Hobbes*, 215–38).

was the first person to translate Thucydides into English directly from the Greek, and while he was an excellent Latinist – as he would have had to be given his education and occupation – and while Roman thinkers and themes appear throughout his works, he did not translate or write extensively on any Roman text or author.[42]

This degree of emphasis on Hobbes's Greek interests is corroborated by other evidence. Aubrey, for instance, describes Latimer, Hobbes's first tutor, as "a good Graecian."[43] The most important piece of evidence, however, comes from Hobbes's "scientific" period. Hobbes's encounter with Euclid in Geneva took place in 1630, from which point he is supposed to have put his humanistic interests behind him in order to immerse himself in science. The high point of this period is thus put at some time between 1630 and the late 1640s, when the English *Leviathan* was composed, and *The Elements of Law* is identified as its first major product. Yet, it was several years after his alleged discovery of Euclid and not long before the composition of *The Elements of Law*, a work in which he is supposedly vehemently anti-rhetorical, that Hobbes published a précis of Aristotle's *Rhetoric*.[44] Like its predecessor, his translation of Thucydides' history, this was the first rendition of that work into English. This uncomfortable fact complicates the neat narratives of Hobbes's conversion to science and calls for an explanation. Although he took it very seriously, Strauss nevertheless considered Hobbes's *Briefe of the Art of Rhetorique* one of "the last remnants of the Aristotelianism of his youth."[45] Other commentators have ignored this work or treated it as an inconsequential byproduct of Hobbes's tutorial duties, and Skinner and Schuhmann have even gone as far as to question its authenticity on rather slight evidence.[46]

It bears repeating, therefore, that whereas most of his contemporaries focused on Cicero and Quintilian, Hobbes worked on Thucydides and Aristotle. This difference is sometimes presented as a mere matter of taste, a somewhat peculiar variation on the predictable theme of humanism, and at other times explained away as the youthful, aphilosophical, or reflexive exercises of a humanist scholar.[47] They were, however, the foundations of a sophisticated and systematic attempt to persuade individuals who are programmed to disagree with one another of the consequences of that disagreement, if left unchecked. Hobbes made much of the need to define terms

---

[42] For an assessment of Roman themes in Hobbes's thought, see Struever, "Dilthey's Hobbes and Cicero's Rhetoric."

[43] Aubrey, '*Brief Lives*,' I: 329.

[44] [Thomas Hobbes], *A Briefe of the Art of Rhetorique* (London: Tho. Cotes for Andrew Crooke [1637]).

[45] Strauss, *The Political Philosophy of Hobbes*, 42.

[46] See Chapter 2, in this volume.

[47] See, for instance, Strauss, *The Political Philosophy of Hobbes*, 42, 44; Tuck, *Philosophy and Government*, 282; Skinner, *Hobbes and Republican Liberty*, 13.

carefully and observe those definitions, but as we will see, he was the first to break his own rules when it came to distinguishing between disciplines and methods. Whatever else they may be, Thucydides' history and Aristotle's *Rhetoric* are both works centrally concerned with persuasion, demagoguery, and their consequences, that is, the very characteristics of politics that Hobbes would continue to focus on throughout his own political treatises. As such, they need to be studied in the context of Hobbes's political theory rather than as artifacts of an earlier phase. However, the shift in emphasis suggested by drawing attention to these early works should not be misinterpreted: what is needed is not a "Greek" Hobbes to replace the "Roman," but a Hobbes who should be studied for what he – rather than the schools of thought that surrounded him – was.

In short, classifying Hobbes as a Renaissance humanist, scientist, or member of any other intellectual approach or school may add something to our understanding of his intellectual development, but it does so at a considerable cost: it obscures the way in which he diverges from these conventions, as other clearly identifiable elements of his thought show. While this is the unavoidable consequence of focusing on any single element of a complex set of evolving ideas, in Hobbes's case it is doubly misleading because it diverts our attention away from the method of consistent contrasts that would frame his political treatises and his persistent attempt to persuade as many people as possible of the perils of anarchy and the benefits of order.

SECRETLY INSTRUCTING THE READERS

Hobbes makes no secret of his love for geometry and the neatness of its methods, and his writings are filled with praise for the geometers and their contributions to mankind. Nevertheless, it is a mistake to conclude from this evidence that he aspired to a geometrical politics. There is every reason to think that Hobbes's belief in the power and promise of science was genuine, and that he took his scientific activities seriously. Precisely for these reasons, however, it is necessary to pay close attention to where he drew the boundary between science and politics. In every one of his political treatises, Hobbes begins by praising the virtues of geometry, but he continues by pointing out that its methods do not apply to civil philosophy because the subject matters of the two are radically different. In fact, according to Hobbes's division of the sciences, civil philosophy stands by itself, in isolation from all other sciences, including mathematics.[48]

As Hobbes's own account of his encounter with Euclid points out and Aubrey's anecdote confirms, it was Euclid's ability to persuade Hobbes that

---

[48] See, for example, *Leviathan* IX: 40; cf. *De Corpore* I.1.9, I.6.7; *The Elements of Law*, II.8.13; *De Cive*, Pref. §§ 4–10; *Leviathan*, XXXI: 194. Cf. Sacksteder, "Man the Artificer," 109; Strong, "How to Write Scripture," 141.

stood out to him. How did this result come about? The encounter was a private one: qua author, Euclid guided Hobbes, the reader, through the demonstration. No teacher intervened, and no authority was invoked in order to persuade Hobbes. In fact, the result of Hobbes's first reading was unexpected: Hobbes's incredulity was such that Aubrey felt the need to add, "[h]e would now and then sweare, by way of emphasis."[49] Refusing to accept the conclusion as presented, Hobbes traced his steps back to the beginning, and thus became "demonstratively convinced" of its truth.

In the *Elements of Law*, the first political treatise of his "scientific" period, Hobbes describes geometry as beginning from "most low and humble principles, evident even to the meanest capacity."[50] As Hobbes's Euclidean moment shows, however, this is not entirely true. Despite being armed with a capacity that was far from the meanest, Hobbes had to reexamine Euclid's demonstration backward before he could agree that its conclusion was correct. The appeal of geometry's method, then, lies less in its accessibility and more in the way in which it approaches and engages the observer.[51]

Most writers, especially those dealing with politics and ethics, backed their views with references to revered sources. Hobbes warns of the danger involved in this practice repeatedly, and in *Leviathan*, argues famously, "words are wise men's counters, they do but reckon by them: but they are the mony of fooles, that value them by the authority of an *Aristotle*, a *Cicero*, or a *Thomas*, or any other Doctor whatsoever, if but a man."[52] One who accepts "conclusions on the trust of Authors ... does not know any thing; but onely beleeveth."[53] Unlike statements of other kinds, especially political ones, geometrical propositions do not rely on authoritative sources.[54] By inviting the observer to follow the ascent from postulates to proof, the geometer gives him a sense of agency in the outcome. No longer feeling as though he were merely accepting as valid a claim handed down

[49] Aubrey, 'Brief Lives,' I: 332 (marginal note). As Patapan notes, this reaction contains an element of vanity ("Lord over the Children of Pride," 82). In Cohen's view, the employment of metaphor in such a setting results in the "achievement of intimacy" between the author and reader ("Metaphor and the Cultivation of Intimacy," 8).

[50] *The Elements of Law*, I.13.3.

[51] This distinction bears emphasizing, for even those commentators who note that it was Euclid's method that appealed to Hobbes tend to mean thereby the procedure beginning with small and well-founded steps (see, e.g., Reik, *The Golden Lands of Thomas Hobbes*, 54). If that had been the case, however, neither Hobbes's initial reaction nor his backtracking would have been necessary.

[52] *Leviathan*, IV:15; cf. *The Elements of Law*, I.13.3, I.17.1, I.17.14, II.8.13, II.9.8, II.10.8; *De Cive*, 3.13; *Leviathan*, VII: 32, XV:77, XLVI:370–71, 376, A Review and Conclusion, 395; cf. Hobbes's annotation to I.20 of Thucydides' history, in his translation.

[53] *Leviathan*, V: 19.

[54] On the degree to which argument, especially political argument, was dependent on authoritative sources in the Middle Ages, see Nederman, "Aristotle as Authority"; cf. Blum, *Studies on Early Modern Aristotelianism*, 43–49. See also *The Elements of Law*, I.6.9 and Chapter 2 in this volume.

to him by a person of authority, the observer can verify the reasons for the claim and thus validate its truth in a way that satisfies him.[55] Once again, Aubrey's anecdote is telling: Hobbes's first reaction to Euclid's conclusion was that it was impossible. Yet, everything that Hobbes needed in order to test his reaction and revise his assessment was there, before him. Although it was Euclid who had assembled the evidence and guided Hobbes to the conclusion, Hobbes's eventual acceptance of that conclusion did not result from Euclid's *authority*.

The fact that he found Euclid's method, rather than his theorems, important "strongly suggests that Hobbes's mind was already preoccupied with some philosophical problems to which Euclidean method seemed to supply the solution."[56] It has been claimed that there is no direct evidence from this period as to what those problems might have been, but this is not the case.[57] Not too long before his encounter with Euclid, Hobbes had completed his translation of Thucydides' history, a work he valued for what it could teach his compatriots about the dangers of demagoguery. In the prefatory material to that translation, Hobbes had concurred with Plutarch's praise for Thucydides' ability to turn the auditor into a spectator.[58] That ability had an important effect on the reader, who, despite being guided by Thucydides, was made to feel as though he were witnessing events at first hand, without the interference of Thucydides' or anyone else's opinion. For Hobbes, this quality was crucial in persuading the reader that Thucydides' account of the war was objective, and that any conclusions about the events were the reader's own. As Hobbes puts it in his essay on Thucydides,

Digressions for instruction's cause, and other such open conveyances of precepts, (which is the philosopher's part), he never useth; as having so clearly set before men's eyes the ways and events of good and evil counsels, that the narration itself doth *secretly instruct the reader*, and more effectually than can possibly be done by precept.[59]

The man who walked into the library in which Euclid's *Elements* lay open was already well aware of the challenges posed by audiences and preoccupied

---

[55] See Weinberger, "Hobbes's Doctrine of Method," esp. 1339, 1349–51. Kahn thus describes the first contract of *Leviathan* as a "literary contract," which is "the precondition of the political contract that founds the Hobbesian commonwealth" ("Hobbes, Romance, and the Contract of Mimesis," 8).

[56] Malcolm, *Aspects of Hobbes*, 9. See Patapan's highly insightful analysis of Hobbes's "Euclidean rhetoric" ("'Lord over the Children of Pride'").

[57] Malcolm, *Aspects of Hobbes*, 9.

[58] For Hobbes, this ability made Thucydides "the most politic historiographer that ever writ" (*EW*, VIII: viii). See also Hobbes's Preface to his translation of Thucydides' history (*EW*, VIII: vii–xi) and his essay "Of the Life and History of Thucydides" (*EW*, VIII: xiii–xxxxii).

[59] "Of the Life and History of Thucydides" (*EW*, VIII: xxii), emphasis added. Hobbes repeats this view at the closing of the essay, where he also attributes it to Lipsius (*ibid.*, xxxi–xxxii).

with the need to instruct them effectively and efficiently of the difference between and the consequences of good and evil counsels. He had already encountered one model of how to do so in Thucydides. Euclid provided another.[60]

The methods that made Thucydides and Euclid effective differ in certain obvious respects. One expecting to see them as different might thus miss certain common characteristics. The first of these is that in Hobbes's classification of the sciences, they are both placed under the heading of natural philosophy.[61] More importantly, both make an appeal to the reader as someone who does not require the assistance of others or the authority of revered teachers in order to arrive at the truth. Rather, they invite the reader to use something of his own – his reason, judgment, or experience – in assessing what lies before him. One might think that the science is confined to what is printed on the page – objective history or geometry – but there is some science involved in their respective presentation of the material in relation to its source, audience, and authority. In each case the author – Thucydides or Euclid – is the source of the material, namely the conclusions and the way we are to arrive at them. Despite being completely dependent on Thucydides or Euclid for those conclusions and the journey that led to them, the reader nevertheless feels more involved in the process, even though his actual participation in the demonstration might be no greater than in reading the arguments of John of Salisbury or St. Thomas Aquinas. In this light, the epistemological status of the reader is not very different from the political status of the individual who is asked to accept the proposition that the order to which he is subject resulted from a social contract among all.

Disagreement was the cause of conflict, but what was the cause of disagreement? It has been argued that the "understanding of self-interest as a power greater than reason, and capable of governing it, is scarcely to be found in English political literature before the 1640s," but it was well known to French authors of the 1630s, who are likely to have been the source of Hobbes's inspiration during his exile in France.[62] There are at least two problems with this explanation, however. The first is that Hobbes did not need to travel to France to awaken to the importance of self-interest, for he was already well aware of it from his translation of Thucydides.[63]

---

[60] Thus, Silver argues that self-evidence in *Leviathan* "is first and foremost an aspect of [Hobbes's] own verbal performance, and only secondarily of the reader's intellectual consent" ("The Fiction of Self-Evidence in Hobbes's *Leviathan*," 352).

[61] *Leviathan*, IX. Mathematics and geometry belong under the branch of quantity and motion, whereas "consequences from the Passions of Men" and "Consequences from *Speech*" belong under the branch entitled "PHISIQUES, or Consequences from *Qualities*." Note that this division occurs despite the fact that Hobbes considers geometry and civil science both demonstrable (*Six Lessons to the Professors of the Mathematics, EW*, VII: 183–84).

[62] Skinner, *Reason and Rhetoric in the Philosophy of Hobbes*, 427–28.

[63] See, for example, *Eight Bookes of the Peloponnesian Warre*, pp. 76–77, 167, 175 marginal note, 205, 284, as well as the notorious three greatest motives in the Athenians' speech

Moreover, a catalog in his hand of the Hardwick library, dating from the
1620s, suggests that he was well read in the *ragion di stato* literature, and
corroborates both his contemporary assessment of Thucydides as well as
the one he offered many years later, toward the end of his life.[64] The second problem is that this explanation overlooks something that Hobbes had
noted from the beginning, namely that there is no such thing as a mono-
lithic conception of self-interest. In *Leviathan*, he would famously cast this
observation in the form of a polemical rejection of the *summum bonum*, but
Hobbes knew from the start that not only do different individuals have different and sometimes conflicting interests, but also that the same individual
has interminable and constantly evolving interests.

A multitude of often-conflicting interests already poses a significant hurdle, since it comes with the likelihood that one may be called on to try
to reconcile irreconcilable demands. If a single argument cannot convince
everyone on its own merits, then the author must give the impression of a
tailor-made approach in the midst of mass production: he must create a space
in which each reader can find reasons for agreeing with his conclusions.[65]
This makes for a difficult balancing act because those reasons should be visible to those who wish to find them, yet not so visible as to alienate everyone
else. Moreover, no single reason should carry too much weight, since that
would render the entire edifice as fragile as the evidence purporting to demonstrate it. Given Hobbes's ambitious aim, however, his case would have to
satisfy a further requirement. To form the basis of a radical reexamination
of one's political behavior, its lesson would have to be compressed into a
mnemonic device that would intercede in one's calculations and encapsulate
the benefits of order and the perils of disorder. In short, it would have to be
possible, probable, *and* memorable.[66]

Leviathan is Hobbes's fullest and most mature political treatise, not least
because it reflects the results of his attempts to address these issues. Mindful

before the Peloponnesian League (I.75–76), in which Hobbes renders ὠφελία as "profit"
(twice). Cf. Slomp, "Hobbes, Thucydides, and the Three Greatest Things." On self-interest in
England, see Chalk, "Natural Law and the Rise of Economic Individualism in England" and
Ferguson, *The Articulate Citizen and the English Renaissance*, 304–07.

[64] See Devonshire Mss., Chatsworth HS/E/1A, which includes entries for Boccalini, Bodin,
Botero, and Mariana, as well as several editions of Machiavelli and Tacitus, including the
translations by Dati and Politi. Hobbes cites sources other than the Bible and ancient authors
very rarely, yet he cites both Lipsius and Bodin with approval.

[65] With regard to monarchy and religion, respectively, Strauss and Lloyd note that Hobbes
presents his arguments in a way that will appeal to different individuals or factions, despite
their differences (*The Political Philosophy of Hobbes*, 66; *Ideals as Interests in Hobbes's
Leviathan*: 44–45; cf. Weinberger, "Hobbes's Doctrine of Method"; Collins, *The Allegiance
of Thomas Hobbes*, 33; Hoekstra, *Thomas Hobbes and the Creation of Order*). There are
numerous other examples of this strategy in Hobbes's theory, as we will see.

[66] *Pace* Skinner (*Reason and Rhetoric in the Philosophy of Hobbes*, 188), the image employed
must therefore *not* be far-fetched (see *A Briefe of the Art of Rhetorique*, III.3, III.10; cf.
Aristotle, *Rhetoric*, 1410b31–36, 1412a11–14).

of the ways in which the abilities of readers vary, he goes through a lengthy demonstration of the demands of the law of nature as discoverable through reason, but also notes that those who might have trouble following that demonstration or remembering its various conclusions could do nearly as well by remembering the Golden Rule.[67] In that work, Hobbes also sounds occasionally as though he were addressing a sovereign. His intended audience no doubt included Charles II, but he also knew that "there are very few so foolish, that had not rather governe themselves, than be governed by others."[68] Well aware of the degree to which the Reformation and transformations in scientific inquiry had invited every Tom, Dick, and Harry to pronounce on matters previously reserved for the learned and powers that be, Hobbes understood that a simple variation on argument from authority would no longer suffice.[69] It is no wonder, then, that *Leviathan* makes so much room for eloquence.

How different are the *Elements* and *De Cive* from *Leviathan*? Hobbes's earliest political treatises are anything but hostile to rhetoric. They reveal, rather, a persistent attempt to grapple with these problems. Where his predecessors had asked of their readers to accept their principles "on trust," Hobbes proposed "only to put men in mind of what they know already, or may know by their own experience."[70] Far from supposing that one could eliminate passion from the picture, Hobbes announces his intention to ground his theory on such principles "as passion not mistrusting, may not seek to displace."[71] The desire to discover Hobbes's Archimedean point has led to attempts to distill his thought down to a single method – rhetoric or science; a single force – reason or the passions; or a single passion – fear or vainglory. As devices, such oppositions reflect the measure of Hobbes's success in persuading his readers that simple, neat contrasts are meaningful and instructive.[72] His own approach relies heavily on an opposition of this sort, that between the anarchy of the state of nature and the order of the commonwealth. This most famous of Hobbes's contrasts in turn is founded on a series of antitheses between good things and bad, such as that between reason and the passions and that between the mathematicians and the dogmatists. One might ask oneself whether these distinctions are simply the impartial imposition of order by a dispassionate scientist, or whether they are also terms of approbation and disapprobation calculated to produce a

---

[67] *Leviathan*, XV: 78–79. Cf. *Questions concerning Liberty, Necessity, and Chance*, EW, V: 267.
[68] *Leviathan*, XV: 77. Cf. Malcolm's introduction to *Leviathan*, esp. I: 51–60.
[69] See, for example, *De Cive*, XIV.19, note to "Yet is it to be referred to sins of imprudence"; cf. *Behemoth*, 134–35.
[70] *The Elements of Law*, I.1.2.
[71] *The Elements of Law*, Ep. Ded., xv.
[72] See Biletzki, *Talking Wolves*, 112–35.

certain reaction.[73] After all, what reader would willingly side with the dogmatists and not with reason?

The multitude of contrasts that one encounters in Hobbes's writings betrays their fragility and fluidity. In the midst of all this noise, Hobbes remains remarkably consistent about his aversion to anarchy, his desire for peace, and his willingness to listen to readers and adjust his writing according to their feedback.[74] There is no doubt that the immediate circumstances in which each of these works was composed can tell us something about its form. For instance, the very limited circulation of the *Elements* and the first version of *De Cive* to learned friends and acquaintances with a strong interest in science must have something to do with their respective forms, tone, and examples. This sense is corroborated by the intriguing imagery – both visual, in the frontispieces, and mental, in Hobbes's colorful examples – of the works that were intended for sale, as well as by Hobbes's revisions. As we will see, however, these revisions were consistently driven by Hobbes's desire to render his philosophy useful, for "the utility of moral and civil philosophy is to be estimated, not so much by the commodities we have by knowing these sciences, as by the calamities we receive from not knowing them."[75] To make these calamities plain to his readers, Hobbes would construct a multifaceted account of a condition that any reasonable individual would wish to avoid. This hydra of an image, the state of nature, would have to give each reader, no matter what his point of view, a succinct and powerful reminder of why it makes sense to cede sovereignty over one's conception of good and evil in exchange for peace.

In what follows, we will trace the development of Hobbes's theory from its earliest formulations: his editions of Thucydides' history (Chapter 1) and Aristotle's *Rhetoric* (Chapter 2). We will see that in Hobbes's view, those works are valuable because they capture the ways in which the human mind's perception of the world and of the individual's place in it set the stage for disagreement and conflict, but also because they contain important insights into how to curb the tendencies that bring about these outcomes. Armed with insight from Hobbes's reading of Thucydides' and Aristotle's views on persuasion, we will trace the evolution of the state of nature in his successive political treatises: *The Elements of Law* (Chapter 3), the two versions of *De Cive* (Chapter 4) and the English and Latin *Leviathan* (Chapter 5). The trajectory of this image from relative obscurity to inescapable point of reference reveals the ways in which Hobbes put the lessons of Thucydides, Aristotle, and Euclid to work in the construction of a sophisticated theory of the mind and of the ways in which it can be diverted from belligerent conduct.

---

[73] See Hill's discussion of reason in *Change and Continuity in Seventeenth-Century England*, Chapter 4.

[74] See Chapters 1 and 4 in this volume.

[75] *De Corpore*, I.i.7; cf. *De Homine*, XI.9; Hobbes to William Cavendish, Paris, August 15/25, 1635 (*The Correspondence of Thomas Hobbes*, I: 29).

A KIND OF SCIENCE

In the Introduction to *Leviathan*, Hobbes declares that reading human nature is the hardest challenge. He promises, however, that once he has laid the foundation, all the reader will have to do is examine himself.[76] Yet, this task is not as simple as it sounds, for "men measure, not onely other men, but all other things, by themselves."[77] This Protagorean pronouncement reinforces the message broadcast by the book's title and frontispiece, namely that one's conception of oneself is always standing in the way of one's ability to assess the world – and one's place in it – accurately. To an author with the ambition to bring about peace through an examination of the passions of the soul, pride presents a serious challenge because it distorts the witness's view of himself and, hence, of everything else. Hobbes's great insight, aided by his encounters with Thucydides, Euclid, and Aristotle, was that this is true not just of kings and ambitious noblemen, but of everyone. His solution to this problem began with the realization that pride could be neither ignored nor switched off. Rather, it had to be enlisted and flattered, so as to be prevented from interfering with Hobbes's teaching toward peace.

It is no accident that in his accounts of glory in *The Elements of Law* and *Leviathan*, Hobbes describes it as the *imagination* of our power.[78] When well grounded in our experience of our abilities, it is glory proper, or "confidence," but when it is based on flattery or conceit, it is "VAINE-GLORY."[79] Hobbes observes that "a well grounded *Confidence* begetteth Attempt; whereas the supposing of power does not, and is therefore rightly called *Vaine*."[80] This observation sheds a different light on Hobbes's repeated invitations to the reader to witness his demonstration and assess its validity for himself.[81] The abundant reasons, so ably demonstrated by Hobbes, for doubting the existence of such a universal ability to read mankind, coupled with the excessive confidence that each of us has in deciding what is best for himself, lead to the discovery of another aspect of equality: human beings are effectively equal when it comes to presuming their wisdom superior to most others', especially when it comes to matters of government and the judgment of right and wrong.[82]

---

[76] See *Leviathan*, Introduction: 2; cf. *The Elements of Law*, I.5.14. Cf. Silver, "The Fiction of Self-Evidence in Hobbes's *Leviathan*," 360–63.

[77] *Leviathan*, II: 4.

[78] *The Elements of Law*, I.9.1; *Leviathan*, VI: 26–27. See Lemetti's insightful account of Hobbes on the imagination ("The Most Natural and the Most Artificial").

[79] *Leviathan*, VI: 26–27.

[80] *Leviathan*, VI: 27; cf. Slomp's examination of glory in Hobbes's treatises (*Thomas Hobbes and the Political Philosophy of Glory*, Chapter 3).

[81] Thus, Silver argues that the "self-referring and self-verifying terminology [of *Leviathan*] is Hobbes's version of mathematical method" ("The Fiction of Self-Evidence in Hobbes's *Leviathan*," 366).

[82] *Leviathan*, XIII: 61. See Feldman, "Conscience and the Concealments of Metaphor in Hobbes's *Leviathan*," 27.

In this context, some of the most prominent elements of Hobbes's method acquire a new significance. While a private appeal to the reader is certainly an opportunity for reasonable reflection, introspection, and thus for the calm assessment of Hobbes's arguments against one's experiences and conscience, it is also an opportunity for flattery.[83] On the one hand, Hobbes and the reader are engaged in a process whose whiffs of replicability and universality, method and procedure, make it sound like science.[84] Hobbes's continued references to proper foundations and method, reason, and science reinforce this sense. On the other hand, the privacy of the encounter has two further psychological advantages. It allows the reader to admit certain things that are best kept from the public, and it provides a space in which the reader can imagine himself not simply a competent judge, but one superior to those purporting to treat moral philosophy, those who had tyrannized him with their mindless invocations of authorities for centuries.[85] This private space, therefore, is not simply one in which the reader validates Hobbes's findings, but also, and more importantly, one of nearly unimaginable freedom. In it, the reader is free to roam to new heights, fancying himself the creator of the commonwealth, the equal of Aristotle, a wise being capable of recognizing reason and assenting to it. Hobbes's wager was that by doing so, the reader would be too busy to listen to the calls of those who sought power for themselves by means of his blood.[86]

This emphasis on imagination and vainglory makes it sound as though Hobbes's appeal was based simply on a ruse, but this is not the case. As Hobbes puts it in *The Elements of Law*, his first task is to establish a foundation such that "passion not mistrusting, may not seek to displace."[87] Having gained the reader's trust by distracting his vanity and enlisting him in the cause of proper method and reason, Hobbes could address the next hurdle: the absence of a *summum bonum*. Having noted that previous attempts at civil philosophy had failed to produce consensus on a single conception of the good, Hobbes opted for a different approach altogether. His own attempt would consider that disagreement a given, and focus instead on the prior level: the ability to pursue any good, no matter what it might be. Hobbes notes that three "passions" bring men out of the state of nature: "Feare of

---

[83] See *De Cive*, III.27 and the note to "The exercise of all these laws"; *Leviathan*, XV: 79. Strauss argues that "vanity is co-ordinated with publicity as fear is with solitude" (*The Political Philosophy of Hobbes*, 111). Although this is true, the contrast risks obscuring the degree to which Hobbes takes advantage of the private encounter with the reader, during which he can appeal to his vanity, as he does, for example, in the introduction to *Leviathan*.

[84] See Dear, *Discipline and Experience*, 246.

[85] See *Leviathan*, A Review and Conclusion, 395. Reik thus argues that the "force and directness" of Hobbes's explanations renders them "almost intellectually *coercive*" (*The Golden Lands of Thomas Hobbes*, 71). Cf. Kahn, *Rhetoric, Prudence, and Skepticism*, 157; Silver, "The Fiction of Self-Evidence in Hobbes's *Leviathan*."

[86] *De Cive*, Ep. Ded., § 20.

[87] *The Elements of Law*, Ep. Ded., xv.

Death; Desire of such things as are necessary to commodious living; and a Hope by their Industry to obtain them."[88] Hobbes's approach is thus distinct because it allows individual readers the freedom to determine which things they deem necessary to commodious living, but also because it recognizes that the fear of death is an impediment largely indifferent to the objects of most men's desires.

As we will see, from his translation of Thucydides to the mature sections of his philosophical system, Hobbes would insist continuously that the most effective way to instruct human beings about the benefits of something is to expose them to the calamities of its absence. Where the pursuit of peace was concerned, then, it would be necessary to present readers with an account of disorder sufficiently powerful to convince them to leave good enough alone. Just as the Golden Rule sums up the effective meaning of the laws of nature, the state of nature would serve as the enthymeme of the perils of disorder. As we noted earlier, however, what is powerful for one reader might leave another untouched. Aware of the fact that the mind forms connections between things in a manner "not altogether so casuall as it seems to be," Hobbes would pack his accounts of the state of nature with cues that would allow a wide range of readers to make their way quickly toward images of disorder capable of giving them pause.[89] The variety of images that appear in Hobbes's accounts of the state of nature confirms his stated desire to appeal to as broad an audience as possible, a desire that is also corroborated by his insistence in collecting feedback on his treatises and amending them accordingly. There was much that Hobbes could have drawn from, and an examination of the evolution of the state of nature reveals the extent to which he sought to take advantage of signposts so well entrenched in the minds of his readers as to form reliable starting points of trains of thought all headed toward uncertainty, disorder, and misery. Chief among those was the Biblical account of the natural condition of mankind (Chapter 6), which also contained that most consequential of rebellions, the Fall. Yet, as the earliest examples of the state of nature show, Hobbes's readers would have been prepared to think beyond the Bible for examples of pre-social man, visions of whom they would have encountered in Lucretius and Hobbes's own Thucydides, among numerous other Greek and Roman authors (Chapter 7), as well as in the snapshots of that new and compelling domain of diffidence, America (Chapter 8). These images conform to the standard that Hobbes first laid out in *The Elements of Law*, where he noted that in seeking to appease, "it is no matter whether the opinion be true or

[88] *Leviathan*, XIII: 63.
[89] *Leviathan*, III: 8; cf. *De Corpore*, I.i.3. As Feldman puts it, rhetorical devices such as metaphors "persuade people precisely because they draw upon a reserve of private associations, which follow one from another involuntarily" ("Conscience and the Concealments of Metaphor in Hobbes's *Leviathan*," 33).

false, or the narration historical or fabulous," and restated in *De Homine*, when he observed that the histories that inform the science of causes do so "whether they be true or false, provided that they are not impossible."[90] For most of his readers, these images of anarchy were possible, probable, and memorable. They reveal not simply the process by which Hobbes built the notorious state of nature of *Leviathan*, but also the extent to which he relied on what, departing from Aristotle, he described in the *Briefe of the Art of Rhetorique* as the power of metaphors to beget in us "a kind of *Science*."[91] It was from such a rhetoric of science and such a science of rhetoric that Hobbes began his relentless pursuit of peace.

---

[90] *The Elements of Law*, I.13.7; *De Homine*, XI.10.
[91] *A Briefe of the Art of Rhetorique*, III.9. Cf., for instance, Aristotle, *Rhetoric*, 1356b32–33.

PART I

A GRÆCIAN

[O]ne ought not to elaborate everything in detail, but leave some things for the listener, too, to perceive and infer for himself; for when he perceives what you have left out, he not only is a listener but also becomes your witness, and in addition more favorably disposed. For he thinks himself perceptive, because you have provided him with the occasion to exercise perception.

– Theophrastus, according to Demetrius (*On Style*)

I

Politic Historiography

It has been suggested that to understand Hobbes properly, it is worth noting that had he died in his forty-first year, he would be remembered only as a "rather minor representative of the last generation of Tudor humanists and translators who did so much to appropriate classical culture to the English language."[1] Until then, Hobbes's "interests and intellectual achievements had been far more typical of someone who had been nurtured – as Hobbes had largely been – in the humanist literary culture of the Renaissance."[2] Humanism, however, is a very problematic and controversial term, whose application to Hobbes confuses rather than illuminates. Coined in the nineteenth century by German scholars to describe the Renaissance shift to the study of humanity over divinity by focusing on grammar, rhetoric, poetry, history, and ethics, especially in the works of Greek and Roman authors, the term is rather vague.[3] An attempt to render it a bit more precise introduces an interesting and, for the present purposes, important consideration: the elusive movement to which this term is usually applied had its roots in Italy.[4] A quick survey of individuals and works labeled humanist immediately reveals not just that these studies focused primarily on Roman and Latin material, but also that to the extent that they examined Greek material, they did so through Latin and Italian lenses.[5] While Hobbes studied

[1] The suggestion is Reik's (*The Golden Lands of Thomas Hobbes*, 25), but it has also been repeated more recently by Skinner (*Hobbes and Republican Liberty*, 1).
[2] Skinner, *Hobbes and Republican Liberty*, 1–2.
[3] On the term and its origin, see Kristeller, *Renaissance Thought*, 8–11. Cf. Kristeller, "Humanism," 113. Burke thus defines humanism as "the movement to recover, interpret and assimilate the language, literature, learning and values of ancient Greece and Rome" ("The Spread of Italian Humanism," 2).
[4] For some of the reasons why Italy became the locus of humanism, see Kristeller, "Humanism," 127–30. Cf. Burke, "The Spread of Italian Humanism;" Grafton, "Humanism and Political Theory."
[5] Burckhardt thus insists, and proclaims "one of the chief propositions" of his study of the Renaissance, "that it was not the revival of antiquity alone, but its union with the genius of

his fair share of Latin and dutifully composed some of his most important works in that language, he was primarily interested in Greek sources, with which he engaged directly.

We know from Aubrey, as well as from Hobbes's autobiographies, that for six years Hobbes received an education in Greek and Latin "literis" at home.[6] Aubrey tells us that Hobbes's tutor, Robert Latimer, "was a good Graecian," who used to instruct Hobbes and a couple of other young boys "in the evening till nine a clock."[7] At age fourteen, Hobbes was sent to Oxford, to study at Magdalen Hall, but before leaving, he presented his tutor with a translation of Euripides' *Medea* "out of Greeke into Latin Iambiques."[8] Hobbes claimed that he remained at Oxford for five years, and the only thing that he says directly about what he did during that time is "operam impendens studio logicæ et physicæ Aristotelicæ."[9] By contrast, in his autobiographies Hobbes has quite a bit to say about his classical education in general, his translations of *Medea* and Thucydides' history, and his extensive reading of Greek and Roman authors, including Horace, Virgil, Homer, Sophocles, Plautus, Aristophanes, Plato, Cicero, and Dionysius of Halicarnassus.[10] Upon completion of his studies at Oxford, Hobbes began his life-long association with the Cavendish family by assuming the post of tutor to William Cavendish.

Hobbes devotes a sizeable portion of his autobiography to the fluctuation of his Greek and Latin skills during his early years as a tutor, and to the steps he took to strengthen them. There, he explains that he studied Greek and Roman historians and poets, as well as the commentaries of the most famous grammarians, not in order to cultivate a more florid style, but to be able to write in Latin, and to find the proper power in words and thought, with a view to writing in a way that would be easy to read and

the Italian people, which achieved the conquest of the Western world" (*The Civilization of the Renaissance in Italy*, I: 175). Burckhardt notes that Greek scholarship "was never so general as Latin scholarship, partly because of the far greater difficulties which it involved, partly and still more because of the consciousness of Roman supremacy, and an instinctive hatred of the Greeks more than counterbalanced the attractions which Greek literature had for the Italians" (*ibid.*, 204–05). One obvious reason for the need to distinguish between Greek and Latin sources was the language. As Kristeller points out, "[w]hereas the study of Greek was mainly aimed at the reading of the classics, that of Latin served the additional purpose of mastering it as a written and even as a spoken language" ("Humanism," 121).

[6] Aubrey, '*Brief Lives*,' I: 328; *T. Hobbes Malmesburiensis Vita* (OL, I: xiii); *Thomæ Hobbesii Malmesburiensis Vita*, A2ᵛ: "Sex annis ad verba steti *Græcæ* atque *Latinæ*."

[7] Aubrey, '*Brief Lives*,' I: 328–29. Aubrey's testimony regarding Latimer carries special weight, since Aubrey himself was a student of his, later on. It was on the occasion of a visit to his old master's school, in 1634, that Hobbes met Aubrey as a boy ('*Brief Lives*,' I: 329–30; cf. Powell, *John Aubrey and His Friends*, 178–79).

[8] *Thomæ Hobbesii Malmesburiensis Vita*, A2ᵛ: "Et decimo quarto mittor ad *Oxonium*;" Aubrey, '*Brief Lives*,' I: 328–29.

[9] *T. Hobbes Malmesburiensis Vita* (OL, I: xiii).

[10] See, for example, *Thomæ Hobbesii Malmesburiensis Vita*, 4.

understand.[11] If as reflections at the end of a long life these statements appear suspicious, it is worth remembering that Hobbes's interest in the power of words and clarity of expression figures prominently, consistently, and from the beginning in his various statements of method over the years, as developed in the prefaces to his major works.

Already, the person who emerges from this sparse account is an uncharacteristic humanist. Aubrey's description of Latimer as "a good Graecian" is but the first sign of an unusual emphasis on Greek material. Hobbes's attention to *Medea*, one of the very few works that he would go on to cite repeatedly in his later years, is another.[12] The most compelling evidence, however, comes from Hobbes's output. In his long scholarly career, Hobbes wrote much in Latin, and translated to and from Latin, as he would have been expected to do, but his sights were fixed on Greek authors.[13] Even the partial reading list mentioned by Hobbes in his verse autobiography is uncharacteristically mixed.[14] It bears repeating that Hobbes's first publication was his translation of Thucydides' history, in 1629, and his last publications, some fifty years later, were Homer's *Odyssey* (1675) and *Iliad* (1676).[15] The only other major work published by Hobbes prior to the composition of *The Elements of Law* was his précis of Aristotle's *Rhetoric*.

Those who see distinct and sometimes divergent stages in Hobbes's intellectual development, in particular those who regard this phase of his life as humanist, tend to focus on the form of his work and to contrast it with his subsequent preoccupation with political philosophy. The picture of Hobbes that emerges from this approach is strangely apolitical, and very much at odds with the thinker who placed politics consistently at the center of his

[11] *T. Hobbes Malmesburiensis Vita* (*OL*, I: xiii–xiv).
[12] Hobbes refers to *Medea* four times in his works. Despite Hobbes's juvenile translation of Euripides' version, three are based on other sources, perhaps Apollodorus (*Library*, I.9.27.3), Diodorus Siculus (*Library of History*, IV.52.1–2), Hyginus (*Hygini Fabulae*, XXIV), or Ovid (*Metamorphoses*, VII.297–349). These are found in *The Elements of Law* (II.8.15), *De Cive* (XII.13), and *Leviathan* (XXX: 177). The fourth, which Hobbes ties explicitly to Ovid's *Metamorphoses* (VII.297–349), occurs in "Of Liberty and Necessity," § 23 (*EW*, IV: 269). In this instance, however, Hobbes is merely responding to Bramhall, who quotes Medea from that work in the corresponding paragraph of his own essay (*Hobbes and Bramhall on Liberty and Necessity*, p. 12). Rogow, who offers some interesting speculations regarding the significance of *Medea* for Hobbes, claims that "no other dramatic or literary work is referred to as often in his writings" (*Thomas Hobbes*, 38).
[13] His most unusual compositions in Latin were a poem, *De Mirabilibus Pecci*, composed to commemorate a tour of the Peak District in Derbyshire, and his *Historia Ecclesiastica*.
[14] Compared, for instance, with the almost exclusively Latin purchases of two Oxford undergraduates in the early seventeenth century, cited by Malcolm (*Reason of State, Propaganda, and the Thirty Years' War*, 3).
[15] *Eight Bookes of the Peloponnesian Warre, etc.* (1629); *The Travels of Ulysses, etc.* (1673); *Homer's Iliads in English, etc.* (1676); cf. Macdonald & Hargreaves, *Thomas Hobbes: A Bibliography*, nos. 1, 75, 79.

concerns.[16] This is perhaps the unavoidable consequence of focusing on difference, rather than continuity, and yet it risks obscuring certain clues that might shed light on the curious development of Hobbes's political thought. It is true that Hobbes would not compose an original political treatise for another ten years, but in his verse autobiography he insists that Thucydides captured his attention for purely political reasons.[17] There Hobbes claims that of the many ancient authors he read Thucydides pleased him most because "he teaches me how foolish democracy is / and how much more than an assembly one man knows," and that he "made him speak to the English so that those inclined to consult the rhetoricians [demagogues]

[16] Thus, for example, Skinner claims,

> Soon after his translation of Thucydides appeared in 1629, Hobbes's intellectual interests began to undergo a marked change, in the course of which his earlier humanist preoccupations were largely left behind. But even at this stage he did not immediately turn his attention to the problems of political philosophy (*Hobbes and Republican Liberty*, 13; cf. Tuck, *Philosophy and Government*, 282).

> Robertson (*Hobbes*, 39) and Cromartie ("*The Elements* and Hobbesian Moral Thinking," 22) also see a difference between the earlier period and Hobbes's later interest in politics, although the former sees a "political instinct" in Hobbes at the time of the translation (*Hobbes*, 17); cf. Sommerville, *Thomas Hobbes*, 27. The material that accompanied Hobbes's translation of Thucydides shows that his attention was fixed from the beginning on the political consequences of demagoguery. As we will see below, this remained Hobbes's central preoccupation throughout the ensuing decades, and in works as diverse as his précis of Aristotle's *Rhetoric* and the allegedly scientific *Elements of Law*.

[17] *Pace* Watkins, *Hobbes's System of Ideas*, 31; Skinner, *Reason and Rhetoric in the Philosophy of Hobbes*, 242; and Tuck, "Hobbes and Tacitus," 110. Unlikely agreement regarding the continuity is found in two accounts. The first is Strauss's, who concludes, "that there was no change in the essential content of the argument and aim of Hobbes's political philosophy from the introduction to his translation of Thucydides up to the latest works" (*The Political Philosophy of Hobbes*, 112), despite the fact that he divides Hobbes's development into stages and describes one of them as humanist (although he does acknowledge that its form is "peculiar") (*ibid.*, 44). The second is Sommerville's, who despite warning repeatedly against the dangers of placing too much emphasis on continuity, concludes that Hobbes's political theory is largely consistent throughout, and formulated prior to the Civil War (*Thomas Hobbes*, 162); cf. Scott, "The Peace of Silence," 117. Robertson notes,

> A natural bent towards political study, and a disposition to take the side of settled and visible authority, are both disclosed in the first work of his pen – disclosed withal so plainly, that, should there now be roused in him the ambition to become, with his native vigour of thought and trained powers of expression, an original investigator and teacher, it might be predicted that a political purpose would be uppermost in his mind (*Hobbes*, 24–25).

> On Thucydides' standing prior to Hobbes's translation, see Schlatter, "Thomas Hobbes and Thucydides," 355–56. For Schlatter, "it appears that Hobbes' reading of Thucydides confirmed for him, or perhaps crystalized for him, the broad outlines and many of the details of his own thought" (*ibid.*, 362).

might flee them."[18] A contemporary translation of Hobbes's autobiographical poem into English does not convey the latter claim accurately, however. As a result, the former is usually taken as Hobbes's last word on Thucydides, despite the fact that Hobbes's chief interest lay consistently in the dangers of demagoguery.[19]

Even so, Hobbes's mature judgment of this work strikes some as suspicious, for the Civil War was still far off.[20] Yet there were plenty of good reasons to be concerned about the perils of democracy and demagoguery in the late 1620s.[21] Hobbes does not tell us when he conceived of the idea of translating the history of the Peloponnesian War, nor when he actually began working on the translation, though he does claim that a long time passed between its completion and publication.[22] We do know, however, that the translation was registered with the Company of Stationers of London on March 18, 1628.[23] Hobbes's first charge and longtime master, the second Earl of Devonshire, died in June of that year. In a letter to his widow, written in November, Hobbes announced that he had completed a draft of an epistle dedicatory that was addressed to her son, the third Earl, and which he submitted to her for her approval, "because the Presse will shortly be ready for it."[24] The work was published in 1629, and in the epistle Hobbes explains to the third Earl that he had no choice but to dedicate the work to

---

[18] *Thomæ Hobbesii Malmesburiensis Vita*, 4. In his entry on Hobbes, Wood writes: "Inter historicos græcos *Thucydidem* præ cæteris dilexit, & vacuis horis, in sermonem anglicum paulatim conversum, cum multa laude an. MDCXXIIX. in publicum edidit, eo fine ut ineptiæ Democraticorum *Atheniensium* nostris hominibus patefierent" (*Historia et Antiquitates Vniuersitatis Oxoniensis*, II: 377). For a prominent example of a contemporary who read Thucydides this way, see Harrington, *The Prerogative of Popular Government*. In *The Common-Wealth of Oceana* (p. 175), Harrington quotes Thucydides from Hobbes's translation.

[19] Cf. Strauss, *The Political Philosophy of Hobbes*, 59.

[20] Stephen, for example, argues that "Hobbes was probably crediting himself with intentions suggested by later experience" (*Hobbes*, 9). Taylor expresses the same view in stronger terms (*Thomas Hobbes*, 5). Cf. Tuck, *Philosophy and Government*, 283.

[21] See Sommerville, *Thomas Hobbes*, 9–10. In criticizing Hobbes's attack on the allegedly seditious doctrines of the ancients, in *Leviathan*, Clarendon noted that "had Mr. *Hobbes* bin of this opinion when he taught *Thucydides* to speak English, which Book contains more of the Science of Mutiny and Sedition, and teaches more of that Oratory that contributes thereunto, then all that *Aristotle* and *Cicero* have publish'd in all their Writings, he would not have communicated such materials to his Country-men" (*A Brief View and Survey*, 85).

[22] *EW*, VIII: ix, xi.

[23] Arber, ed., *A Transcript of the Registers of the Company of Stationers of London*, IV: 161; cf. Martinich, *Hobbes*, 77. Reik (*The Golden Lands of Thomas Hobbes*, 36–37) therefore argues that the translation was published in response to the Petition of Right, which was proposed on May 6, 1628, and received the approval of the House of Lords on May 27 of that year. Cf. Relf, *The Petition of Right*, 36, 47; Rushworth, *Historical Collections, etc.*, 557–58.

[24] Hobbes, Letter to Christian Cavendish, London, November 6, 1628 (*The Correspondence of Thomas Hobbes*, I: 6).

his late father, "by whose indulgence [he] had both the time and ammunition to perform it."[25] Even for someone of Hobbes's scholarly abilities, such a project would have required a substantial amount of time, which means that its beginning cannot be located much later than about the middle of the 1620s.[26] Although it is possible that Hobbes decided to publish Thucydides' history in English for different reasons than those that led him to translate it, his explanation of the role of the translation is nevertheless puzzling.

The answer to this question lies in Hobbes's preface to the translation and essay "Of the Life and History of Thucydides," which are usually examined only in relation to stylistic matters. Hobbes may not have devoted much space therein to conventional political terms, but he has much to say on persuasion and manipulation, in ways that prefigure his epistemology and political theory. Twice in his essay Hobbes uses a phrase of Plutarch's to explain that Thucydides' chief virtue as a historian lies in his ability to make the auditor a spectator.[27] This seemingly innocent remark has a special significance for Hobbes, who identifies two opposite and equally dangerous extremes in the formation of one's understanding of the world. On the one side lies absolute self-reliance – the collection of information about the world based solely on one's senses – and on the other side lies absolute authority – the uncritical acceptance of the doctrines of revered masters.

Each of these comes with its own dangers. The former results in a point of view that is necessarily partial and swayed by one's interests. In the latter case, information comes from someone else, who is not only subject to the same limitations as oneself, but whose interests might also be opposed to one's own. Hobbes liked Thucydides because he not only identifies these extremes, but also charts a path between the dangers that result from them. By offering a narrative consisting only of what appears necessary, and promising to keep his own views out of it as much as possible, Thucydides allows his reader to feel as though he were striking a balance between the disadvantages stemming from having his thoughts corrupted by someone else's judgment and having them clouded by his own emotions or deceived by his senses. Thus, Hobbes's adoption of Plutarch's description is far from accidental. It signals Hobbes's realization that Thucydides has discovered a way to present his history to the reader as objective and unadulterated, even though Thucydides' own role in selecting the episodes and composing the narrative had clearly been formative. The impression that the reader is simply witnessing events as they are unfolding, without the historian's interference, is central to Thucydides' claim to be able to protect his readers'

---

[25] *EW*, VIII: iii. Malcolm cites evidence that it was available on January 1 (*Reason of State, Propaganda, and the Thirty Years' War*, 11 and note 44).

[26] The task took Valla, admittedly a lesser Grecian than Hobbes, some four years to complete (see, for example, Ferlauto, *Il testo di Tucidide e la traduzione latina di Lorenzo Valla*, 3, 8, 56; cf. Powell, "The Papyri of Thucydides and the Translation of Laurentius Valla," 11).

[27] *EW*, VIII: viii, xxii.

ears from the corrupting influence of others, and to his invitation to them to observe events for themselves and reach their own conclusions. Hobbes, who shares Thucydides' apprehension of demagogues, would eventually build his civil philosophy on these foundations.

THE UNRELIABILITY OF SELF-RELIANCE

In the epistle dedicatory addressed to the third Earl of Devonshire, Hobbes praises the second Earl not so much for having studied history and civil knowledge – the most worthy subjects for great persons – but rather for having applied them "to the government of his life and the public good."[28] Hobbes therefore recommends Thucydides' history to the third Earl because it contains "profitable instruction for noblemen, and such as may come to have the managing of great and weighty actions."[29] Hobbes argues that even though the younger William has much to learn from the example of his late father and from others around him, there is a particular quality in history that renders it a necessary supplement to one's education, "[f]or in history, actions of *honour* and *dishonour* do appear plainly and distinctly, which are which; but in the present age they are so disguised, that few there be, and those very careful, that be not grossly mistaken in them."[30] History introduces distance between the events and their assessment, and for Hobbes there are several reasons why this distance is necessary if useful lessons are to be drawn from the past.

A first set of reasons for mistrusting one's assessment and interpretation of contemporary events has to do with the mechanics of the way in which that assessment is formed. In subsequent works, in which Hobbes develops his theory of human nature in detail, he argues that the ways in which our organs of sense perceive the qualities of the motions of objects in the outside world should make us suspicious of our conclusions about that world. This fact should alert us to the possibility that different actors perceive the same thing in different ways, if only because they observe it from different vantage points, for example.[31] Things become even more complicated, however, once the motion of the external object ceases. Hobbes likens this sequence to the ripples in a pool of water that continue after the motion that caused them has ceased. Accordingly, he defines "imagination" as "conception remaining, and little by little decaying from and after the act of sense."[32] This process of decay is inevitable and results in a loss of clarity with respect to the object remembered. For example, its parts are no longer as clear as they were at the

---

[28] *EW*, VIII: iv. Hobbes's comments here presage his subsequent emphasis on utility. See, notably, his description of the utility of philosophy in *De Corpore*, I.i.7; cf. *De Homine*, XI.9.
[29] *EW*, VIII: v.
[30] *EW*, VIII: vi.
[31] *The Elements of Law*, I.2; *Leviathan*, I: 3–4.
[32] *The Elements of Law*, I.3.1.

time of conception; therefore, any assessment of this object or its relation to other objects is bound to be faulty.[33]

Hobbes argues that for the most part our conceptions follow one another as cause and effect, so that those who desire an end can proceed backward to the means necessary for its attainment and thereby construct a series of steps that are necessary to get from where they are to the desired object.[34] The more information one possesses regarding antecedents and consequents, therefore, the more likely will one be to find a connection to a particular object.[35] This is one of the main reasons why Hobbes prefers those who have the most experience, but also why he considers good history an important tool, because it adds to the stock of such connections.[36] One's store of conceptions and the circumstances in which an incoming conception manifests itself, however, will affect the way in which that new conception will be handled. Thus, for example, a ship will mean very different things to one person who has just returned from a pleasant cruise than to another who has just seen a loved one sail away.

As if the practical limitations involved in our perception of the outside world were not enough, a further set of constraints is introduced by the way in which our interests affect our judgment.[37] An individual present in popular assemblies, seditions, and fields of battle such as those described by Thucydides is unlikely to be an impartial spectator. Even if he were, the speed, violence, and passions involved in such events would most likely leave him with a strong yet distorted impression. At the very least, then, the nature of such events as are worthy of being retold by a historian renders them too powerful for dispassionate observation and assessment. When one adds the fact that most observers are likely to be involved in them somehow, it becomes clear that their assessments of those events are in turn likely to be partial. It is for this reason that in the epistle dedicatory Hobbes recommends good history as a supplement to one's own experience, even if the latter derives from the observation of subjects worthy of emulation, such as the third Earl's father and acquaintances.

THE HISTORIAN'S PARTIALITY

The opening of Hobbes's preface to the translation is quite unconventional. Whereas a humanist scholar would have been expected to adhere to the demands of the *topos* and commence with an attempt at *captatio benevolentiæ*,

---

[33] *The Elements of Law*, I.3.7.
[34] *The Elements of Law*, I.4.2. Cf. *Leviathan*, VIII: 35; Review and Conclusion: 389.
[35] *The Elements of Law*, I.4.6, I.4.10; *De Cive*, XIII § 17; *Leviathan*, III: 10–11.
[36] Aubrey tells us that Hobbes would rather be treated by "an experienced old woman, that had been at many sick people's bed-sides, then from the learnedst but unexperienced physitian" ('*Brief Lives*,' I: 350).
[37] *Leviathan*, XV: 79–80.

to secure the goodwill of his reader, Hobbes begins by announcing that his work has already received the approval of those whom he esteems.[38] "[Y]et," he continues, "because there is something, I know not what, in the censure of a multitude, more terrible than any single judgment, how severe or exact soever, I have thought it discretion in all men, that have to do with so many, and to me, in my want of perfection, necessary to bespeak your candour."[39] Hobbes's description of the judgment of a multitude is interesting because it contains two elements that coexist uneasily. On the one hand, he expresses his fear of it, and this may not be surprising. His trepidation here presages his view of the relative advantages of monarchy and democracy that emerges in the rest of the preface to the translation and in his essay on Thucydides, as well as in his political treatises. It is also the first indication of the sentiment that Hobbes would eventually express in connection with Thucydides, in his verse autobiography. On the other hand, he also finds reasons not to be content with the private approbation that his work has received and to brave the "terrible" censure of the multitude. This kind of undertaking, he claims, is beneficial to those who "have to do with so many," the very task that Hobbes would eventually set for himself in his own political treatises.[40]

To increase his chances of reaping the benefits of this judgment, Hobbes promises to explicate his reasons for embarking on the translation. He calls Thucydides a master of his craft, in whose work "the faculty of writing history is at the highest."[41] Hobbes argues that the "principal and proper work of history" is to use the past in order to instruct men "to bear themselves prudently in the present and providently towards the future," and Thucydides does this more "naturally and fully" than anyone else.[42] Hobbes considers narrative to be the very nature of history, and Thucydides' superiority stems from his ability to construct a narrative that is free of unnecessary and distracting elements. In so doing, he avoids the particularly treacherous pitfalls that usually consume historians. First, many historians sprinkle their accounts with discourses on manners and policy that add nothing to the readers' understanding of the events at hand. Second, histories often include conjectures regarding the aims and motives of the actors whose actions they are chronicling. Thucydides, however, seems to "never digress to read a lecture, moral or political, upon his own text, nor enter into men's hearts further than the acts themselves evidently guide him."[43] Hobbes's aversion to

---

[38] According to Aubrey, "Benjamin Johnson" [Ben Jonson] and "Aiton" [Sir Robert Ayton] were among those whom Hobbes asked to judge his translation (*'Brief Lives,'* I: 365; cf. *ibid.*, I: 25–26; I: 332).

[39] *EW*, VIII: vii.

[40] *EW*, VIII: vii. Cf. the Epistle Dedicatory of *The Elements of Law.*

[41] *EW*, VIII: vii.

[42] *EW*, VIII: vii.

[43] *EW*, VIII: viii.

these practices extends well beyond their stylistic and substantive consequences for the writing of history. In his view, they go to the heart of politics
and in their own way contribute to the outbreak of conflict.

Hobbes's dislike of conjectures not warranted by the evidence follows
directly from his theory of perception. While it is impossible to know the
future, one can use one's own store of connections between antecedents
and consequents to form an expectation of what is likely to follow.[44] The
same connections work backward as well, so that an encounter with something known as a consequent will lead one to conclude that it was preceded
by what one knows to be its antecedent. Hobbes illustrates this process
through the example of fire: one who has seen fire followed by ashes, will,
upon encountering ashes once again, conclude that there had been fire; this
he calls a conjecture of the past.[45] The greater the frequency with which one
sees the same antecedent followed by the same consequent, the closer the
association one will draw between the two. This frequency can be problematic, however, since the observer may have *better* reason to think that
the antecedent will once again be followed by the usual consequent, even
though he has no reason to conclude that it *must* or that it always has. For
Hobbes, "[e]xperience concludeth nothing universally," even if one can draw
prudent conclusions.[46] The fragile connection between any single antecedent
and consequent reveals the difficulty involved in reconstructing a chain of
causes and effects composed of several such pairs. For this reason, Hobbes
values Thucydides' reluctance to go too far in attempting to decipher the
intentions of actors from their actions.[47] Deliberation consists of a succession of appetites for and aversions from an object, and, as the manifestation
of the actor's will, an action tells us only what the culmination of his deliberation – that is, his last appetite or aversion – was.[48]

Conjecture, however, can lead one astray in more ways than one. Having
drawn conclusions, right or wrong, about an actor's motives, one can err
still further in evaluating them. While Hobbes grants that "it is prudence to
conclude from experience, what is likely to come to pass, or to have passed
already," he warns that "so is it an error to conclude from it, that it is so or
so called." The reason is that "we cannot from experience conclude, that any
thing is to be called just or unjust, true or false, nor any proposition universal whatsoever, except it be from remembrance of the use of names imposed
arbitrarily by men."[49] According to Hobbes, the names of things emerge

---

[44] See, for example, *The Elements of Law*, I.4.7. Cf. *Leviathan*, III, V, VI, XII: 56, XIII: 60–61,
    XXV: 134–35.
[45] *The Elements of Law*, I.4.8.
[46] *The Elements of Law*, I.4.10; *Leviathan*, III: 11.
[47] *EW*, VIII: viii.
[48] *The Elements of Law*, I.12.1–2; *Leviathan*, VI: 28–29; "Of Liberty and Necessity," §§
    25–33.
[49] *The Elements of Law*, I.4.11.

as it becomes necessary to manage the influx of information delivered by the senses and classify it with reference to information already possessed.[50] Coupled with the fact that perception of the same external object can take place in a variety of circumstances, this means that a single object can come to be characterized in a variety of ways, for "there is scarce any word that is not made equivocal by divers contextures of speech, or by diversity of pronunciation and gesture."[51] In the end, one should not lose sight of the fact that a historian is but an ordinary human being, and as such is subject to these perceptual limitations on top of any limitations imposed by partiality.[52]

History, then, can be equivocal, and both Thucydides and Hobbes are acutely aware of the political dangers inherent in words. In a famous passage from his description of the civil war in Corcyra, Thucydides describes how the simplest and most familiar of terms came to lose their meaning: terms of approbation and disapprobation were applied according to self-interest, and even the clearest words, such as father or brother, became empty when father killed son and brother slew brother. This fratricide was the simplest sign of how bad things had gotten, a powerful indicator that Hobbes would eventually place at the center of his own account of disorder and the state of nature. Thucydides' virtue lies in his ability to not only recognize the dangers inherent in and resulting from the ambiguity of words, but also in allowing the reader to feel as though he were reaching the same conclusion on his own, by not interrupting his narrative with his own discourses. Hobbes marvels at Thucydides' ability to be "accounted the most politic historiographer that ever writ," by filling his narrations with the right material, ordering them with judgment, and expressing himself with "such perspicuity and efficacy" as to make the reader believe that he is actually witnessing the events for himself, without any interference from the historian.[53] Hobbes confesses, "[t]hese virtues of my author did so take my affection, that they begat in me a desire to communicate him further."[54]

THUCYDIDES' SOLUTION: LETTING EVENTS SPEAK FOR THEMSELVES

The most significant evidence of Hobbes's interest in demagoguery comes from his essay, "Of the Life and History of Thucydides," which was published between the preface and translation of the history of the Peloponnesian War. Though hardly unknown at the time, Thucydides was not as popular among

---

[50] *The Elements of Law*, I.5.2.
[51] *The Elements of Law*, I.5.1–5; I.5.7.
[52] See, for example, *The Elements of Law*, I.5.14; *Leviathan*, XV: 79–80.
[53] *EW*, VIII: viii.
[54] *EW*, VIII: viii.

the English as he has become since. Hobbes therefore tells the readers that he felt the need to justify his project somehow, and to introduce the historian to those who might not know very much about him or see the utility of an English translation of his history. Accordingly, the opening section of Hobbes's essay on Thucydides is devoted to biographical information and to a defense of Thucydides from the charge that he was an atheist.

In his first mention of rhetoric, Hobbes informs the reader that Thucydides was a disciple of Antiphon, "one ... for power of speech almost a miracle, and feared by the people for his eloquence."[55] With such a teacher, argues Hobbes, Thucydides would have been "sufficiently qualified to have become a great demagogue, and of great authority with the people."[56] However, Thucydides did not want to pursue this path, because "in those days it was impossible for any man to give good and profitable counsel for the commonwealth, and not incur the displeasure of the people."[57] For Hobbes, Thucydides' time was one of radical transvaluation, in which those proposing the most dangerous and desperate enterprises were the ones who were seen as the best citizens and the ones with the most power to sway the people.[58] Someone more moderate, willing to offer "temperate and discreet advice," would have been seen as a coward.[59] Hobbes would soon find himself in a similar situation, and Thucydides offered a model of how to navigate these straits. As the reader of the history would soon come to see, the inconstant signification of terms, which would become a central preoccupation of Hobbes's, already figured prominently in Thucydides' account. In hindsight, it is not entirely surprising that Hobbes portrays Thucydides as a victim of that tendency. He believes that it was to avoid these consequences that Thucydides chose to withdraw from public life and devote his energies to the writing of history.[60] More importantly, however, Thucydides chose not to follow this path in the writing of his history. As Hobbes notes repeatedly and with approval, Thucydides refrains from interrupting the narrative with his own discourses, and offers his personal view of the outcomes of events only rarely and when there is good reason.[61]

Given Thucydides' diagnosis, for Hobbes "it is manifest that he least of all liked the democracy."[62] Hobbes points to many passages in the history, where Thucydides

noteth the emulation and contention of the demagogues for reputation and glory of wit; with their crossing of each other's counsels, to the damage of the public; the

[55] *EW*, VIII: xv.
[56] *EW*, VIII: xvi.
[57] *EW*, VIII: xvi.
[58] *EW*, VIII: xvi.
[59] *EW*, VIII: xvi.
[60] *EW*, VIII: xvi.
[61] *EW*, VIII: viii, xxii.
[62] *EW*, VIII: xvi.

inconsistency of resolutions caused by the diversity of ends and power of rhetoric in the orators; and the desperate actions undertaken upon the flattering advice of such as desired to attain, or to hold what they had attained, of authority and sway amongst the common people.[63]

Hobbes does not find much evidence of praise for aristocracy; he concludes that Thucydides seems to like monarchy best, since the Athenian government under Pericles was, in effect, monarchical. Thus, Hobbes's claim, in his much later verse autobiography, regarding Thucydides' views about the various regime types is but a repetition of the conclusion that Hobbes had drawn at the time of the translation.

Hobbes recounts the story of Thucydides' brief and unfortunate involvement in the war, and then devotes almost as much space to the description of his resultant banishment. There, he describes Cleon, its alleged instigator, as a "most violent sycophant in those times, and thereby also a most acceptable speaker amongst the people."[64] Hobbes's defense of Thucydides here is interesting not only because it is a response to the problem of the inconstant signification and consequent abuse of terms, but also because it contradicts Hobbes's earlier insistence on conjecturing only so far as the evidence permits. Despite that insistence, here he chastises those who "judge only upon events" and do not take into account the actor's intentions.[65]

From his defense of Thucydides' actions, Hobbes turns to a lengthy consideration of his writings. Lost as they are in the midst of an essay usually bypassed as a mandatory, conventional exercise on the way to the main event, Hobbes's remarks regarding Thucydides' method are invaluable and merit close attention, as they presage his own views regarding eloquence and method, which he would develop along the same lines in the years to come. To assess Thucydides' writing, Hobbes argues that one needs to examine it for truth and elocution, since the former is the soul and the latter the

---

[63] *EW*, VIII: xvi-xvii.

[64] *EW*, VIII: xix. Hobbes's characterization of Cleon is modeled after Thucydides' "ὢν καὶ ἐς τὰ ἄλλα βιαιότατος τῶν πολιτῶν τῷ τε δήμῳ παρὰ πολὺ ἐν τῷ τότε πιθανώτατος," which Hobbes renders as "being of all the citizens most violent and with the people at that time far the most powerful" (III.36).

[65] *EW*, VIII: xix. It should be noted that this view is broadly consistent with the way in which Thucydides decided to solve the problem of reproducing speeches. See *Eight Bookes of the Peloponnesian Warre*, I.22, which Hobbes translates as follows:

> What particular persons have spoken when they were about to enter into the war or when they were in it, were hard for me to remember exactly; whether they were speeches which I have heard myself, or have received at the second hand. But as any man seemed to me, that knew what was nearest to the sum of the truth of all that had been uttered, to speak most agreeably to the matter still at hand, so I have made it spoken here.

> However one interprets this complicated statement, it is clear that Thucydides' reconstruction involves conjecture based on the speaker's character and history. See, for example, Gomme, *A Historical Commentary on Thucydides*, 139-48.

body of history. A good history needs both, because "[t]he latter without the former, is but a picture of history; and the former without the latter, unapt to instruct."[66] Hobbes's analogy and view of elocution here is, once again, prophetic, and should be borne in mind.

Where the truth of Thucydides' history is concerned, Hobbes finds that little needs to be said in its defense. Hobbes is by no means alone in considering Thucydides' veracity to be beyond reproach. His defense of Thucydides here, however, is striking, not simply because it displays none of Hobbes's usual suspicion of motives, but also because it shows the extent to which Thucydides' statement of method had succeeded in persuading his readers that he was doing something different – producing a credible account of events as they happened – rather than reproducing legends, hearsay, or personal views. Thucydides was well aware that the extent and complexity of the events he was recounting would have caused a reasonable reader to be credulous, and had accordingly chosen to address the status of his evidence head on.[67] His direct handling of that matter succeeded in convincing Hobbes and many others that an apparent weakness of such a sweeping history did not stand in the way of an objective account.

Hobbes goes one step further, and concludes that the most obvious of Thucydides' difficulties were actually advantages. No one, he claims, challenges Thucydides' veracity, and there is no need to do so, since Thucydides seems to have had no reason to lie. Hobbes also finds that the scope of Thucydides' project adds to his credibility, since it is confined to events about which he could collect data. The requisite information was available to him and he did not lack the means to collect it.[68] Although the events related by Thucydides took place during his lifetime, he was neither present nor directly involved in many of them, and hence he is not as prone to the errors resulting from perceptual limitations and the interference of the passions that Hobbes addressed in the preface. The most important proof of Thucydides' impartiality, however, is to be found in his own statement of intent. Because the history of the Peloponnesian War was written as an "everlasting possession," there is no reason to suspect that Thucydides was trying to reap immediate and tangible benefits from it.[69] One might object here that given his own ill-fated involvement in the war and his subsequent banishment, Thucydides would have had ample reason to portray Athens in an unfavorable light. Hobbes, however, finds no evidence of such a bias and concludes that "no word of his, but [the Athenians'] own actions do sometimes reproach them."[70] Thus, Hobbes concludes that "if the truth of a

---

[66] *EW,* VIII: xx.
[67] *Eight Bookes of the Peloponnesian Warre,* I.20–22.
[68] *EW,* VIII: xx–xxi.
[69] *Eight Bookes of the Peloponnesian Warre,* I.22; *EW,* VIII: xxi.
[70] *EW,* VIII: xxi.

history did ever appear by the manner of relating, it doth so in this history: so coherent, perspicuous and persuasive is the whole narration, and every part thereof."[71]

How Thucydides achieves this remarkable result becomes clear when one follows Hobbes and divides elocution into disposition – or method – and style. Where the method is concerned, he suggests that Thucydides proceeds in a sensible way, beginning with a summary of the development of Greece from its beginnings up to the start of the war, continuing by examining its causes, "both real and pretended," and then following "distinctly and purely" the events themselves as they unfold, dividing the narrative into years, and then into summer and winter.[72] When it comes to actions and the motives behind them, Thucydides either presents the motives before the actions, in the sequence of the narrative, or he has the actors themselves explain them in orations, but always adhering to the principle of conjecturing no further than the actions themselves permit.[73] Thucydides adds his own judgment of these actions "when there is just occasion," but he never digresses to instruct the reader himself. Were he to do so, he would be speaking to his audience himself. Instead, he lets his readers see the "ways and events of good and evil counsels" and thereby allows the narrative itself to "*secretly instruct the reader*, and more effectually than can possibly be done by precept."[74] Where eloquence and method are concerned, then, Hobbes has learned important lessons from Thucydides. His recognition of the need for eloquence and of the power of proper method here marks the beginning of his own quest for the means to instruct as effectively as Thucydides had done, by making the reader feel as though he had arrived at the right conclusions on his own.

Hobbes promises to leave the assessment of Thucydides' style to "ancient and competent judges."[75] As it turns out, however, this is not entirely true. He begins this section with Plutarch, who, as he had noted in the preface, captures Thucydides' perspicuity in his observation that the history of the Peloponnesian War turns the auditor into a spectator, a view that Hobbes shares and considers Thucydides' greatest strength.[76] Plutarch also notes that Thucydides manages to "cast his reader into the same passions that they were in that were beholders."[77] Hobbes then cites Cicero's approval of Thucydides' style, before turning to Dionysius of Halicarnassus, to whom he devotes the bulk of the remainder of his essay. This is an interesting choice, given that Dionysius is critical of Thucydides and, according to Hobbes's judgment, not a very competent judge. Hobbes's choice

---

[71] *EW*, VIII: xxi.
[72] *EW*, VIII: xxi.
[73] *EW*, VIII: viii, xxi.
[74] *EW*, VIII: xxii, emphasis added.
[75] *EW*, VIII: xxii. But see *Leviathan*, A Review and Conclusion: 394–95.
[76] *EW*, VIII: viii, xxii.
[77] *EW*, VIII: xxii.

is important, however, for two reasons. First, because it allows Hobbes to distinguish between rhetoric and elocution, and second because it reveals that his division of elocution into method and style is, in the end, untenable. Ultimately, Hobbes's comments on Dionysius's criticisms of Thucydides show that a writer's stylistic choices will affect his ability to persuade and instruct his audience.

The difference between elocution and rhetoric is manifested in Hobbes's description of Dionysius. Having been led to expect a competent judge, the reader instead finds here a rhetorician who "would no further commend [Thucydides] than of necessity he must," and who in fact had "taken so much pains, and applied so much of his faculty in rhetoric, to the extenuating of the worth" of Thucydides' work.[78] In considering Dionysius's case, Hobbes already reveals himself as an apt student of Thucydides: "I have thought it necessary to take out the principal objections he maketh against him; and without many words of mine own to leave them to the consideration of the reader."[79] Just as Thucydides invites the reader to behold events for himself and make up his mind, Hobbes will do the same with Dionysius's arguments. This ruse would mark the beginning of this practice, which would soon become the centerpiece of Hobbes's own method.

The list of Dionysius's allegedly stylistic charges soon reveals that there is in fact no essential difference between method and style where elocution is concerned. The first charge is that Thucydides' history is not as noble and beneficial as Herodotus's, because it treats but a single war and one that is "neither honourable nor fortunate."[80] If anything, however, Hobbes sees Thucydides' scope as much more conducive to the writing of good history than Herodotus's, since it is manageable and affords him a chance to gather the necessary evidence. He also considers the nature of that war far more appropriate for instruction because it teaches men the calamities that they should avoid, a lesson that Hobbes himself would take to heart in constructing his own system.[81] Dionysius also finds fault with Thucydides for not knowing where to begin and end his account. He argues that there is no need for the extensive prehistory that Thucydides provides, and chastises him for laying the blame for the war with his own city when he could have avoided

[78] *EW*, VIII: xxiii.

[79] *EW*, VIII: xxiii.

[80] *EW*, VIII: xxiii.

[81] *EW*, VIII: xxvi. In comparing Thucydides to Herodotus, Hobbes argues, "men profit more by looking on adverse events, than on prosperity: therefore by how much men's miseries do better instruct, than their good success; by so much was Thucydides happy in taking his argument, than Herodotus was wise in choosing his" (*EW*, VIII: xxiv). Hobbes's own negative system is summed up best in his denial of a *summum bonum* and his insistence that it would be easier to build consensus around the undesirability of a *summum malum*, a project in which the opposition of the state of nature to civil society will be central. We will return to this matter.

doing so. Hobbes's response to these charges is easy to predict. He argues that a discussion of causes is necessary insofar as it sheds light onto the main event, and praises Thucydides for laying blame where he finds it and remaining equally impartial toward the actors throughout the history.[82]

Having addressed Dionysius's two most fundamental criticisms, Hobbes pauses to remind the reader that he devoted as much space to them as he did because he wanted to let Dionysius's views on history speak for themselves. The reader's assessment of those views, however, is far from unaided. On the one side of the argument lies Dionysius, and on the other his opposition, which is quite formidable. At its head, far from silent, is Hobbes himself, who declares, "there was never written so much absurdity in so few lines," supported by practically everyone else who has spoken on the matter, as well as by common sense. Whether any reader would muster the courage to take Dionysius's side in this fight is unclear, but that is as it should be, because of Dionysius's "[m]ost manifest vices" – his expectation that the historian should be loyal to his country and conceal any information that might malign it: "He was a rhetorician; and it seemeth he would have nothing written, but that which was most capable of rhetorical ornament."[83]

The third objection raised by Dionysius concerns Thucydides' dutiful adherence to proceeding by years and seasons, rather than by sequences of events, which makes the history hard to follow at times. In responding, once again Hobbes invokes Thucydides' claim that his history is presented as a possession for all time, rather than for the present. Hobbes argues that this approach is more natural in that it allows Thucydides to present a single narrative of the whole war. The attentive reader who devotes some time to it, he suggests, will draw the right conclusions.[84] The distinction between attentive and inattentive readers would become a regular feature of Hobbes's works. In *The Elements of Law*, which was addressed to a few learned readers, Hobbes would reprimand those who are too "confident of their own knowledge [and] weigh not what is said," and proclaim that "the fault is not mine but theirs," since just as his task was to show his reasons, "so it is theirs to bring attention."[85] Addressing a much broader and more diverse audience in *De Cive*, Hobbes would invite the reader to consider the highest secrets of state, hidden by the allegories and myths of the ancients.[86] Going one step further, Hobbes would open *Leviathan* by proclaiming the task at hand "harder than to learn any Language, or Science," but would add immediately that with his help, all the reader would have to do to is introspect, "[f]or this kind of Doctrine, admitteth no

---

[82] *EW*, VIII: xxiv-xxvi.
[83] *EW*, VIII: xxvi.
[84] *EW*, VIII: xxvii.
[85] *The Elements of Law*, I.1.3.
[86] *De Cive*, Pref.

other Demonstration."[87] Hobbes's censure of Dionysius here presages his own attempts at *captatio benevolentiæ*.

Next, Dionysius objects to Thucydides' method in the first book of the history, wherein he finds him devoting too much time to the "archeology" of Greece and of treating the events related to Epidamnus and Potidaea before addressing the "true cause" of the war. As to the first issue, Hobbes notes that an author must either suppose that the reader possesses knowledge of these early times and of the origins of cities and customs, or supply it as "a necessary preface."[88] Where the cause of the war is concerned, Hobbes finds the objection absurd. As Thucydides makes clear in Book I, the relationship between the pretext and "truest cause" of the war is a stepping stone toward understanding everything that followed. Hobbes's concern, however, extends even further, since the relationship between the two types of causes involves conjecture, and the abuse of conjecture is one of the chief vices of most histories. The exposition of the events regarding Epidamnus and Potidaea, therefore, is an essential complement to the elucidation of the truest cause, which is conjectural and thus depends on evidence of this sort. For Hobbes, "a more clear and natural order cannot possibly be devised."[89]

For Dionysius, Thucydides' history was unclear not only in its structure and procedure, but also in the way in which it was written, with its long and obscure sentences. This criticism might strike one as purely stylistic, but Hobbes's rebuttal shows once more that when it comes to eloquence, style and method go hand in hand. Hobbes concedes that some sentences in Thucydides' work are long, but thinks that the attentive reader will be able to make sense of them. Their difficulty stems from the profundity of their subject matter, treating as they do "those human passions, which either dissembled or not commonly discoursed of, do yet carry the greatest sway with men in public conversation."[90] This, however, is as it should be, since as Hobbes had noted in both the epistle dedicatory and the preface to the translation, Thucydides' history is not for everyone. Those who cannot follow his descriptions of seditions and other such events are unable to do so because they cannot "penetrate into the nature of such things."[91]

As Hobbes describes it, Thucydides' history represents for him an attempt to navigate treacherous extremes: on the one side, absolute liberty through reliance only on one's own conceptions and experience of the world, and on the other side, absolute subjection to the authority of another. Each of these is fraught with danger. The former is dangerous because one's ability to perceive is subject to practical and mechanical limitations, as well as to

---

[87] *Leviathan*, Introduction: 2.
[88] *EW*, VIII: xxvii.
[89] *EW*, VIII: xxvii-xxviii.
[90] *EW*, VIII: xxix.
[91] *EW*, VIII: xxx. Cf. *ibid.*, iii-vi, x-xi, where Hobbes is interested in the "few and better sort of readers," and "all men of good judgment and education."

the influence of passions, fear, honor, and interest. The latter is even worse, because others are subject to the same limitations and interests likely to be opposed to one's own. If one is to profit from history and acquire the means to live "prudently in the present and providently towards the future," one needs a guide such as Thucydides, who is able to instruct the reader secretly by turning him from an auditor into a spectator, thereby showing him what he needs to see, but allowing him to feel that he drew the right conclusions on his own.[92] For Hobbes, Plutarch's observation is especially apt, for it captures Thucydides' paradoxical virtue: he centers his story around speeches, yet he makes the reader observe, rather than listen, thereby protecting him from the authority of received wisdom and the dangers of demagoguery. By setting the action before the reader's eyes, Thucydides offers him the advantages of direct experience all the while shielding him from the dangers involved in actually being present as orators attempt to sway their audiences. This silence would prove crucial if men were to hear the one thing that matters, for

as men, for the atteyning of peace, and conservation of themselves thereby, have made an Artificiall Man, which we call a Common-wealth; so also have they made Artificiall Chains, called *Civill Lawes*, which they themselves, by mutuall covenants, have fastned at one end, to the lips of that Man, or Assembly, to whom they have given the Soveraigne Power; and at the other end to their own Ears.[93]

[92] *EW*, VIII: vii; xxii.
[93] *Leviathan*, XXI: 108–09.

2

Winning Belief in the Hearer

[B]efore some audiences not even the possession of the exactest knowledge will make it easy for what we say to produce conviction. For argument based on knowledge implies instruction, and there are people whom one cannot instruct. Here, then, we must use, as our modes of persuasion and argument, notions possessed by everybody ...

      – Aristotle, *Rhetoric*

A RHETORICIAN

Hobbes left the Cavendish household after his Thucydides was published, and assumed a new post as tutor to the son of Sir Gervase Clifton, whom he accompanied on a Grand Tour to France and Switzerland.[1] It was during that trip, according to Aubrey, that Hobbes took notice of geometry, "the onely Science that it hath pleased God hitherto to bestow on mankind," and there that he had his Euclidean moment.[2] We have noted that Hobbes's encounter with Euclid is seen as having transformed his thought by opening his eyes to the possibilities of a scientific approach to politics that could be as successful as geometry. Precisely because science figures so prominently in Hobbes's writings from this point forward and because his interest in it was very serious, it is necessary to approach the relationship between science and politics with circumspection.[3]

---

[1] According to the verse autobiography, Hobbes spent eighteen months in Paris during this trip (*Thomæ Hobbesii Malmesburiensis vita*, 4); cf. *T. Hobbes Malmesburiensis Vita* (*OL*, I: xiv), where Hobbes describes it as "in Galliam," although his correspondence puts him in Geneva in the spring of 1629 (*The Correspondence of Thomas Hobbes*, I: 7–14, but see note 23 on p. 10).

[2] *Leviathan*, IV: 15; cf. Aubrey, '*Brief Lives*,' I: 332.

[3] The relationship of geometry to Hobbes's scientific approach to politics is often misunderstood. See, for example, Bramhall, *The Catching of Leviathan*, Chapter 2 (*The Works of the Most Reverend Father in God, John Bramhall D.D.*); Clarendon, *A Brief View and*

Hobbes's fascination with all aspects of science, his admiration for the achievements of the geometers, and his contention that natural philosophy was in his day young, but civil philosophy much younger, having begun only with his *De Cive*, are but a few of the many reasons for thinking that the episode related by Aubrey marked the beginning of a radically new phase in Hobbes's thinking.[4] As we have seen, several commentators have alleged a break between Hobbes's early, "humanist" period, and this new, post-Euclidean phase.[5] But if the publication of Hobbes's translation of Thucydides offers a convenient signpost for the end of his so-called humanist period and his "discovery" of Euclid another for the beginning of his scientific phase, it is worth bearing in mind that the real story is more complicated. Although it is possible to read Aubrey's anecdote as suggesting that this was Hobbes's first encounter with Euclid, it is unlikely that this was the case.[6] What appealed to Hobbes in this instance was the effect that Euclid's method could have on an observer in Hobbes's position.

The setting is crucial, for upon entering a library, one finds oneself surrounded by authorities on all sides, with none as formidable as the one that lies open on the lectern. Therein, Hobbes traced the proof on his own, and Euclid demonstrated the truth of his claim without any appeal to authority. Yet, according to Aubrey's account, Hobbes first expressed his disbelief at

Survey, 79, 117; Harrington, *Politicaster*, 23; Bignone, *Studi sul pensiero antico*, 40–41; Goldsmith, *Hobbes's Science of Politics*, 9–11; Skinner, *Hobbes and Civil Science*, 75–76, 319–20. Notable exceptions are Kahn, *Rhetoric, Prudence, and Skepticism*, 156–57; Sorell, "The Science in Hobbes's Politics"; Strauss, *The Political Philosophy of Hobbes*, 129–70. Cf. Oakeshott, *Hobbes on Civil Association*, esp. 146–47; Keller, "In the Service of 'Truth' and 'Victory.'"

[4] See *De Corpore*, Ep. Ded., *EW*, I: ix.

[5] Strauss, *The Political Philosophy of Hobbes*; cf. Skinner, *Reason and Rhetoric in the Philosophy of Hobbes*. The main distinction tends to be between a "humanist" and a "scientific" phase, but there are other criteria, for example, those employed by Remer, who focuses on the difference between a "rhetorical epistemology" and the "certainty of science" ("Hobbes, the Rhetorical Tradition, and Toleration").

[6] Jesseph points to two reasons for doubting that this was Hobbes's first encounter with Euclid. The first is that Hobbes was apparently able to follow the demonstration of the Pythagorean theorem which, according to Jesseph, "is sufficiently complex to be largely incomprehensible to a complete novice." The second is a list of books (Devonshire Mss., Chatsworth HS/E/2), including many on mathematics, attributed by Pacchi to Hobbes ("Una biblioteca ideale di Thomas Hobbes"). However, Malcolm has challenged the attribution, arguing that the list is in the hand of Robert Payne, and suggesting that it "may have been compiled in 1631 as an aid to Hobbes when he undertook the tuition of the Earl of Devonshire; alternatively, it may have come into Hobbes's possession only after Payne's death" (*The Correspondence of Thomas Hobbes*, II: 874; cf. *Aspects of Hobbes*, 82, 143). The catalogue of the Hardwick Library in Hobbes's hand lists two volumes of Euclid (Devonshire Mss., Chatsworth HS/E/1A). Tellingly, the outside back cover of the catalogue's contemporary binding bears the imprints of several geometrical shapes clearly made with a ruler and compass. According to Aubrey, Hobbes used to "say that he was wont to draw lines on his thigh and on the sheetes, abed, and also multiply and divide" (*'Brief Lives,'* I: 333).

Euclid's conclusion, and had to retrace the steps backward, so as to become "demonstratively convinced" of the truth. Hobbes's two reactions indicate Euclid's appeal. The initial disbelief contains something of the suspicion of authority and confidence in one's own judgment that resides more or less in everyone – the very attitudes that Hobbes would eventually place at the head of his account of vainglory and conflict.[7] Relying not on Euclid's reputation or the authority of other noted geometers or philosophers, but on logical steps that a careful reader could confirm on his own, the proof offers itself to any well-intentioned observer who wishes to test it. By doing so, that observer can satisfy himself of its truth, and retain the sense of having had some measure of agency in the process. The crucial point about this sort of demonstration, of course, is that the observer's sense of achievement is far greater than the achievement itself, for it is Euclid's discovery and ability to present the evidence in such a manner that makes the demonstration possible. Whether true or not, Aubrey's anecdote captures something that Hobbes saw in Euclid, and which was already fresh in his mind from the recently completed translation of Thucydides. Euclid succeeded in his demonstration by rendering the observer of the proof a witness in the proceedings, just as Thucydides succeeded by giving his reader the sense that he was witnessing the events he was describing. Although very different in other ways, both procedures eliminated the dubious and self-interested middlemen that so frustrated Hobbes.

Focusing on 1629 as the point at which Hobbes allegedly broke with humanism and turned to science thus causes us to lose sight of the fact that Hobbes had been and continued to be primarily concerned with persuasion. A notebook from the 1630s, belonging to Hobbes's pupil and found among Hobbes's papers at Chatsworth, shows that Hobbes used a Latin précis of Aristotle's *Rhetoric* to teach the future Earl.[8] The strongest evidence of a continued interest in persuasion, however, lies in the fact that some eight years into this scientific phase, and well before Hobbes composed and circulated his first major treatise, he composed and published a précis of Aristotle's *Rhetoric*. An entry in the Register of the Company of Stationers of London dated February 1, 1636–37 lists Andrew Crooke's name alongside the following description: "Entred for his Copie vnder the hands of Master WEEKES and Master Downes warden a Booke called *A breife of the Art of Rhetorique, conteyninge in substance, all that* ARISTOTLE *hath written in his three Bookes of that subiect* by T: H: [*i. e.* THOMAS HOBBES]."[9]

---

[7] *Leviathan*, XIII: 60–61.

[8] Devonshire Mss., Chatsworth HS/D/1.

[9] Arber, ed., *A Transcript of the Registers of the Company of Stationers of London*, IV: 346. The first edition of the *Briefe of the Art of Rhetorique* bears no date, so it is on the basis of this registration date that the publication is thought to have taken place in 1637. On the attribution to Hobbes, see Macdonald & Hargreaves, 7–9; Dodd, "The Rhetorics in Molesworth's Edition of Hobbes," esp. 37, n. 8; Harwood, *The Rhetorics of Thomas Hobbes*

Despite the fact that the title page does not name its compiler, there is little doubt that the précis was Hobbes's. We have substantial evidence of his active involvement and strong views during the publication of his works, which suggests that it is unlikely that he would have continued to work with a publisher who had tried to credit him with a work that was not his, and yet Hobbes made Crooke – the publisher of the *Briefe* – his English publisher.[10] On the publisher's side, and assuming that "T.H." refers to Thomas Hobbes, it is hard to see what Crooke could have gained by misattributing the work to an author who, at that point, had no reputation to speak of. Moreover, two years after Hobbes's death, William Crooke published *The Art of Rhetoric, with a Discourse of the Laws of England*. In the Preface, Crooke attributed the work to Hobbes.[11] Then there is Aubrey, who claims, "[t]here is also a small peece in English called *A Breefe of Aristotle's Rhetorick* printed by Andrew Crooke, which was his, though his name be not to it."[12]

This work has had an awkward place in accounts of Hobbes's intellectual development. With few exceptions, commentators have found it difficult to fit it into the neat story of Hobbes's turn to science, and have rejected it, passed it by, or considered it a byproduct of Hobbes's tutorial duties.[13] The

---

and Bernard Lamy, 1–3. There is a broad consensus that the first major work in Hobbes's scientific period was *The Elements of Law*, and that the "Tractatus Opticus" and Hobbes's critique of White's *De Mundo Dialogi Tres* were composed subsequently (see, for example, Tuck, "Hobbes and Descartes"; Malcolm, *Aspects of Hobbes*, 12–13, on the former, and Jacquot & Jones's introduction to *Critique du De Mundo de Thomas White* and Jones's introduction to *Thomas White's De Mundo Examined*, on the latter).

[10] See *The Correspondence of Thomas Hobbes*, II, 823–24. Where Hobbes's involvement in the publication of his works is concerned, we will consider the notable case of *De Cive*.

[11] Hobbes, *The Art of Rhetoric, with a Discourse of the Laws of England*, A3[r-v], but see Cromartie's introduction to *A Dialogue between a Philosopher and a Student, of the Common Laws of England*, lxvii.

[12] Aubrey, 'Brief Lives,' I: 359.

[13] The most notable exception is Strauss, who argues, "[i]t would be difficult to find another classical work whose importance for Hobbes's political philosophy can be compared with that of the *Rhetoric*" (*The Political Philosophy of Hobbes*, 35), although it should be noted that Strauss accepts as genuine not only the *Briefe*, but also *The Art of Rhetoric*, which has been attributed to Hobbes mistakenly (see Dodd, "The Rhetorics in Molesworth's Edition of Hobbes," esp. 42). In his own account, Skinner cites Strauss with approval, although he considers Aristotle less important in Hobbes's intellectual development than his Roman counterparts, arguing that Hobbes "clearly possessed an intimate knowledge of Aristotle's *Rhetoric*, but ... made use of it only in connection with analysing the passions of the soul" (*Reason and Rhetoric in the Philosophy of Hobbes*, 38, n. 183). Among those who consider it a mere product of Hobbes's instruction of the future Earl of Devonshire, Martinich suggests that "[p]erhaps Hobbes thought that his labors with Aristotle's rhetoric could spare other people the potentially corrupting activity of reading that book" (*Hobbes: A Biography*, 97; cf. Struever, *Rhetoric, Modality, Modernity*, 14). It is worth noting that the Hardwick library catalog lists two copies of Aristotle's *Rhetoric*, one containing both Greek and Latin, as well as

challenge posed by this work is multifaceted and obvious. Its publication date comes too far into Hobbes's scientific phase to allow us to classify it as a mere product of his humanist phase.[14] That Hobbes chose not merely to publish this work well into his scientific phase, but that it was the only thing on this scale that he published between 1629 and 1647, makes it unlikely that this was just a handbook for fellow tutors. The *Briefe* is yet another example of why trying to understand the development of Hobbes's thought in phases is ultimately unhelpful.

Among the better known characteristics of the enduring image of Hobbes the scientist are his aversion to rhetoric and his antipathy toward Aristotle.[15] Despite Hobbes's vociferous statements against both, however, some of the most important contributions to our understanding of his theory have begun precisely by calling our attention to how important rhetoric and Aristotle

---

another just in Latin, in addition to a Latin edition of Aristotle's works (Devonshire Mss., Chatsworth HS/E/1A). Regardless of the extent to which the *Briefe* was motivated by Hobbes's tutorial duties, Hobbes's decision not simply to use Aristotle, rather than Cicero or Quintilian, but also to publish this précis is telling. Given that he published nothing of this magnitude between Thucydides and *De Cive*, this fact must have some significance.

In assessing Skinner's *Reason and Rhetoric*, Schuhmann has argued that whereas the Latin summary of the dictation book can be linked to Hobbes, "the English version published in the *Briefe* should not be ascribed to Hobbes, and the *Briefe* should correspondingly not be used for the study of Hobbes's thought" ("Skinner's Hobbes," 118). However, in his chronicle of Hobbes, which was published that year and which contains references to Skinner's *Reason and Rhetoric*, Schuhmann considers the *Briefe* a translation based on the Latin précis of the notebook and, hence, presumably a work of Hobbes's (*Hobbes une chronique*, 57). Schuhmann's suggestion in his review of Skinner's book is the only such challenge to the attribution of the *Briefe* to Hobbes of which I am aware. That challenge appears to be based mainly on Schuhmann's view that the *Briefe* contains "a few remarks that are not in line with what is known to be Hobbes's thought" ("Skinner's Hobbes," 118). This test, however, is problematic because the *Briefe* is an idiosyncratic summary of Aristotle's *Rhetoric*, not simply a presentation of Hobbes's views. Other interpreters, such as Harwood (introduction to *The Rhetorics of Thomas Hobbes and Bernard Lamy*) and Sorell ("Hobbes's UnAristotelian Political Rhetoric") have argued persuasively that the *Briefe* displays patterns of addition and omission (cf. Rayner, "Hobbes and the Rhetoricians," 87–89; Wildermuth, "Hobbes, Aristotle, and the Materialist Rhetor," 77). The evidence from the registers of the Company of Stationers, from Aubrey, and from Crooke, coupled with the fact that not only did Hobbes not disavow the work, but he continued onto a long and highly successful relationship with its publisher, Crooke, seems to me to prevail over Schuhmann's objection. Cf. Malcolm's introduction to *Leviathan*, I: 92.

[14] Although Strauss, for example, concludes that it is "more correct to assume that the use and appreciation of Aristotle's *Rhetoric* which may be traced in Hobbes's mature period are the last remnants of the Aristotelianism of his youth" than to consider it a late discovery, as in the case of Euclid (*The Political Philosophy of Hobbes*, 42).

[15] On rhetoric, see, for example, *The Elements of Law*, Ep. Ded. and II.8.14; *De Cive*, XII.12; on Aristotle, see, *The Elements of Law*, I.13.3, I.17.1, I.17.14, II.8.3, II.8.13, II.9.8, II.10.8; *De Cive*, Pref., § 7, I.2, III.13, V.5, X.2, X.8; *Leviathan*, XII: 59, XV: 77, XVII: 86, XXI: 110–11, XLIV: 334, and XLVI.

are for Hobbes.[16] Hobbes's statements regarding Aristotle may often sound like "a declaration of war," but the "attitude that is conveyed by his published writings, taken as a whole, is closer to respectful opposition than warlike contempt."[17] More importantly, even though he disagrees with both, Hobbes distinguishes between Aristotle and his scholastic exegetes and followers, and it is the latter in particular to which he takes exception.[18] In assessing the place of Aristotelianism in Hobbes's thought, therefore, it is necessary to try to clarify when the designation of something as Aristotelian refers to Aristotle himself, and when to his followers. Hobbes is especially averse to attempts by the "schoolmen" to render Aristotelian philosophy compatible with Christian doctrine.[19] This distinction, which is in no way

[16] Strauss compared passages from Hobbes's *Elements of Law*, *Leviathan*, and *De Homine* to Aristotle's *Rhetoric*, and argued that Hobbes's formulations "betray in style and contents that their author was a zealous reader, not to say a disciple of the *Rhetoric*" (*The Political Philosophy of Hobbes*, 35; cf. *ibid.*, 36–43; Pacchi, "Some Guidelines into Hobbes's Theology," 89–90). The curriculum that Skinner describes, on the other hand, is one dominated by the Roman teachers of rhetoric, especially Quintilian, and one from which Aristotle is largely absent (*Reason and Rhetoric in the Philosophy of Hobbes*, 35–38). This picture, however, is problematic both in general and especially in the case of Hobbes, who mentions Quintilian only once in his entire corpus: in the prefatory essay to his translation of Homer's *Odyssey* (*Homer's Odysses*, B7ʳ). Between the end of the fifteenth century and the time when Hobbes matriculated at Oxford, Cicero was by far the most widely read of the ancient theorists of rhetoric, and while Quintilian was popular, Aristotle was far from unknown. In Skinner's story, it is hard to see how Aristotle could have come to play the role that he did in Hobbes's thought, and even harder to understand why Hobbes would have turned to Aristotle, rather than to Cicero or Quintilian, when it came to the study and teaching of rhetoric. Cf. Vickers, "'Tis the Goddesse of Rhetorick," 27; Garsten, *Saving Persuasion*, 28–31.

[17] Sorell, "Hobbes and Aristotle," 364. Cf. Weinberger, "Hobbes's Doctrine of Method," 1348; Shapiro, "Reading and Writing in the Text of Hobbes's *Leviathan*," 148.

[18] On the difficulties involved in defining Aristotelianism more generally, see especially, Mercer, "The Vitality and Importance of Early Modern Aristotelianism"; Schmitt, *Aristotle and the Renaissance*, 6–7, 89–109; Nederman, "The Meaning of 'Aristotelianism' in Medieval Moral and Political Thought." Although any term encompassing such breadth over such a long period is bound to become problematic, it is also worth bearing in mind Schmitt's observation that "all things considered, Aristotelianism still represented a more comprehensive and internally coherent system than any that was available to replace it" ("Philosophy and Science in Sixteenth-Century Universities," 490; cf. *ibid.*, 531; Kristeller, *The Classics in Renaissance Thought*, 33–34, 46–47). On Aristotelianism in Hobbes, in particular, see Sorell, "Hobbes and Aristotle," 371; Leijenhorst, *The Mechanisation of Aristotelianism*, esp. 219–22; Jesseph, "*Scientia* in Hobbes," 125–26.

[19] In *Leviathan*, for example, Hobbes claims that "the study of Philosophy it hath no otherwise place, then as a handmaid to the Romane Religion" (XLVI: 370). Jolley ("The Relation between Philosophy and Theology," 363) notes that Hobbes's use of the term "Vain Philosophy" in the title of the chapter devoted to his most vehement attack on Aristotelianism (*Leviathan*, XLVI), aligns him with a trope that has its origins in Paul's warning, "Beware lest any man spoil you through philosophy and vain deceit, after the tradition of men, after the rudiments of the world, and not after Christ" (Colossians, 2:8). As Leijenhorst observes, Hobbes first connects the two explicitly in *The Elements of Law* (II.6.8); he adds that this line of interpretation was well established by Hobbes's time and had appeared in Luther

meant to diminish Hobbes's real disagreements with Aristotle himself,
should be borne in mind because it points to a source of far greater annoy-
ance to Hobbes than any particular Aristotelian doctrine, namely the tendency to defend arguments not on their merits, but by reference to authority.
Hobbes insists that one of the main flaws of earlier writings on politics
was their uncritical reliance on the authority of revered sources, such as
Aristotle and Cicero. In *Leviathan*, he writes of words that pass from mouth
to mouth like yawning, and of the deceitful practices of those who "stick
their corrupt Doctrine with the Cloves of other mens Wit."[20] We will return
to this matter, but for now we should note that for Hobbes, Aristotelianism
is often emblematic of the tendency to adopt views about important matters without deciding for oneself whether those views make sense – the kind
of attitude to which Thucydides' and Euclid's respective methods offered
appealing alternatives.

Nevertheless, Hobbes's hostility toward Aristotelianism adds a new
layer of complexity to the *Briefe*. To summarize the problem: How ought
one interpret the publication of a précis of Aristotle's *Rhetoric* – the first
attempt to render that work into English, no less – by someone who is
alleged to have left humanism behind, to have become consumed by science, and who is generally thought of as an enemy of the author and subject
matter of the book he has translated and summarized? Seen not in the narrow and artificial confines imposed in hindsight by Hobbes's "turns," but in
the broader setting of his literary output and his stated aims, the *Briefe* is
not as puzzling as it seems. The work that preceded it – the translation of
Thucydides' history – was a warning against the political dangers of demagoguery. The work that would follow it, *The Elements of Law*, would be
a treatise intended to communicate views whose acceptance "would be an
incomparable benefit to commonwealth."[21] Throughout his career, Hobbes

and Melanchthon, a fact that Hobbes was aware of, as evidenced by his summary history,
in his *Questions concerning Liberty, Necessity, and Chance, EW,* V: 63–65 (Leijenhorst, *The
Mechanisation of Aristotelianism,* 27–34).

[20] *Leviathan,* A Review and Conclusion, 395. Hobbes is emphatic about the distinction between
the originals and their imitators in the *Historia Ecclesiastica* (401–14), the *Decameron
Physiologicum* (*EW,* VII: 76), *Leviathan,* IV: 15, and the Appendix to the Latin *Leviathan*
(*OL,* III: 540). Cf. *The Elements of Law,* I.13.3, I.17.1, I.17.14, II.8.13, II.9.8, II.10.8; *De
Cive,* 3.13; *Leviathan,* III: 11, V: 19, V: 22, XV:77, XLVI:370–71, 376; *Answer to the Preface
to Gondibert,* 140–41, 149, 156–57; *Behemoth,* 179, 318; Hobbes's annotation to I.20 of
Thucydides' history, in his translation (*Eight Bookes of the Peloponnesian Warre,* 12). In
his Preface to *The Advancement of Learning,* Bacon had raised a similar objection to the
authority of the ancients (*The Works of Francis Bacon,* III: 321–22). See also Rummel, *The
Humanist-Scholastic Debate in the Renaissance & Reformation,* 153–54; Ross, "Hobbes
and the Authority of the Universities," 73–75. Strong suggests that "this argument has its origin in the attacks on the Roman church made by the early Reformers," and cites the example
of Calvin's *Institutes* ("How to Write Scripture," 148).

[21] *The Elements of Law,* Ep. Ded.

would consistently state that the greatest threat to order comes from words and disagreement about their meaning. He would also describe himself as a man with a "devotion to peace," whose aim was to convince his fellow citizens to not pay attention to the false entreaties of preachers, confessors, and casuists, but to "patiently put up with some inconveniences in [their] private affairs ... rather than disturb the state of the country."[22] Persuasion was always the problem, and persuasion would be the solution. Aristotle's *Rhetoric* was thus a natural next stop.[23]

To begin to understand the significance of Aristotle's *Rhetoric* for Hobbes, it is important to remember two things that in some ways point in opposite directions: that Hobbes was in many ways exceptional, and that Aristotle was still a major presence in the curriculum in Hobbes's day.[24] As we have seen, to the extent that it makes sense to speak of Hobbes's humanism, it is necessary to do so with several qualifications.[25] Whereas his contemporaries tended to focus on Latin texts, even when they studied Greek authors, Hobbes was educated by "a good Graecian," and was the first to translate both Thucydides' history and Aristotle's *Rhetoric* from Greek into English.[26]

---

[22] *De Cive*, Pref. §§ 24, 20.

[23] Schuhmann, for instance, contends that "[t]o a *philosopher* of that time, 'rhetoric' should in the first place be expected to mean Aristotelian rhetoric" ("Skinner's Hobbes," 117); cf. Kristeller, *The Classics and Renaissance Thought*, 34.

[24] See, for example, Malcolm, *Aspects of Hobbes*, 4–5. Green & Murphy, *Renaissance Rhetoric Short-Title Catalogue 1460–1700*, 33–44 (Aristotle), 107–38 (Cicero), 351–60 (Quintilian). According to Green & Murphy, from the end of the fifteenth century until the time Hobbes matriculated at Oxford, there were 107 editions of *De inventione* paired with the *Rhetorica ad Herennium* and fifty editions of the latter alone, as well as 101 editions of Aristotle's *Rhetoric*. During the same period, there were forty-three editions of Quintilian's *Institutio oratoria* (twenty-one of these with commentary), and fifty-four of the *Institutio oratoria* along with the *Declamations* (twenty-two of these with commentary). Despite excluding various editions listed by Green & Murphy, Mack nevertheless deems it "safe to assume that more editions (a total of 300–400) were printed of commentaries on Cicero than of any classical or renaissance rhetoric manual" (*A History of Renaissance Rhetoric, 1380–1620*, 30). By Mack's count, Quintilian is a distant second, and Aristotle a distant third, although Mack excludes twenty-six editions of Aristotle in Greek, with which he overtakes Quintilian. Cf. Schmitt, "Philosophy and Science in Sixteenth-Century Universities," 498–99; Green, "Aristotle's *Rhetoric* and Renaissance Views of the Emotions." On the popularity of the *Rhetoric* from the thirteenth century onward, especially with regard to political questions, see Ward, "From Antiquity to the Renaissance," 55–56.

[25] See Condren, *Thomas Hobbes*, 11. Skinner acknowledges that Hobbes's interest in Greek authors and works stood in marked contrast to the dominant trend of the age (*Reason and Rhetoric in the Philosophy of Hobbes*, 25–26). Cf. Strauss, *The Political Philosophy of Hobbes*, 44.

[26] On the latter, see Harwood's Introduction to *The Rhetorics of Thomas Hobbes and Bernard Lamy*, 2. Citing Wallace (*The Life of Sir Philip Sidney*, 327), who in turn cites Hoskins, who had allegedly seen the manuscript of a translation of the first two books of Aristotle's *Rhetoric* done by Sidney around 1585, Skinner claims that Sidney, "a student at Oxford ... made what appears to have been the first English translation of Aristotle's text" (*Reason and Rhetoric in the Philosophy of Hobbes*, 36). Wallace notes, however, that this translation

The preeminence of Cicero and the significance of other Latin authors in the late sixteenth-century and early seventeenth-century English curricula are beyond dispute, but recent accounts of Hobbes's intellectual surroundings give the impression that his was a world dominated by Latin. Yet as late as *Leviathan*, in his notorious attack on vain philosophy, Hobbes describes the university of his day as a place in which the authority of Aristotle was so dominant as to render study "not properly Philosophy ... but Aristotelity."[27] More importantly for our purposes, we know that Hobbes himself summed up his studies at Oxford as exercises in Aristotelian logic and physics.[28] Indeed, Aristotle's presence was well established at Oxford long before Hobbes matriculated there. According to McConica,

By the *Nova statuta* of 1564/5, the major part of the course leading to the Bachelor of Arts degree was given over to the *trivium*, as it was at Cambridge. The authors were as follows: in grammar, Linacre, Virgil, Horace or some of Cicero's letters; in rhetoric either Cicero's *Orationes* or *Praeceptiones*, or Aristotle's *Art of Rhetoric*; in dialectic, the *Institutiones* of Porphyry or part of Aristotle's *Dialectic*.[29]

Not long thereafter, John Rainolds delivered his famous lectures on Aristotle's *Rhetoric* there.[30] Rainolds's lecture notes suggest "that his auditors, or some of them at least, had the Greek text before them."[31] In short, by Hobbes's time there, Aristotle's *Rhetoric* was far from invisible at Oxford, and Aristotle continued to enjoy preeminence in general.[32] This background

"was probably never published," and adds, "[f]rom what we know of Sir Philip's acquaintance with Greek it is not likely that this translation was made directly from the original" (*The Life of Sir Philip Sidney*, 327). On the reception of the *Rhetoric* in England, see Green's introduction to *John Rainolds's Oxford Lectures on Aristotle's Rhetoric*, 10–11. Be this as it may, when considered alongside other evidence, Sidney's interest in the *Rhetoric* several years before Hobbes matriculated there confirms that this work was far from exotic at Oxford. Cf. McConica, "Elizabethan Oxford," 707, 712.

[27] *Leviathan*, XLVI: 370.

[28] *T. Hobbes Malmesburiensis Vita* (OL, I: xiii).

[29] McConica, "Humanism and Aristotle in Tudor Oxford," 292; cf. Gibson, *Statvta Antiqva Vniversitatis Oxoniensis*, 389–90; Hatcher, ed. G. *Haddoni Legum Doctoris, etc.*, 347–48; Fletcher, "The Faculty of Arts," 172. Wood (*Historia et Antiquitates Vniversitatis Oxoniensis*, II: 376) reports that Hobbes was admitted to the degree of Bachelor of Arts on February 5, 1608 ("admissus fuit ad lectionem cujuslibet libri logices v. *Febr*. an. VII"). According to Herrick, the Oriel College Library contained a copy of Aristotle's *Rhetoric* as early as 1375 ("The Early History of Aristotle's *Rhetoric* in England," 246).

[30] See Green, ed., *John Rainolds's Oxford Lectures on Aristotle's Rhetoric*. Rainolds had to lecture three times a week "on Greek grammar or rhetoric" (McConica, "Humanism and Aristotle in Tudor Oxford," 303).

[31] McConica, "Humanism and Aristotle in Tudor Oxford," 304.

[32] As Malcolm notes, even though academics spent much of their time on endeavors beyond the official curriculum, "[t]here had been a definite revival of Aristotelianism in England in the latter part of the sixteenth century, and extra decrees were issued in Oxford in 1586 to exclude the use of authors who disagreed with the 'ancient and true philosophy' of Aristotle" (*Aspects of Hobbes*, 5, but cf. Schmitt, "Philosophy and Science in Sixteenth-Century

perhaps helps explain why Hobbes devotes little attention to Roman thinkers and so much to Aristotle and his followers. Further evidence from Aubrey explains why, when he sought to understand and teach rhetoric, Hobbes turned to Aristotle. Hobbes's biographer claims that he had heard Hobbes "say that Aristotle was the worst teacher that ever was, the worst polititian and ethick – a countrey-fellow that could live in the world <would be> as good: but his rhetorique and discourse of animals was rare."[33]

True to its title, the *Briefe of the Art of Rhetorique* is about one third of Theodore Goulston's 1619 translation into Latin, the first edition of Aristotle's *Rhetoric* to be printed in England, whose divisions it follows.[34] The *Briefe*'s length announces that much of the original is missing, and that what is there is delivered in a terse style. Even if we were to grant that one of Hobbes's aims in composing the *Briefe* was to teach Latin and rhetoric to his charge, his broader interest in Aristotle and rhetoric more generally force us to ask: What changes did Hobbes make to the original, and why?

To begin with, the *Briefe* lacks most of Aristotle's examples and often omits important details from the original analysis.[35] In the abstract, it may be tempting to conclude that these economizing strategies simply reflect an attempt to render a complex subject intelligible to a young pupil. The history of the reception of Aristotle's *Rhetoric*, however, shows evidence of serious disagreement and often bewilderment about some of its most fundamental elements.[36] On occasion, therefore, such changes may reflect not simply a teacher's economizing strategy, but particular lines of interpretation, in which "the larger understandings of Aristotle's treatise directly shape what the several commentators have to say about the details of the text."[37] Commentators have suggested several possible sources of influence

Universities," 490). For a description of these decrees, see Gibson, *Statvta Antiqva Vniversitatis Oxoniensis*, 437.

[33] Aubrey, *Brief Lives*, I: 357.

[34] Aristotle, Ἀριστοτέλους τέχνης ῥητορικῆς βιβλία τρία. *Aristotelis de Rhetorica Seu Arte Dicendi Libri Tres, Græcolat., etc.*; Dodd, "The Rhetorics in Molesworth's Edition of Hobbes," 37, n. 10; Harwood's introduction to *The Rhetorics of Thomas Hobbes and Bernard Lamy*, 2, 5.

[35] See Harwood's introduction to *The Rhetorics of Thomas Hobbes and Bernard Lamy*, 14.

[36] The difficulties begin with the very first sentence, in which Aristotle describes rhetoric as "ἀντίστροφος τῇ διαλεκτικῇ" (1354a1), leaving generations of commentators in confusion over the precise relationship of the two (see Green, "The Reception of Aristotle's *Rhetoric* in the Renaissance," 337–40). See, for example, Rainolds' lecture on this issue (Green, ed., *John Rainolds's Oxford Lectures on Aristotle's Rhetoric*, Lecture on Chapter 1, 102–15). Green discusses several examples of such contentious passages, noting that disagreement over Aristotle's meaning often extended to other passages whose translation was not in dispute ("The Reception of Aristotle's *Rhetoric* in the Renaissance," 343; cf. "Aristotle's *Rhetoric* and Renaissance Views of the Emotions").

[37] Green, "The Reception of Aristotle's *Rhetoric* in the Renaissance," 341; cf. *ibid.*, 344. Green notes that the possibilities are numerous here. Thus, some interpreters have seen the *Briefe*'s blurring of the distinction between arguments leading to probable and certain conclusions, and between method and art, as evidence of a Ramist influence. In the very opening lines

on Hobbes in this regard, but the evidence points once again to a practice that is "too eclectic, too idiosyncratic, to allow easy classification[;] Hobbes was especially resistant to all systems but his own."[38] As with his other works, here, too, it is ultimately counterproductive to attempt to make sense of Hobbes by means of schools of thought.

In substance, the work reveals two important characteristics that indicate a certain divergence from Aristotle and point to ideas that Hobbes would develop in his original works. The first of these has to do with the *Briefe's* definition of rhetoric. Where Aristotle defines it as "the faculty of observing in any given case the available means of persuasion," Hobbes considers it "that Faculty, by which wee understand what will serve our turne, concerning any subject, to winne beliefe in the hearer."[39] Without precluding Aristotle's academic and detached understanding, Hobbes's definition nevertheless emphasizes that every rhetorical opportunity is a contest, often with much at stake. Whereas Aristotle's rhetorician is a student interested in understanding and mapping the nuances of persuasion, Hobbes's is a politician with his eyes set on victory.[40] With this mindset, too much attention to nuance may in fact become a liability. How does one achieve victory? Condensing Aristotle's handful of pages into a dozen lines, Hobbes explains that

Of those things that beget beleefe; some require not the help of Art; as *Witnesses, Evidences,* and the like, which wee invent not, but make use of; and some require Art, and are invented by us.

The beleefe, that proceedes from our invention, comes partly from the *behaviour* of the *speaker;* partly from the *passions* of the *hearer:* but especially from the *proofes* of what we alledge.[41]

---

of the *Briefe,* for example, Hobbes claims, "to discover *method* is all one with teaching an Art" (*A Briefe of the Art of Rhetorique,* I.1). See Harwood's introduction to *The Rhetorics of Thomas Hobbes and Bernard Lamy,* 8–9; cf. Ong, "Hobbes and Talon's Ramist Rhetoric in English." Zappen concludes that "Hobbes's rhetorical method defies classification as Aristotelian, Ramist, anti-Ramist, or counterreformist," ("Aristotelian and Ramist Rhetoric in Thomas Hobbes's *Leviathan,*" 90).

[38] Harwood, introduction to *The Rhetorics of Thomas Hobbes and Bernard Lamy,* 13. Cf. Biletzki, "Thomas Hobbes," 60–61.

[39] Aristotle, *Rhetoric,* 1355b25–26: "Ἔστω δὴ ἡ ῥητορικὴ δύναμις περὶ ἕκαστον τοῦ θεωρῆσαι τὸ ἐνδεχόμενον πιθανόν;" *A Briefe of the Art of Rhetorique,* I.2. Hobbes uses a nearly identical formulation in *The Elements of Law* (II.8.14).

[40] Cf. *A Briefe of the Art of Rhetorique,* I.3. Aristotle in fact states explicitly that the function of rhetoric "is not so much to persuade, as to find out in each case the existing means of persuasion" (*Rhetoric,* 1355b9–11, Freese translation). The quality of Aristotle's definition was not lost on Hobbes's contemporaries. See, for example, Rainolds's lecture on Chapter 5, wherein Rainolds paraphrases Vives's *De Causis* (Green, ed., *John Rainolds's Oxford Lectures on Aristotle's Rhetoric,* 160–65).

[41] *A Briefe of the Art of Rhetorique,* I.2. Green points out that in his own preface, Goulston claims "that the enthymeme is a structure in which logical, ethical, and pathetic persuasives work upon one another reciprocally to create belief" ("The Reception of Aristotle's *Rhetoric* in the Renaissance," 340).

To the rhetorician, these proofs are examples – namely short inductions or enthymemes, that is, short syllogisms – aimed at conveying only what is necessary, "to avoid prolixity, and not to consume the time of the publique businesse needlessly."[42] Regardless of whether Hobbes's summary of Aristotle was shaped primarily by pedagogical or ideological considerations, it is interesting that its brevity and tone are in accordance with its understanding of rhetoric as urgent business with little patience for nuance.

This brings us to the second key feature of the *Briefe*: its particular emphasis on the audience. In a well-ordered commonwealth, in which the sovereign has laid down universal rules and the task of the speaker is to decide in a crimination whether *"Tis so*; or *not so*," the rhetorician, forbidden from playing on the judges' emotions, "could have nothing at all to say."[43] In most cases, however, the circumstances are not quite so happy, for "ordinarily those that are Judges; are neither patient, nor capable of long *Scientificall proofes*, drawne from the *Principles* through many *Syllogismes:* and therefore had neede to be instructed by the *Rhetoricall*, and shorter way."[44] Once again, then, economy is of the essence; this time not simply because the public business demands it, but also because of the audience's limitations.

Throughout the *Briefe*, one encounters numerous reminders of the ways in which the audience's opinions, interests, and physical and mental limitations will require that the speaker attune his message in certain ways if he hopes to succeed in persuading. Thus, Hobbes argues that the speaker must use common opinions as principles, "such as the Judge is already possessed with: because the end of *Rhetorique* is victory, which consists in having gotten *beleefe*" and must take aim at the *"passions* of the *Hearer."*[45] Given

---

[42] *A Briefe of the Art of Rhetorique*, I.2. As this idiosyncratic, general definition of enthymemes shows, Hobbes is not adhering to the textbooks. Ong notes that a broad Ramism, which he defines as "intellectual absolutism in terms of a simplistically conceived and popularly implemented scientism," was sufficiently widespread at the time as to constitute a subconscious influence, but adds that it is difficult to determine whether this was a factor in Hobbes's interpretation of Aristotle ("Hobbes and Talon's Ramist Rhetoric in English," 268). It is worth noting, however, that Tenison invokes Ramus to criticize Hobbes (*The Creed of Mr. Hobbes Examined*, 102 [misnumbered as 202]–03).

[43] *A Briefe of the Art of Rhetorique*, I.1.

[44] *A Briefe of the Art of Rhetorique*, I.1. In his introduction to the *Briefe*, Harwood claims that Hobbes here "makes a point not found in Aristotle" (19), but this is not correct. Hobbes is rendering, more or less accurately, Aristotle's view:

> before some audiences not even the possession of exact knowledge will make it easy for what we say to produce conviction. For argument based on knowledge implies instruction, and there are people whom one cannot instruct. Here, then, we must use, as our modes of persuasion and argument, notions possessed by everybody, as we observed in the *Topics* when dealing with the way to handle a popular audience (Aristotle, *Rhetoric*, 1355a24–29, W. Rhys Roberts translation; Aristotle's internal reference appears to be to *Topics*, 101a30–34).

[45] *A Briefe of the Art of Rhetorique*, I.3; II.1; cf. *ibid.*, I.8: "And because *beleefe* is not gotten onely by *proofes*; but also from *manners*; the *manners* of each sort of Common-wealth ought

this goal and constraints, the enthymeme – as Hobbes, following Aristotle, understands it – acquires a special significance as the device that allows the speaker to appeal to the audience in the most expedient and effective manner.[46]

This less than charitable description of the capacity of the audience to follow complicated arguments reads like a foretaste of Hobbes's mistrust of readers, but it stands out in the *Briefe* only because it is among those issues highlighted in the *Rhetoric*, whose Aristotelian emphasis Hobbes chose to preserve. Hobbes is not inserting his own view here, but rather reproducing one that Aristotle expresses more than once in the first Book of the *Rhetoric*. Having already warned of the fact that some people are simply beyond instruction, Aristotle states that "[t]he duty of rhetoric is to deal with such matters as we deliberate upon without arts or systems to guide us, in the hearing of persons who cannot take in at a glance a complicated argument, or follow a long chain of reasoning."[47] Renaissance commentators understood that Aristotle refers to the limitations of the audience, but disagreed about what those limitations were and to whom they applied.[48] Some, no doubt taking their cue from his reference to the *Topics*, understood Aristotle as distinguishing between certain readers and others, but many understood him as pointing to limitations true of all human beings, such as an inability to focus on things that are not immediately before one's eyes, or issues that are not of immediate concern to oneself. These are precisely the kinds of shortcomings that Thucydides had dealt with so effectively, in Hobbes's view.[49]

If the difference in tone between Aristotle's and Hobbes's definitions of rhetoric gives the impression of a radical shift from academic study to the practice of persuasion, it is important to emphasize that Hobbes once again merely underscored something that was already there in Aristotle. As his focus on the limitations imposed by the capacity of the audience shows, Aristotle was himself interested in this side of rhetoric. To the practically minded rhetorician, however, the ultimate determination of who exactly is incapable of following complicated arguments matters little, since any large audience will include some individuals who, for one reason or another, will pose a challenge. At the very least, therefore, prudence requires that one concerned with persuading rather than simply understanding the mechanics

---

to be well understood by him that undertaketh to perswade, or disswade in matter of State." On what Hobbes means by "manners," see *Leviathan*, XI.

[46] See Aristotle, *Prior Analytics*, 70a–b.

[47] Aristotle, *Rhetoric*, 1357a1–4 (W. Rhys Roberts translation): "ἔστιν δὲ τὸ ἔργον αὐτῆς περί τε τοιούτων περὶ ὧν βουλευόμεθα καὶ τέχνας μὴ ἔχομεν, καὶ ἐν τοῖς τοιούτοις ἀκροαταῖς οἳ οὐ δύνανται διὰ πολλῶν συνορᾶν οὐδὲ λογίζεσθαι πόρρωθεν."

[48] See Green, "The Reception of Aristotle's *Rhetoric* in the Renaissance," 345–47.

[49] In the *Topics*, Aristotle speaks of "τῶν πολλῶν" (101a31). On the focus on human limitations, see Green, "The Reception of Aristotle's *Rhetoric* in the Renaissance," 346–47.

of persuasion will have to assume that he will be addressing some such auditors. As Hobbes would point out in *De Cive*, one need not expect that all men are evil in order to take precautions; the mere existence of a few evil men whose identity is unknown suffices.[50] Similarly, the suspicion that certain members of the audience are incapable of following a complicated ratiocination should encourage the prudent rhetorician to use certain simplifying mnemonic devices in order to get his point across. But there is also good reason for thinking that Hobbes saw no one as fully immune to this type of inability. Just as everyone is more or less capable of guidance in accordance with reason at some point, everyone – even the most rational of human beings – is occasionally incapable of following reason.[51] This realization elevates appeals to the passions by means of mnemonic devices to a matter of the highest priority.

Equally importantly, having separated rhetoric from the other sciences at the outset of his treatise, Aristotle had thereby led several commentators to the conclusion that rhetoric as he saw it was divorced from ethical concerns. Thus, whereas in Cicero's view rhetoric is inextricably intertwined with virtue, for Aristotle it is construed as epistemologically indifferent to it and, hence, equally open to good use and bad.[52] Although seemingly aloof, this neutrality with regard to questions of good and evil paradoxically redirects attention to the practical consequences of rhetoric, by alerting us to the fact that rhetoric need not be seen as coterminous with demagoguery, but that it can be harnessed toward beneficial ends, just as it can be rendered dangerous and pernicious.[53]

As we have seen, commentators have suggested that had Hobbes died after Thucydides, he would be remembered merely as a minor representative of the Tudor humanist tradition. Already problematic with Thucydides, this suggestion becomes much more difficult with the *Briefe*, for by 1637, Hobbes's two main publications had been first translations into English of two Greek authors. These intellectual pursuits are sufficiently close to what one might describe as those of a typical humanist as to make the designation seem unproblematic. Yet, "[i]f Hobbes can be shown to move in some sense in the climate of Renaissance thought, and more specifically of Renaissance

---

[50] *De Cive*, Pref. § 12.

[51] See, for example, Malcolm, *Aspects of Hobbes*, 228.

[52] According to Ward, "[i]t may well be that Aristotle's *Rhetoric* presented a more powerful challenge to the primacy of Christian humanism (than the Ciceronian tradition) because it divorced rhetoric more thoroughly from ethical and moral issues" ("The Medieval and Early Renaissance Study of Cicero's *De inventione* and the *Rhetorica ad Herennium*," 52, n. 248).

[53] Thus, Struever sees Hobbes's definition of rhetoric in the *Briefe* as the result of pessimism stemming from the essentially "*tangential* nature" of rhetoric, whose persuasive power may be harnessed toward a variety of purposes, some of them ethical, others not (*The Language of History in the Renaissance*, 156).

humanism and naturalism, one still may not forget that, by appropriating
certain elements deriving from earlier traditions, Hobbes recast them and
made them quite uniquely his own."[54] Hobbes's Thucydides and Aristotle
challenge the story of the humanist-turned-scientist by reminding us of the
fact that whatever other interests Hobbes may have had, his principal concern was with persuasion for order. This concern, which remained alive and
well during Hobbes's scientific phase, must inform the way in which we
approach Hobbes's attempts to articulate a distinct science of politics, if we
wish to make sense of them.

That Hobbes's interest in Aristotle's *Rhetoric* was far from a passing one
becomes evident in the very next major work that he composed: his first
comprehensive treatise on politics, a work that has come to be known as
"The Elements of Law, Natural and Politic."[55] Although generally classified
as the first major product of Hobbes's scientific phase, and as the inaugural
statement of his "civil science," this work bears a direct connection to the
Briefe of the Art of Rhetorique.[56] A side-by-side examination of Hobbes's
account of "the pleasures of the sense," of "honour," and of "the passions
of the mind" in *The Elements of Law* shows that it is heavily indebted "in

---

[54] Schuhmann, "Hobbes and Renaissance Philosophy," 349.

[55] According to Hobbes:

> When the Parliament sate, that began in *April* 1640. and was dissolved in *May* follow-
> ing, and in which many points of the Regal Power, which were necessary for the Peace
> of the Kingdom, and the safety of His Majesties Person, were disputed and denied, M^r
> *Hobbes* wrote a little Treatise in English, wherein he did set forth and demonstrate,
> That the said Power and Rights were inseparably annexed to the Soveraignty; which
> Soveraignty they did not then deny to be in the King; but it seems understood not, or
> would not understand that Inseparability. Of this Treatise, though not Printed, many
> Gentlemen had Copies, which occasioned much talk of the Author; and had not His
> Majesty dissolved the Parliament, it had brought him into danger of his life (*Mr. Hobbes
> Considered*, 4–5).

> This is believed to be referring to a work in two parts, "Human Nature" and "De Corpore
> Politico," first published in 1650 as *Human Nature, etc.*, and *De Corpore Politico, etc.*,
> respectively, although it appears that these publications were unauthorized (see Macdonald
> & Hargreaves, *Thomas Hobbes: A Bibliography*, p. 9, and items 15 and 17; cf. Tönnies'
> introduction to his edition of *The Elements of Law*, esp. p. vii). It is important to note
> that *Human Nature* consisted of Chapters 1–13 of Part I of the *Elements*, and *De Corpore
> Politico* the remainder, and did not follow Hobbes's division of the material in the manu-
> scripts (for example, Devonshire Mss., Chatsworth HS/A/2A, HS/A/2B, HS/A/2C, British
> Library Egerton MS 2005, Harl. MSS 1325, 4235, 4236; cf. British Library Harl. MS 6858).
> We will consider the significance of this division later. On the history and circulation of
> the manuscript, see Dzelzainis, "Edward Hyde and Thomas Hobbes's *Elements of Law,
> Natural and Politic.*" The two parts were eventually united in what came to be known as
> *The Elements of Law Natural and Politic*, as edited by Ferdinand Tönnies in 1889.

[56] See, for example, Skinner, *Reason and Rhetoric in the Philosophy of Hobbes*, 426. Johnston
finds evidence, in the *Elements*, of a contribution to science and to political debate, but
concludes that "these two dimensions of the manuscript are at least partially heterogeneous
rather than complementary" (*The Rhetoric of Leviathan*, 29).

themes, mode of presentation, and even in details," to the *Briefe*.[57] This evidence of continuity with the *Briefe* may strike the reader of the *Elements* as problematic. In the latter work, Hobbes mentions the term "rhetoric" but once – in the Epistle Dedicatory – and only to explain to his patron that the awkward style of the work is the unfortunate consequence of the fact that in composing it, he was "forced to consult … more with logic than with rhetoric."[58] Beyond the Epistle, Hobbes's lavish praise for the mathematicians and his sustained and forceful attack on the dogmatists appears to confirm the impression that this is the work of someone who is striving to extend the benefits of science to the realm of politics. This impression, however, is mistaken. Hobbes's talk of science in the *Elements* is part of an overall Aristotelian rhetorical strategy aimed at persuading his readers that agreement and order are possible, so long as human beings begin from foundations to which no one could object.[59]

---

[57] Strauss, *The Political Philosophy of Hobbes*, 35. The subjects in question are treated in Chapters 8 and 9 of the first part of the *Elements*. By juxtaposing passages from the *Briefe* to equivalents from the *Elements*, *De Homine*, and *Leviathan*, Strauss shows that Hobbes repeats this basic pattern in his subsequent works as well (*ibid.*, 35–43). In his edition of Hobbes's works, Molesworth included, in addition to the *Briefe* (printed therein under the title "The Whole Art of Rhetoric,") two other works, "The Art of Rhetoric plainly Set forth," and "The Art of Sophistry" (*EW*, VI: 511–36). In so doing, Molesworth was following the 1681 collection published by William Crooke, *The Art of Rhetoric, with a Discourse of the Laws of England*. As Dodd shows, Strauss was mistaken in considering all of the works on rhetoric in Molesworth genuine, for only the *Briefe* was by Hobbes ("The Rhetorics in Molesworth's Edition of Hobbes, 42"). Nevertheless, Strauss's observation regarding Hobbes's account of the passions is not affected by this mistake, since it was based solely on a comparison of Hobbes's later works with "The Whole Art of Rhetoric," that is, with the *Briefe of the Art of Rhetorique*.

[58] *The Elements of Law*, Ep. Ded., xvi.

[59] As we will see, Hobbes returns to Aristotle explicitly in the chapter in which he considers "How by Language Men Work upon Each Other's Minds" (*The Elements of Law*, Chapter 13). Cf. *ibid.*, II.8.14.

PART II ·

A DEVOTION TO PEACE

[T]here is scarce a Common-wealth in the world, whose beginnings can in conscience be justified.

      – Hobbes, *Leviathan*

3

Unobjectionable Foundations

The Elements of Law, Natural and Politic

Nature opens the door to *The Elements of Law*.[1] The contrast between
the two principal parts of human nature – reason and passion – contains
everything that one needs to understand order and disorder, agreement and
disagreement, concord and discord, and peace and war.[2] At first glance, one
finds nothing objectionable in Hobbes's suggestion that the realm of reason
is ruled by mathematics, and is concerned only with the comparison of figures and motion, whereas that of passion is characterized by unending dispute, because it pertains to man's right and profit. Yet, Hobbes's contrast is
not as innocent as it seems. Each side bleeds into the other since in practice,
reason is as involved as passion in the determination of issues of right and
justice, just as the comparison of figures and motion, which in the abstract
sounds innocent enough, can in fact inflame the passions. How the order
of the one realm can be brought to bear on the other becomes evident in
Hobbes's promise to put "such principles down for a foundation, as passion
not mistrusting, may not seek to displace; and afterward to build thereon
the truth of cases in the law of nature (which hitherto have been built in
the air) by degrees, till the whole be inexpugnable."[3] But what would those
principles be and how could passion be brought to trust them?

Hobbes's solution to this problem involves an optical illusion. Even
though in practice the boundaries between the realms of reason and passion,
where they exist, are porous, he will speak to his readers as though it were
perfectly possible to separate the two into neat, hermetically sealed domains.
Having conjured these receptacles, he will proceed to rearrange the world

---

[1] Nature makes an appearance in the title of the work, in the first sentence of the Epistle
Dedicatory, as well as in the opening paragraphs of the first chapter of Part I.

[2] *The Elements of Law*, Ep. Ded. Hobbes explains that "THE true and perspicuous explication of the elements of laws, natural and politic, ... dependeth upon the knowledge of what
is human nature, what is a body politic, and what it is we call a law" (*The Elements of Law*,
I.1.1).

[3] *The Elements of Law*, Ep. Ded.

neatly into them, so as to restore reason to reason and passion to passion, and yet behind that very contrast he will continue to smuggle elements of one into the other in order to achieve his purpose. The principles that will serve as the foundation of the "true and perspicuous explication of the elements of laws, natural and politic" are knowledge of human nature, of a body politic, and of law. As writings on these topics have multiplied, so have controversies and doubts. This is a sign, for Hobbes, that their authors have not understood the subject.[4] As we have seen, Hobbes was not shy about his abilities and contributions to knowledge, so the way in which he situates himself in this continuum of writers on politics is worth a close look:

> Harm I can do none, though I err no less than they. For I shall leave men but as they are, in doubt and dispute. But intending not to take any principle upon trust, but only to put men in mind of what they know already, or may know by their own experience, I hope to err the less; and when I do, it must proceed from too hasty concluding, which I will endeavour as much as I can to avoid.[5]

Authors err, then, and persuasion will require the reader's participation. Hence, Hobbes's relatively modest ambition: to speak to the reader in terms that are within reach, either because of experience amassed, or because of experience that can be attained. The essentially scientific nature of this method should be clear: the procedure by which the claims will be tested and replicated is available to all, and the success of Hobbes's proposed approach hinges on that availability. Combining lessons from the successes of Thucydides and Euclid in persuading their audiences, Hobbes would seek to transform his reader into a witness who would verify the veracity of his claims, even though he would have arrived at his conclusions under Hobbes's close but unobtrusive guidance.

With this basic statement of method, Hobbes embarks on the construction, step-by-step, of his edifice. The first step is innocent enough: human nature, he tells us, is "the sum of [man's] natural faculties and powers" – those of the body, and those of the mind.[6] The second step shows that Hobbes meant what he said when he laid out his method; because the ground on which this battle will be fought is the mind of the reader, the powers of the body are irrelevant, and thus dismissed. Those of the mind he divides into (1) the "cognitive, or imaginative, or conceptive", and (2) the "motive."[7] Chapters 2–6 of Part I are devoted to the former, and Chapters 7–9 of Part II to the latter.

Hobbes's analysis of these powers is strange. Having stated at the outset that he will leave it to the reader to confirm the validity of his claims on his own, one might expect him to begin with a strong vote of confidence in the reader's ability to do so, which would lay the foundation for such an

---

4 *The Elements of Law*, I.1.1.
5 *The Elements of Law*, I.1.2.
6 *The Elements of Law*, I.1.4–5.
7 *The Elements of Law*, I.1.6–7.

investigation. That vote, however, is rather tepid. Hobbes finds that "there be few men which have not so much natural logic, as thereby to discern well enough, whether any conclusion I shall hereafter make ... be well or ill collected."[8] A small amount of natural logic will, in fact, confirm that the reader has several reasons for doubting his conceptions and, therefore, the experiences formed from them.[9] Thus, as he prepares us to feel as though we were assuming the responsibility of making up our own minds about matters of the highest significance, Hobbes alerts us to the ubiquity of "seemings and apparitions," and to the many ways in which our mind moves from the conception of something without, to an ever-fading memory of it, and then onto a chimerical dream in which that object has been transformed into a fiction, and suggests gently that it may even be impossible, in some cases, to tell the difference between a dream and reality.[10] In many cases, the mind may indeed jump from one thing to another in a way that signals incoherence, but in many others it follows a specific order that can be identified. Even the latter, however, is suspicious because it is shaped by preexisting connections. This can assume surprising forms, as, for example, when the mind goes from St. Andrew to tumult, for, "from St. Andrew the mind runneth to St. Peter, because their names are read together; from St. Peter to a stone, for the same cause; from stone to foundation, because we see them together; and for the same cause, from foundation to church, from church to people, and from people to tumult."[11] As a result, "the mind may run almost from any thing to any thing," a mechanism that serves man well in his attempt to satisfy his needs.[12] Though economical, however, this ability is also dangerous because it may cause one to draw connections where they are not appropriate. To make matters worse, "*ratio*, now, is but *oratio*, for the most part, wherein custom hath so great a power, that the mind suggesteth only the first word, the rest follow habitually, and are not followed by the mind."[13]

In short, by the end of Chapter 5, any confidence one may have had in one's experience – that is, one's ability to form accurate conceptions of things and to reason properly about them – has been shattered. Hobbes's summary of his findings is devastating:

Now, if we consider the power of those deceptions of sense, mentioned chapter 2 section 10, and also how unconstantly names have been settled, and how subject they

---

[8] *The Elements of Law*, I.5.11.
[9] See, for example, *The Elements of Law*, I.2.4–5.
[10] *The Elements of Law*, I.2.10; I.3.1–4; I.3.10. Hobbes directs the reader's attention to I.2.10 again, at I.4.11 and I.5.14. Cf. Shapiro, *Probability and Certainty in Seventeenth-Century England*, 5; Tuck, "Optics and Sceptics."
[11] *The Elements of Law*, I.4.2.
[12] *The Elements of Law*. I.4.2.
[13] *The Elements of Law*, I.5.14. In *Leviathan*, Hobbes notes that "When a man thinketh on any thing whatsoever, His next Thought after is not altogether so casuall as it seems to be," and proceeds to examine trains of thought "unguided" and "regulated" (III: 8–9). On the formula *ratio non oratio*, see Somos, *Secularisation and the Leiden Circle*, 297–300.

are to equivocation, and how diversified by passion, (scarce two men agreeing what is to be called good, and what evil; what liberality, what prodigality; what valour, what temerity) and how subject men are to paralogism or fallacy in reasoning, I may in a manner conclude, that it is impossible to rectify so many errors of any one man, as must needs proceed from those causes, without beginning anew from the very first grounds of all our knowledge, sense; and, instead of books, reading over orderly one's own conceptions: in which meaning I take *nosce teipsum* for a precept worthy of the reputation it hath gotten.[14]

All this sounds dispiriting in regard to the new science announced at the outset, and yet it is worth remembering that it is but one half of the problem, for these peculiarities are limited to the cognitive powers of the mind. The motive powers make matters even more complicated by introducing differences of perspective stemming from the differences in the vital constitutions of human beings, which, in turn, lead to a universe of nearly infinite appetites and aversions.[15] If, in turn, this degree of complexity were not enough, it should be borne in mind that, up to this point, Hobbes's examination of the powers of the mind regarded the mind in isolation. That is, it explained how the mind navigates a world with innumerable stimuli, but one lacking the most important source of interaction: other minds. Moving from this relative isolation to a social world, however, is a crucial next step because it is conflict that Hobbes is interested in, and his goal in writing the *Elements* is to offer such opinions as would be acceptable to "every man."[16]

PRIVATION

Hobbes takes this next step in Chapter 13 of Part I, the chapter devoted to "How by language men work upon each other's minds." The location and content of this discussion are not accidental. For the reader who follows the table of contents, Hobbes's discussion of the state of nature in the *Elements* is to be found in I.14.[17] That designation is, of course, correct, but the first sign of the state of nature is in fact offered in the preceding chapter. Hobbes begins it with a strange observation: the mind reads signs in order to understand what other minds are thinking. Some of those signs, such as sudden gestures, are hard to counterfeit, but others, such as words, are not.[18] This is a problem of the first order, since teaching and persuading are both the subject and aim of Hobbes's treatise. Teaching "exactly, and without error" may be too much to ask, but even hoping to offer opinions that will be

---

[14] *The Elements of Law*, I.5.14.

[15] *The Elements of Law*, I.10.2. Cf. Evrigenis, *Fear of Enemies and Collective Action*, 102–09.

[16] *The Elements of Law*, Ep. Ded., p. xvi.

[17] Tönnies's designation in his edition is confirmed by the surviving manuscripts (for example, Devonshire Mss., Chatsworth HS/A/2A; HS/A/2B; HS/A/2C).

[18] *The Elements of Law*, I.13.1–2.

acceptable to all sounds like a tall order.[19] How, then, does one seek the truth, and where?

Hobbes argues that one must survey the various subjects "wherein men have exercised their pens," to see how much disagreement there is between them.[20] The one who does so will find that those who have focused on

nothing else but the comparison of magnitudes, numbers, times, and motions, and their proportions one to another, have thereby been the authors of all those excellences, wherein we differ from such savage people as are now the inhabitants of divers places in America; and as have been the inhabitants heretofore of those countries where at this day arts and sciences do most flourish.[21]

The line has been drawn, then. On the one side lie those whose work is beyond controversy, those to whom mankind owes everything that is good, everything that separates man from the state of nature. Hobbes does not yet use that term to describe the life of the American savages or the ancestors of his most illustrious contemporaries, but he sets the stage in language that should already ring a bell, and gives a first clue as to the means by which he will attempt to persuade his readers:

For from the studies of these men hath proceeded, whatsoever cometh to us for ornament by navigation; and whatsoever we have beneficial to human society by the division, distinction, and portraying of the face of the earth; whatsoever also we have by the account of times, and foresight of the course of heaven; whatsoever by measuring distances, planes, and solids of all sorts; and whatsoever either elegant or defensible in building: all which *supposed away*, what do we differ from the wildest of Indians?[22]

If this list sounds familiar, that is because it is the near antithesis of Hobbes's notorious description of things absent from the state of nature in *Leviathan*. In this earlier instance, it is worth pausing for a moment to think about the nature and terms of the distinction proposed by Hobbes. To make it possible to distinguish between everything that is contentious and everything that is not, he has delimited a sphere that is inhabited *only* by those who do *nothing else* than compare magnitudes and numbers. This rather curious constituency, the *mathematici*, he credits with *everything* that is good.[23]

---

[19] Hobbes argues, "The infallible sign of teaching exactly, and without error, is this: that no man hath *ever* taught the contrary; not that few, how few soever, if any" (*The Elements of Law*, I.13.3, emphasis added). Cf. Tuck's discussion of Charron ("Optics and Sceptics").

[20] *The Elements of Law*, I.13.3.

[21] *The Elements of Law*, I.13.3.

[22] *The Elements of Law*, I.13.3, emphasis added. Cf. *Leviathan*, XIII § 9.

[23] *The Elements of Law*, I.13.3–4. Hobbes's choice of appellation calls to mind Sextus Empiricus's Πρὸς Μαθηματικούς (*Against the Professors*). Although Hobbes's later work against the professors of mathematics makes it clear that he is playing on the association, there are two reasons for concluding that he is not following Sextus here. First, as Hobbes's description of the "*mathematici*" shows, he has in mind those who deal with magnitudes and numbers rather than those concerned with μαθήματα (*Against the Professors*, I § 1),

Hobbes emphasizes that it is the fruits of their labor that distinguish his audience from the savages of America. His emphasis is offered in the form of the peculiar invitation to engage in a thought experiment in which the readers would strip themselves of all those excellences and their attendant benefits, and look at themselves anew.

Hobbes's invitation is not accidental. He argues that the best starting point for the teaching of natural philosophy – that is, the philosophy that concerns itself with the very subject matter of his Promethean comparers – is "from *privation*; that is, from feigning the world to be annihilated."[24] It is important to note, however, that even though privation is the method employed in both cases, the privation of *De Corpore* is very different from that of the *Elements*. The difference is obvious, but nevertheless worth emphasizing: whereas in the case of natural philosophy the privation is radical, in the case of the *Elements* the privation removes everything that is beneficial to human society, but *not* human society itself, nor some of the other things that that society entails. Thus, at the end of the thought experiment proposed in the *Elements*, the mind is not left alone with its phantasms, but rather staring into a picture by John White.[25]

---

namely, what one might describe as the arts and sciences. Second, in his only comments on Sextus Empiricus (*Six Lessons to the Professors of the Mathematics*, *EW*, VII: 184, 317–18), Hobbes claims that his own geometrical definitions have "removed the grounds for skeptical doubts about geometry that had been raised by Sextus Empiricus in his treatise *Against the Mathematicians*" (Jesseph, *Squaring the Circle*, 81). In Lesson V, Hobbes accuses Sextus of the most serious crime, namely of having misunderstood Euclid's most fundamental definition, that of a point, and thereby having "utterly destroyed most of the rest, and demonstrated, that in geometry there is no science" (*EW*, VII: 317–18). Hobbes accuses Wallis and Ward, the targets of his attack, of having committed the same errors, and thereby "betrayed the most evident of the sciences to the sceptics" (*ibid.*, 318). Hobbes was far from alone in expressing the hope that the mathematicians' success could be replicated in politics. In *The Iesuites Catechisme*, Pasquier argued that "although there can be no certaine iudgement giuen of future things, yet I dare say, & it is true, that in matter of State, the predictions of good or ill, are no lesse infallible then iudgements Mathematicall" (231). Not everyone was as sanguine, of course. In *The Catching of Leviathan*, Bramhall mocked Hobbes's assertion that politics was unlike tennis play and like arithmetic and geometry, arguing that the opposite was the case, but declaring no surprise that Hobbes, who had no experience in the matter, would make such a mistake (see Bramhall, *The Works of the Most Reverend Father in God, John Bramhall D.D.*, 883–84).

[24] *De Corpore*, II.7.1. Toward the end of his first Meditation, Descartes proposes a similar thought experiment by supposing that everything around him was merely the attempt of an evil demon to deceive him (*Meditations, Objections, and Replies*, 12). Hobbes's objection to this Meditation was that it added nothing new to a topic well rehearsed by "Plato and other ancient philosophers" (*ibid.*, 100).

[25] This point has crucial implications for the character of the state of nature, which on the basis of an erroneous identification with the annihilation of the world proposed in *De Corpore* is often turned into a completely barren and solitary place, in which cooperation, for example, is not possible. On why this picture is incorrect, see Evrigenis, *Fear of Enemies and Collective Action*, 111–19; cf. Biletzki, "Thomas Hobbes," 65–66.

The contrast between reason and passion that was promised at the outset of the *Elements* is now ready. Its hyperbolic nature is apparent in Hobbes's matter-of-fact assertion that the comparison of magnitudes has continued to grow and yield fruit, and "[y]et to this day was it *never* heard of, that there was *any* controversy concerning *any* conclusion in this subject."[26] On the other side of this neat and peaceful realm are those who have written on "the faculties, passions, and manners of men," the moral and civil philosophers, the *dogmatici*. Their domain is the antithesis of order. The reason is one that we have encountered before, and the one that Hobbes would return to again and again, namely, their uncritical reliance on the authority of others. The only thing these dogmatists can agree on, it seems, is that they know no more than what Aristotle had taught them. Beyond that, Hobbes repeats, every new contribution to the debate only serves to confuse matters further.[27] Their role in the perpetuation of controversy amounts to a crime, and it is with them alone that the responsibility rests.[28]

Buried as it is in a chapter on the workings of language, the distinction between the mathematicians and the dogmatists is easy to miss or misunderstand. Yet there must be some reason why Hobbes singled it out as an apt metaphor for his task in the Epistle Dedicatory. The language with which he fills in the details here provides a further clue. These groups are no mere polar opposites in some innocuous scientific domain. Their respective actions make the world a better or worse place, not simply by furthering or hindering the advancement of knowledge and the pursuit of discoveries and inventions, but by making the world peaceful and commodious or violent and unpleasant. Sitting above this contest of good and evil, Hobbes passes judgment:

> those we call the mathematici are absolved of the crime of breeding controversy; and they that pretend not to learning cannot be accused; the fault lieth altogether in the dogmatics, that is to say, those that are imperfectly learned, and with passion press to have their opinions pass everywhere for truth, without any evident demonstration.[29]

The dogmatists who disseminate their views widely, however, are but the tip of the iceberg. For when it comes to the domains of moral and civil philosophy, "every man thinks that ... he knoweth as much as any other; supposing there needeth thereunto no study but that it accrueth to them by natural wit."[30]

One could read Hobbes's diagnoses of the perils confronting the individual mind, let alone the difficulties regarding the examination of moral and civil

[26] *The Elements of Law*, I.13.3, emphasis added. But cf. *Leviathan*, XI: 50.
[27] *The Elements of Law*, I.13.3–4; cf. Ep. Ded.
[28] *The Elements of Law*, I.13.4.
[29] *The Elements of Law*, I.13.4.
[30] *The Elements of Law*, I.13.3; cf. *ibid.*, II.10.8.

matters, as a rather elaborate attempt to do what every writer addressing such topics does: pronounce everyone else wrong, and claim singular insight into the truth. Hobbes, however, has done much more than simply dismiss those who have preceded him and with whom he disagrees.[31] He has identified problems in places where the very possibility of solutions is now in question. For, if he is correct, then there can be no hope of transferring the method of natural philosophy to the study of moral and civil matters because the latter will not admit of the former. This point needs to be emphasized because Hobbes's admiration for geometry makes it easy to misunderstand his belief in how far it can help reform moral and civil philosophy. Thus, just as privation means one thing when applied to natural philosophy but quite another when applied to civil philosophy, "evident demonstration" and proof will mean very different things in the context of a geometrical proof than in support of a political argument.[32] In the latter context, evident demonstration takes place "either from experience, or from places of Scripture of uncontroverted interpretation."[33]

As it turns out, there are precious few Biblical passages that pass the latter test, so the demonstrative weight falls on experience. Hobbes had warned the reader that he intended merely to alert us to what we know already, and it is now possible to begin to realize the full significance of that promise. Running alongside Hobbes's contrast between the mathematicians and the dogmatists is a parallel division between teaching and persuasion. Both teaching and persuasion describe the effect of one mind on another, but the similarity ends there. Each practice employs its own means and method to achieve its effect. Those who could be described as teachers, according to this distinction, proceed methodically from experience and invoke the same kind of evidence in the listener, who thereby learns. When no such evidence exists, however, what is transmitted is nothing more than bare opinion. The latter process is persuasion.[34] Thus, despite Hobbes's term, "persuasion" refers to the realm of disagreement and conflict, and not to the consensus that one might associate with the term. The difference to which Hobbes here wishes to draw attention is that between teaching and its opposite (persuasion), which is an activity centered on the transmission of opinion, rather than truth. His usage here is thus part of his strategy of artificially neat contrasts, in which rhetoric belongs on the side of the passions. Related activities, described as "INSTIGATION and APPEASING"

---

[31] He is not shy about doing so explicitly, both in the *Elements of Law* (Ep. Ded.), and elsewhere (for example, *De Cive*, Ep. Ded.; *De Corpore*, Ep. Ded.; OL: I, ix).

[32] See, for example, *The Elements of Law*, I.13.4. Cf. *Leviathan*, VIII–IX, A Review and Conclusion, § 4; *De Corpore*, I.1.9.

[33] *The Elements of Law*, I.13.4. Cf. *Leviathan*, XLIII: 326.

[34] *The Elements of Law*, I.13.2.

give rise to passion. Hobbes describes the relationship between the two as follows:

For the begetting of opinion and passion is the same act; but whereas in persuasion we aim at getting opinion from passion; here, the end is, to raise passion from opinion. And as in raising an opinion from passion, any premises are good enough to infer the desired conclusion; so, in raising passion from opinion, *it is no matter whether the opinion be true or false, or the narration historical or fabulous. For not truth, but image, maketh passion; and a tragedy affecteth no less than a murder if well acted.*[35]

It should now be clear precisely what Hobbes had in mind when he suggested in the Epistle Dedicatory that "it would be an incomparable benefit to commonwealth, if every man held the *opinions* concerning law and policy here delivered."[36] Passion gives rise to opinion, and opinion gives rise to passion, and at the heart of this process lies not truth, but an image that may be true or false, historical or fabulous – an image like that of the state of nature, which Hobbes will begin to paint in the very next chapter.[37]

A CERTAIN EQUALITY, AN UNCERTAIN ANARCHY

If, in accordance with the method that has been emerging up to Chapter 14, the purpose of the state of nature is to make a compelling case for the benefits of order by painting a horrific picture of disorder, then Hobbes's first sketch fails. The state of nature of *Elements* I.14 contains all the basic ingredients of the better known, later versions. Equality, diffidence, vanity, comparison, appetite, natural right, and the state of war all make an appearance here, combining to compose a picture of disorder, but their roles are underdeveloped, and their arrangement premature. The different order of presentation and relationship of one concept to the others in *Elements* I.14 are the reasons why it is difficult to map the first account of the state of nature neatly onto its equivalents in *De Cive* and *Leviathan*. The resulting image of disorder is accordingly less powerful than in the later accounts, and even though in essence the argument is the same, the state of nature of *The Elements of Law* fails to persuade the reader of the perils of anarchy.

The table of contents of the *Elements* identifies the chapter in question as treating "Of the Estate and Right of Nature."[38] Hobbes's description of its subject matter is worth noting. He suggests that having examined the "whole nature of man … it will be expedient to consider in what estate of security this our nature hath placed us, and what probability it hath

---

[35] *The Elements of Law*, I.13.7, emphasis added. Cf. *A Briefe of the Art of Rhetorique*, III.16.
[36] *The Elements of Law*, Ep. Ded., p. xvi, emphasis added.
[37] The claim regarding truth here refers not to the content of the argument, but to the image used to convey it. This is a crucial distinction to which we will return.
[38] Devonshire Mss., Chatsworth HS/A/2A; HS/A/2B; HS/A/2C.

left us of continuing and preserving ourselves against the violence of one another."[39] The "nature" in question, then, is human nature, as described in the opening chapters of the work, rather than nature personified. The "state" in question is not some abstract natural condition, but rather the condition of our security given that nature.

Surveying the basic parameters of that condition, Hobbes concludes that "men in mere nature, ought to admit amongst themselves equality."[40] This is because even though disparities of strength and wit abound, they are insufficient to ensure anyone's supremacy for long. Each individual is susceptible to the potential for destruction at the hands of another, "since there needeth but little force to the taking away of a man's life."[41] It is tempting to say that there is equality in the state of nature, but what kind of equality is this? It seems to be based on vulnerability, and yet it stems from apparently widespread inequalities in physical strength and wit. Moreover, what sort of equality is it if it requires Hobbes's urging to be recognized?[42]

The reason why it is not recognized by all is that some individuals are vainglorious and seek to dominate others, even if those others are their equals or their superiors. To such individuals, even the moderate seem obnoxious. Their attempts to act on their desire for domination are sufficient, claims Hobbes, to produce "a general diffidence in mankind, and mutual fear one of another."[43] By presenting these attributes as sufficiently widespread to bring about conflict, but not as universal, Hobbes is able to reap a further psychological benefit. He can provide a space of reason that the reader can occupy as he assents to Hobbes's assessment of the unreasonable. A reasonable author and a reasonable reader can thus agree with one another that the world is full of vainglorious individuals, without thereby accusing themselves in the process.

If the reader is skeptical that such widespread diffidence can result from the work of so few, Hobbes proceeds to offer other reasons to think conflict likelier, if not inevitable. The vainglorious may be few, but "every man" thinks well of himself and hates to see the same in others. When such feelings are present, one can expect that insults and other provocations will result in conflict.[44] If this too seems farfetched, there is a further, more common tinderbox: many individuals are likely to desire the same good, one that can neither be divided nor enjoyed in common. Hence, "the greatest part of men, upon no assurance of odds, do nevertheless, through vanity,

[39] *The Elements of Law*, I.14.1–2.
[40] *The Elements of Law*, I.14.2.
[41] *The Elements of Law*, I.14.2.
[42] For an account of the many difficulties involved in Hobbes's conception of equality in the state of nature, see Kinch Hoekstra, "Hobbesian Equality." For the reasons pointed out earlier, as well as several others identified by Hoekstra, I will refer to it as "effective equality."
[43] *The Elements of Law*, I.14.3.
[44] *The Elements of Law*, I.14.4.

or comparison, or appetite, provoke the rest, that otherwise would be contented with equality."[45]

Conflict might seem a little likelier than it did at first. Still, a moderate reader of the kind favored by Hobbes might nevertheless be excused for not thinking this list compelling. Yet Hobbes means it to apply to everyone, because everyone is interested in his own well-being and everyone wishes to avoid harm, and in particular, "that terrible enemy of nature, death, from whom we expect both the loss of all power, and also the greatest bodily pains in the losing."[46] The presence of this *summum malum* forms the basis of Hobbes's account of natural right – a right to the means toward the avoidance of death that cannot be denied to anyone.[47] Thus, one may use all one's power in preserving one's life and limb, but also anything else that one judges necessary toward that end. In such a condition, the judgment of the end and means rests with the individual, and Hobbes's justification for this allocation is simple: if a man be denied any link in this chain, he is being denied the right to self-preservation.[48]

Hobbes's granting of such extensive rights to individuals, especially in a condition characterized by equality, is potentially very problematic for his edifice. Although it sits well with his declared intention to lay his argument at the feet of every single one of his readers, it also opens the door to imposing constraints on the sovereign, a move that some of his critics would gladly make.[49] Rather than deny either equality or the existence of extensive natural rights, Hobbes chooses a different strategy: he diffuses them by pointing out that when held by everyone, in a condition of effective equality, such rights amount to nothing at best, and to a major inconvenience

---

[45] *The Elements of Law*, I.14.5. Tricaud raises the issue of the compatibility of this triad with those offered in *De Cive* I.4–6 and *Leviathan* XIII § 6, and sees important differences between the three accounts ("Hobbes's Conception of the State of Nature from 1640 to 1651," esp. 117–23). As we will see, however, this impression is not the result of any significant change in the substance of the account, but rather of certain modifications in the arrangement and presentation of the central concepts. Cf. Eggers, *Die Naturzustandstheorie des Thomas Hobbes*, 562–63.

[46] *The Elements of Law*, I.14.6.

[47] Hobbes uses the phrase in *De Cive*, Ep. Ded. § 10. According to Thucydides,

> either some greater terror than death must be devised, or death will not be enough for coercion. For poverty will always add boldness to necessity; and wealth, covetousness to pride and contempt. And the other [middle] fortunes, they also through human passion, according as they are severally subject to some insuperable one or other, impel men to danger. But hope and desire work this effect in all estates.…In a word, it is a thing impossible and of great simplicity to believe when human nature is earnestly bent to do a thing that by force of law or any other danger it can be diverted (I.45, Hobbes's translation).

[48] *The Elements of Law*, I.14.6–9.

[49] See, for example, Bramhall, *The Works of the Most Reverend Father in God, John Bramhall D.D.*, 883; Filmer, *Observations Concerning the Originall of Government*, Pref.

at worst.[50] The absurdity of this condition is captured in the realization
that both those who invade *and* those who resist do so "with right," which
makes for perpetual insecurity. This paradox prompts Hobbes to declare
that the state of men in natural liberty is a state of war, since "WAR is nothing else but that time wherein the will and intention of contending by force
is either by words or actions sufficiently declared."[51]

The promise of life in a condition of "liberty and right of all to all" should
therefore be corrected by the realization that this condition amounts to one
of "hostility and war ... such, as thereby nature itself is destroyed, and men
kill one another."[52] With the whole picture in mind, it becomes apparent
that anyone who wishes to live in such a condition contradicts himself, since
man "by natural necessity" desires his own good, something that he cannot
hope to pursue in a condition of such pervasive hostility and uncertainty.[53]
Anticipating the need to prove this condition real, Hobbes points to

> both the experience of savage nations that live at this day, and by the histories of our
> ancestors, the old inhabitants of Germany and other now civil countries, where we
> find the people few and short lived, and without the ornaments and comforts of life,
> which by peace and society are usually invented and procured.[54]

Before considering the efficacy of these examples, it is necessary to note that
they point to a direct connection between Hobbes's two dichotomies: the one
between the mathematicians and the dogmatists, and the one between the
state of nature and civil society. The link is the one that Hobbes had alluded
to in the previous chapter, when at the end of his exercise in privation he
had concluded that the antithesis of everything good, of a world constructed
by reason and by the mathematicians, was the condition of "the wildest of
Indians."[55] The chasm between a condition of order and commodious living
on the one hand, and one of disorder and privation on the other hand, is
based on the earlier chasms that Hobbes constructed between the passions
and reason, and between the dogmatists and the mathematicians.[56]

---

[50] For example, Hobbes argues, "that right of all men to all things, is in effect no better than
if no man had right to any thing," because "there is little use and benefit of the right a
man hath, when another as strong, or stronger than himself, hath right to the same" (*The
Elements of Law*, I.14.10).

[51] *The Elements of Law*, I.14.11. The reader familiar with Hobbes's subsequent definitions of
war will recognize the seeds of those definitions in this one. Its tone, however, is considerably
less menacing. We will return to this matter, especially in regard to Chapter 1 of *De Cive*.

[52] *The Elements of Law*, I.14.12.

[53] *The Elements of Law*, I.14.12.

[54] *The Elements of Law*, I.14.12.

[55] *The Elements of Law*, I.13.3.

[56] Thus, even though the *Elements* falls outside the scope of his study, Kraynak is correct when
he suggests that "the primary theme of Hobbes's studies in civil history is the distinction
between barbarism and civilization" (*History and Modernity in the Thought of Thomas
Hobbes*, 12).

The examples of the savages of Hobbes's day and of the ancestors of civilized nations were meant to persuade his readers that his image of the state of nature was not simply "fabulous," but that it had some "historical" grounding as well.[57] A fastidious reader might object that Hobbes is misrepresenting the condition of the Indians of America and of the ancient Germans, but that sort of objection misses the obvious rhetorical force of these examples, which appeal to a basic contrast between the commodious living that comes from civilization and the hardship that is generally associated with primitive conditions. Hobbes's emphasis on the "ornaments and comforts of life" is noteworthy because it points to the fact that this account of the state of nature does not address the issue of anarchy explicitly. As a consequence, the reader is asked to think about ways of life that are more or less desirable, but is hardly faced with the starker and more explicitly sinister choice between life and violent death.

On the most basic level, the problem with these examples is obvious: they might prove that such a condition has existed or that it even exists, but they do not prove that it is one that Hobbes's readers need to worry about. Even if one were to concede the debatable claim that the lives of the Indians and of the ancient Germans were shorter and more uncertain than those of the readers of the *Elements*, one could still point out that the latter had no reason to fear that they would find themselves in such a condition. The benefits of the mathematicians had already been bestowed on them, and were here to stay. This impression is reinforced as one explores the difference between the two sets of examples. If that of the contemporary savages shows that the state of nature still existed, it nevertheless did so by showing that it existed far away. If anything, the example of the savage ancestors of "now civil countries" would lead a contemporary inhabitant of those countries to the conclusion that the state of nature had been left behind for good.

Perhaps because of the small and scientifically-minded audience he was addressing in the *Elements*, Hobbes appears less concerned with providing examples of the state of nature and more interested in conveying to his reader the frame of mind that such a condition ought to engender. Once again, he shies away from speaking explicitly of anarchy, but he points out that reliance on one's own abilities coupled with an effective equality should lead one to recognize the necessity of preemptive strikes, so as to avoid having to face prospective adversaries later. This may seem like a small rational step away from the basic description of this natural condition, but its significance is great, for it justifies otherwise unthinkable conduct. It requires that one eliminate anyone whom one subdues "either by infancy, or weakness, ... unable to resist him."[58] To do so, argues Hobbes, is to act "by right of nature," and to refuse is, once more, to contradict oneself by

[57] Using Hobbes's terms, from *The Elements of Law*, I.13.7.
[58] *The Elements of Law*, I.14.13.

allowing another to "gather strength and be our enemy."[59] Perhaps the purpose of this thought is to get the reader to understand just how unpleasant such a condition would be. Regardless, the conclusion that Hobbes draws from it is striking: "irresistible might in the state of nature is right."[60] This is the first instance, in Hobbes's writings, of the term "state of nature."

It is in the very midst of the domain in which might makes right, however, that Hobbes locates the means by which one may exit the darkness of the state of nature, since the selfsame effective equality which made that condition possible is what will lead one to the conclusion that "no man is of might *sufficient*, to assure himself for any long time, of preserving himself thereby, whilst he remaineth in the state of hostility and war."[61] Even the most confident among the vainglorious ought to realize that under such circumstances, lasting security or reliable rule over others is simply impossible. By pointing to the fact that no man is capable of preserving himself on his own, reason – which is the law of nature – directs man to seek peace where that is possible, "and to strengthen himself with all the help he can procure, for his own defence against those, from whom such peace cannot be obtained; and to do all those things which necessarily conduce thereunto."[62] One comes to this realization by considering the prospects for agreement in a condition in which each is judge of what is right and wrong and there is no universal standard because "*right* reason is not existent."[63] Disorder will give way to order once "the reason of some man, or men," namely "he or they that have the sovereign power," has established such a standard by promulgating civil laws.[64]

All this talk of reason, built as it is on a contrast between a world of productive, ordered inquiry and one of dogmatism and disagreement, might fool one into thinking that the *Elements* is indeed the predominantly scientific treatise it is often taken to be. Hobbes mentions the word "rhetoric" only once in the entire treatise, and only to explain to his patron that its style is "the worse" because of his focus on logic, rather than rhetoric.[65] There are several reasons, however, for being skeptical of such an interpretation. Recall, for example, that in the Epistle Dedicatory, Hobbes also refers to the content of the *Elements* as "the *opinions* concerning law and policy here delivered."[66] Recall, further, that he declares his intention to begin with such a foundation

[59] *The Elements of Law*, I.14.13. Cf. *ibid.*, II.1.16; II.3.2; II.3.9; II.4.3.
[60] *The Elements of Law*, I.14.13. The second part of the work contains a further four instances (II.1.16; II.3.2; II.3.9; II.10.8), as well as three instances of "estate of nature" (I.16.4; II.1.6; II.4.3).
[61] *The Elements of Law*, I.14.14, emphasis added.
[62] *The Elements of Law*, I.14.14. On reason as the law of nature, see *ibid.*, I.15.1.
[63] *The Elements of Law*, II.10.8, emphasis added.
[64] *The Elements of Law*, II.10.8.
[65] *The Elements of Law*, Ep. Ded., xvi.
[66] *The Elements of Law*, Ep. Ded., xvi, emphasis added.

"as passion not mistrusting, may not seek to displace."[67] By the very contrast between reason and passion, this trust cannot be established through reason, but must involve some kind of deception. What, exactly, that procedure entails becomes clear in Chapter 13, when Hobbes turns to consider the ways in which men affect one another's minds by means of words, and notes that one category of speech consists of "INSTIGATION and APPEASING, by which we increase or diminish one another's passions."[68] As we have seen, to effect instigation and appeasing, one must raise passion from opinion. Hobbes characterized his views in the *Elements* as "opinions" concerning law and policy, and declared his intention to appease his readers. So which passions would he have to raise, and by what means?

When Hobbes composed the *Elements*, he included the first nineteen chapters in the first part, under the heading "Human Nature."[69] When the work was divided into two parts for its unauthorized publication in 1650, *Humane Nature* only contained Chapters 1–13.[70] This division, which drew the cutoff point between I.13 and I.14 – rather than where Hobbes had, at the end of I.19 – was reproduced by Molesworth in his edition of Hobbes's English works.[71] This accounts, perhaps, for the fact that readers have failed to associate Hobbes's astonishing statement in the former, that "in raising passion from opinion, it is no matter whether the opinion be true or false, or the narration historical or fabulous," with the narration that follows in the very next chapter, namely, Hobbes's account of the state of nature.[72] To anyone but the privileged few who had access to the full manuscript of the *Elements of Law*, the former statement would have concluded the volume entitled *Human Nature*, and the narration of the state of nature would have opened the separate volume entitled *De Corpore Politico*. Keeping the two in mind together, however, allows one to see how Hobbes proposes to appease his readers. Hobbes had already drawn the distinction between the state of nature and civil society in Chapter 13, when he had juxtaposed the world of the mathematicians, with all its attendant benefits, to that of the "wildest of Indians."[73]

[67] *The Elements of Law*, Ep. Ded., xv.
[68] *The Elements of Law*, I.13.7.
[69] See Devonshire Mss., Chatsworth HS/A/2A; HS/A/2B; HS/A/2C; British Library Mss. Egerton 2005; Harl. 1325; 4235; 4236; 6858.
[70] See *Humane Nature*; cf. *De Corpore politico*.
[71] See *EW*, IV. Recall that the two parts were not reunited until Tönnies published his edition of the *Elements* in 1889.
[72] *The Elements of Law*, I.13.7. The chapter diagram that forms the table of contents of the entire work marks Chapters 14 and 15 of Part I as treating "Of the condition of men in mere nature" and thereby contributes to the impression that I.13 contains nothing relevant to the state of nature, despite the fact that Hobbes introduces the distinction between civil society and an antecedent state represented by "the wildest of Indians" therein (I.13.3). Cf. *De Homine*, XI.10.
[73] *The Elements of Law*, I.13.3. The initial division of the work and the table of contents perhaps account for the fact that several commentators hold the mistaken view that Hobbes

In the context of a narrative in which passion is the cause of conflict and reason the force for peace, the notion that peace might result from raising passion sounds counterintuitive. Even though such a narrative is appealing, the radical divide that it imposes between reason and the passions is too neat and simplistic to be true. Hobbes's suggestion that appeasing might involve raising passion, rather than eliminating it, runs counter to such a narrative, but is in accordance with his view that the passions cannot be eliminated from the equation. Already aware of the fact that human beings think in terms of a *bonum sibi*, rather than a *summum bonum*, Hobbes realized that his narration, somewhat historical and fabulous, would have to persuade his readers that the objects of their desire, no matter what they might be, would presuppose the ability to acquire them, itself subject to "that terrible enemy of nature, death," which deprives us of all power.[74] By presenting the state of nature as a condition of "general diffidence in mankind, and mutual fear one of another," Hobbes provides a foundation that passion cannot mistrust since the logic that gets him there is one that cannot be refuted by anyone driven by a *bonum sibi*, whatever that might be.[75] The passion, therefore, that needed to be raised was the fear of death, but Hobbes's first attempt, in *The Elements of Law*, fell short.[76]

---

only added the example of the Indians to his account of the state of nature in *De Cive*. Skinner, for instance, claims that the "only significant difference" between the *Elements* and *De Cive* is that in the latter, "Hobbes fills out his earlier observations about the experience of ancient nations with the specific claim that 'the peoples of America provide us with an example of this way of life even at the present time'" (*Hobbes and Republican Liberty*, 98). Cf. Goldsmith, "Picturing Hobbes's Politics?" 234; "Hobbes's Ambiguous Politics," 642; Baumgold, "The Difficulties of Hobbes Interpretation," 841, table 1. The only exceptions I am aware of are Landucci (*I filosofi e i selvaggi*, 128) and Gliozzi who follows him (*Adamo e il nuovo mondo*, 412), Ashcraft ("*Leviathan* Triumphant," 163), and Sorell (*Hobbes*, 37–38).

[74] *The Elements of Law*, I.14.6.
[75] *The Elements of Law*, I.14.3. Cf. *ibid.*, Ep. Ded., xv.
[76] When he considers the generation of a commonwealth, Hobbes argues that "the wills of most men are governed only by fear, and where there is no power of coercion, there is no fear" (*The Elements of Law*, II.1.6).

FIGURE 1. Title page of Hobbes's *De Cive* (1642).
Source: [Thomas Hobbes], *Elementorum Philosophiæ Sectio Tertia De Cive* (Paris, 1642), *EC65 H6525 642e, Houghton Library, Harvard University.

4

The Birth of Civil Philosophy

De Cive

[T]he first grounds of all science are not only not beautiful, but poor, arid, and, in appearance, deformed.

– Hobbes, *De Corpore*

Shortly after composing and circulating *The Elements of Law*, Hobbes fled to France, where he spent the next eleven years.[1] Before two years had passed, he had composed a new political treatise, entitled *Elementorum Philosophiæ Sectio Tertia De Cive*, roughly corresponding in subject matter to *De Corpore Politico*, though with the addition of a substantial section on religion. In 1642, printed copies of this new work were distributed to certain friends and acquaintances, but the work was not made available for sale.[2] This fact has some significance, given Hobbes's explicit aim to appeal to the widest possible audience, and helps account for the ways in which it evolved.[3] Nevertheless, there is evidence to suggest that *De Cive* made an impression sufficient to cause word about it to spread, and to necessitate,

---

[1] *Mr. Hobbes Considered*, 6.

[2] This is the edition that Warrender designates as "L1." According to the *Vitæ Hobbianæ auctarium*, "pauca duntaxat exemplaria Parisiis 1642 evulgaverat" (*OL*, I: xxxii). In letters written within days of each other, in 1646, Pierre Gassendi and Marin Mersenne urged Samuel Sorbière to find a publisher for a corrected version of *De Cive*, noting that the private printing of 1642 had been insufficient. Mersenne urged, "See then that some outstanding printer brings to light that golden book, augmented and adorned with jewels, and do not let us longer be wanting it," and Gassendi wrote, "Obviously so few copies of the book were printed, that they produced rather than satisfied a thirst for it; since indeed I see many who eagerly seek the book, but without success" (letters to Sorbière, Orléans, April 25, 1646 and Paris, April 28, 1646, respectively, in *De Cive, The Latin Version*, 297–98). On this basis, Warrender puts the number of copies printed at "probably no more than 100" (*De Cive, The Latin Version*, 40). Very few copies of the 1642 edition survive, and even fewer are intact.

[3] See *The Elements of Law*, Ep. Ded., xvi; *Thomæ Hobbesii Malmesburiensis vita*, 8.

a few years later, the publication of an edition for sale.[4] That edition was published by Elzevir in 1647 to great acclaim.[5]

Hobbes declared that *De Cive* marked the beginning of civil philosophy, and that it was the work that made him famous internationally.[6] Despite the fact that he went on to publish his English *Leviathan* and a Latin version of that work later still, Hobbes declined the opportunity to revise *De Cive* before its reissue, and included it in the works published in the Latin collection of 1668.[7] Between 1642 and 1647, Hobbes made four important changes to this work. The first three were immediately apparent: the 1647 edition had a new title, a different frontispiece, and a substantial Preface to the Readers, which the earlier version had lacked.[8] In addition to these changes, the reader soon discovered that Hobbes had added a series of explanatory notes, in which he addressed some of the most important issues raised by readers of the 1642 edition.[9]

[4] See Warrender's introduction to his edition of *De Cive, The Latin Version*, esp. p. 7, as well as Appendix B, which contains correspondence related to *De Cive*.
[5] Thomas Hobbes, *Elementa Philosophica De Cive* (Amsterdam: Elsevier, 1647). Warrender designates this edition as "L2" (*De Cive, The Latin Version*, ed. Howard Warrender, 37, 41–43, 47–51). Cf. Macdonald and Hargreaves, *Thomas Hobbes: A Bibliography*, numbers 25, 26.
[6] In the Epistle Dedicatory of the later *De Corpore*, Hobbes dismisses what passed for philosophy in "old Greece" as "a certain phantasm, for superficial gravity, though full of fraud and filth," and proclaims, "Natural Philosophy is therefore but young; but Civil Philosophy yet much younger, as being no older … than my book *De Cive*" (*EW*, I: ix). In his verse life, Hobbes writes that two years after arriving in France,

> edo *De Cive* libellum,
> Qui placuit Doctis, & novus omnis erat;
> Versus & in varias Linguas cum laude legebar,
> Gentibus & latè nomine notus eram.
> Laudabat mediis in Erynnibus *Anglia*, & illi
> Quorum consiliis cognitus hostis eram.
> Sed quod consiliis præsentibus utile non est
> (*Thomæ Hobbesii Malmesburiensis vita*, 6–7).

Citing Euphemus's speech to the Camarinæans in Thucydides' history, among other examples, Tenison mocks Hobbes's claim to novelty in *The Creed of Mr. Hobbes Examined* (171–72).
[7] Sorbière wrote twice (Samuel Sorbière to Thomas Hobbes, Leiden August 19, 1647; Samuel Sorbière to Thomas Hobbes, Leiden, October 4, 1647, in *The Correspondence of Thomas Hobbes*, I: 161–63), to let Hobbes know that Elzevir was planning a second edition of *De Cive*, and to ask whether Hobbes had any changes to make. Along with his response (Thomas Hobbes to Samuel Sorbière, Saint-Germain, November 27, 1647), Hobbes sent a sheet with "nothing … except errors of the previous printing," adding that he had "nothing to add or subtract" (*The Correspondence of Thomas Hobbes*, I: 163–65).
[8] Whereas the former title declared that the work was the third part of a system, the new title, *Elementa Philosophica De Cive*, presented the work as independent. The change was prompted by Elsevier's reasonable objection to the publication of the third part of a system whose two first parts had yet to be written. See Thomas Hobbes to Samuel Sorbière, Paris, June 1, 1646 (*The Correspondence of Thomas Hobbes*, I: 131–34).
[9] In the Preface, Hobbes writes, "[b]ut for the sake of those who have been perplexed by my principles, namely the nature of man, the right of nature, the nature of agreements and the

For the present purposes, the change to the frontispiece is significant. The private version of 1642 opens with an arresting representation of the book's three parts: *libertas, imperium*, and *religio* (see Figure 1). The frontispiece is divided into two horizontal panels, the lower of which contains a banner with the title of the work given as *Elementorum Philosophiae Sectio Tertia De Cive*, Proverbs 8.15 as the epigraph, and with Paris 1642 as the place and date of the printing, but without any mention of the author. In the foreground, on either side of this banner, are figures representing the first two parts of the book, liberty (*libertas*) and government (*imperium*). The state of nature is represented on the right-hand side by an armed Algonquian Indian flanked by scenes of savage cruelty, including a manhunt and cannibalism. Civil society is represented by a female regal figure holding a sword in one hand and the scales of justice in the other, and reigning over scenes of tranquility and industry in the background. The top panel represents the third part of the work – religion – through a depiction of the Last Judgment.[10]

By contrast, while the frontispiece prepared for the 1647 edition retains the basic structure, representing each of the three parts of the work, its design is far less striking (see Figure 2). At its center, atop a pedestal that announces the new title and full publication information of the work, including its author's name, sits a female figure with the Sacred Heart in one hand and a large cross in the other, representing religion. On her left stands a figure in regal dress representing government, while on her right the state of nature is this time represented by a female figure in simple dress bearing a staff in her right hand and holding up a Dutch liberty cap with her left.[11] Far less impressive and clear than its predecessor, the revised frontispiece nevertheless offers us, inadvertently, two important pieces of information: first, that Hobbes most likely had a hand in the original design, but not in its successor, and second, that most of Hobbes's readers would not have seen the original frontispiece with its striking depiction of the state of nature.[12]

generation of a commonwealth, as they have not followed their passions but their own real understanding in making their comments, I have added notes in some places, which I thought might satisfy my critics" (§ 24). See also the language in the note to I.10, in which Hobbes refers to subsequent chapters in the past tense.

[10] The 1642 edition's frontispiece is very similar to that of a manuscript copy at Chatsworth, dating from 1641. That copy bears the author's initials as "T.H." See *De Cive, The Latin Version*, Frontispiece, 38–40. Warrender accepts the respective dates as accurate (39).

[11] In the 1644 Dutch edition of Ripa's *Iconologia*, a popular source of iconography throughout Europe during the first half of the seventeenth century, the figure of liberty holds a Dutch liberty cap, rather than a pileus, as in the Italian editions (cf. Ripa, *Iconologia*, II: 375; *Cesare Ripa's Iconologia of Uytbeeldinghen des Verstants*, http://www.dbnl.org/tekst/persoo1c-esao1_01/persoo1cesao1_01_1113.php). On liberty caps and their symbolism, see Harden, "Liberty Caps and Liberty Trees," esp. 68, 73–74, 90–91; cf. Schama, *The Embarrassment of Riches*, 98–100.

[12] On Hobbes's involvement in the production of his works, see Goldsmith, "Picturing Hobbes's Politics?" 232, 234.

ELEMENTA
PHILOSOPHICA
de
CIVE,
Auctore
THOM. HOBBES
Malmesburienſi.

Amſterodami,
Apud Ludovicum Elzevirium. Anno 1647.

FIGURE 2. Title page of Hobbes's *De Cive* (1647).
Source: Thomas Hobbes, *Elementa Philosophica De Cive*, (Amsterdam: Elzevir, 1647). Ioannis D. Evrigenis.

THOM. HOBBES Nobilis Anglus
Ser. Principi Walliæ a studiis præp

FIGURE 3. Portrait of Hobbes.
Source: Thomas Hobbes, *Elementa Philosophica De Cive* (Amsterdam: Elzevir, 1647). Ioannis D. Evrigenis.

The surviving correspondence tells us that the production of this new edition was problematic. Over the years, Mersenne, Gassendi, and others had been pushing for the publication of *De Cive*. In 1646, the task was assigned to the Amsterdam publishing house of Elzevir, and Samuel Sorbière, who was nearby, in Leiden and The Hague, undertook its supervision on behalf of Hobbes, who was still in France.[13] During production, Hobbes became tutor in mathematics to the Prince of Wales, a fact that Sorbière noted with approval and proceeded to highlight by placing it under a portrait of Hobbes that adorned the new edition (see Figure 3). When Hobbes received the proof of the sheet that included this portrait, he wrote to Sorbière to express his considerable dismay at the prospect that the association would damage the prince and prevent Hobbes from returning to England. So upset

---

[13] See Thomas Hobbes to Samuel Sorbière, Paris, May 16, 1646; Samuel Sorbière to Thomas Hobbes, The Hague, May 21, 1646 (*The Correspondence of Thomas Hobbes*, I: 125–30).

was Hobbes, that he offered to plead with the Elzevirs and even pay to have the sheets in question removed from any copies that remained with them, as well as to ask booksellers he knew to do the same with their stock.[14]

One need not assume that an author was either interested or directly involved in the design of a book's frontispiece and iconography, but there is considerable evidence to suggest that Hobbes was both interested and personally involved in the production of several of his works.[15] In the case of the 1647 *De Cive*, his letters to Sorbière confirm Hobbes's interest and show that he was not directly involved in the book's design, which means that he was most likely not responsible for the new frontispiece. One further piece of evidence reinforces the view that the original 1642 design is the one that Hobbes preferred.

There were some copies of the 1647 edition – only very few of which survive – that bear a different frontispiece, but which are otherwise indistinguishable from the main issue of 1647.[16] In those copies the front matter that had caused Hobbes such consternation is missing. In its place, one finds a frontispiece that is a crude, hastily composed version of the original design (see Figure 4). The provenance of this replacement is not known, but the evident haste in its composition and its placement suggest that it was put together in response to Hobbes's objections. This return to the original design of 1642 makes it probable that that design represented Hobbes's choice.[17]

The tone and contents of *De Cive* confirm the sense that the original frontispiece was the right one. In its first version, which lacks the prefatory material, the reader's eye moves immediately from the menacing Indian scene that monopolizes the title page to the first chapter, which describes the state of man without civil society.[18] Even in the published version, however, in which this transition is interrupted by the prefatory material, the tone of the work is distinctively more sinister. Whereas the *Elements*, with its emphasis on reason, invites the reader to compare the worlds of mathematics and dogmatism and conclude that the former is preferable to the latter, *De Cive*, with its talk of prejudice and rapacity, focuses on persuading the reader that life "without civil society" is undesirable. There is little

[14] See Thomas Hobbes to Samuel Sorbière, Paris, March 22, 1647 (*The Correspondence of Thomas Hobbes*, I: 155–59).

[15] See, for example, Hobbes's description of his work in preparing his translation of Thucydides (*EW*, VIII: ix-xi). Cf. Corbett and Lightbown, *The Comely Frontispiece*, 222; Goldsmith, "Picturing Hobbes's Politics?" 232; "Hobbes's Ambiguous Politics," 642.

[16] This is the edition that Warrender designates as "L2a."

[17] It is worth bearing in mind that despite the fact that "liberty" has positive connotations for many people, including some of Hobbes's contemporaries, for Hobbes the condition of natural liberty is undesirable. Thus, the alternative design of 1647, with its symbols of republican liberty, is not as antithetical to Hobbes's message as one might think at first. Nevertheless, there is no evidence to indicate who chose that design and why.

[18] *De statu Hominum extra Societatem civilem.*

FIGURE 4. Title page of Hobbes's *De Cive* (1647).
Source: Thomas Hobbes, *Elementa Philosophica De Cive* (Amsterdam: Elzevir, 1647), Keynes, A.16.01. By permission of the Provost and Scholars of King's College, Cambridge.

doubt that this change in tone was the result of the different circumstances in which the two works were composed.[19] Indeed, as we will see, Hobbes invokes these events in order to explain the timing of *De Cive*. It seems reasonable, therefore, to assume that exile and growing political unrest in England contributed to the shift. Nevertheless, the prefatory material to *De Cive* shows that Hobbes is still first and foremost concerned with order and disorder, and that he continues to identify rhetoric as both a key part of the problem and of its potential solution.

A MIRROR OF PRINCES

Hobbes's first account of *De Cive* comes in the form of the Epistle Dedicatory, composed as 1641 was drawing to a close.[20] Written, as they were, by a royalist in exile, the opening lines of the dedication of *De Cive* to the Earl of Devonshire could easily be mistaken for a vindication of monarchy. Therein, Hobbes notes that Cato used to speak for the Roman people when he classed kings as predatory animals, even though "[b]y the agency of citizens who took the names Africanus, Asiaticus, Macedonicus, Achaicus and so on from the nations they had robbed, that people plundered nearly all the world."[21] Hobbes's defense of monarchy, however, is incidental. The main point is that prejudice rendered the Roman people unable to see in themselves something that they condemned readily in others. To illustrate this tendency, Hobbes points to two famous maxims that seem contradictory, but which are "surely both true: *Man is a God to man*, and *Man is a wolf to Man*."[22]

---

[19] As Sommerville notes, "[b]etween 1640 and 1642 political divisions increased within and outside parliament" (*Thomas Hobbes*, 19); cf. Sommerville, *Politics and Ideology in England*, 173–88.

[20] Warrender reproduces the last page of the Epistle from the manuscript copy at Chatsworth, which is signed in Hobbes's hand, as from Paris, but without a date (see *De Cive: The Latin Version*, Plate II and p. 38). The Epistle is dated November 1, 1641 in the printed version.

[21] *De Cive*, Ep. Ded. § 1 (Silverthorne translation). Tuck and Silverthorne's version of the Epistle Dedicatory and Warrender's version of the Preface to the Readers are printed mainly in italics, reflecting a small subset of the editions printed during Hobbes's lifetime. In quoting from either, therefore, I have used italics only to preserve emphasis in the original.

[22] *De Cive*, Ep. Ded. § 1 (Silverthorne translation); cf. *Behemoth*, 322. The latter maxim is, most famously, found in Plautus's *Asinaria*, where the Merchant says, "lupus est homo homini, non homo, quom qualis sit non / nouit. [Man is a wolf and not a man toward a man when he doesn't know what he's like]" (495–96), although Laird considers it "obviously an adaptation of Aristotle's aphorism" in Book I of the *Politics* (1253a26–29; see Laird, *Hobbes*, 66, n. 1). As Laird points out, the first part of the maxim occurs in the *Vindiciæ Contra Tyrannos* (p. 184) and the second in Hooker's *Of the Laws of Ecclesiastical Polity* (I.x.12). Citing Tilley (see *A Dictionary of the Proverbs in England in the Sixteenth and Seventeenth Centuries*, M245, M247), Tricaud notes that the two maxims appear numerous times before *De Cive*, both in England and elsewhere. Tricaud points to Bacon's use of the latter maxim in *The Great Instauration*, and argues that Hobbes is likely to have seen the two maxims together in a collection compiled by Erasmus ("'Homo homini Deus,' 'Homo

For Hobbes, the former refers to the relationships among human beings within civil society, whereas the latter refers to the state of nature, wherein, as we have seen, "on account of the wickedness of evil men, the good must have recourse, if they wish to protect themselves, to the virtues of war, which are force and fraud, that is, to a brutal rapacity."[23] Natural right dictates that behavior conducive to self-preservation cannot be a vice, yet human beings have a natural tendency to judge themselves differently from others in this regard.[24] Thus, even though the Roman people ravaged the nations, Cato assigned kings to the genus of rapacious beasts.[25] "It may seem surprising," Hobbes adds,

> that prejudice should so impose upon the mind of Cato, a man renowned for wisdom, and partiality should so overcome his reason, that he censured in Kings what he thought reasonable in his own people. But I have long been of the opinion that there was never an exceptional notion that found favor with the people nor a wisdom above the common level that could be appreciated by the average man; for either they do not understand it, or in understanding it, they bring it down to their own level.[26]

If the latter view seems at odds with a civil philosophy that promises to speak to everyone, it is worth remembering that it is nevertheless consistent with Hobbes's assessment of readers and audiences in his translation of Thucydides, in the *Briefe*, and in *The Elements of Law*.[27] This pessimism is owing, in part, to the fact that to arrive at the truth regarding these matters,

homini Lupus,'" 63–67, 70). One cannot rule out the latter possibility, but it is worth pointing out that the frequent occurrence of the two maxims – often together – in English works in the sixteenth and seventeenth centuries points to the likelihood that they were well known and widely used. On *Homo homini Deus*, see, for example, Andrewes, *XCVI. Sermons*, I: 496, II: 95, 147. Among those who quote the maxims side by side, in works that Hobbes is likely to have read, Charron and Montaigne consider them apt descriptions of marriage (Charron, *Of Wisdome Three Bookes, etc.*, 178; Montaigne, *Essayes*, 511). Despite this statement, Bramhall accused Hobbes of considering human nature "worse than the nature of Bears, Wolves, or the most savage wild beasts" (*Castigations of Mr. Hobbes*, 509–10).

23 *De Cive*, Ep. Ded. § 2; cf. *The Elements of Law*, I.14.13. Hobbes is usually associated with the second maxim, although as Biletzki points out, it should not be taken out of context (*Talking Wolves*, 115). Hobbes's description, here, of force and fraud as "virtues" is doubtless a nod to Machiavelli, as is their ascription to the rapacity of beasts (*ad ferinam rapacitatem*). Cf. Machiavelli, *The Prince*, chapter XVIII.

24 Hobbes often casts issues of perception in terms of vision. In this case, he observes that "men have a natural tendency to use rapacity as a term of abuse against each other, seeing their own actions reflected in others as in a mirror where left becomes right and right becomes left" (*De Cive*, Ep. Ded. § 2). In the original, Hobbes's natural juxtaposition of right (dextra) and left (sinistra) conveys its moral connotations more clearly.

25 *De Cive*, Ep. Ded. § 1. In Plutarch's account, Cato says, "by nature this animal, the king, is carnivorous" (Plutarch, *Marcus Cato*, VIII.8).

26 *De Cive*, Pref. § 3 (Silverthorne translation).

27 See, for example, *EW*, VIII: vii; *A Briefe of the Art of Rhetorique*, I.1; *The Elements of Law*, I.5.14; II.8.14.

one must bear in mind how easy it is to misread history. Very few have the ability to engage in the deep meditation that is required for learning the truth.[28] As he had noted in his edition of Thucydides, Hobbes argues that events and individuals often stand out for the wrong reasons, in this case "by their grandeur and often by that very wolf-like element which men deplore in each other."[29] True wisdom, however, cannot depend on such whimsical foundations, but must rest upon remembrance originating in "fixed and definite names."[30] Executed properly, this method constitutes philosophy, and it "opens the way from the observation of individual things to universal precepts."[31] Like rhetoric, philosophy is indifferent to subject matter and can be applied to anything.

The appearance of reason and the antithesis between proper and improper methods here is reminiscent of Hobbes's earlier attempt to describe order and disorder in the *Elements*. This suspicion is confirmed when Hobbes announces his exemplary philosophers – a subset of the *mathematici*, whom he had credited with everything good in the *Elements* – the geometers. The rationale is the same:

whatever benefit comes to human life from observation of the stars, from mapping of lands, from reckoning of time and from long-distance navigation; whatever is beautiful in buildings, strong in defence-works and marvellous in machines, whatever in short distinguishes the modern world from the barbarity of the past, is almost wholly the gift of *Geometry*; for what we owe to *Physics*, *Physics* owes to *Geometry*.[32]

Predictably, the other side of this divide is inhabited by the moral philosophers. Hobbes notes that had the latter emulated the success of the geometers, they would have made the greatest contribution to human happiness because they would have been able to tame ambition and greed, "whose power rests on the false opinions of the common people about right and wrong," thereby granting the human race "such secure peace that … it seems unlikely that it would ever have to fight again."[33] Despite having accorded them the title "philosophers," Hobbes attributes their failure to the fact that they have not begun their inquiries into natural law and natural right from the right starting point. Instead, they have engaged in a perpetual war of the pens, in which the same action that is praised by one party is criticized by another. Each defends his position and miscasts that of his opponent, backing it only with the opinions of other philosophers.[34]

---

[28] *Leviathan*, XXX: 179.
[29] *De Cive*, Ep. Ded. § 3. Cf. *EW*, VIII: vii–viii.
[30] *De Cive*, Ep. Ded. § 4: "*appellationes certas & definitas.*"
[31] *De Cive*, Ep. Ded. § 4.
[32] *De Cive*, Ep. Ded. § 5. Cf. *The Elements of Law*, I.13.3–4.
[33] *De Cive*, Ep. Ded. § 6.
[34] *De Cive*, Ep. Ded. §§ 7–8.

Hobbes's immodest claim that *De Cive* marked the foundation of civil philosophy is based on a suitable starting point, which he discovered in the "darkness of doubt itself," the domain in which human beings dispute one another's claims to property.[35] Hobbes does not explain why he turned his attention to the question of natural justice, but his choice to couch the starting point of his inquiry in the language of property shows that this coin has two sides: one is negative – marked by darkness, doubt, privation, and death – but the other is positive, and contains the hope not just for life, but for commodious living. That the two go hand in hand is indicated by the fact that Hobbes discovered not a single Archimedean Point, but "two absolutely certain postulates of human nature, one, the postulate of human greed by which each man insists upon his own private use of common property; the other, the postulate of natural reason, by which each man strives to avoid violent death as the supreme evil in nature."[36] In any case, the right starting point was a necessary but not a sufficient prerequisite for success. It would allow Hobbes to hope that he could succeed where others had failed, but without the right method, it would not suffice to persuade everyone – including the "average man" – of the benefits of order.[37]

The conclusion of the Epistle Dedicatory is completely conventional in its deferential tone, but it contains a clue as to what that method might entail. Therein, Hobbes lauds his patron and expresses doubts about the worth of his work, as he would have been expected to do. The manner in which he does so, however, is interesting, because it calls to mind Aubrey's anecdote regarding Hobbes's Euclidean realization. Hobbes tells the Earl of Devonshire that he does not know what he has achieved in *De Cive*, "for we are all poor judges of our own discoveries because we love them."[38] This remark is consistent with the emphasis on partiality that opens the Epistle, but it also reminds us of the significance of becoming "demonstratively convinced" of a truth.[39] Beyond the right starting point, Hobbes would need to proceed through his demonstration in a manner that would allow any reader to follow him to the conclusion, while leaving him with the impression that he had done so on his own, even if the result would have been impossible without Hobbes's guidance. His summary of his achievements in *De Cive*

---

[35] *De Cive*, Ep. Ded. §§ 8–9. On the basis of evidence of a variety of primitive arrangements regarding property, Tierney argues that the "problems about property that are central to our Western tradition of political thought are not universal human problems" (*The Idea of Natural Rights*, 134). Hobbes's observation, however, concerns not specific types of property arrangements, but the very notion of property itself.

[36] *De Cive*, Ep. Ded. § 10: "Nactus ergo duo certissima naturæ humanæ postulata, vnum cupiditatis naturalis, qua quisque communium vsum postulat sibi proprium; alterum rationis naturalis, qua quisque mortem violentam tanquam summum naturæ malum studet euitare."

[37] *De Cive*, Ep. Ded. § 3.

[38] *De Cive*, Ep. Ded. § 12.

[39] Aubrey, '*Brief Lives*,' I: 332.

makes it clear that this objective is driving his method. He announces that he has "demonstrated by the most evident inference ... the necessity of agreements and of keeping faith, and thence the Elements of moral virtue and civil duties."[40] What reasonable reader could disagree with these goals?

The Preface to the Readers that Hobbes added for publication some five years later is remarkable for a number of reasons. Although addressed to a very different audience than the Epistle Dedicatory, it continues the themes of the latter and develops them in a manner reminiscent of the prefatory material to the translation of Thucydides. Far from being reticent about revealing his reservations regarding the capacity of most readers to read carefully and to understand what they have read, Hobbes engages in a startling critique of the average reader's ability to comprehend civil affairs. No longer addressing a man of privilege in confidence, Hobbes announces to the average reader that "[t]he wise men of remotest antiquity believed that this kind of teaching ... should be given to posterity only in the pretty forms of poetry or in the shadowy outlines of Allegory, as if to prevent what one might call the high and holy mystery of government from being contaminated by the debates of private men."[41]

If the narrative according to which Hobbes believed in the possibility of a civil philosophy founded solely on reason and accessible to everyone were true, we ought to expect this statement to be followed by a denunciation of this practice. Yet, what follows is a story about how this highest of the sciences has become the domain of every man. Socrates was the first to devote all of his energy to investigating it, but he was promptly followed by Plato, Aristotle, Cicero, and thereafter "all the Philosophers of all nations, and not only philosophers, but gentlemen also in their leisure hours, have attempted it, and continue to do so, as if it were easy and accessible without effort, open and available to anyone naturally inclined to it."[42] This interest is but one of several signs that this is the most esteemed of the sciences. Perhaps a better sign, however, is that everyone wants to claim it for himself. Whether they possess knowledge of it or not, men are happy to have "even a false semblance of it," and while they will allow others to claim honor and preeminence in the other sciences, they will not allow them to be called "*Prudentes*."[43] A third sign comes from weighing its consequences. In

---

[40] *De Cive*, Ep. Ded. § 10.

[41] *De Cive*, Pref. § 2. Toward the end of his *Comparative Discovrse of the Bodies Natvral and Politiqve*, a work that was known to Hobbes and available at Hardwick (see Devonshire Mss., Chatsworth HS/E/1A), Forsett discusses the curiosity of simple men who wish to look into "state businesse," using as examples Cato and Plautus (98). Hobbes's language here is reminiscent of Bacon's in his Preface to *De Sapientia Veterum* (*The Works of Francis Bacon*, VI: 625–28, 695–99).

[42] *De Cive*, Pref. §§ 2–3.

[43] Tuck and Silverthorne translate the term as "Statesmen," and give the original in brackets (*On the Citizen*, Pref. § 3). This translation, however, obfuscates the meaning of the sentence

the radical chasm that framed *The Elements of Law*, Hobbes emphasized the positive contributions of the mathematicians, and invited his readers to consider what their condition would look like if those were taken away. In *De Cive*, he argues that the worth of knowledge about matters political can be understood by considering "what damage to mankind follows from a false and rhetorical semblance of it."[44] Although nothing has changed in substance, this shift in perspective announces the very different tone of Hobbes's second attempt.

If everyone believes, on some level, that he has a monopoly on the truth when it comes to political matters, the consequences can be dire. Hobbes lists a few examples of the type of disorder that can result from such a belief. He also notes that the prevailing moral philosophy of his day contains many other views that can lead to similar outcomes, and concludes that "those ancients foresaw this who preferred that the knowledge of Justice be wrapped up in fables rather than exposed to discussion."[45] This epoch, during which power and obedience were simply matters of fact, rather than the subjects of debate, was "peace, and a golden age, which ended not before that *Saturn* being expelled, it was taught lawfull to take up arms against Kings."[46] Lacking learned stupidity, the men who inhabited that world could see that there was no point in opposing the force that provided them with security. In their eyes, sovereign power became "a certain visible divinity."[47] It was this truth that the ancients grasped and sought to protect by delivering it "to posterity, either curiously adorned with Verse, or clouded with Allegories," in the fable of Ixion, whose presumptuousness amid the Gods

---

because it focuses on the practice of politics rather than on prudence or good sense, and hence fails to explain why everyone, including philosophers and common men, who have nothing to do with government, might claim the title for themselves. In this regard, Cotton's 1650 translation, which renders the term as "prudent," is preferable (*Philosophical Rudiments concerning Government and Society*, Pref., A12ʳ). In the *Elements*, Hobbes argues that "generally, not he that hath skill in geometry, or any other science speculative, but only he that understandeth what conduceth to the good and government of the people, is called a wise man" (II.8.13). In his answer to Bramhall, Hobbes warns of a further difficulty, when he points out that "[i]t is one thing to know what is to be done, another thing to know how to do it" (EW IV: 286). In *Leviathan*, he claims, "Men that have a strong opinion of their own wisdome in matter of government, are disposed to Ambition" (XI: 49).

[44] *De Cive*, Pref. § 4.

[45] *De Cive*, Pref. § 6.

[46] *De Cive*, Pref. § 6; cf. Hesiod, *Works and Days*, 109–26; Aratus, *Phaenomena*, 100–36; Ovid, *Metamorphoses*, I.89–112, XV.96ff.; Tibullus, *Elegies*, I.3.35–36; Virgil, *Georgics*, I.121ff.; *Aeneid*, VI.792–93, VIII.314–29; Lovejoy and Boas, *Primitivism and Related Ideas in Antiquity*, 53–70. As Giamatti notes, later in *Works and Days* (225–37), Hesiod presents the benefits of Saturn's reign as reward for just behavior (*The Earthly Paradise and the Renaissance Epic*, 19–20).

[47] *De Cive*, Pref. § 6. This, along with the "Homo homini Deus" of the Epistle Dedicatory (§§ 1–2), presages Hobbes's description of the sovereign as a "*Mortall God*" in *Leviathan* (XVII: 87).

had yielded him a cloud from which had sprung the belligerent race of the Centaurs.[48] Changing the names in this story, suggests Hobbes,

is as much as if they should have said, that private men being called to the Counsels of State desired to prostitute justice, the only sister and wife of the supreme, to their own judgments, and apprehensions, but embracing a false and empty shadow instead of it, they have begotten those hermaphrodite opinions of morall Philosophers, partly right and comely, partly brutall and wilde, the causes of all contentions, and blood-sheds.[49]

The cloud has continued to yield Centaurs until Hobbes's day. Hobbes promises to dispel it, by showing that questions of right and wrong, just and unjust, and good and evil can only be answered by "those mandated by the commonwealth to interpret its laws."[50] As he had pointed out at the start of the *Elements*, Hobbes sought to make his teaching useful.[51] In *De Cive*, he declares that his demonstration will "not only shew us the high way to peace, but will also teach us how to avoyd the close, darke, and dangerous by-paths of faction and sedition, [than] which I know not what can be thought more profitable."[52]

Announcing his intention to explain his method, Hobbes then turns to a more detailed explication of the search for the right starting point that he had described only briefly to his patron. There, as we have seen, Hobbes had hinted at the need for a correct starting point and a method by which to persuade all his readers, including the "common" ones. In the Preface, the two elements are presented in reverse order. As before, persuasion is necessary, but not sufficient: far from embracing a scientific approach to politics and dismissing rhetoric, Hobbes begins by stating that "the conventional structure of a rhetorical discourse, though clear, would not suffice by itself."[53] To supplement it, he inquired into the right starting point, which he discovered by looking at the matter and formation of a commonwealth, as well as "the first beginning of justice."[54] The principle behind this approach is simple: just as to understand the workings of any complex device, one must take it apart

---

[48] *De Cive*, Pref. § 2; Pindar, *Pythian* II.21–49; Tibullus, *Elegies*, I.3.73.
[49] *De Cive*, Pref. § 7. Hobbes's language and imagery here show the difficulties that would be involved in any attempt to disentangle reason from the passions fully.
[50] *De Cive*, Pref. § 8.
[51] *The Elements of Law*, Ep. Ded., xvi.
[52] *De Cive*, Pref. § 8.
[53] *De Cive*, Pref. § 9 (Silverthorne trans.). The original term is "orationis." Among those who locate *De Cive* in Hobbes's "scientific" phase, Skinner, for example, claims that "[b]oth *The Elements of Law* and *De Cive* had been founded on the conviction that any genuine science of politics must aim to transcend and repudiate the purely persuasive techniques associated with the art of rhetoric" (*Reason and Rhetoric in the Philosophy of Hobbes*, 334). As his opening statement regarding his method shows, however, in *De Cive*, as in the earlier *Elements*, Hobbes saw rhetoric as inescapable.
[54] *De Cive*, Pref. § 9.

so to make a more curious search into the rights of States, and duties of Subjects, it is necessary, (I say not to take them in sunder, but yet that) they be so considered, as if they were dissolved, (i.e.) that wee rightly understand what the quality of humane nature is, in what matters it is, in what not fit to make up a civill government, and how men must be agreed among themselves, that intend to grow up into a well-grounded State.[55]

Readers familiar with the *Elements* had already encountered something similar in the invitation to suppose away all the trappings of commodious living that had yielded a picture of the "wildest of Indians."[56] In *De Corpore*, Hobbes would eventually describe the analytical method as a process of resolution.[57] In this case, the resolution lands Hobbes in an anarchic situation, where he discovers a principle "by experience well known to all men, and denied by none," namely that where there is no common power to fear, individuals will fear and distrust one another.[58] In such circumstances, one will do everything in one's power to look out for oneself, and in doing so will be acting in accordance with right.

Hobbes is able to back up the latter of his two bold claims here by pointing to the actions of human beings, which speak louder than words. Even in the best of commonwealths in situations in which there is no power to keep all in awe, diffidence prevails and dictates that we take precautions in order to protect ourselves and our interests. Defenders of mankind may deny that in an anarchic situation individuals will act in this way, but they will still arm themselves when they travel, and lock their doors and chests to protect their property. Hobbes calls on the reader to compare the defenders' words with their actions and realize that they contradict themselves.[59] By invoking these ordinary actions, Hobbes is able to prove that there is universal distrust even amid relative order, thereby bringing before the reader the obvious conclusion that a condition of anarchy is a condition of diffidence. More importantly, the choice of these mundane situations accomplishes something crucial with regard to what follows. It prepares the reader to accept the extraordinary proposition that the state of nature is not simply the distant and indifferent condition of the ancient Germans or of the Indians of America, but one that he encounters day in, day out.

Equally remarkable, however, is Hobbes's evidentiary standard here. Commentators have made much of Hobbes's conclusion in the *Elements* that "[e]xperience concludeth nothing universally," yet it is precisely on the

---

[55] *De Cive*, Pref. §§ 9–10.

[56] *The Elements of Law*, I.13.3.

[57] Hobbes argues that knowledge of universal things is "acquired by reason, that is, by resolution" (*De Corpore*, I.6.4).

[58] *De Cive*, Pref. § 10.

[59] Hobbes takes the relationship between words and deeds very seriously. See, for example, his statement regarding his aim in *Leviathan* (XXX: 180).

reader's experience that Hobbes calls for proof.[60] Recall that in the *Elements* Hobbes announces his intention to persuade his readers by putting them "in mind of what they know already, or may know by their own experience."[61] The Preface to *De Cive* shows that Hobbes's method has not changed, but the intensity of its application and consequent tone have. Coupled with the familiar examples from everyday life, his renewed call to rely on experience in *De Cive* signals a more vigorous and direct appeal to the readers' experiences than may be found in the *Elements*. Once again, the story of Hobbes's "civil science" clashes with the evidence from the text. If philosophy is the realm of universals, then it seems that there is no room for experience in civil philosophy since experience cannot be relied on to produce universal conclusions. Yet, Hobbes's discussion of human vanity in relation to political wisdom tells us that we should be wary of such expectations. On the one hand, the use of the term "philosophy" to describe both the teachings of philosophers proper and the pronouncements of dogmatists signals that Hobbes is applying the term in both its proper and its conventional senses.[62] On the other hand, the object of everyone's envy in matters political is not certainty, but prudence, and "PRUDENCE is nothing else but conjecture from experience."[63] Recall that it is the title "*Prudentes*" that human beings deny even to those whose superiority in intellectual pursuits they recognize.[64] One can conjecture from things past "what is likely to come to pass, or to have passed already" without taking the extra, unwarranted step of thinking that the conjecture is tantamount to certainty.[65]

Far from constructing a philosophical account that will yield universal conclusions in conformity with the demanding standards of *De Corpore*, in appealing to experience in the *Elements* and *De Cive*, Hobbes is merely extending the principles that he had expounded in his analysis of history where he had identified prudence toward the present and providence toward the future as the benefits of good history.[66] Still, one might wonder why certainty is never an option. One answer may be gleaned from thinking about what the regime would look like, under which there would be no uncertainty, and, hence, no insecurity. As we will see, for Hobbes no such regime has ever existed, and no such regime can ever exist. Hobbes's own answer is more straightforward: the kind of certainty that is possible in geometry is impossible in civil philosophy because the two are different *kinds* of

---

[60] *The Elements of Law*, I.4.10. See, for example, Goldsmith, *Hobbes's Science of Politics*, 234; Skinner, *Reason and Rhetoric in the Philosophy of Hobbes*, 260–61. Cf. Shapiro, *Probability and Certainty in Seventeenth-Century England*, 39–40, 83–84.

[61] *The Elements of Law*, I.1.2.

[62] See, for example, several instances of both uses in *De Cive*, Ep. Ded. §§ 5, 6; Pref. §§ 2, 5.

[63] *The Elements of Law*, I.4.10; cf. *Leviathan*, III: 10.

[64] *De Cive*, Pref. § 3

[65] *The Elements of Law*, I.4.11; cf. *De Homine*, XI.10.

[66] *EW*, VIII: vii.

knowledge. We have noted that, according to Hobbes's classification of the sciences, civil philosophy stands apart from natural philosophy, which even includes rhetoric, logic, and ethics.[67] Hobbes's reason for this distinction is that the matter of the two branches is very different, being bodies natural in the one case, and bodies artificial in the other.[68] When he contrasted the achievements of the geometers to the inability of the moral philosophers to emulate their success, Hobbes wondered about the benefits we might reap "were the nature of humane Actions as distinctly knowne, as the nature of *Quantity* in Geometricall Figures."[69] His distinction between the domains of natural and civil philosophy makes one wonder whether the "were" refers to something that is possible but which has not happened, or to something that is impossible. The latter scenario need not mean that something like a civil philosophy is in turn impossible, but rather that such a philosophy would function differently and look different than natural philosophy.

How all this enters into the civil philosophy that Hobbes is putting together in *De Cive* becomes evident immediately. Having called on the experience of his reader to confirm what one ought to expect in a condition of anarchy, Hobbes claims boldly that commonwealths and individuals alike behave in this way, and thereby "professe their mutuall feare and diffidence."[70] Some jump to the conclusion that this view means that human beings are evil by nature. Hobbes is willing to concede the former, "since it is so clearly declar'd by holy writ," but certainly not the latter.[71] The point, however, is that the uncertainty that defines politics renders the question irrelevant and the conclusion regarding human nature far from necessary. What matters is that "though the wicked were fewer [than] the righteous, yet because we cannot distinguish them, there is a necessity of suspecting, heeding, antici-pating, subjugating, selfe-defending, ever incident to the most honest, and fairest condition'd."[72] As the mundane actions that Hobbes invoked in order to make his point show, even under the ablest of sovereigns communal life

---

[67] See Hobbes's table of the sciences in *Leviathan* (IX: Table between folios 40 and 41). In *De Corpore*, Hobbes retains the fundamental division between natural and civil philosophy, but adds, "civil philosophy is again commonly divided into two parts, whereof one, which treats of men's dispositions and manners, is called *ethics*; and the other, which takes cogni-zance of their civil duties, is called *politics*, or simply *civil philosophy*" (I.1.9). It is worth noting that the place of ethics does not affect the distinct status of politics. Strauss points rightly to the distinction between political philosophy and natural science in Hobbes's table, but suggests that the classifications are best understood as "under nature on the one side, and under man as productive and active being on the other" (*The Political Philosophy of Hobbes*, 8). Cf. Sacksteder, "Man the Artificer," 109; Strong, "How to Write Scripture," 142 and note 40.

[68] *De Corpore*, I.1.9.

[69] *De Cive*, Ep. Ded. §§ 5–6.

[70] *De Cive*, Pref. § 11.

[71] *De Cive*, Pref. § 12.

[72] *De Cive*, Pref. § 12.

involves some uncertainty. Therefore, prudence and providence must always constitute the bottom line.

That it is prudence and providence, rather than certainty, that we are after in civil philosophy matters greatly in devising the means by which one can protect oneself. This fact corresponds to Hobbes's method. By granting the validity of Hobbes's principle, the reader has allowed him to establish a foundation on the basis of which he can proceed to show that the state of nature is a war of all against all, in which all men have a right to all things, and that this condition is one that all men, "as soone as they arrive to understanding of this hatefull condition, doe desire (even nature it selfe compelling them) to be freed from this misery."[73] The solution to this problem lies in agreements to surrender their natural right to all things. By its very nature this surrender will entail some uncertainty, but one's calculus will be driven by the alternative, and the alternative in this case is always worse because the state of nature will always be more dangerous.[74] The details of this exit strategy will complete the first part of the work, *libertas*. The second part, *imperium*, will be devoted to the commonwealth, while the third part, *religio*, is intended to show that what Hobbes has demonstrated through reason is not in conflict with Scripture.

Having completed this preliminary and enlightening description of the work, and before proceeding to its main body, Hobbes wishes to offer his reasons for having composed it. As we know from the controversy surrounding its publication, *De Cive* started out as the third part of a three-part system. Hobbes confirms its status in the Preface, and describes how the third part happened to appear first. He explains that he arranged the first elements of philosophy into three sections: one devoted to matter and its general properties (*De Corpore*), a second to man and his faculties and passions (*De Homine*), and a third to the commonwealth and the duties of citizens (*De Cive*). Hobbes makes a point of stating that he went about this task slowly and painstakingly since he was not disputing, but reasoning, when he was interrupted by the seething debates regarding sovereignty and subjection, precursors of the war that was to come. The urgency of those debates caused Hobbes to disregard the order he had devised, and turn to *De Cive*. As he did so, he made a discovery that explains why he considers civil philosophy distinct from the other branches of knowledge: the third part did not need the preceding parts, as it could stand on its own principles, which can be discovered by experience.[75]

---

[73] *De Cive*, Pref. § 14. The original terms are "statum naturæ" and "bellum omnium contra omnes."

[74] See, for example, *De Cive*, Pref. § 20; cf. *Leviathan*: "For man by nature chooseth the lesser evil" (XIV: 70).

[75] *De Cive*, Pref. §§ 18–19; cf. *De Corpore*, I.1.9 (*EW*, I: 11–12). Where § 19 is concerned, Cotton's 1650 translation is preferable to Tuck and Silverthorne's since in the original Hobbes describes his mode of proceeding as follows: "non enim dissero, sed computo,"

Hobbes closes by explaining to the readers that he composed the work for their sake, hoping that after they have considered his doctrine they will realize that it is better to put up with some inconvenience in their private affairs than disturb public affairs, reminding them that *"human affairs cannot possibly be without some"* inconvenience.[76] Hobbes urges the readers to weigh their intentions against the laws, rather than the words of those ambitious men who are out to get power at their expense. He hopes that anyone who follows his suggestion will realize how much better it is to enjoy his present state, even if it is not optimal, rather than go to war. He thus invites readers to turn in anyone who preaches seditious doctrines.[77] Underscoring that his doctrine is presented as a defense of the commonwealth, regardless of its form, and that no part of his argument should be taken as a critique either of existing commonwealths or of theological doctrines, except insofar as theologians advocate disobedience, Hobbes asks readers to be patient with his shortcomings, since his words are not those of a partisan, but of one who has a "devotion to peace," and "whose just grief for the present calamities of his country, may very charitably be allowed some liberty."[78]

THE STATE OF MEN WITHOUT CIVIL SOCIETY

Unlike its predecessor of 1642, but even the unauthorized *De Corpore Politico*, whose structure it resembles, the published version of *De Cive* opens with no allusion to either a system of which the work is a part, or to an account of human nature on which it is based.[79] Instead, the reader is confronted immediately with the state of nature.[80] Reducing human nature to four faculties – physical force, experience, reason, and passion – Hobbes sets himself the task of determining whether men are born fit for society, and of determining what is necessary to bring it about.[81] In the *Elements*,

---

and says nothing about reason, but points to "experientia." As Strauss notes, Hobbes's discovery here is consistent with his evaluation of politics as a distinct domain (*The Political Philosophy of Hobbes*, 6–7). This consistency makes it hard to dismiss this statement as an opportunistic response to Elzevir's suggestion that the book not be presented as the third part of a system whose first two parts had yet to be completed. Nevertheless, the coincidence begs the question regarding the status and extent of the work's purported independence.

[76] *De Cive*, Pref. § 20, emphasis added.
[77] *De Cive*, Pref. § 21.
[78] *De Cive*, Pref. § 24.
[79] Compare, for instance, the beginning of I.14.1 of *The Elements of Law* with that of *De Corpore Politico*, I.1, p. 2 (B^v). The 1642 version begins, "Exposita est, præcedente sectione, natura humana vniuersa ..." (*Elementorvm Philosophiæ Sectio Tertia De Cive*, 2); cf. *De Cive, The Latin Version*, p. 89, note to line 11.
[80] The title of the first chapter is *"De statu Hominum extra Societatem civilem."* The English translator's decision to render "extra" as "without" is sound, so long as one bears in mind that the English word is intended as both "in the absence of" and "outside of."
[81] *De Cive*, I.1.

Hobbes had already dismissed extant moral philosophy for hesitating to go any further than Aristotle had gone.[82] This time around, the charge is more specific: most of those who write on public affairs pronounce man "an animal by nature fit for society," that which the Greeks call a "Ζῶον πολιτικòν."[83] The reference appears unmistakable, yet, as Hobbes's use of the plural throughout this paragraph shows, he is not pointing to Aristotle's pronouncement that man is "φύσει πολιτικòν ζῷον." Instead, he is referring to its Scholastic appropriation.[84]

Where Aristotle had proclaimed man an animal in need of the polis, following William of Moerbeke, Aquinas had gone a little further, declaring that "it is natural for man, more than for any other animal, to be a social and political animal, to live in a group."[85] Aquinas's broadening of Aristotle's pronouncement was perhaps warranted by the very narrow sense that the term "political" would have conveyed to his readers, but it nevertheless contributed to a slight, yet important, shift away from Aristotle's emphasis on need and toward the view that man is naturally social.[86] This shift was exacerbated by Aristotle's idiosyncratic, if influential, understanding of the pivotal concept, nature. If in invoking "Ζῶον πολιτικòν," in *De Cive* Hobbes were implying that Aristotle is guilty of considering man "an animal born fit for Society," however, then one might object that the implied association is based on a distortion of Aristotle's teleological conception of nature, which Aristotle sees as a disposition toward the fulfillment of a potential, rather than the existence, at birth of a fully realized capacity.[87]

Hobbes is able to attribute this alleged misunderstanding to "our too slight contemplation of Humane Nature," which would have us believe

---

[82] *The Elements of Law*, I.13.3.

[83] *De Cive*, I.2: "Hominem esse animal aptum natum ad Societatem."

[84] See Aristotle, *Politica*, 1253a2–3. On Aquinas's indebtedness to Aristotle's conception of nature, see Ullman, *Principles of Government and Politics in the Middle Ages*, 244–50; cf. Canning, *A History of Medieval Political Thought, 300–1450*, 125–27. As Hoekstra notes, this objection was raised by Eachard and Tyrrell (*Thomas Hobbes and the Creation of Order*; cf. Eachard, *Mr. Hobb's State of Nature Considered*, 63; Tyrrell, *A Brief Disquisition of the Law of Nature*, 253–66). Examples of scholastic appropriations are: Oresme, John of Paris, Dante (see, for example, *Monarchy*, I.iii), Vazquez de Menchaca, and Marsilius of Padua. Cf. Ullman, *Principles of Government and Politics in the Middle Ages*, 243–52; Nederman, "Aristotelianism and the Origins of 'Political Science' in the Twelfth Century"; Black, *Political Thought in Europe*, 20–22; Quillet, "Community, Counsel and Representation," 526–45; Brett, *Liberty, Right and Nature*, 172–73; Syros, *Die Rezeption der aristotelischen politischen Philosophie bei Marsilius von Padua*, 63–99; Syros, *Marsilius of Padua*, 28–35.

[85] St. Thomas Aquinas, *On Kingship*, I.1. Cf. *Sententia libri Politicorum*, A78–79. Cf. Finnis, *Aquinas*, 246, notes 135, 137.

[86] See Sigmund, "Law and Politics," 218–19. Cf. the related discussion of "community" in Quillet, "Community, Counsel and Representation," 526–29.

[87] *De Cive*, I.2. See, for example, Aristotle, *Physics*, 199a8–9; *Metaphysics*, 1049b5–1051a3. Both Cotton and Silverthorne render Hobbes's "aptum natum" as "born fit." For the reasons pointed out earlier, it ought to be translated as "by nature fit."

that men are born ready to consent to "certaine Covenants and Conditions together which themselves should then call Lawes."[88] Despite the reference to "Ζῷον πολιτικὸν," then, Hobbes's disagreement cannot be with Aristotle since he and Aristotle agree that it is man's inability to be self-sufficient that drives him toward association with others, rather than any native love of other men qua men.[89] More importantly, although the degree of man's natural sociability is the subject of considerable debate, there is hardly any prominent school of thought that goes as far as to advocate the position that Hobbes is describing here. Even in the most influential of accounts, that of Genesis, man's natural propensity toward obedience does not last long. Hobbes's opponents here are, once again, the mindless imitators of Aristotle.

This very first substantial pronouncement of *De Cive* is already "a stumbling block in front of the reader on the very threshold of civil doctrine."[90] In addition to being irreverent toward Aristotle and the moral philosophers, and offensive toward God and humanity, it appears to defy the very standard that Hobbes ascribes to civil philosophy since it seems to contradict experience. We know that readers must have stumbled here because this is the locus of the first of Hobbes's explanatory notes. In explaining his claim that men are not by nature fit for society, Hobbes notes that he is not denying the obvious fact that no man lives outside society, nor that human beings dislike solitude and seek the company of others.[91] He adds, however, that *"Civil societies are not mere gatherings, but Alliances, the making of which*

---

[88] *De Cive*, I.2. As previously, Hobbes uses the plural here.

[89] See Aristotle, *Politica*, 1253a26–29; cf. *De Cive*, I.2: "For if by nature one Man should Love another (that is) as Man, there could no reason be return'd why every Man should not equally Love every Man, as being equally Man, or why he should rather frequent those whose Society affords him Honour and Profit." Hobbes adds, "[w]e doe not therefore by nature seek Society for its own sake, but that we may receive some Honour or Profit from it; these we desire Primarily, that Secondarily" (Warrender ed.). As we shall see, Leibniz, who had corresponded with Hobbes and knew his works well, thought that the Iroquois and Hurons had "overthrown the most universal political maxims of Hobbes and Aristotle" (*Die Philosophischen Schriften*, 424, but cf. *ibid.*, 271).

On the meaning of Aristotle's conception of man as "φύσει πολιτικὸν ζῷον," see Yack, *The Problems of a Political Animal*, esp. 51–52, 62; Simpson, *A Philosophical Commentary on the Politics of Aristotle*, 24; Evrigenis, *Fear of Enemies and Collective Action*, 32–34. That Hobbes is well aware of Aristotle's meaning in the *Politics* becomes evident in his discussion of the Aristotelian distinction between men, ants, and bees as political animals (*De Cive*, V.5; *Leviathan*, XVII: 86; *Questions Concerning Liberty, Necessity, and Chance, EW*, V: 80), which takes into account Aristotle's *Historia animalium* (487b33–488a14), a work which, along with the *Rhetoric*, Hobbes held in high esteem (Aubrey, *Brief Lives*, I: 357). Pacchi is thus correct, when in a different context he declares, "anche Hobbes infatti pensa che l'uomo sia destinato a vivere in communità" (*Scritti Hobbesiani*, 44).

[90] *De Cive*, I.2, note to "Born fit."

[91] *De Cive*, I.2, note to "Born fit."

requires good faith and pacts. Children and the uneducated are ignorant of their force, as are those who are unaware of what would be lost by their absence and ignorant of their utility.[92] Experience tells us that men gather together for mutual benefit, but it also tells us that many among them are ignorant of the full utility of good faith and compacts because they "*do not know what would be lost by the absence of Society.*"[93]

As in the Preface, Hobbes's evidence consists of a series of mundane experiences that will be more or less familiar to every reader, but which Hobbes reinterprets and casts in a particularly negative light. Thus, the very things that one might point to as delights of society – things such as gatherings, discussions, and the exchange of stories that often symbolize the fruits of sociability – Hobbes presents as opportunities for competition and honor. The reluctant move that Hobbes had initiated in the *Elements*, from *bonum sibi* to a *summum malum*, is now well on its way to becoming a radical break. Hobbes notes that everyone, including those who because of pride do not deign to acknowledge equality, desires society, but not everyone is ready to accept it, for "[w]anting is one thing, ability another."[94] The difference between "mere gatherings" and civil societies proper is the *summum malum*. No one, argues Hobbes, would dispute that if fear were eliminated, men would seek to dominate one another, rather than associate with each other peacefully. Hence, it must be established that "the Originall of all [large], and lasting Societies, consisted not in the mutuall good will men had towards each other, but in the mutuall fear they had of each other."[95]

The equally offensive and provocative claim that mutual fear establishes and preserves large and lasting societies posed a second stumbling block to Hobbes's readers. In his second note, Hobbes explains that those who disagree with his contention do so because they interpret fear as nothing but fright. Hobbes's understanding of it, however, is far more expansive. Those who object to his claim, he argues,

presume, I believe, that to fear is nothing else then to be affrighted: I comprehend in this word Fear, a certain foresight of future evill; neither doe I conceive flight the sole property of fear, but to distrust, suspect, take heed, provide so that they may not fear, is also incident to the fearfull. They who go to Sleep, shut their Dores; they who Travell carry their Swords with them, because they fear Theives. Kingdomes guard their Coasts and Frontiers with Forts, and Castles; Cities are compast with

---

[92] *De Cive*, I.2, note to "Born fit."

[93] *De Cive*, I.2, note to "Born fit": "Societates autem civiles non sunt meri congressus, sed Fœdera, quibus faciendis fides & pacta necessaria sunt. Horum, ab infantibus quidem & indoctis, Vis; ab iis autem qui damnorum à defectu Societatis inexperti sunt, utilitas ignoratur."

[94] *De Cive*, I.2, note to "Born fit."

[95] *De Cive*, I.2. I have changed the translation of "magnarum" from "great" to "large," so as to clarify that this is not intended to be a judgment of their greatness, but an assessment of their capabilities.

Walls, and all for fear of neighbouring Kingdomes and Townes; even the strongest Armies, and most accomplisht for Fight, yet sometimes Parly for peace, as fearing each others power, and lest they might be overcome. It is through fear that men secure themselves.[96]

Prudence requires that those who find themselves in the midst of such uncertainty take precautions to secure themselves. Hobbes argued in the *Elements* that the ornaments of life that "usually" result from peace and security will tend to be absent from the state of nature because of this very uncertainty.[97] As this passage makes clear, the key to this condition is precisely its uncertainty. The precautions that individuals will take in order to secure themselves *can* yield sophisticated implements and social arrangements, such as alliances, but cannot be counted on to do so, and what may come about cannot be relied on for lasting security.[98]

In its essential components, Hobbes's first published account of the state of nature is similar to its predecessors, in the *Elements* and the privately circulated *De Cive*. As before, here, too, the chief characteristics of the state of nature are an effective equality among men – a universal natural right to all things – coupled with the attendant ability to judge everything for oneself, which taken together make for radical uncertainty and, ultimately, a condition of war.[99] The 1647 edition departs from its predecessors in two important ways. First, its tone is more sinister. Thus, whereas in the *Elements* Hobbes had ascribed the uncertainty of the state of nature to equality and to man's tendency to "provoke" others, in *De Cive* he locates the causes of mutual fear in equality and a willingness to "hurt."[100] Throughout Chapter I, Hobbes revisits the main points of the earlier accounts, but recasts them so as to convey how undesirable a condition of anarchy can be. This time the focus is less on the benefits of peace and order that are missing from the state of nature and more on the widespread and devastating harms that can result from uncertainty. Hobbes has already signaled his intention to move from an account of *bonum sibi* toward one of the *summum malum*, and it is precisely this *summum malum* that captures the tone of *De Cive* best: from a single mention of fear in *Elements* I.14, Hobbes moved to five in the privately circulated version of 1642, and to sixteen in the published edition.[101]

---

[96] *De Cive*, I.2, note to "The mutuall fear."

[97] *The Elements of Law*, I.14.12.

[98] See, for example, *De Cive*, I.4, where Hobbes writes of property, and I.14, where he writes of allies. Cf. Ashcraft, "Political Theory and Political Action"; Evrigenis, *Fear of Enemies and Collective Action*, 120–28; Hoekstra, *Thomas Hobbes and the Creation of Order*.

[99] *De Cive*, I.3 is devoted to equality, I.8–12 to natural right. Hobbes summarizes the latter in his note to I.10.

[100] Hobbes uses the term "provoke" in I.14.4 and I.14.5. In *De Cive*, by contrast, the term is "lædendi" (I.3; I.4).

[101] *The Elements of Law*, I.14.3; *De Cive*, I.2 (2), I.3, I.13, I.14, and eleven instances in Hobbes's note to "In men's mutual fear."

Second, the published account is designed so as to make it clear that the state of nature is a condition that should matter to everyone. To that end, whereas in the *Elements* Hobbes had tried to make the case for effective equality by simply noting that even the weakest has the means to hurt the strongest, in *De Cive* he repeats the observation, but adds "how brittle the frame of our humane body is."[102] The psychological force of this slight shift is significant: this is not just an example in the service of a highfalutin philosophical argument, but rather, food for thought for every aspiring combatant. If focusing on the Davids and Goliaths of the state of nature rendered the consequences of effective equality too abstract, a reminder of the fragility of every human body serves as a warning to all those who might contemplate stepping outside the boundaries of reliable protection. In the same vein, as the Preface shows clearly, *De Cive* makes explicit what had been largely implicit in the *Elements*, namely, that in a condition of fear "all men" wish to hurt others.[103] The vainglorious because they fancy themselves superior to others, and the moderate because they will need to defend their lives, liberty, and property from them.[104] Hobbes is thus able to not only render that condition relevant to everyone, but also to expand its reach to include those things necessary for life and commodious living, over and above bare survival.

Hobbes had indicated his intention to broaden the scope of the state of nature and ensure its relevance to his readers with the insertion of mundane examples from everyday life in the Preface. Chapter I continues this trend by adding a new cause of conflict to which anyone can relate: disagreement.[105] Having already captured everyone in his division of the world into the vainglorious and the moderate, Hobbes nevertheless suggests that the "mere act of disagreement is offensive," and continued disagreement is "tantamount to calling [one] a fool."[106] In a battle of the wits, trifles such as laughter, words, and gestures can become signs of contempt, of "which there is no greater vexation of mind; and then from which there cannot possibly arise a greater desire to doe hurt."[107] The inclusion of disagreement among the causes of the state of war points toward one of the central features of anarchy – the lack of established, enforceable terms – but also brings that condition closer to home.[108] Even one who has not armed himself to ride through

[102] Cf. *The Elements of Law*, I.14.2; *De Cive*, I.3 (Warrender ed.).
[103] *De Cive*, I.4: "Voluntas lædendi omnibus quidem inest in statu naturæ …."
[104] *De Cive*, I.4; cf. Pref. § 12; *The Elements of Law*, I.14.3–4.
[105] This from the point of view of the reader of *De Cive*, since the order of composition is, of course, the reverse, with the Preface having been composed long after chapter I.
[106] *De Cive*, I.5.
[107] *De Cive*, I.5 (Warrender ed.).
[108] In a letter to Hobbes on the status of the natural condition, Peleau would offer parliaments and disagreements among philosophers as examples of the state of nature "in the civil state" (François Peleau to Thomas Hobbes, Bordeaux, December 25, 1656/January 4, 1657, in *The Correspondence of Thomas Hobbes*, 422–25).

a forest knows the rage that can arise from the simplest of quarrels. No one, neither the modest nor the vainglorious, is completely immune to its dangers. One particular branch of disagreement, however, stands out among others as the most frequent cause of a desire to inflict harm: disagreement about property. In the absence of an authority that can determine what belongs to whom, and given a universal natural right to all things, sooner or later everyone will disagree with someone about something. Their unwillingness to acknowledge each other's right and either yield or divide the good in question will leave them with no option, in the absence of a judge, but to fight for it. The dynamics of this system are such that two individuals with unchecked powers to judge everything for themselves will suffice to bring about a state of war. Any more, and that war becomes one of all against all.[109]

Hobbes's explicit examples of states of nature in Chapter I are the same as in the previous versions. To prove that a condition exists that is marked by perpetual war, in which not even the victor of any single battle may feel secure, Hobbes points once again to the "Americans" of his century, and to the ancient inhabitants of contemporary civilized countries, who "were then few, fierce, short-lived, poor, nasty, and who lacked all the comforts and adornments of life that *peace* and society make possible."[110] Unlike the previous versions, however, in the published edition of *De Cive*, the reader encounters the state of nature beyond the narrow confines of the chapter in which it is treated. Thus, in Chapter V, which opens the section of the book devoted to *imperium*, Hobbes considers the status of the laws of nature in the state of nature.[111] Here, Hobbes elaborates on a theme that he had developed in the *Elements*, captured by the dictum, "*inter arma silent leges.*"[112]

In *De Cive*, Hobbes returns to this theme in examining how commonwealths emerge. Having placed considerable emphasis on the existence and significance of natural laws, Hobbes must explain why they are nevertheless insufficient to bring about lasting civil societies.[113] As *rectæ rationis dictamen*, the laws of nature are known to anyone who can reason,

---

[109] *De Cive*, I.13: "*bellum ... omnium contra omnes.*" Hobbes's assessment of this source of conflict explains, in part, his starting point (see *De Cive*, Pref., § 9).

[110] *De Cive*, I.13: "Exemplum huius rei sæculum præsens Americanos exhibet, sæcula antiqua cæteras gentes, nunc quidem ciuiles florentesque, tunc verò paucos, feros, breuis æui, pauperes, fœdos, omni eo vitæ solatio atque ornatu carentes, quem *pax* & societas ministrare solent."

[111] The title of the chapter is "Of the Causes and Generation of Commonwealths."

[112] *The Elements of Law*, I.19.2. The formulation in *De Cive*, V.2 is different: "*inter arma silere leges.*"

[113] In addition to his preliminary treatment, in Chapter I, Hobbes devotes the remainder of Part I (*Libertas*) to an examination of the laws of nature (*De Cive*, II–IV). On natural law in relation to the state of nature more generally, see Eggers, *Die Naturzustandstheorie des Thomas Hobbes*.

but they are insufficient by themselves because human beings will violate them if they judge that to be more beneficial than abiding by them.[114] Hobbes explains that even a rational being that understands these laws may nevertheless conclude that the security they promise is not immediate. In such cases, natural right prevails, and that which natural right demands immediately may well clash with the natural laws' long-term dictates toward peace.[115] Crucially, Hobbes states that a man is in compliance with natural law so long as he is "prepared in mind to embrace Peace when it may be had," since natural laws oblige only in the court of conscience.[116]

The harsh silence of the laws amid arms might give the reader reason to dismiss Hobbes's positive account of the laws of nature as mere window dressing. After all, if self-preservation is the bottom line, what is the point of a mental disposition toward peace that cannot be enforced? Hobbes, however, is serious about the force of the laws of nature qua dictates of reason. A reasonable man will come to see that in the long run, and with the exception of cases in which his self-preservation is under immediate and compelling threat, his best interest lies in establishing peace. One can see evidence of such restraint in the way in which human beings actually behave in such circumstances. To demonstrate that this is the case, Hobbes proposes a comparison. At the extreme, posit the pure state of nature as a war of all against all, in which laws are completely silent.[117] Moving away from this extreme, one observes that customarily, when one nation fights another, the combatants display a certain amount of moderation since by definition wars involving groups cannot be as extreme as a war of all against all.[118] But even smaller groups, in more anarchic settings, display a certain amount of moderation in their pursuit of self-preservation. Those who in ancient times had to resort to plunder in order to survive, Hobbes suggests, would nevertheless spare the lives of their victims, whenever possible, and allow them to keep the implements necessary to ensure their own sustenance. When plunder was acceptable, and even honorable, this practice was not the result of some vague benevolence, but rather the consequence of prudence, for cruelty toward their victims would have signaled to others

---

[114] See, for example, *De Cive*, I.15, II.1, V.1.

[115] *De Cive*, V.1: "Ex quo intelligitur *leges naturales* non statim vt cognitæ sunt securitatem cuiquam præstare ipsas obseruandi, & proinde, quamdiu cautio ab inuasione aliorum non habetur, cauendi sibi quibuscunque modis voluerit & potuerit, vnicuique manere *Ius* primæuum...." This mechanism is predicted by the fundamental law of nature, which commands that one seek peace, where that is possible, and pursue defense by all means, where it is not (II.2). Cf. *Leviathan*, XVIII: 94.

[116] *De Cive*, V.1 (Warrender ed.): "paratus animo sit ad pacem habendam, vbi haberi potest;" cf. *ibid.*, III.27–29; *The Elements of Law*, I.17.10. Cf. *Leviathan*, XIV: 79.

[117] *De Cive*, V.2: "bellum tale intelligatur, vt sit omnium contra omnes; qualis est *status naturæ meræ....*"

[118] *De Cive*, V.2.

that the perpetrators were weak and afraid, thereby rendering them less secure in the long term.[119]

Hobbes's generosity in allowing the reader some hope that the laws of nature will impose limits is itself restrained. In keeping with the generally bleaker tone of *De Cive*, Hobbes gives his example of plunder a more sinister twist. In *The Elements of Law*, Hobbes had invoked the ancient plunderers, but his account of their conduct was detached and focused on the rationale behind their actions.[120] There was nothing that could identify them, and certainly nothing that would suggest that their actions, understandable though they might be, could be approved. When Hobbes returns to this example in *De Cive*, he writes of "ληστρικὴν" and "*Rapto vivere*," adding that this way of life was not only *not* against the law of nature, but also *not* without glory.[121] Hobbes's allusion to Greece and use of an example in which plunder was "neque sine gloriâ" call to mind Thucydides, according to whom:

> For the *Grecians* in old time, and such *Barbarians* as, in the Continent, liued neere vnto the Sea, or else inhabited the Ilands, after once they beganne to crosse ouer one to another in Ships, became Theeues, and went abroad vnder the conduct of their most puissant men, both to enrich themselues, and to fetch in maintenance for the weake: and falling vpon Towns vnfortified, and scatteringly inhabited, rifled them, and made this the best meanes of their liuing; Being a matter at that time no where in disgrace, but rather carrying with it something of glory.[122]

It is possible that Hobbes's invidious addition of honor into the picture of primitive uncertainty was inspired by Thucydides' "archeology."[123] Hobbes's

---

[119] *De Cive*, V.2; *The Elements of Law*, I.19.2. Hobbes's emphasis on security here ensures that this example is not open to misinterpretation as evidence of pity or natural sociability, of the kind that would come to play such an important role in subsequent accounts of the state of nature. Rousseau, for instance, began his own famous account of pity as a natural disposition by attacking Hobbes (*Discourse on the Origin and Foundations of Inequality among Men*, I §§ 35–36).

[120] *The Elements of Law*, I.19.2.

[121] *De Cive*, V.2; cf. Bodin, *Method for the Easy Comprehension of History*, 297–99. Hobbes's term, "ληστρικὴ," which contributes to the impression that his source here is Thucydides, is relatively rare. In Thucydides, it occurs only once, not in I.5, where he writes of "ληστείαν," but in IV.9, where it is used to refer to a pirate vessel. Few authors use it in the sense that Hobbes writes of in *De Cive*, among them Plutarch, Josephus, Heliodorus, and Dionysius of Halicarnassus, and these only very rarely.

[122] Thucydides, *Eight Bookes of the Peloponnesian Warre*, I.5, p. 4. Brown ("Thucydides, Hobbes, and the Derivation of Anarchy," 58) and Tuck and Silverthorne (*De Cive*, V.2, p. 70, note 2) note the connection explicitly; cf. Schlatter, ed., *Hobbes's Thucydides*, I.5, notes 5 and 6 (on p. 576). Hornblower (*A Commentary on Thucydides*, I: 23) refers to Davies' excellent analysis of piracy in Greece, according to which the tendencies that Thucydides and Hobbes describe here extend well beyond the earliest times ("Cultural, Social and Economic Features of the Hellenistic World," esp. 286–87). Cf. Forbes, ed., *Thucydides Book I*, Part II: pp. 12–13; Ormerod, *Piracy in the Ancient World*, esp. chapter 2.

[123] Commenting on this issue, Bodin writes, "[w]ithout any shame travelers usually asked whether those they encountered were robbers or pirates or not" (*Method for the Easy Comprehension of History*, 298).

translation of this passage does not preclude Thucydides' original distinction between the Greeks of old and the barbarians of his day, but it does not convey it clearly either.[124] This formula, however, is reminiscent of Hobbes's examples of the state of nature in both the *Elements* and *De Cive*, of the ancient ancestors of civilized nations and contemporary savages, so that Hobbes's ancestors of the civilized countries of his day correspond to Thucydides' Greeks "in old time," and Hobbes's Indians of America to Thucydides' "Barbarians."

It is also clear, however, that the primary inspiration behind his discussion of the silence of laws amid arms is Cicero, whose famous dictum, "silent enim leges inter arma," was occasioned by conditions reminiscent of the state of nature.[125] In the midst of a period already characterized by increasing violence in Rome, a long-standing feud between Titus Annius Milo and Publius Clodius Pulcher came to a head when armed gangs led by the two men met and fought in 52 BC, near Bovillae. Clodius, who was injured during this fight, was eventually killed, most likely on Milo's orders.[126] Clodius's rioting supporters eventually got hold of his corpse, which they returned to Rome, carried into the Senate House, and set on fire, thereby destroying the building itself. Milo was put on trial for the" murder of Clodius, and Cicero undertook to defend him. On the day of the trial, however, and in the face of Pompey's soldiers and an angry mob, Cicero only managed to utter a few words before Milo was exiled to Marseilles. Cicero's *Pro T. Annio Milone*, the source of Hobbes's *inter arma silent leges*, was an expanded version that was composed after the fact.[127]

That version begins with fear. Cicero notes the intimidating presence of armed men and the unusual circumstances of the tribunal, and confesses that even the presence of guards is insufficient to render his fearlessness entirely free of fear.[128] Cicero grounds his defense in the natural right to self-defense, a right that both reason and Roman history show to be

---

[124] According to Forbes, I.5 "gives some particulars of the rude state of the early Hellenes ('who in many ways resembled the Barbarians of to-day')" (*Thucydides Book I*, Part II p. 12).

[125] Cicero, *Pro T. Annio Milone oratio*, 11. The connection is noted by Tuck and Silverthorne (*De Cive*, V.2, p. 69, note 1). Hobbes took Bramhall to be referring to *Pro Milone* (see *EW*, V: 53–54, 184), yet Chappell finds it doubtful that Bramhall "intended to allude to Cicero" (*Hobbes and Bramhall on Liberty and Necessity*, 77, n. 8). In any case, Hobbes's conjecture is evidence that he knew *Pro Milone* well. Citing the nearly universal agreement among historians in viewing Cicero's age as one of "decay and disintegration leading to the final collapse," Wood argues, "[n]othing so nearly resembled the Hobbesian *bellum omnium contra omnes* in which everyone must be the eventual loser" (*Cicero's Social & Political Thought*, 31–32). Cicero himself relates incidents in which his life was in danger (see, for example, Rawson, *Cicero*, 125).

[126] The details are contained in an account by Quintus Asconius Pedianus (Commentary on Cicero's *Pro T. Annio Milone oratio*); cf. Cary and Scullard, *A History of Rome*, 302; Badian, "Annius Milo," 99.

[127] Rawson, *Cicero*, 138–39.

[128] Cicero, *Pro T. Annio Milone oratio*, 1–2.

self-evident.[129] After citing a series of examples intended to demonstrate that even those who ought to feel aggrieved by a killing acknowledge that nothing can be said against the perpetrator so long as he acted in self-defense, Cicero points to the many weapons around him, and asks why we would be allowed to carry them, if we were not allowed to use them? That we are, in fact, allowed to use them in self-defense is evident from

a law not of the statute-book, but of nature; a law which we possess not by instruction, tradition, or reading, but which we have caught, imbibed, and suckled in at Nature's own breast; a law which comes to us not by education but by constitution, not by training but by intuition – the law, I mean, that, should our life have fallen into any snare, into the violence and the weapons of robbers or foes, every method of winning a way to safety would be morally justifiable. When arms speak, the laws are silent; they bid none to await their word, since he who chooses to await it must pay an undeserved penalty ere he can exact a deserved one.[130]

It is precisely this Catch-22 that individuals in Hobbes's state of nature find themselves in. Natural law requires peace, but peace requires security, and security only comes about when one has become sufficiently dangerous to potential attackers to cause them to refrain, rather than attack him.[131] The threshold of security is determined by the size of the threat. The precarious security established by Pompey's troops, in the face of Clodius's angry supporters, was clearly not sufficient to assure Cicero of his safety. Rather, as Hobbes points out, one's group must be sufficiently large that a few defections would not cause the enemy to think that he has achieved sufficient numbers for victory.[132] Hobbes's emphasis on sufficiency here indicates the degree to which his account of the emergence of civil society rests on the same principle as Aristotle's. Perhaps most importantly, however, this emphasis on sufficiency signals that the difference between the state of nature and civil society is not fixed, but rather a matter of degree, since, as we will see, the state of nature never disappears from the picture. As Hobbes has already indicated, such associations for mutual safety are necessary but not sufficient for the establishment of civil society, since to begin to act in accordance with the law of nature, individuals need to remain focused on the common good. What prevents them from becoming distracted by their sense of their own good is fear.[133]

[129] Cicero, *Pro T. Annio Milone oratio*, 6–10.
[130] Cicero, *Pro T. Annio Milone oratio*, 10–11. Cf. *De officiis*, I.iv, § 11.
[131] *De Cive*, V.3.
[132] *De Cive*, V.3. Cf. *The Elements of Law*, I.19.3: "And therefore before men have sufficient security for the help of one another, their number must be so great, that the odds of a few which the enemy may have, be no certain and sensible advantage," as well as Hobbes's description of the purpose of *Leviathan*, which was to convince his compatriots of the need for an army sufficiently large to compel them to concord (*T. Hobbes Malmesburiensis vita* [OL, I: xv]). See also Evrigenis, *Fear of Enemies and Collective Action*, 122–23.
[133] *De Cive*, V.4; cf. *ibid.*, I.2 and note to "In men's mutual fear."

Hobbes explains why fear is necessary in a passage that reads like another invective against Aristotle, but which in fact shows once again that Hobbes is a very careful reader of Aristotle, with whom he agrees more than he disagrees. In his *History of Animals*, Aristotle describes as "political" the subset of gregarious creatures that have one common end in sight.[134] This definition, however, leads Aristotle quickly to the strange conclusion that, alongside man, bees, wasps, ants, and cranes are political animals. Hobbes finds that this classification is incorrect because the agreement one observes among these creatures is merely a concurrence of many wills, rather than a single will, which is the characteristic of commonwealths. Hobbes offers six reasons for rejecting Aristotle's appellation, all of which ultimately boil down to man's possession of λόγος – speech and reason.[135] In so doing, however, he is agreeing with the *Politics*, wherein Aristotle declares,

That man is more of a political animal than any bee or any other gregarious animal is clear. Nature, as we say, makes nothing in vain, and only man, of all the animals, has λόγον. For voice is but a sign of the unpleasant and pleasant, and thus exists in other animals (for their nature only extends as far as having a sense of the unpleasant and pleasant, and communicating these to each other), whereas λόγος exists to demonstrate the advantageous and disadvantageous, and thus also the just and unjust. For it is particular to human beings, in contrast with the other animals, that they alone have a sense of the good and evil, and of the just and unjust, and the like.[136]

In Hobbes's famous formulation, the combination of speech and reason renders man's tongue a "trumpet of war and sedition," presenting countless opportunities for one's conception of one's own good and the common good to diverge. Unlike the other gregarious animals, for which consent is natural, human beings must therefore declare their consent by agreement, and must

---

[134] "Πολιτικὰ δ'ἐστὶν ὧν ἕν τι καὶ κοινὸν γίνεται πάντων τὸ ἔργον· ὅπερ οὐ πάντα ποιεῖ τὰ ἀγελαῖα" (*Historia animalium*, 488a7–9). Aristotle's classifications here are strange for several reasons. For instance, they render the various nests and hives in question *poleis*, and include species that Aristotle considers anarchic among "political" beings pursuing a common end.

[135] *De Cive*, V.5. The causes include competition for honor, a desire for preeminence, a desire to judge and try to alter one's institutions, and the ability – and concomitant vulnerability – to misrepresent things as better or worse than they are. Cf. *The Elements of Law*, I.19.5.

[136] Aristotle, *Politica*, 1253a7–18. Translators render "λόγος" as "speech" with such frequency and persistence that I have opted for the unsatisfactory alternative of leaving the term untranslated here. This passage demonstrates why the usual translation is inadequate and misleading. Yack, whose analysis of the passages from the *Historia Animalium* and *Politics* is excellent, uses the term "reasoned speech and argument," which is far preferable to "speech" (*The Problems of a Political Animal*, 52). It is clear that Aristotle's contrast between φωνὴ and λόγος begins with the difference between animal cries and human speech, but it is also clear that limiting λόγος to speech leaves out the purely internal processes whereby human beings come to see good and evil, justice and injustice, and which complement their communications with others about them, but can also be independent of them. Hobbes addresses λόγος in *Leviathan* (IV: 16).

also render it reliable by instituting a common power that will rule through fear of punishment.[137]

It is frequently thought that Hobbes's account of the state of nature constitutes a thought experiment.[138] Yet, up to this point, in both the *Elements* and *De Cive*, Hobbes has only associated the state of nature with actual conditions. It is here, midway through *Imperium*, that Hobbes first suggests such a thought experiment, by inviting the reader to return to the state of nature, to consider fully grown human beings "as if but even now sprung from the earth, and suddainly (*like* Mushromes) come to full maturity without all kind of engagement to each other."[139] As the Preface promises, the crucial difference, where human associations are concerned, is that between mere aggregations for temporary security and lasting societies, or, in Hobbes's terms, that between a multitude and a union, which arises through the submission of individual wills to the will of a sovereign, thereby becoming a single will.[140] Hobbes claims that such lasting societies can arise in two ways: (1) naturally, which refers to submission through fear, or (2) by institution, referring to an agreement by individuals to join together and submit to the will of the sovereign.[141]

---

[137] *De Cive*, V.5. Goldschmidt (*La doctrine d'Épicure et le droit*, 47) wonders whether Hobbes has in mind Epicurus's Maxim XXXII here, which reads, "Those animals which are incapable of making covenants with one another, to the end that they may neither inflict nor suffer harm, are without either justice or injustice. And those [nations] which either could not or would not form mutual covenants to the same end are in the like case" (Diogenes Laertius, *Lives of the Eminent Philosophers*, X.150). I have amended Hicks's translation slightly, in light of Goldschmidt's discussion (*La doctrine d'Épicure et le droit*, 61). On the difference between man and the other animals regarding speech, see *De Homine*, II.x.3 (*OL*, II: 91).

[138] See, for example, Hood, *The Divine Politics of Thomas Hobbes*, 74; Kavka, *Hobbesian Moral and Political Theory*, 84; Macpherson, *The Political Theory of Possessive Individualism*, 28; Medick, *Naturzustand und Naturgeschichte der bürgerlichen Gesellschaft*, 34–35; Warrender, *The Political Philosophy of Hobbes*, 237–42; Watkins, *Hobbes's System of Ideas*, 72.

[139] *De Cive*, VIII.1 (Warrender ed.). This reproduces most of *The Elements of Law*, II.3.2, although the mushroom simile is new with *De Cive*. In his edition of Lucretius, Creech singles out accounts of "men springing out of the *Earth*" as evidence of the fact that the "*Epicurean* Principles are pernicious to *Societies*" (*T. Lucretius Carus the Epicurean Philosopher, His Six Books De Natura Rerum*, Notes, p. 39).

[140] *De Cive*, V.4–10, VI.1; cf. *The Elements of Law*, I.19.5–9. Rousseau's distinction between the will of all and the general will corresponds to the one Hobbes draws here between the multitude as a mere aggregation of particular wills and the union as possessing a single will (*Of the Social Contract*, II.iii.2).

[141] *De Cive*, V.12. Following the thought experiment at VIII.1, Hobbes suggests a third way, by generation, which he considers in chapter IX. As it turns out, however, obligation to parents is not the result of birth, but of the power that parents have over infants, which Hobbes considers equal to the power that lords have over servants, and sovereigns over

The idea that solitary or loosely associated individuals congregated in a state of nature and decided to subject their wills to that of another is the distinctive element of Hobbes's analysis of the rise of civil society. It is also one of the most difficult, since it introduces a serious challenge to the notion of the state of nature and, hence, to the very foundation of Hobbes's theory. If the social contract were removed from Hobbes's account, the suggestion that isolated human beings or small bands had led a precarious existence prior to the establishment of reliable civil societies would have been far less problematic. A depiction of the state of nature as a primitive and perilous condition would still be in tension with several mainstream interpretations of the natural condition of mankind as depicted in the opening chapters of Genesis, but it would certainly not seem entirely incredible to those who believed that natural man was postlapsarian, or to those who based their understanding of the state of nature on the accounts of the ancient Greeks and Romans. Democritus, Protagoras, Thucydides, Plato, Aristotle, Cicero, Plutarch, Diodorus Siculus, and many others had described pre-social man in much the same terms.[142] In this context, Hobbes's examples, of the Indians of his day and of the ancient ancestors of civilized countries, would have sufficed to render his contrast between civilization and barbarism credible, even if one disagreed about the particulars.

Perhaps more importantly, the suggestion that civil society was the result of the gradual development of natural processes, such as conquest and submission, is a reasonable one, whereas the idea of a primitive gathering in which otherwise savage individuals act as though they were reasonable delegates with a firm view of their long-term interest is simply absurd.[143] As we will see, objections along these lines were legion, even if superfluous. All this begs the question: Why introduce this element into the theory when it gives rise to so many complications without necessarily adding something of value? If the natural account of the emergence of commonwealths – which is based on propositions that both experience and history can approve of, and thus takes such obvious facts of life as family and conquest seriously – suffices to justify Hobbes's argument for order, what is to be gained by inviting readers to think about this hypothetical contract?

To begin to answer this question, it is necessary to compare Hobbes's two accounts. In the first, the rise of civil society by institution, Hobbes notes that it is not sufficient for several individuals to consent to band together,

---

subjects (IX.1–7). The affinity between the two is already hinted at in VIII.1, where Hobbes likens a kingdom to a large family and a family to a small kingdom. In *Leviathan*, Hobbes corrects his classification, placing dominion "paternall" and "despoticall" under the same heading (XX).

[142] See, for example, Thucydides, I.5–7; Aristotle, *Politica*, 1253a28–29; Plato, *Protagoras*, 322b; *Laws*, 678b1–4; Cicero, *De inventione* I.ii.2; Lucretius, *De rerum natura* V.925–1010; Seneca Epistle XC; Diodorus Siculus, I.8.1–10.

[143] One indication of their difference along these lines is the space that Hobbes devotes to each. In *De Cive* VIII.1, Hobbes writes of "*ciuitate naturali.*"

but rather essential that they also subject their wills "in such things as are necessary to Peace and Defence."[144] The first prerequisite for peace and defense, according to Hobbes, is that each individual be protected from the violence of other men, so long as he refrains from harming them. Hobbes adds immediately, however, that such protection can never be guaranteed absolutely. The best we can hope for is a reasonable assurance of safety, for "to make men altogether safe from mutuall harmes, so as they cannot be hurt, or injuriously kill'd, is impossible," and is thus out of the question.[145] Since, however, security is the reason why men subject themselves to the will of another, subjection can be achieved through the elimination of the reasonable causes of such fear. The elimination of fear of harm at the hands of one's neighbors, however, is not tantamount to the elimination of all fear.

When Hobbes pointed out in the opening chapter that the cause of lasting societies is mutual fear, he was not referring merely to the fear that individuals in the state of nature have of one another, and which is eliminated once reliable civil societies come into being, but also to the fear that replaces it, namely the fear of punishment at the hands of the sovereign. The mere elimination of fear would result in only temporary associations, since the promises to refrain from injuring one's fellows would soon give way to depravity, as experience would lead us to expect.[146] A reliable and predictable fear of punishment at the hands of the sovereign, and the concomitant hope of commodious living, are preferable to the constant fear of harm in the state of nature, which is why human beings, who by "a necessity of nature" choose what appears to be good for themselves, will opt to submit to the sovereign.[147] What Hobbes does not state explicitly in this context, but nevertheless follows from this reasoning, is that in addition to the fear of punishment at the hands of the sovereign, the potential transgressor must also consider the possibility that similar behavior by a sufficient number of his fellows will result in a return to the condition of lawlessness that he so wished to leave behind. This, of course, is what Hobbes has in mind in the Preface to *De Cive*, when he urges readers to put up with some inconvenience rather than risk returning to the worse of the two evils.[148]

Yet, natural commonwealths arise from contracts as well.[149] These contracts are tacit agreements arising out of trust between the victor and the vanquished, when the former allows the latter to live in physical liberty. Had

---

[144] *De Cive*, VI.3.
[145] *De Cive*, VI.3.
[146] *De Cive*, VI.4. This is one of many examples of the centrality of experience that sets civil philosophy apart from the other sciences.
[147] *De Cive*, VI.4. This is but the negative formulation of the principle expressed in *The Elements of Law*, I.14.12.
[148] *De Cive*, Pref., § 20.
[149] The term in *De Cive* is "contractu" (VIII.1). In the equivalent passage, in the *Elements*, it is "covenant" (II.3.2). Cf. *De Cive*, VIII.1, where, as we have seen, Hobbes writes of "natural commonwealths."

the victor simply spared the life of the vanquished and then imprisoned him, the latter would be considered a slave. By sparing his life *and* allowing him to remain physically unconstrained, however, he indicates that he trusts him to obey, and thereby binds him through obligation.[150] One might object here that this is a perverse conception of a contract, since the vanquished have no choice but to comply. Hobbes, however, counters that "agreements are universally valid once the benefits have been accepted, and if the act and the content of the promise are licit," promises we make in exchange for our life and safety are also licit, even if they are distasteful.[151] The man who is asked to choose with a sword to his neck has no less of a choice to make with the threat than without.[152] As the example of the ancient plunderers shows, his decision to submit may well be reinforced by the knowledge that a prudent conqueror will have more reasons to wish to spare him than not.

Hobbes's curious description of the process of submission could be construed as a means of extending the language of contracts beyond the hypothetical scenario of institution, and into the more likely natural alternative. It is also possible, however, to interpret this extension as a way of rendering the two allegedly distinct processes effectively the same, either because they both involve a contract of some sort, or because they both involve submission through fear.[153] In fact, in his discussion of paternal power, Hobbes

---

[150] *De Cive*, VIII.1–3. At VIII.3, Hobbes refers to II.9, where he had defined a pact (*"pactum,"* in both instances) as a promise from one who is trusted to perform in the future.

[151] *De Cive*, II.16.

[152] This conception of submission as a contract is a corollary of Hobbes's view of liberty as consistent with necessity. See "Of Liberty and Necessity," §§ 23–32; cf. Evrigenis, *Fear of Enemies and Collective Action*, 110–11. See also Hobbes's two examples at the end of the second note to *De Cive*, I.2.

[153] This move has been noticed by several interpreters. Ashcraft, for example, observes that Hobbes "does not set aside the alternative explanations; he merely *redefines* them in terms of consent, leaving intact the assumptions and framework themselves (*"Leviathan* Triumphant," 156). Ashcraft cites Strauss (*The Political Philosophy of Hobbes*, 65) and Willey (*The Seventeenth Century Background*, 117), who draw attention to Hobbes's redefinition, although only Strauss does so in regard to the establishment of the commonwealth; Willey focuses on Hobbes's scriptural interpretation. As we will see, Hobbes will acknowledge that they in fact amount to the same thing in *Leviathan*, XX. Hoekstra notes that

> Hobbes's requirement that all obligation depends on consent ... is often cited to show that he is, foundationally, a liberal of some kind, or that, more particularly, he is a consent theorist. However, the very ubiquity of consent, as the foundation of all obligations, has an opposite effect. Whereas Hobbes is often understood to use consent as the test of whether or not there is obligation, at times he instead infers consent from a situation in which there must be obligation. In this sense, one *has* consented when one *ought* to have consented ("The *de facto* Turn in Hobbes's Political Philosophy," 68–69).

> Hoekstra observes rightly that Hobbes's view rests on his conception of human nature as much as it does on the facts of power, and thus opts for characterizing Hobbes as a "political naturalist," rather than a *de facto* theorist (*ibid.*, 72).

states that although a patrimonial kingdom differs from monarchy by institution in the manner in which each comes about, once formed, "it has all the same properties, and both have the same right of government; they do not need to be discussed separately."[154]

If anything, however, treating the two processes as effectively equivalent renders even more pressing the question regarding the purpose of thinking about the rise of commonwealths by institution. The fact that both processes involve an element of submission through fear allows Hobbes to bridge the gap between the incredible social contract and the credible story of submission. Similarly, the translation of submission into a contract allows Hobbes to maintain the otherwise implausible notion that his readers are somehow bound to obey their sovereigns because of an agreement. Even if there never had been a gathering at which their savage ancestors had committed themselves to obeying their sovereign, thereby binding their offspring along with themselves, their own tacit acceptance of their sovereign and the protection he provides constitutes a pact.

Still, nothing thus far requires that one buy into the story of the commonwealth by institution. That story is the political consequence of Hobbes's individual appeal to the reader. Hobbes promised to diverge from the failed method of his predecessors by presenting an argument not based on someone else's authority, but one that the reader could accept on his own, and based on his personal experience. The invitation to "return to the state of nature" and consider men as though they had sprung from the earth, fully formed and without any ties to one another, is an invitation to the reader to consider what he himself ought to do under such circumstances and to recognize that he has already consented. The reader who, on the basis of experience, validates Hobbes's account of what the transition from the state of nature to civil society ought to look like will thereby offer the equivalent of his authorization of the political order that results from this thought experiment and from his recognition of the facts. If that reader were persuaded to choose the lesser evil of submitting to his sovereign over the return to the state of nature, as Hobbes hopes he will be, then his acceptance of the existing order would constitute much more than tacit consent. By opting not to follow those who call on citizens to "take part in any rebellion, conspiracy or covenant prejudicial to the commonwealth," but to turn them in to the authorities, the reader would show his approval of Hobbes's edifice.[155]

---

[154] *De Cive*, IX.10. Cf. *The Elements of Law*, II.4.10: "whatever rights be in the one, the same also be in the other." Hobbes adds, "therefore I shall no more speak of them as distinct, but as of monarchy in general."
[155] *De Cive*, Pref., § 21: "Hæc qui probat, is meum quoque in scribendo consilium probum esse existimabit." King points out that Hobbes's emphasis on sovereignty by institution was also a means of disarming antimonarchical arguments (*The Ideology of Order*, 239).

It is important to remember, however, that this mechanism by which the reader can be persuaded to signal his authorization of Hobbes's system is not confined to the thought experiment of *De Cive*, chapter VIII, but that it also depends crucially on verisimilitude, which is gained by giving the reader ample reason to believe that the state of nature is grounded in reality and can be confirmed not simply by reason, but also by experience. On the level of personal experience, every man knows what it is to be a subject and every man knows what it is to be a king, because every man has found himself in each position, by virtue of having been a son and a father. To persuade the reader that this is the case, Hobbes invites him once more to "return to the state of nature," this time not to engage in a thought experiment, but to think about the nature of dominion in the family.[156] What one finds there is enlightening. As we should expect, given the account of the state of nature in the *Elements*, dominion over children is not based on generation, as most suppose, but on power.[157] As the state of nature is a condition of equality, "all adults are to be taken as equal to each other," which means that dominion over children belongs to the mother, who first has the child in her power.[158] Experience shows that whatever inequality of strength may exist between the sexes is insufficient for any claim to superiority of men over women. Indeed, one can find examples of women exercising dominion, such as the Amazons, as well as "several places today where women have *sovereign power.*"[159]

The trademark of Aristotelian political science is the classification of constitutions in Book III of the *Politics*. Hobbes has signaled his intention to depart from the practices of those who have considered civil philosophy

---

[156] *De Cive*, IX.2: "Redeundum igitur est ad statum naturalem...." On the combination of the two approaches, see Schochet's comments on Strauss and Warrender ("Hobbes on the Family and the State of Nature," 437–45), although his summary of Strauss's position on the status of the state of nature, at 437–38, does not take account of the whole of Strauss's view of the matter (see, for example, Strauss, *The Political Philosophy of Hobbes*, 102–07; cf. Warrender, *The Political Philosophy of Hobbes*, 237–42).

[157] *De Cive*, IX.1; cf. *The Elements of Law*, I.14.13. Schochet points to the probable connection between the child's future consent and the precept of the law of nature regarding gratitude ("Hobbes on the Family and the State of Nature," 433–34). In *De Cive*, this is the third precept (III.8).

[158] *De Cive*, IX.2. Hobbes supplies several additional arguments at IX.3.

[159] *De Cive*, IX.3. This is a loose application of Hobbes's standard formula for specific examples of the state of nature, according to which he offers an ancient and a contemporary example. Although he refers here to the ancient practices of the Amazons, Hobbes is well aware of the fact that the name was applied routinely by his contemporaries to women either found or thought to exist in uncharted territories. Thus, his contemporaries would have known of the Amazons through their reading of ancient sources, such as Apollonius Rhodius, Homer, Pliny the Elder, Seneca, Virgil, and Xenophon, but they would have also encountered them in the writings of Botero (*Relations of the Most Famous Kingdomes*, 454, 496), Mercator (*Historia mundi*, 847), and Purchas (*Purchas His Pilgrimes*, I: 13, 20, 73, 84, 357, et passim), among many others.

before him, and his own classification of regimes is presented in open defiance of Aristotle. Unlike many of the other places in which Hobbes names Aristotle only to attack the views of his followers, here it is the Greek philosopher himself who is the target of Hobbes's criticism. Hobbes rejects Aristotle's distinction between good and bad regimes, and reminds the reader that the only meaningful distinction between good and bad is the fundamental distinction between actions tending to peace and actions tending to war.[160] As Hobbes surveys the ways in which civil society emerges, he invites the reader to return to the state of nature twice, first to consider men singly and then in families. Each of these returns is designed to remind the reader of what is lost by such a return. Mindful of the need to remind individuals of the benefits of civil society constantly, Hobbes proposes to compare the advantages and disadvantages of a commonwealth, "lest some perhaps should think it better, that every man be left to live at his own will, then to constitute any civill society at all."[161] Hobbes grants that in the state of nature one has unfettered liberty, but reminds the reader that that liberty is useless because one is simultaneously subjected to the equally boundless liberty of others. As the subject of a commonwealth, every individual loses enough liberty so as to no longer constitute a threat to others, but retains as much liberty as he needs in order to live well and in peace.[162] In the state of nature,

> every man hath such a Right to all, as yet he can enjoy nothing; in [a commonwealth], each one securely enjoyes his limited Right; Out of it, any man may rightly spoyle, or kill one another; in it, none but one. Out of it we are protected by our own forces; in it, by the power of all. Out of it no man is sure of the fruit of his labours; in it, all men are. Lastly, out of it, there is a Dominion of Passions, war, fear, poverty, slovinlinesse, solitude, barbarisme, ignorance, cruelty. In it, the Dominion of reason, peace, security, riches, decency, society, elegancy, sciences, and benevolence.[163]

This contrast is a necessary reminder of the dangers inherent in discussions of alternative institutional arrangements and other signs of discontent with the existing order, that Hobbes has identified as the principal sources of danger to the commonwealth from within.[164]

Hobbes has already given the reader a preview of these internal causes of dissolution when he discussed the differences between man and the other gregarious animals.[165] When he returns to them in Chapter XII, his extended examination gives the impression that they are numerous and complicated.

---

[160] *De Cive*, X.2.

[161] *De Cive*, X.1 (Warrender ed.).

[162] *De Cive*, X.1: "ad bene & tranquillè viuendum."

[163] *De Cive*, X.1 (Warrender ed.). Hobbes's contrast here builds on that of *The Elements of Law*, I.14.10–12.

[164] See the third arguments in *The Elements of Law*, I.19.5 and *De Cive*, V.5, respectively.

[165] *De Cive*, V.5.

All of them, however, boil down to the same thing: the erroneous notion that one has retained more of the rights that one had in the state of nature than civil society will allow. It is no surprise, then, that first and foremost among seditious opinions is the illusion that "*knowledge of good and evil is a matter for individuals.*"[166] While this opinion is true in the state of nature, and an indispensable part of natural right, "in the civil state it is false."[167] With its focus on the benefits of peace and civilization, Hobbes's earliest contrast between civil society and the state of nature made the commonwealth appear like Paradise, yet he never made the allusion explicit. It is here, in *De Cive*, XII, that the obvious is stated: "The oldest of God's commands is (Gen. 2.17): *Do not eat of the tree of the knowledge of good and evil*, and the oldest of the devil's temptations is (3.5): *You will be as gods knowing good and evil.*"[168] If the commonwealth is like the Garden of Eden, the presumption that a subject has the right to judge good and evil is tantamount to the Fall.[169]

The less pious implication of this analogy, however, is that the sovereign is in some ways like God. Hobbes would wait until *Leviathan* before coming close to admitting as much, but some of the seditious opinions that he lists here confirm this suspicion.[170] Thus, subjects can sin in obeying the sovereign, the sovereign is subject to the laws, his power can be divided, and the subject's faith is the result of supernatural infusion, rather than a superior's precept or reason.[171] A subject who acts on these seditious opinions disobeys what Hobbes would eventually describe as a "Mortall God," and thereby opens the door for his expulsion from the commonwealth. Civil society is not quite Paradise, but the state of nature is worse than life outside the Garden of Eden, where industry was at least possible, if taxing.

Rebellious spirits misunderstand the difference between a multitude and a people, and thus the difference between the temporary and unreliable associations that were possible in the state of nature, and a union into a single will that constitutes a lasting civil society.[172] This tendency is neither surprising nor remarkable, given the inability of most people to evaluate their

---

[166] *De Cive*, XII.1. This includes, of course, the determination of what belongs to whom, since private property did not exist in the state of nature (XII.7).

[167] *De Cive*, XII.1. Hobbes refers to his proof of the former claim in I.9.

[168] *De Cive*, XII.1.

[169] We will consider the connection between the state of nature and Genesis in Chapter 6.

[170] In *Leviathan*, Hobbes refers to the commonwealth as "that great LEVIATHAN," but adds immediately, "or rather (to speake more reverently) of that *Mortall God*, to which wee owe under the *Immortal God*, our peace and defence" (XVII: 87).

[171] *De Cive*, XII.2–6. This is a common line of argument. See, e.g., Sommerville, "John Selden, the Law of Nature, and the Origins of Government," 441–42; Tuck, *Philosophy and Government*, 216.

[172] *De Cive*, XII.8.

circumstances properly. As Hobbes had noted consistently since the translation of Thucydides, individuals have an inability to weigh their own good in relation to the common good, and a concomitant incapacity to weigh short-term advantages and disadvantages against the long term. In practice, this means that taxes and other burdens imposed by civil society will always be felt as heavier than they are, in part because the benefits that they pay for are taken for granted or are too far removed from the payment.[173] Hobbes has warned the reader from the start, however, that he should be willing to put up with some inconvenience, rather than act in a way that will eventually bring about the worst alternative.[174] It is clear that these tendencies render a reminder of that alternative necessary, and Hobbes's task is to supply it, through the specter of the state of nature.

In addition to the discontented, the ferment of rebellion includes those who have too much time on their hands, as well as those whose inability to weigh things well fills them with a hope of victory, regardless of the odds.[175] Among them, an ambitious rabble-rouser will find the makings of a faction by manipulating the very characteristics that separate man from the other gregarious animals and render him political. Once again, Hobbes erects a sharp contrast between the realms of reason and the passions, but this time he admits openly that there are two kinds of eloquence, one corresponding roughly to each realm.[176] Although Hobbes maintains the fiction of a realm of pure reason here, he concedes that there are cases in which the eloquence that speaks to the passions is not divorced from wisdom.[177] The existence of the discontented, the men of leisure, the vainglorious, and the naive, explains why such eloquence is necessary. Even if the reader can see what reason dictates, he knows that there are many who cannot, or will not. Hoping that reason alone can appeal to them is to hope for something that has already proven impossible. Hobbes admired Thucydides for his ability to turn his auditors into spectators, but here he notes that under the right circumstances, rhetoricians can turn theirs "out of fools into madmen."[178]

---

[173] Hobbes returns to this matter in *Leviathan* (XVIII: 94), where he describes this human tendency to misjudge the demands of the present vis-à-vis those of the future using a brilliant image that we will consider later. Questions centered on taxation had figured prominently in the disputes between the King and his subjects in the preceding decades, of which the case of Ship Money was the most notorious (see Sommerville, *Thomas Hobbes*, 17–19; Evrigenis, *Fear of Enemies and Collective Action*, 96, n. 9).

[174] See, for example, *De Cive*, Pref., §§ 20–21. Cf. *Leviathan*, XIV: 70.

[175] *De Cive*, XII.10–11. This hope is indispensable to rebellion. Hobbes argues that without it "no sedition will follow; individuals will hide their feelings and put up with a bad situation rather than risk a worse" (XII.11). In such a case, the clarity of the alternative renders the choice obvious.

[176] *De Cive*, XII.12. Cf. *The Elements of Law*, Ep. Ded.; I.13; *De Cive*, XII.1.

[177] *De Cive*, XII.12: "For one [kind of eloquence] is never separated from *wisdom*; the other almost always is." This division rests on that between *ratio* and *oratio*, discussed earlier.

[178] *De Cive*, XII.12.

How, then, does one bring them to the truth? By employing eloquence coupled with wisdom, which can show "whence the Lawes derive their power,
which are the Rules of *just* and *unjust, honest* and *dishonest, good* and *evill*;
what makes and preserves Peace among men, what destroyes it; what is *his*,
and what *anothers*," as well as persuade them of the utility of the Golden
Rule.[179]

As in the *Elements*, Hobbes's manner of proceeding here allows the
reader to walk away from his portrayals of the disobedient thinking that
nothing therein applies to him. Thus, the reader is the reasonable interlocutor to whom Hobbes is presenting the facts as they are, and no reasonable
person would disagree with such a presentation. That he was seeking such
a reaction was already clear from the Preface to *De Cive*, where Hobbes
made it clear that his arguments about the need to protect oneself through
anticipation could rest on the very modest assumption that most people are
in fact good, and that it is only our inability to tell the good and bad apart
that makes anticipation necessary.[180] At the end of Chapter XII, the reader
can continue to indulge in the fiction that the language in which Hobbes is
addressing him is that of pure reason. As a prudent man, however, Hobbes is
anticipating the possibility that every reader will in fact need to be addressed
in a different language. As a result, a powerful metaphor is never far away.
Enlisting one of his favorite tales, Hobbes likens the eloquence of the rabble-
rouser and the stupidity of the rabble that follows him to the eloquence of
Medea and the stupidity of the daughters of Pelias, who thought that they
could rejuvenate their father by cutting him to pieces and boiling him.[181]

The changes Hobbes made from the *Elements*, through the first version
of *De Cive*, to the published version of 1647 reveal that he continued to
revise his works on the basis of his readers' reactions. This should come as
no surprise given his stated intention to frame the thinking of the widest
possible audience. Yet too much attention to his allegedly geometrical politics has caused commentators to lose sight of the fact that Hobbes's primary
concern in writing was not science for its own sake, but utility.[182] Like its
predecessor, *De Cive* shows that one should be wary of following Hobbes's
labels too closely. His tables of contents and headings would have us believe
that his examination of the natural condition of mankind is confined to
Chapter 14 of the *Elements*, and Chapter I of *De Cive*. However, explicitly
or through the use of subtle enthymemes, Hobbes invokes it continuously
and increasingly to achieve his purpose. Its omnipresence is most obviously
evident in Hobbes's successive invitations to the reader to consider what a

---

[179] *De Cive*, XII.12.

[180] *De Cive*, Pref., §§ 12–13.

[181] *De Cive*, XII.12. Opting for a more exotic example, Rousseau makes the same point in *Of
the Social Contract* (II.ii.2).

[182] The two, of course, need not be mutually exclusive. We will return to the relationship
between them later.

commonwealth should look like by returning to the state of nature. Yet, the state of nature to which the reader returns in each of these cases is different. Sometimes it is inhabited by isolated individuals, and at other times by groups.[183] Perhaps most importantly, it is a condition that even the solitary reader can find himself in, all by himself; for a thought experiment will yield the same basic truth as one's recollection of episodes from across history, or one's own past experiences with others.[184]

Still, Hobbes's expanded portrayal of this uncertain condition in *De Cive* does not take full advantage of what is perhaps the most obvious example of the natural condition. Although he describes the state of nature as a state of war, and even as a war of all against all, Hobbes does not invoke either the example of warfare in general, or examples of particular wars, in order to buttress his claim and render it vivid and compelling. Twice, in the second half of the book, he comes close to doing so, but these instances are buried in rather obscure locations. The first of these occurs in Hobbes's treatment of the sovereign's duties. He declares that the pursuit of *salus populi* requires that one be forewarned and forearmed, "for the condition between commonwealths is *natural*, that is, one of hostility."[185] Sovereigns must therefore develop networks of spies in the manner in which spiders cast their webs, so that at the center they may be forewarned about the slightest outmost movement. Invoking the arts of the gladiator, Hobbes adds that sovereigns must also take care to forearm themselves, and do so promptly, long before any particular threat manifests itself, since doing so on short notice is difficult and the potential consequences of negligence are great.[186]

Hobbes returns to this language in a chapter in which he examines the Kingdom of God according to the New Covenant. There, he considers whether it could ever make sense for a sovereign to submit his subjects'

---

[183] For example, that of *De Cive*, Pref., § 11, VIII.1, and that of X.2. For analyses of why Hobbes's characterization of the state of nature as "solitary" should not be taken literally, see Ashcraft, "Political Theory and Political Action;" Hoekstra, *Thomas Hobbes and the Creation of Order*.

[184] As, for example, *De Cive*, VIII.1, I.13, and Pref., § 11, respectively, show. Thus, as we have seen earlier, several commentators pronounce the state of nature a thought experiment. This view is supported not simply by the present evidence, but also by Hobbes's later statement, in *Leviathan*, in which he proclaims the state of war an inference from the passions (XIII: 62). Faced with the obvious problem of the historical examples that Hobbes places alongside his description of the natural condition, some commentators see different phases or states of nature, as, for example, did Leibniz, when he wrote of a "pure" state of nature (Gottfried Wilhelm Leibniz to Thomas Hobbes, Mainz, July 13/23, 1670 [British Library Add. MS 4294, fol. 64v]). Cf. Verdon, "On the Laws of Physical and Human Nature," 657, and Pettit, who writes of a "state of second nature" (*Made with Words*, 99).

[185] *De Cive*, XIII.7.

[186] *De Cive*, XIII.8. Hobbes notes that the difficulty lies in the fact that people consider it a great injury to have to part with their property in order to contribute to the public good; cf. *ibid.*, III.32; *Leviathan*, XVIII: 94.

consciences to an enemy, as, for example, a Catholic king might to the Pope.[187] That a condition of war is not limited to actual fighting is evident in interstate relations, for,

[n]ever mind that they are not always fighting (for enemies too make truces); hostility is adequately shown by distrust, and by the fact that the borders of their commonwealths, Kingdoms and empires, armed and garrisoned, with the posture and appearance of gladiators, look across at each other like enemies, even when they are not striking each other.[188]

Among seditious doctrines, "the first, without question, is: *that knowledge of good and evil is a matter for individuals.*"[189] Hobbes directs his readers to the first example that would have crossed their minds: This was the crux of God's first command to man, this was the essence of the devil's first temptation, and this is what had led to man's expulsion from the Garden of Eden. The dividing line between the Garden of Eden and the miserable existence that human beings were exiled to was to be guarded by "Cherubims, and a flaming sword which turned every way," much as the dividing line between the state of nature and civil society would be guarded by an ever-vigilant, hybrid being, with superhuman powers and sword in hand.[190]

---

[187] *De Cive*, XVII.27. Hobbes refers to V.5, where he argues that a single will is necessary in matters of peace and defense.

[188] *De Cive*, XVII.27.

[189] *De Cive*, XII.1.

[190] Genesis, 3:24. On the sword, see Hendel, "'The Flame of the Whirling Sword.'" According to Duncan, the posting of the Cherubim was seen as "the crucial problem" by writers who tried to interpret the meaning of the expulsion either "literally as part of a historical narrative or as a figurative representation of the theological concept of change in man's condition" ("Paradise as the Whole Earth," 179; cf. 179–83). In addition to using the image of the posture of gladiators to describe sovereigns, Hobbes also emphasizes that the sword of the sovereign is ever-ready to be aimed in any direction since it is both the sword of justice and peace, domestically, and the sword of defense and war, abroad (see, for example, *De Cive*, VI.6–7; *Leviathan*, XVIII: 90–91).

FIGURE 5. Title page of Hobbes's *Leviathan*.
Source: Thomas Hobbes, *Leviathan* (London: Andrew Crooke, 1651), f AC85.
J2376.Zz651h, Houghton Library, Harvard University.

5

Reason of State

Leviathan

[T]he unlearned, that is most men, are content to believe, rather than
be troubled with examining ...
– Hobbes, "An Answer to Bishop Bramhall"

A being of this sort is the first thing that the reader of *Leviathan* encounters (see Figure 5).[1] It is a giant crowned figure, hovering over an orderly
landscape. His torso made up of smaller men, and holding a sword in the
right hand and a crozier in the left, he presides over a complex set of panels
that contain examples of his respective powers.[2] From a distance, the initial

---

[1] To a reader who has had the opportunity to read *Leviathan*, the frontispiece is a remarkably
rich summary of its contents, and doubtless the work of someone intimately familiar with
them. Corbett and Lightbown (*The Comely Frontispiece*, 221–22) and Bredekamp (*Thomas
Hobbes Der Leviathan*, 52) argue persuasively that the design was conceived by Hobbes and
executed by Abraham Bosse. A hand-drawn version of the frontispiece adorns a presentation
copy of *Leviathan* that is held to have been the one that Hobbes prepared for Charles II
(British Library Mss. Egerton 1910; cf. Clarendon, *A Brief View and Survey*, 8–9). The two
versions differ in some important ways, not the least of which is that the faces of the persons
that make up the sovereign face him in the printed version, whereas they face the reader in
the manuscript. In comparing the two, Brown argues that they were executed by different artists, and attributes the manuscript version to Wenceslas Hollar ("The Artist of the *Leviathan*
Title-Page," esp. p. 29, but cf. Bredekamp, *Thomas Hobbes Der Leviathan*, p. 31–36, 39–52).
Bredekamp argues that Bosse produced the hand-drawn version as well, but following
Hollar's portrait of Charles II, which accounts for the stylistic similarity between the two
(*Thomas Hobbes Der Leviathan*, 52).
[2] For a detailed explanation, see Corbett and Lightbown, *The Comely Frontispiece*, 219–30,
esp. 219–21. Cf. Martinich, *The Two Gods of Leviathan*, 362–67. As we have noted earlier,
Hobbes's catalog of the Hardwick library contains an entry for Forsett's *A Comparative
Discovrse of the Bodies Natvral and Politiqve* (1606), a work whose title bears a strong
resemblance to Hobbes's *Elements of Law*. That work is remarkable for several other reasons
related to Hobbes, not the least of which is its extended parallel between the natural body

impression is one of nearly perfect order. The reader who compares the frontispiece of *De Cive* to that of *Leviathan* might be forgiven for thinking, at first glance, that the panel representing *imperium* in the earlier work appears to have taken over the later one, displacing *libertas* and *religio*. The state of nature appears to have vanished, and religion seems to have been plucked from the heavens and deposited in the sovereign, from whom it flows. Closer inspection, however, reveals that the changes are more subtle.

Underneath the sovereign's extended arms stretches a peaceful landscape, in the heart of which lies a commonwealth displaying evident signs of prosperity. The sovereign's posture and the manner in which he bears his implements cast a protective aura over the scene below, thereby symbolizing the lesson from the end of *De Cive*, a lesson that would be given a much more prominent role in *Leviathan*: by assuming the posture and appearance of a gladiator, the sovereign makes it possible for his subjects to live commodiously.[3] The sword and crozier signal how and in which domains the sovereign does so, and the panels underneath each symbol of his authority show what that authority means in practice. On the left-hand side, underneath the sword, is a series of panels pertaining to war. On the right, beneath the crozier, a series of corresponding panels depicts matters of doctrine. By contrast, inside the commonwealth, in the middle, reminders of the disorder on either side are barely noticeable amid the peace: walls, fortresses, and outposts, a handful of soldiers engaged in a drill and two barely visible sentries.[4] The effect of this presentation is paradoxical. On the one hand, the state of nature seems more remote than in the case of *De Cive*. On the other hand, it is nearer and more likely. No longer located in the distant American

---

and the body politic. Forsett's account anticipates Hobbes's description of the relationship between the two bodies in the Introduction to *Leviathan*, most notably in its emphasis on the sovereign as the soul of the commonwealth. It also includes the following description of the commonwealth according to Hermes Trismegistus: "*an huge and mightie Gyant, whose head was aboue the firmament, his necke, shoulders and upper parts in the heauens, his armes and hands reaching to the East and West, his belly in the whole spaciousnesse vnder the Moone, his legges and feet within the earth*" ("To the Reader," sig. iij^(r-v)), which as Prior notes, bears a striking resemblance to the image on Hobbes's frontispiece ("Trismegistus 'His Great Giant,'" 369). In the bibliography that accompanies his survey of English political thought, Smith characterizes Forsett's treatise "The Source of much of Hobbes" ("English Political Philosophy in the Seventeenth and Eighteenth Centuries," Bibliography, p. 965), a characterization to which Laird takes exception (*Hobbes*, 77). Laird sees "no internal evidence that Hobbes had read" Forsett's work and is "confident that if he did read it, it could not have impressed him," citing several noted instances of arguments regarding the body politic (*ibid.*, 77–78). The similarities between Forsett's work and Hobbes's *Elements* and *Leviathan*, as well as Hobbes's access to it at Hardwick, however, offer sufficient reasons for considering it a possible source of influence, even if not a formative one. *See also* 1 Corinthians 12:12; *Vindiciæ Contra Tyrannos*, 88.

[3] *De Cive*, XVII.27; cf. *Leviathan*, XIII: 63.

[4] Indeed, in comparing the printed version of the design to one drawn by hand, in the presentation copy, Brown finds a "deadness," which he goes so far as to characterize as "an objectively demonstrable characteristic of the engraving" ("The Artist of the *Leviathan* Title-Page," 26).

wilderness, the state of nature of *Leviathan* lies all around Hobbes's reader: just beyond the reach of the sovereign's sword, in the battlefields of the left-hand panel, or in the disputations of the right. The same is true of the third panel from *De Cive*, representing religion. The dreadful but distant deterrent of the Last Judgment has been replaced by reminders of the immediate dangers inherent in religious disagreement. Each of the panels on the right corresponds to one on the left, suggesting that the controversy surrounding religious doctrine smacks of war, a war of the minds that could turn into the worst kind of conflict: civil war.[5] Yet, heavenly agency has not been eliminated completely, either. The only thing higher than the sovereign is a passage from Scripture, which confirms what the picture suggests: there is no power *on Earth* that compares to him.[6] The passage gives a first and very important clue as to the title of the work. It ties the name Leviathan to the Book of Job, rather than to the Book of Isaiah, and indicates that Hobbes is using it as an example of irresistible power, rather than one of evil. This clarification was necessary because for all its ambiguity and several meanings, by Hobbes's time Leviathan was associated primarily with evil in general and with the Devil in particular.[7]

Among the numerous authors for whom Leviathan signifies evil, one is especially important for the present purposes: Jean Bodin. Bodin mentions Leviathan in several of his works, and commentators on Hobbes's use of the Biblical beast have occasionally mentioned Bodin's *De la démono-manie des sorciers*, a work in which Bodin likens Leviathan to the Devil.[8] As we have seen, Hobbes rarely cites near-contemporary authors, and even more rarely with approval. Yet he accords this rare privilege to Bodin's

---

[5] On the corresponding panels, see Bredekamp, "Thomas Hobbes's Visual Strategies," 32.

[6] "*Non est potestas super Terram quæ comparetur ei*," (Job 41:24 in the Vulgate). Hobbes returns to it and elaborates in Chapter XXVIII (166–67). The passage from the printed frontispiece is absent from the hand-drawn version of the presentation copy. Cf. Bredekamp, *Thomas Hobbes Der Leviathan*, pl. 18, p. 37. The placement of the passage and its provenance also suggest the special status of Scripture, something that Hobbes confirms repeatedly (see, for example, *The Elements of Law*, I.13.4; *De Cive*, Pref., § 16; *Leviathan*, Review and Conclusion: 395). Cf. Strong, "How to Write Scripture," 131.

[7] Job 3:8 and 40:20, Isaiah 27:1, in the Vulgate. All this aside from the question whether Leviathan is a whale, crocodile, snake, or other kind of beast, itself the subject of intense and longstanding debate. For an extensive analysis of the range of meanings, see Schmitt, *The Leviathan in the State Theory of Thomas Hobbes*, esp. Chapter 1, but note Mintz's warnings ("Leviathan as Metaphor," 3–4). Cf. Steadman, "Leviathan and Renaissance Etymology"; Greenleaf, "A Note on Hobbes and the Book of Job"; Stillman, "Hobbes's *Leviathan*," 795. Steadman notes that the sense that Hobbes ascribes to the name was "unconventional, but not unprecedented" ("Leviathan and Renaissance Etymology," 575).

[8] Bodin, *De la démonomanie des sorciers*, II.vi, p. 103ʳ, III.1, pp. 120ʳ⁻ᵛ; Schmitt mentions the *La démonomanie* in connection to Hobbes (*The Leviathan in the State Theory of Thomas Hobbes*, 8, 23); cf. Freund, "Le dieu mortel," 40. Hobbes devotes Chapter XLV of *Leviathan* to this topic.

Six livres de la République.[9] It is to that work that we must turn in order
to understand the frontispiece of *Leviathan* better.[10] In the final chapter
of the *Six livres*, a chapter replete with terms and imagery that one finds
also in *Leviathan*, Bodin considers three kinds of justice and their relationship to the commonwealth.[11] The first feature that anticipates Hobbes is
Bodin's extended, if strange, discussion of geometry, which he relates to
Plato's *Republic* and to distributive justice.[12] In Bodin's classification, geometrical justice is inferior to harmonical justice, a choice that is unsurprising given his view that human societies rest on a foundation of *amicitia*.[13]
As it turns out, this position is not as antithetical to Hobbes's view as it
may sound, for this *amicitia* is only possible in regimes based on harmony,
whose final aim is peace.[14]

If an odd discussion of geometry in the context of a consideration of
justice, and a concurrence on peace as the aim of the well-ordered commonwealth are insufficient to link Hobbes to the *Six livres* definitively, Bodin's
language and imagery in describing that commonwealth are nevertheless
quite striking. Bodin argues that the sovereign prince is "exalted aboue all
his subiects, and exempt out of the ranke of them: whose maiestie suffereth
no more diuision than doth the vnitie it selfe, which is not set nor accounted
among the numbers, howbeit that they all from it take both their force and

---

[9] *The Elements of Law*, II.8.7. Entries in Hobbes's hand, in the Hardwick Library catalogue,
for "*Bodini Methodus Historiar. 16°,*" "*Bodin de Repub. Lat. fol.,*" "*Bodin de Rep. Eng.
fol.,*" "*Bodini methodus Histor. 8°,*" "*Bodin. De La Repub. 8°,*" show that Hobbes had access
to Bodin's *Six livres* in French, Latin, and English, as well as to two different editions of the
Methodus (Devonshire Mss., Chatsworth HS/E/1A). According to Laird, the Knolles translation of the *Six livres* "appear[s] to have been a standard university text-book in England,"
making it clear that "any extensive larceny on Hobbes's part ran a very good chance of being
detected" (*Hobbes*, 73).

[10] The only comment on Bodin's reference to Leviathan in the *Six livres de la republique* I
am aware of is Dowdall's ("The Word 'State,'" 122). Malcolm ("The Name and Nature of
Leviathan") has investigated the possible connection between Boulduc – through Mersenne –
and Hobbes, in regard to the latter's choice of Leviathan for the title of his great treatise.
Although this connection is certainly possible, it is likelier that Hobbes's inspiration came
from Bodin.

[11] Bodin, *The Six Bookes of a Commonweale*, VI.vi. Knolles's English edition of this work
is a composite of Bodin's French and Latin versions, which differ from one another, and
therefore does not correspond fully to either edition (see McRae's introduction to his
1962 edition). I will hence cite the French, Knolles's translation, and the Latin edition of
1609.
The three kinds of justice are: (1) commutative or arithmetical, (2) distributive or geometrical, and (3) harmonical (*The Six Bookes of a Commonweale*, 756; *De Republica Libri
Sex*, 1170).

[12] *The Six Bookes of a Commonweale*, 755–61; *De Republica Libri Sex*, 1169–77.

[13] *De Republica Libri Sex*, 1174; *Les six livres de la republique*, 731: "amitié." Knolles translates "amicitia" as "loue and friendship" (*The Six Bookes of a Commonweale*, 759).

[14] *Six livres de la république*, 757; *De Republica Libri Sex*, 1218; *The Six Bookes of a
Commonweale*, 792.

power."[15] In a well-ordered commonwealth, the three estates will occupy their proper stations, making for a "pleasant harmonie of all the subiects among themselues; as also of them altogether with their soueraigne prince."[16] Using an analogy that the marginal note in the Latin edition sums up as "the most excellent image of the commonwealth," Bodin likens the harmonious kingdom to "the nature of man himselfe, being the verie true image of a well ordered Commonweale: and that not in his bodie onely, which still hath but one head, and all the rest of the members aptly fitted thereunto."[17] Bodin elaborates on this analogy by explaining how the different parts of the commonwealth correspond to the organs and limbs of the human body and to the parts of the human mind, and concludes that "a souereigne prince, ... with his authoritie and power might (as doth the vnderstanding) reconcile all the parts, and so vnite and bind them fast in happinesse together."[18] The union of all under the sovereign gives rise to this giant man that is the commonwealth, the repository and source of all power.[19]

The image of the body politic brings us one step closer to Hobbes's frontispiece, but the strongest evidence of a connection between the *Six livres* and *Leviathan* comes from Bodin's conclusion. In enumerating the parts of the commonwealth and relating them to the parts of the body, Bodin describes some of them in less than flattering terms. Still, not only do they have a place in the well-ordered commonwealth, but they also are in fact necessary to it, much in the way that good music contains some dissonance, "cunning cookes ... to give the better tast vnto their good meates, serve in therewith certaine dishes of sharpe and vnsauerie sauces," and cunning painters mix in black and other dark colors, to bring out the brighter ones.[20] The principle is simple: contrast allows the better elements to shine and receive the recognition they deserve. Thus, the harmonious commonwealth contains "fools, vitious, and wicked men," and elements of geometrical and arithmetical justice, all of which combine with the good to bring about peace. This earthly construction mirrors God's creation, in which "Matter

[15] *The Six Bookes of a Commonweale*, 790; *Six livres de la republique*, 756; *De Republica Libri Sex*, 1216.

[16] *The Six Bookes of a Commonweale*, 790; *Six livres de la republique*, 756; *De Republica Libri Sex*, 1216. The highest order is "Ecclesiastique," which Knolles translates as "Ecclesiasticall."

[17] *De Republica Libri Sex*, 1217: "Præstantissimæ ciuitatis imago;" *The Six Bookes of a Commonweale*, 790; *Six livres de la republique*, 756: "l' homme, qui est la vraye image de la Republique bien ordonnee;" *De Republica Libri Sex*, 1216.

[18] *The Six Bookes of a Commonweale*, 791; *Six livres de la republique*, 757; *De Republica Libri Sex*, 1217.

[19] *The Six Bookes of a Commonweale*, 791. Bodin argues that individuals have no power other than what they receive from the union, itself the result of the sovereign's power on which "all others orderly depend" (*ibid.*).

[20] *The Six Bookes of a Commonweale*, 791; *Six livres de la republique*, 757; *De Republica Libri Sex*, 1217.

and Forme" maintain one another to produce a harmony of the whole.²¹ On that scale, God has

> mingled the bad with the good, and placed vertues in the middest of vices, bring-
> ing forth also certain monsters in nature … to the end that thereof might arise the
> greater good, and that by such meanes the power and beautie thereof might be the
> better knowne, which might otherwise haue beene hid and folded vp in most thicke
> and obscure darknesse.²²

Bodin's example of such a monster is the Pharaoh, "the worker and father of all mischiefe, whome the sacred Scriptures declare by the name of *Leuiathan.*"²³

Bodin's Leviathan may be the Devil, whereas Hobbes's is a "Mortall God," but the two are remarkably close. Both offer ready means of distin-guishing between good and evil, and both contain webs of associations that convey the essence of a doctrine of absolute sovereignty based on power. Bodin mentions Leviathan in the context of a discussion of political geom-etry, using man as a metaphor for the well-ordered commonwealth, and employing language that contains every single word from the title and sub-title of Hobbes's masterpiece. Perhaps the most suggestive feature of Bodin's analysis, however, is his attention to the power of contrast to illuminate.²⁴ As we have seen, Hobbes's earlier political writings display evidence of this technique at work. Beginning with the relatively unobjectionable chasm between reason and the passions, and moving from that to the curious con-trast between the mathematicians and the dogmatists, Hobbes paved the way for his most central antithesis between the state of nature and civil society, one that would persuade his reader that the horrors of the former render the inconveniences of the latter tolerable.

Leviathan represents the culmination of this technique, itself part of a gen-eral rhetorical strategy that was in place since the very beginning, whereby

---

²¹ *The Six Bookes of a Commonweale,* 792; *Six livres de la republique,* 758: "de la matiere, & de la forme"; *De Republica Libri Sex,* 1218: "materia & forma." This, of course, is the language that Hobbes uses to describe the subject of *Leviathan,* in the subtitle of the work.

²² *The Six Bookes of a Commonweale,* 793; *Six livres de la republique,* 758–59; *De Republica Libri Sex,* 1220.

²³ *The Six Bookes of a Commonweale,* 793; *De Republica Libri Sex,* 1220. This passage is not in the French edition. Although Bodin claims here that the Scriptures use the name Leviathan for the Pharaoh, he goes on to associate it with the Devil, demons, or evil in general, as he does in his other works, such as the *De la démonomanie des sorciers* (cf. *Colloquium of the Seven about Secrets of the Sublime,* 42, 105, 107, 118, 217; on the connection to Egypt, see Kluger, *Satan in the Old Testament,* 86). The marginal note in the Latin edition reads: "Job 40 and Psalm 104. They often call [Leviathan] הׁשטן. Ezekiel 29 and 30 interprets [Leviathan] most correctly." The two Latin editions that I have examined contain different misspellings of the Hebrew, but it is clear that the intention was to print הׁשטן (ha-shatan). Without the definite article, the term is often used to denote an opponent or enemy (see Kluger, *Satan in the Old Testament,* esp. 25–53).

²⁴ A characteristic captured by the oppositional quality of Bodin's choice of Leviathan.

Hobbes avails himself of the weapons of rhetoric while disavowing it for its reputation. The name and frontispiece set the stage for what follows by pitting an image of commodious living against suggestive reminders of its opposite. As Bodin's near-contemporary use of Leviathan illustrates, that name had several connotations, but was associated first and foremost with evil. The contrast between the predominant meaning of the name and the image on the frontispiece was the first link in the processes that Hobbes had described as "INSTIGATION and APPEASING" in the *Elements*.[25]

The strongest evidence of Hobbes's continued use of contrast comes in the Introduction to the work, which begins with the word "NATURE," and which it contrasts to artifice. This particular contrast is so well established and unproblematic that one would never think to question it. In Hobbes's hands, however, it contains the seeds of its own destruction, since nature herself is the product and means of artifice (God's), and the artificer in Hobbes's contrast (man) is himself a product of nature. Hobbes defines nature as "the Art whereby God hath made and governes the World," and adds that it "is by the *Art* of man, as in many other things, so in this also imitated, that it can make an Artificial Animal."[26] The word "it" toward the end of this sentence is but the most obvious problem: Who is it who makes this artificial animal – nature or man? The point of Hobbes's project, however, is less to resolve the question of the chicken or the egg, and more to predispose the reader by introducing a series of fruitful suggestions all headed in an improbable direction: to persuade the reader of his nearly divine status.

In the context of his own Leviathan, Bodin had noted a divine element in men, by virtue of which he placed them between the animals and angels in the order of Creation.[27] Hobbes had hinted at something like this in the Epistle Dedicatory to *De Cive*, when he used Plautus to describe man as a wolf to man in the state of nature, and as a god to man in civil society. Building on the subtle contrasts of the frontispiece, in the introduction to *Leviathan*, Hobbes mentions no beasts other than the one for whom the book is named, and that only to exalt the divine qualities of man by likening him to God. Just as God created man, man creates the "great LEVIATHAN" that is the commonwealth, whose business is the *"peoples safety."*[28] This approach is atypical, insofar as it does not mix praise with blame. Unlike the earlier works, wherein as we have seen Hobbes's praise was modest and his criticism abundant, *Leviathan* accords its reader a god-like status: it

[25] *The Elements of Law*, I.13.7.

[26] *Leviathan*, Introduction: 1. Cf. the opening to the epistle to the reader of *De Corpore* (*EW*, I; *OL*, I), where Hobbes first urges the reader to imitate a sculptor and then to fashion his procedure after the order of Creation.

[27] *The Six Bookes of a Commonweale*, 793.

[28] *Leviathan*, Introduction: 1. In Chapter X, Hobbes adds: "The Greatest of humane Powers, is that which is compounded of the Powers of most men, united by consent, in one person" (41).

proclaims him the creator of the greatest power on Earth.[29] Already impressive, this achievement reaches hubristic proportions when Hobbes notes that art goes even "further, imitating that Rationall and most excellent worke of Nature, *Man*."[30] If the contrast between nature and artifice were intended in earnest, then the lesser artificer has excelled his Maker. But as the opening sentence of the work shows, the contrast is ultimately meaningless, since whatever man does is ultimately attributable to his Maker.[31] Hobbes's reason for invoking it is to uphold the antithesis between the state of nature and civil society. For, if not nature but man is the artificer of Leviathan, then Hobbes can continue to suggest that the state of nature is devoid of order and that the commonwealth is artificial.[32]

This excessive flattery eases the path toward the main objective, which is to recreate Hobbes's Euclidean moment by persuading the reader that armed only with his copy of *Leviathan* and the fruits of his experience and introspection, he can decipher mankind. This kind of knowledge, argues Hobbes, is necessary to one who is to govern a whole nation. It has been argued, on the basis of this statement and other evidence, that Hobbes wrote *Leviathan* for Charles II.[33] This theory has considerable merit, but even if true, it leaves us with an important puzzle: Why did Hobbes choose to publish *Leviathan*? If the work were intended solely for his former pupil, then a presentation copy, such as the one mentioned by Clarendon, would have sufficed. Moreover, as we have seen earlier, as late as 1647 when Elzevir inquired whether he had anything to add or subtract to *De Cive* prior to its reissue, Hobbes had replied in the negative. This suggests that *Leviathan* was not intended as an amendment of his earlier political theory, but had another purpose. Hobbes's own account is helpful here. He claims that he published *Leviathan* in England, while he himself remained in Paris so that it could be made clear that peace in the Christian world was impossible without the adoption of his doctrine and a military force of sufficient magnitude

[29] See, for example, *EW*, VIII: vi; *The Elements of Law*, I.2.10; I.5.14; *De Cive*, Pref., §§ 3, 6. I intend "creator" here, rather than "co-creator." As Kantorowitz points out, in his report on Calvin's Case, Coke makes the "striking observation that the mortal king was God-made, but the immortal King, manmade" (*The King's Two Bodies*, 423). Coke writes of the "politic, body or capacity, so called, because it is framed by the policy of man" (*The Selected Writings and Speeches of Sir Edward Coke*, I: 189, but see also the rest of his description). Calvin's case was published in Part VII of Coke's reports, which is listed in Hobbes's catalogue of the holdings of the Hardwick Library (Devonshire Mss., Chatsworth HS/E/1A).

[30] *Leviathan*, Introduction: 1.

[31] Cf. *Leviathan*, XII: 52–53.

[32] This point is emphasized rightly by Strauss, *The Political Philosophy of Hobbes*, 7–8; Sacksteder, "Hobbes: Man the Maker," 77; cf. Strong, "How to Write Scripture," 140–41. Hobbes's language here contradicts that of *De Cive* (VIII.1).

[33] See Miller, "The Uniqueness of *Leviathan*," 91 and Malcolm's introduction to his edition of *Leviathan* (I: 51–60). Cf. *Leviathan*, XXXI: 193.

to compel citizens to concord.[34] Even if Charles II had been the impetus for *Leviathan*, the book still had an important role to play in advancing Hobbes's plan to persuade everyone of his views.[35]

The clue to this motive comes once again from the name and frontispiece of the work. As the subject of Leviathan, the reader is one of the proud, and Hobbes begins his effort to appease with the right note of flattery of the reader's pride.[36] Hobbes casts his invitation to the reader in the form of the familiar *nosce teipsum*, a call that he had first issued in the *Elements*.[37] In that earlier work, Hobbes's invitation had been preceded by reasons for being pessimistic about one's capacity to judge. Hobbes's pessimism had continued in *De Cive*, where he had cited the ancients' practice of wrapping discussion about justice in fables, before describing his own role in illuminating the path to peace as the most important achievement.[38] In *Leviathan*, Hobbes addresses the creator of a mortal god, of the greatest power on earth, a being who despite all that power cannot decode the intentions and motives of his fellows. Hobbes offers the reader a key to solve this problem: by considering one's own actions in relation to one's thoughts, opinions, reason, and passions, one can decipher the passions of other men in similar situations, since the objects of the passions may differ from one man to another, but the passions "are the same in all men."[39]

In the Preface to Book I of his *Discourses on Livy*, Machiavelli tells the reader that "[a]lthough this enterprise may be difficult, nonetheless, aided by those who have encouraged me to accept this burden, I believe I can carry it far enough so that a short road will remain for another to bring it to the destined place."[40] Only slightly more modest than in his previous treatise, Hobbes puts the matter in almost identical terms: the task at hand is harder than the mastery of any language or science, but with Hobbes's help, the reader will only have to consider "if he also find not the same in himself" because "this kind of Doctrine, admitteth no other Demonstration."[41] Recall that in Aubrey's anecdote, Euclid's appeal for Hobbes lay in the manner

---

[34] *T. Hobbes Malmesburiensis vita* (OL I: xv). Hobbes's explanation here also accounts for the decision to publish the work in English.

[35] Recall, for instance, the Epistle Dedicatory of the *Elements*, in which Hobbes declares it "an incomparable benefit to commonwealth, if every man held the opinions concerning law and policy" delivered in that treatise (p. xvi).

[36] Job 41:25 (41:34, KJV).

[37] *The Elements of Law*, I.5.14; *Leviathan*, Introduction: 2.

[38] *De Cive*, Pref., § 8.

[39] *Leviathan*, Introduction: 2. This is why Hobbes renders "nosce teipsum" as "read thyself," rather than "know thyself." On Hobbes's choice of term in relation to his method, see Strong, "How to Write Scripture," Silver, "A Matter of Interpretation," and Strong, "When Is a Text Not a Pretext?"

[40] Machiavelli, *Discourses on Livy*, I, Pref., § 2.

[41] *Leviathan*, Introduction: 2. On the similarity to Machiavelli, see Evrigenis, "Hobbes's Clockwork."

in which it allows the reader to become "demonstratively convinced" of the truth. Knowing that "men measure, not onely other men, but all other things, by themselves," Hobbes must allow each reader the space in which he can consider himself the measure of all things.[42]

Two further features of Hobbes's method are noteworthy. First, that it involves a thought experiment insofar as one is required to put oneself in another's shoes, if only to compare that hypothetical situation with one he has experienced himself. Second, it occurs in private. The reader is asked to consider the evidence by himself, on the basis of his experience, and come to his own conclusions. This isolation allows the reader to be more honest in his assessment than he might be in public, while at the same time affording him the option of distinguishing himself from most other men; the reader could grant that most men are vulgar or selfish without admitting, thereby, that he was either. This tendency to think oneself special would become one of Hobbes's criteria for effective equality, in *Leviathan* XIII. Equally importantly, however, as in the *Elements* and *De Cive*, it allows him to feel as though he were a witness, rather than the passive recipient of some authority's view, thereby continuing to accord him an epistemic status befitting his role as creator of the mortal god.[43] No other entreaty could entertain higher hopes of *captatio benevolentiæ*.

By appearing to put the author in the background – casting him as an aid rather than an authority – by presenting the argument without reliance on established authorities, such as Aristotle, and by inviting the reader to participate in the demonstration, a process of this sort has the added advantage of making one feel as though he were progressing toward the truth independently. It is important to remember, however, that just as Euclid guided Hobbes through the proof that rendered him demonstratively convinced of the truth, Hobbes is guiding his reader to the desired conclusion. Hobbes expressed his disbelief at having arrived at Euclid's conclusion, but a reexamination convinced him that the conclusion was sound. Not long after the publication of *Leviathan*, Hobbes wrote that his notorious book "hath framed the minds of a thousand gentlemen to a conscientious obedience to present government, which otherwise would have wavered in that point."[44] Hobbes knows that "all men by nature reason alike, and well, when they have good principles," which include the apt imposition of names and "a good and orderly Method."[45] These principles form the foundation of science, which Hobbes presents as the antidote to the absurdities emanating from abuses of speech, all of which conform to the impression that a civil philosophy so founded mirrors geometry.[46]

---

[42] *Leviathan*, II: 4.
[43] Farr thus writes aptly of the "sovereign reader" ("Atomes of Scripture," 185–88).
[44] *Six Lessons to the Professors of the Mathematics* (*EW*, VII: 336).
[45] *Leviathan*, V: 21.
[46] On abuses of speech, see *Leviathan*, IV: 13; on absurdities and science, V: 20–21, and cf. VIII: 39, on insignificant speech, and IV: 15, on geometry. Recall that in the latter, Hobbes

Every bit of *Leviathan*, however, cries out against this story. The title and frontispiece are not mere gimmicks, advertising the civil science that would follow, but accurate reflections of the sequence of metaphors, allegories, and imagery that dominate the rest of the work. Hobbes classifies metaphor as an abuse of speech, yet he does so in the midst of a series of allegories contained within that greatest of all his metaphors, Leviathan.[47] As we noted earlier, the passage from Job at the head of the frontispiece makes it clear that Hobbes wishes to use Leviathan as a symbol of irresistible power. Hobbes's attention, from the very beginning, to the problem of vainglory and conclusion that the solution to conflict rests with a power able to "keep all in awe," make the Book of Job – a book that Hobbes considers not a history, but a treatise on theodicy – an obvious source of symbolism.[48] Framed appropriately, the protagonists and main contours of the story could convey the essence of Hobbes's doctrine from the start, allowing him, in turn, to frame the minds of his readers toward conscientious obedience.

The way in which the subject matter of the opening chapters of *Leviathan* has been recast shows that everything is directed toward that goal. Dispensing very quickly with sense, Hobbes turns immediately to the mind. Therein, memories of particular instances of sense accumulate to make experience. The recollection of any one of these constitutes simple imagination. The combination of two or more makes for compounded imagination, which is the mechanism that enables the mind to conceive of a composite image like that of the frontispiece, but also that which makes vainglory possible. Hobbes notes that just as he who compounds the memory of a horse and of a man can envision a centaur, he who mixes his image of himself with the actions of another can come to see himself as a Hercules or an Alexander.[49]

More promising or dangerous is the process that Hobbes describes as a "*Consequence*, or TRAYNE of Thoughts," a "*Mental Discourse*," because the transition from one thought to the next is "not altogether so casuall as it seems to be."[50] Examples of "unguided" and "regulated" trains of thought show that the mind builds stories by connecting antecedents and consequents

declares geometry "the *onely* Science that it hath pleased God hitherto to bestow on mankind" (emphasis added), which confirms that whatever civil philosophy may be, it is not science. See Goldsmith, *Hobbes's Science of Politics*, 229, but cf. Sorell, *Hobbes*, 146.

[47] *Leviathan*, IV: 13. Most readers notice immediately that Hobbes's self-proclaimed hostility to such devices is odd in the face of his extended use of them. See, for example, Stillman, "Hobbes's *Leviathan*," 795–96, 807; Mintz, "Leviathan as Metaphor," 6–7; Shapiro, "Reading and Writing in Hobbes's *Leviathan*," 148; Springborg, "Hobbes's Biblical Beasts," 368. Not everyone does, though; in a discussion of metaphor, Cohen cites Hobbes's opposition to the device as emblematic, but does not mention the context in which Hobbes registers it ("Metaphor and the Cultivation of Intimacy"; cf. Hull, "'Against this *Empusa*,'" n. 44; Sorell, "Hobbes's UnAristotelian Political Rhetoric," 101–02).

[48] See, for example, *The Elements of Law*, I.9.1; I.19.4; II.1.8. On Job, see *Leviathan*, XXXIII: 202.

[49] *Leviathan*, II: 5–6.

[50] *Leviathan*, III: 8.

from its store of experience. Hobbes sums up regulated trains of thought as "seeking," since regardless of whether the starting point is the cause or the effect, the mind hunts for "the causes, of some effect, present or past; or of the effects, of some present or past cause."[51] A greater store of experience of cause-and-effect relationships thus makes it likelier that one will be able to get to where one wishes to go. Hobbes warns repeatedly that conjecture based on the past is nothing but a guess, since no amount of precedent will yield certainty about the future. His example is telling:

> he that hath seen by what courses and degrees, a flourishing State hath first come into civil warre, and then to ruine; upon the sight of the ruines of any other State, will guesse, the like warre, and the like courses have been there also. But this conjecture, has the same incertainty almost with the conjecture of the Future; both being grounded onely upon experience.[52]

Hobbes's aim, then, dictates that he speak to the reader's experience and imagination, in order to persuade him of the advantages of conscientious obedience and of the disadvantages of disobedience. By definition uncertain, such an appeal pertains not to science, but to prudence.[53]

The mechanism that allows the mind to connect antecedents to consequents is also at work in the satisfaction of one's desires, "[f]or the Thoughts, are to the Desires, as Scouts, and Spies, to range abroad, and find the way to the things Desired."[54] This logic of means and ends extends to the desires themselves, and paves the way for one of Hobbes's most notorious claims, that "there is no such *Finis ultimus*, (utmost ayme,) nor *Summum Bonum*, (greatest Good,) as is spoken of in the Books of the old Morall Philosophers."[55] Despite appearances, this is no mere declaration of relativism. First and foremost, it is the simple conclusion of the realization that human beings continue to experience desires as long as they are alive, and hence can never reach a point at which they can declare themselves satisfied once and for all.[56] This is thus no controversial description of insatiable monsters, but rather an account of beings whose most basic desires recur regularly, and require continuous satisfaction. So long as one lives, one will need to eat, and there is no way to ensure one's supply of food for the rest of one's life.[57] As Hobbes would put it in *De Homine*, "man is famished even

---

[51] "*Seeking*, or the faculty of Invention, which the Latines call *Sagacitas*, and *Solertia*" (*Leviathan*, III: 9–10).
[52] *Leviathan*, III: 11; cf. Thucydides, *Eight Bookes of the Peloponnesian Warre*, I.10, p. 7; *De Cive*, IX.14.
[53] *Leviathan*, V, esp. p. 22; cf. VIII: 34.
[54] *Leviathan*, VIII: 35.
[55] *Leviathan*, XI: 47.
[56] *Leviathan*, XI: 47; cf. VIII: 35.
[57] Hobbes argues that it is not the quest for a "more intensive delight," but rather the uncertainty regarding the preservation of one's present means that leads men to acquire more (*Leviathan*, XI: 47).

by future hunger."[58] Moving beyond these basic needs only adds to the multitude of desires one has to satisfy, prompting Hobbes to declare that there is in all mankind a "perpetuall and restlesse desire of Power after power, that ceaseth onely in Death."[59] This perpetual desire would suffice to turn a solitary and peace-seeking being into a menace for others, as it did for Cacus, who turned everything into a state of war.[60]

Hobbes's rejection of the *summum bonum*, however, is also the fullest articulation of a groundbreaking principle that allows him to claim for himself a new kind of civil philosophy. As we have seen already, the failure of previous political writers is evident in the persistence of the wars of the swords and of the pens.[61] The reason behind their failure lies in their futile attempts to persuade others that what they perceive as desirable ought to be universally acknowledged as a *summum bonum*. This, however, is impossible for both senses of the concept. First, because even though the passions are universal, the objects of the passions differ from one person to another, according to experience and circumstances, which means that no single thing can become the highest aim of all.[62] Second, the persistence of desire means that no single thing can ever become the final good for any one individual. To use Hobbes's metaphor from the *Elements*, life is an ongoing race that only ends for a runner when he forsakes it, in death.[63] In light of these assumptions, any attempt to find yet another *summum bonum* and try to persuade others to accept it as such is bound to end in frustration.[64]

Having identified the failure of the old moral philosophers in the Epistle Dedicatory to *De Cive*, Hobbes noted that the remedy lay in a proper starting point, one that he located in darkness.[65] Employing his fundamental technique of sharp contrasts, Hobbes then juxtaposed that darkness to the light that proper method could yield, thereby implying that the region that marked the start of his inquiry was the state of nature, a condition in which there is community of property. An examination of the consequences of such

---

[58] *De Homine*, X.3.

[59] *Leviathan*, XI: 47. Hobbes defines power as present means for the attainment of some apparent good (X: 41). On Hobbes's account of human nature, see Evrigenis, *Fear of Enemies and Collective Action*, 99–111.

[60] See Virgil, *Aeneid*, VIII.184–305; cf. Augustine, *Concerning the City of God against the Pagans*, XIX.12. As we will see, Hobbes refers to Cacus in his answer to the Preface to *Gondibert* (152–5[3]).

[61] *De Cive*, Ep. Ded., § 7; cf. *Leviathan*, XLIV: 333–34.

[62] *Leviathan*, Introduction: 2. Cf. *De Homine*, XI.4, where Hobbes elaborates on this matter, especially in relation to Aristotle (*OL*, II: 96–97); cf. Cicero, *De finibus*.

[63] *The Elements of Law*, I.9.21.

[64] Hobbes explains the difference between primary and secondary appetites, as well as the basic reasons why the objects of men's desires differ, even though their desires and their passions are the same, in *Leviathan*, VI (23–24).

[65] *De Cive*, Ep. Ded., § 8. The theme of darkness is repeated in the Preface to the Readers (§ 8).

a state led him to the realization that violent death is the greatest evil in nature, one that all men would seek to avoid.[66] The solution to the problem of consensus, then, lies not in the pointless pursuit of the *summum bonum*, but in agreement regarding the *summum malum*, a hindrance that is indifferent to values, standing in every man's way, no matter the good for which he is striving.[67] Rather than becoming entangled in a pointless effort to persuade others of the merits of a particular *summum bonum*, this approach counts on agreement on a prior level at which everyone can concur that war hinders the pursuit of all goods, and should thus be avoided.[68] Hence, peace emerges as a special kind of good, a prerequisite for the pursuit of other goods that could meet with universal approval, but not a *"Finis ultimus,* (utmost ayme,) nor *Summum Bonum,"* because of this very intermediary quality.[69]

Most people will not admit to fear in public, but Hobbes had no reservations about doing so, a confession that is rather unsurprising in light of his notorious statement in *Leviathan*, that the "Passion to be reckoned upon, is Fear."[70] There is a degree of fear for one's life that is so immediate and overpowering that the only natural reactions to it are fight or flight. For Hobbes, those reactions capture something that even a calmer and more detached assessment will grant, namely, that death is the supreme evil because it deprives one of the power to do anything else.[71] Indeed, as Hobbes pointed out in the note he added to *De Cive* on this topic, it is fear in this broader sense that he is interested in primarily, the kind that a reasonable reader who considered the prospects of satisfying his own desires could associate with readily. Hobbes had paved the way for this kind of appeal in *De Cive* through his very broad definition of fear, his provocative suggestion that great and lasting societies owe their foundation to men's mutual fear, and through the invocation of a series of examples of uncertain, if mundane, situations. His account in *Leviathan* of the qualities that enable men to live in peace and unity builds on those earlier appeals.[72] It offers the reader,

[66] *De Cive*, Ep. Ded., §§ 9–10: "*summum naturæ malum.*"
[67] See *Leviathan*, A Review and Conclusion, 396.
[68] See Sorell, "Hobbes's UnAristotelian Political Rhetoric," 106; "Hobbes Overcontextualized," 134.
[69] *Leviathan*, XI: 47.
[70] See *Thomæ Hobbesii Malmesburiensis vita*, 2:

> Atq; metum tantum concepit tunc mea mater,
> Ut pareret geminos, méque metúmque simul
>   (cf. Aubrey, 'Brief Lives,' I: 353; *Leviathan*, XIV: 70).

[71] *De Cive*, II.18: "timiditatis summus" over the "malum … maximum." Cf. "Of Liberty and Necessity," § 14.
[72] *Leviathan*, XI. In that chapter, Hobbes lists the fears of death, of wounds, of oppression, of being circumvented, of punishment, and of powers invisible. The latter, which is the cause of religion and superstition, explains the presence of Chapter XII, "Of Religion," in which the discussion of all manner of fear continues, and wherein Hobbes describes anxiety as

regardless of who he is or his circumstances, something that speaks to him, and prepares him to accept that "the Passions that encline men to Peace, are Feare of Death; Desire of such things as are necessary to commodious living; and a Hope by their Industry to obtain them."[73]

THE NATURAL CONDITION OF MANKIND

Hobbes's notorious discussion of the state of nature in *Leviathan* occurs in a chapter entitled *"Of the* NATURALL CONDITION *of Mankind, as concerning their Felicity, and Misery."*[74] Sufficiently different from its predecessors, this title already offers a foretaste of what is to follow. Whereas the equivalent section of the *Elements* spoke of the "condition of men in mere nature," and of the "estate and right of nature," and that of *De Cive* of the state of men without or outside civil society, respectively, *Leviathan* promises yet another contrast that will soon turn out to be deceptive, for in Hobbes's account that condition is one of nearly complete misery.[75]

Whereas Hobbes opened *De Cive* by emphasizing the importance of fear for the establishment of lasting civil societies, in *Leviathan* he returns to the model of the *Elements* and begins his account of the state of nature by explaining why it is a condition of effective equality. Although in essence the arguments Hobbes offers in *Leviathan* are based on those of the *Elements*, the language of the later work is different in subtle, yet important ways. Where its predecessor is succinct and detached, as one would expect a scientific treatise to be, *Leviathan* spells things out. For example, in the *Elements* Hobbes writes of the weaker destroying the power of the stronger, whereas in *Leviathan* he changes it to strength enough to kill. Thus, Hobbes acknowledges that some men are "manifestly stronger in body, or of quicker mind" than others, but notes that such differences are insufficient to render one so predominant as to guarantee his supremacy over others.[76] Hobbes's argument seems compelling: however great the difference, the weakest can kill

---

follows: "it is impossible for a man, who continually endeavoureth to secure himselfe against the evill he feares, and procure the good he desireth, not to be in a perpetuall solicitude of the time to come." Thus, "every man, especially those that are provident, are in an estate like to that of *Prometheus*" (XII: 52).

[73] *Leviathan*, XIII: 63. Hobbes sets the stage for this list in Chapter XI.

[74] *Leviathan*, XIII: 60.

[75] Cf. Hoekstra, "Hobbes on the Natural Condition of Mankind," 109. The former is the title given to *Elements* I.14 and I.15 collectively, and the latter the title of I.14, in the table of contents of the manuscripts. Individual chapters of the *Elements* are only given titles in the table of contents (see Devonshire Mss., Chatsworth HS/A/2A; HS/A/2B; HS/A/2C; British Library Mss., Egerton 2005, Harl. 1325, 4235, 4236, 6858).

[76] *Leviathan*, XIII: 60. Recall that according to Hobbes's own summary, *Leviathan* sought to teach his compatriots the need for an army that was "satis magnus" to compel them to concord (*T. Hobbes Malmesburiensis vita* [OL, I: xv]).

the strongest, "either by secret machination or by confederacy with others, that are in the same danger with himselfe."[77]

More remarkable, however, is Hobbes's argument for effective equality in the qualities of the mind. This side of things, which was given short shrift in the *Elements*, where it was lumped together with strength, is now a far more important part of the argument. Here, Hobbes observes that when it comes to the faculties of the mind, there is "yet a greater equality amongst men, than that of strength."[78] The reason is that not science, but prudence informs human conduct, and prudence is "but Experience; which equall time, equally bestowes on all men, in those things they equally apply themselves unto."[79] If this statement seems overly optimistic in light of Hobbes's consistent reservations regarding most men's ability to comprehend what they read and reason properly from it, it bears repeating that *Leviathan* is addressed to the children of pride.

Where the *Elements* suggested meekly that men "ought to admit amongst themselves equality; and that he that claimeth no more, may be esteemed moderate," *Leviathan* emphasizes vanity.[80] Hobbes knows that most will refuse to concede that men are by nature effectively equal, because of

a vain conceipt of ones owne wisdome, which almost all men think they have in a greater degree, than the Vulgar; that is, than all men but themselves, and a few others, whom by Fame, or for concurring with themselves, they approve. For such is the nature of men, that howsoever they may acknowledge many others to be more witty, or more eloquent, or more learned; Yet they will hardly believe there be many so wise as themselves: For they see their own wit at hand, and other mens at a distance. But this proveth rather that men are in that point equall, than unequall. For there is not ordinarily a greater signe of the equall distribution of any thing, than that every man is contented with his share.[81]

Knowing that "there are very few so foolish, that had not rather governe themselves, than be governed by others," Hobbes needs to address every reader – not just Charles II – as though he were a ruler, regardless of how

---

[77] *Leviathan*, XIII: 60.
[78] *Leviathan*, XIII: 60.
[79] *Leviathan*, XIII: 60–61. Cf. *The Elements of Law*, I.8.13, where Hobbes distinguishes between experience and science, and offers arguments that show why seditious behavior contravenes both. Hobbes's distinction and emphasis on the arguments from science should not divert attention away from the fact that, even if meaningful, on the question of sedition the distinction is of no practical import. Cf. *De Homine*, XI.10.
[80] *The Elements of Law*, I.14.2.
[81] *Leviathan*, XIII: 61. Cf. *ibid.*, XXVII: 154; XXX: 176; *De Cive*, Pref., § 3; recall *The Elements of Law*, II.8.13: "For generally, not he that hath skill in geometry, or any other science speculative, but only he that understandeth what conduceth to the good and government of the people, is called a wise man." In *The Prince*, Machiavelli argues, "[f]or the vulgar are taken in by the appearance and the outcome of a thing, and in the world there is no one but the vulgar" (XVIII: 71).

modest he might be, for he is, after all, the creator of Leviathan.[82] Hobbes's approach preserves the theoretical possibility that only a few men are vainglorious and think themselves better than their fellows. This move is necessitated by the very vanity in question, which causes one to see oneself as reasonable, even as one recognizes unreasonable, vainglorious behavior in others. Here, too, the logic of Hobbes's argument is compelling, for it does not matter whether men are *in fact* equal by nature, but only that they be treated as though they were. The reason is that if they are, then their equality should be acknowledged, but if they are not, then the desire of those who are inferior and yet think themselves the equals of others will lead them to require that they be treated as such, and prudence would require that everyone else oblige them.

Hobbes's indifference to whether equality actually obtains in the state of nature is crucial, for it demonstrates that the issue is primarily one of perception, rather than fact. His suggestion in the *Elements* that men "ought to admit amongst themselves equality" sounded either like an appropriate response to evidence of equality, or like a normative appeal. His explanation of the same facts in *Leviathan* is more persuasive, precisely because it takes seriously both vanity in general and the reader's own assessment of himself. Yet, most important is his effort to draw the reader's attention to the fact that whether equality obtains or not, presumption of equality is enough to render it relevant. Hence, regardless of whether men are in fact equal, the ninth law of nature requires that each man acknowledge others as equal by nature, and "breach of this Precept is *Pride*."[83]

It is not hard to see how an environment populated by beings whose desires are perpetual, whose abilities are more or less equal, and who must in any case treat others as though they were equal, will amount to a condition of continuous uncertainty. Where even a single man constitutes a threat to the fruits of one's labor, life, and liberty, one would do well to expect opportunistic gangs to come after him as well.[84] The absence of a reliable authority that can put an end to such threats, however, means that along with his victim's seat and goods, the successful invader will also inherit the fear that he will be next.[85] In an attempt to free himself from the diffidence of this condition, one must anticipate, that is, one must augment

[82] *Leviathan*, XV: 77.
[83] *Leviathan*, XV: 77.
[84] Recall that in *De Cive*, Hobbes argues that temporary alliances enable men in the state of nature to pursue particular goals, but points out that those alliances are a far cry from the reliable protection of large and lasting societies. See, for example, *De Cive*, I.2, note to "Born fit" (*fœdera*), and I.13 (*socii*). The suggestion recurs in Hobbes's argument regarding effective physical equality, which results from confederacies among those who are exposed to common enemies (*Leviathan*, XIII: 60; cf. Evrigenis, *Fear of Enemies and Collective Action*, 111–26).
[85] *Leviathan*, XIII: 61.

one's power by any means possible, until there is no power sufficient to threaten him.[86]

Yet, so long as actors continue to acknowledge the effective equality of the state of nature, this threshold will be impossible to meet, either because no accumulation of power will be sufficiently reliable, or because prudence will demand that the significance of the remaining threats be exaggerated. Returning to his fundamental distinction between the moderate and the vainglorious, Hobbes shows that the logic of the situation compels everyone to do more than he might be inclined to do. Some, he notes, take pleasure in their own power and conquest, and will hence pursue them "farther than their security requires."[87] Their presence in turn forces the moderate to join the arms race and go farther than they would otherwise be inclined to go, since doing nothing in the face of aggressive expansionism would leave them vulnerable to the vainglorious.

In assessing this condition, Hobbes draws a polemical conclusion: "men have no pleasure, (but on the contrary a great deale of griefe) in keeping company, where there is no power able to over-awe them all."[88] Extreme though it may sound, this assertion is justified by the psychology on which it is founded. Hobbes notes that every man "looketh that his companion should value him, at the same rate he sets upon himselfe."[89] The recognition that there are moderate and vainglorious men should lead to the conclusion that the value sought from others would depend on one's assessment of one's own worth, so that the vainglorious would seek more appreciation than they deserve, but the moderate only an appropriate amount. As in the case of power, however, the logic of equality renders the one type offensive to the other, for the moderate would remind the vainglorious that men are equal, but the vainglorious would complain of not receiving the recognition that befits their greatness from the moderate.[90] The outcome is secured by Hobbes's great insight, that human beings "hardly believe there be many so wise as themselves: For they see their own wit at hand, and other mens at a distance."[91] The discrepancy between one's fuller view of one's own abilities and the partial view of other people's abilities thus ensures that even the perfectly moderate individual – if such a being existed – might still misjudge his worth and, with it, the adequacy of other people's appreciation of it. Hobbes's repeated emphasis on the numerous other ways in which one can reach wrong conclusions only reinforces the sense that there are too

---

[86] *Leviathan*, XIII: 61. The possible means include force and wiles. This type of behavior, notes Hobbes, "is no more than his conservation requireth, and is generally allowed."

[87] *Leviathan*, XIII: 61.

[88] *Leviathan*, XIII: 61.

[89] *Leviathan*, XIII: 61.

[90] These signals are likeliest to emerge as these individuals pursue their natural right, since the vainglorious will consider any amount of appropriation by others excessive.

[91] *Leviathan*, XIII: 61.

many uncertainties in this environment to ever allow one to let down one's guard fully.[92]

Reverting back to the language of the opening of the *Elements*, where "natural condition" referred to human nature, Hobbes identifies three principal causes of conflict: "First, Competition; Secondly, Diffidence; Thirdly, Glory."[93] Without "a common Power to keep them all in awe," individuals who have reasons to assume that others pose a threat to their well-being find themselves in the condition of a war of "every man, against every man."[94] This pronouncement has been the source of substantial criticism. Hobbes had written of a war of all against all repeatedly in *De Cive*, and several commentators interpreted the extremism of his assertion as part of his polemic against the Aristotelian tradition of natural sociability.[95] This is not, however, the asocial battle cry that it has been taken to be. First, because as we have seen already, the state of nature is not a condition devoid of cooperation and collective action, but merely one in which whatever cooperation comes about is serendipitous and cannot be relied on to last.[96] Second, because it is based on Hobbes's idiosyncratic definition of war, which is even broader than his definition of fear:

> For WARRE, consisteth not in Battell onely, or the act of fighting; but in a tract of time, wherein the Will to contend by Battell is sufficiently known: and therefore the notion of *Time*, is to be considered in the nature of Warre; as it is in the nature of Weather. For as the nature of Foule weather, lyeth not in a showre or two of rain; but in an inclination thereto of many dayes together: So the nature of War, consisteth not in actuall fighting; but in the known disposition thereto, during all the time there is no assurance to the contrary. All other time is PEACE.[97]

The difficulties involved in reading correctly the motives of others, and in interpreting the significance of their actions and postures, leaves individuals

[92] See, for example, *The Elements of Law*, I.2.10, I.5.1–5, I.5.7, I.5.14, I.13.1–2; *De Cive*, I.5; as well as Hobbes's account of the formation of the will, especially in "Of Liberty and Necessity," § 11. One's ability to discern another's motives is complicated by the fact that the process of appetites and aversions that lead to an outcome constitutes a black box, about which one can tell several more or less plausible stories, but still never be sure that any one of those corresponds to the truth. See Evrigenis, *Fear of Enemies and Collective Action*, 110.

[93] *Leviathan*, XIII: 61; cf. *ibid.*, XXX: 179. As Slomp points out, this list represents Hobbes's version of Thucydides' "three greatest things" (I.76): honor, fear, and profit ("Hobbes, Thucydides, and the Three Greatest Things").

[94] *Leviathan*, XIII: 62; cf. *ibid.*, XIV: 68–69, XVII: 85–87.

[95] See, for example, *De Cive*, Pref., § 14, I.13, V.2.

[96] For a full account of the evidence against this common misperception, see Hoekstra, *Thomas Hobbes and the Creation of Order*, Part I.

[97] *Leviathan*, XIII: 62; cf. *ibid.*, XVIII: 91: "For those men that are so remissely governed, that they dare take up Armes, to defend, or introduce an Opinion, are still in Warre; and their condition not Peace, but only a Cessation of Armes for feare of one another; and they live as it were, in the procincts of battaile continually;" *De Cive*, I.2, note to "The mutuall fear;" *De Cive*, XIII.7.

unsure as to the extent to which someone constitutes a threat. For this reason, in examining the consequences of effective equality, Hobbes argued that even moderate individuals will be compelled to exercise prudence. Hobbes describes this condition of uncertainty as a war of all against all because it lacks the *"assurance"* that something that appears threatening is, in fact, not. His explanation thus casts the frontispiece of *Leviathan* under a different light. The multiple evidence of a disposition to fighting, as evidenced in the sovereign's posture, the numerous fortifications, drills, and men of war, and symbolized aptly by the clouds of foul weather over the sovereign's head, show that the eerily peaceful scene below is not simply one of peace, but that war – as defined by Hobbes – is in fact all around.

That contrast between peace and war thus signals the culmination of Hobbes's numerous antitheses. Having begun with reason and the passions, and gone through the opposition between the mathematicians and the dogmatists, the Indians of America and his Northern European contemporaries, Hobbes has arrived at the antithesis that can convey readily how much felicity lies in the inconveniences of order, by painting a vivid picture of the misery that accompanies disorder. When all one can do is attempt to decipher the signals of others for oneself, and rely only on one's own means for security, then one finds oneself in a condition in which,

there is no place for Industry; because the fruit thereof is uncertain: and consequently no Culture of the Earth; no Navigation, nor use of the commodities that may be imported by Sea; no commodious Building; no Instruments of moving, and removing such things as require much force; no Knowledge of the face of the Earth; no account of Time; no Arts; no Letters; no Society; and which is worst of all, continuall feare, and danger of violent death; And the life of man, solitary, poore, nasty, brutish, and short.[98]

Although clearly based on Hobbes's list of what separates civilization from "the wildest of the Indians," in the *Elements*, this list reflects Hobbes's increasing dependence on the *summum malum*.[99]

The two lists have four items in common, with only minor differences: navigation, building, an account of time, and knowledge of the face of the earth.[100] In accordance with the work's scientific tone, the list of the *Elements* focuses on benefits that can be portrayed in the technical language that Hobbes uses to describe the neat and methodical activities of the mathematicians. Everything on that list flows from mathematics and geometry: activities such as navigation, cartography, horology, astronomy, and architecture, described with terms such as "division," "measuring," "plains," and

---

[98] *Leviathan*, XIII: 62.
[99] *The Elements of Law*, I.13.3.
[100] In the *Elements*, the account of time is joined with "foresight of the course of heaven" (I.13.3). The formulation regarding the benefits of navigation is a little more explicit in *Leviathan* (XIII: 62).

"solids." What the practical benefits of these activities are is not hard to imagine, but just to be sure, Hobbes fixes the opposite end of the spectrum among the wildest of the Indians. The list itself, however, contains nothing of the messiness of human life, with its disagreements and conflicts, all of which he has consigned to the world of the dogmatists.

In *Leviathan*, by contrast, the list is more extensive. It is filled with examples of the benefits of order, the trappings of commodious living, and the makings of felicity – except that this time around Hobbes lists them as missing. The first important change to the list is thus the addition, before each item, of the word "no." Spelling out what their absence means for the life of the reader, Hobbes rules out industry, since there is no point to investing in something that might be snatched away at any moment. Those unfortunate enough to find themselves in this condition have no time for activities that promise a payoff far into the future, and hence will see no benefit in cultivating the earth, or bothering with tasks so demanding as to require planning, preparation, and complicated implements. All those activities that enrich life in society, but which cannot point to any immediate contribution to security, are thus cast aside, leaving this barren landscape not only without arts and letters, but even without society itself. Trapped in the mindset that Hobbes has been analyzing, an individual who is surrounded by others whom he sees as capable of inflicting harm on him, but lacking a defender whose protection would free him of these constraints, is saddled with the "worst of all," the *summum malum*, a "continuall feare, and danger of violent death."[101]

Given Hobbes's diagnosis of the shortcomings of arguments based on some conception of the *summum bonum*, and his proposition that common ground might be found on the *summum malum*, his task here is to persuade the reader that where the danger of violent death looms and fear reigns, life is "solitary, poore, nasty, brutish, and short," making for a condition that ought to be avoided at all costs. To do so, he must first persuade him that such a condition is possible. Then, he must persuade him that it is probable and, hence, worth taking seriously as he contemplates his political options. To make matters more difficult, Hobbes must do all this in a way that is memorable so that the reader may carry the lesson of the state of nature with him every time he considers what the best course of action – or inaction – might be. Perhaps the greatest difficulty, however, is to do so for *every* reader. Recall that according to Hobbes's analysis of the *summum bonum*, one of the two chief difficulties lies in one's inability to persuade different individuals with different goals to pursue one and the same object.

[101] *Leviathan*, XIII: 62. As Hobbes goes on to show in Chapter XXIV, the relationship between industry and security is mutually reinforcing. While in the state of nature security is necessary for industry, it is industry that nourishes and sustains the commonwealth, allowing it to grow, and thereby ensures that it can fulfill its role as the provider and guarantor of security.

The most important changes between the earlier accounts of the state of nature and that of *Leviathan* are those that attempt to address these concerns. Hobbes paved the way by putting the reader in a diffident mood through his compelling account of effective equality, and by emphasizing the *summum malum*. Hardly anything in the first half of *Leviathan* XIII is new, but everything is now negative. Hobbes's powerful description of the misery of this condition succeeds in capturing and holding the reader's attention. Yet, the reader wonders, is man's natural condition "solitary, poore, nasty, brutish, and short?" Even if it were, what significance should that have for him? Hobbes's meager references to actual manifestations of the state of nature in his earlier works indicate an awareness of the problem of its status and a willingness to assuage the reader's concerns. Chapter XIII of *Leviathan* indicates that in his previous works Hobbes had underestimated the difficulty involved in persuading the reader that the state of nature is a condition worth taking seriously.

As we know from his translation of Thucydides and *De Cive*, Hobbes sought feedback from readers and amended his works in order to address their concerns.[102] The most substantial change to his account of the state of nature in *Leviathan* comes in the form of three paragraphs devoted to manifestations of that condition. The volume and richness of these examples is their first notable characteristic. Equally important and telling is the fact that in the first two of these paragraphs Hobbes gives voice to the reader's concern explicitly. The first takes up the basic objection of a reader who, raised on the vaguely scholastic principle of human sociability, might find Hobbes's description of human nature fundamentally mistaken: "It may seem strange to some man, that has not well weighed these things; that Nature should thus dissociate, and render men apt to invade, and destroy one another."[103] Therein Hobbes describes the preceding analysis as an "Inference, made from the Passions," and urges the reader who mistrusts it to confirm it "by Experience."[104]

Hobbes's use of "mistrust" and "experience" here is interesting, for it calls to mind the statement regarding his method that he made at the beginning of the *Elements*. Recall that there Hobbes promised to "put such principles down for a foundation, as passion not mistrusting, may not seek to displace," and proceeded to explain what that entails: "But intending not to take any principle upon trust, but only to put men in mind of what they know already, or may know by their own experience, I hope to err the less."[105] The reader who considers Hobbes's step-by-step analysis of effective

---

[102] See, for example, *Eight Bookes of the Peloponnesian Warre*, Preface to the Readers; Aubrey, 'Brief Lives,' I: 365; *De Cive*, Pref., § 24.

[103] *Leviathan*, XIII: 62.

[104] *Leviathan*, XIII: 62.

[105] *The Elements of Law*, Ep. Ded., xv; I.1.2.

equality and its consequences might find himself in the paradoxical position of reaching a conclusion that contravenes the widespread belief, itself supported by weighty authority, that men are by nature social. To persuade the reader that that inference from the passions ought to be trusted, Hobbes refers him to experience, which corroborates his claims. Repeating a series of examples of the most mundane but telling precautions, examples that he had also invoked in the Preface to *De Cive*, Hobbes urges the reader to consider what his own actions say about his view of mankind. To travel, the reader arms himself and brings company. In his own home, and despite the protection of his sovereign, he nevertheless locks his doors and chests.[106] The reader's actions speak louder than Hobbes's words, but both point in the same direction.

Still, even if accepted, this argument and the appeal to experience merely confirm that prudence and precautions are the necessary consequences of uncertainty. This hardly amounts to a war of all against all. Once again, Hobbes gives a voice to these objections: "It may peradventure be thought, there was never such a time, nor condition of warre as this;" his answer is puzzling: "I believe it was never generally so, over all the world: but there are many places, where they live so now."[107] Hobbes offers three examples to prove the latter part of his assertion. The first is the familiar case of the "savage people in many places of *America*," whom he describes as having no government other than that of small families, and hence live in the kind of "brutish manner" he described earlier.[108] The second is no longer that of the savage ancestors of civilized nations, as in the previous two works, but the much more powerful and relevant example of those who have made the dreadful leap from peaceful government to civil war, as Hobbes's compatriots and many of his readers in the rest of Europe had.[109] The term that Hobbes uses to describe this transition – "degenerate" – and the example itself are, once again, indicative of the centrality of the *summum malum*. Whereas in the case of the savage ancestors the contrast was between an earlier condition that was worse and a later condition that is better, in the case of civil wars, the reader is asked to imagine the opposite. In addition to referring to a state of affairs that his readers were still experiencing at first hand, this example parallels the structure of the state of nature, which

---

[106] *Leviathan*, XIII: 62; cf. *De Cive*, Pref., § 11. As he had in *De Cive*, Hobbes notes that this diagnosis does not constitute an indictment of human nature since these actions are not sins, nor violations of the law until a law exists that forbids them.

[107] *Leviathan*, XIII: 63.

[108] *Leviathan*, XIII: 63. Hobbes's use of the term "families" here is consistent with his contemporaries' and refers to the fact that clans and other kinship groups constituted the primary forms of political organization among Native Americans, especially in the East. Explorers often used the term "family" as a synonym for "nation" (see, for example, Smith, *The Generall Historie of Virginia, New-England, and the Summer Isles*, 23, 214).

[109] Cf. *Leviathan*, XVIII: 94; XXI: 107.

in Hobbes's theory is not an account of how the commonwealth came into being, but rather an exercise in privation yielding an account of what life without the commonwealth would be like.[110] As Hobbes would argue in *De Homine*, this approach is more effective because regaining a good that has been lost is better than not having lost it, since the memory of the evil suffered makes one appreciate it all the more.[111]

Hobbes's third and most powerful example centers on the image of sovereigns in the posture of gladiators, which Hobbes introduced in *De Cive* XVII, and which became the center of *Leviathan*'s frontispiece. Hobbes argues that even if individual men were never "in a condition of warre one against another;

> yet in all times, Kings, and Persons of Soveraigne authority, because of their Independency, are in continuall jealousies, and in the state and posture of Gladiators; having their weapons pointing, and their eyes fixed on one another; that is, their Forts, Garrisons, and Guns upon the Frontiers of their Kingdomes; and continuall Spyes upon their neighbours, which is a posture of War.[112]

The existence of sovereigns willing and able to assume this posture has a transformative impact on the lives of the individuals under their protection. Hobbes explains that "because they uphold thereby, the Industry of their Subjects; there does not follow from it, that misery, which accompanies the Liberty of particular men."[113]

This last caveat is crucial. It clarifies Hobbes's puzzling assertion at the start of the paragraph: it is because they are the subjects of sovereigns that individuals are never in a condition of war one against another.[114] In his account of effective equality, Hobbes makes a persuasive case for why an anarchic condition in which individuals must provide for their own security, and in which, even if they manage to cooperate with others, they can never *rely* on their help, will be miserable. Itself anarchic, the state of nature inhabited by sovereigns such as the one who adorns the frontispiece of *Leviathan* is a condition in which a certain amount of felicity is possible, precisely because in it effective equality and its consequences no longer obtain. To envisage how this might come about, one need not engage in complicated ratiocinations of the sort that have discovered in Hobbes the precursor to the prisoner's dilemma.[115] Hobbes explains how even the most prudent and

[110] See Sorell, *Hobbes*, 146–47; Hoekstra, *Thomas Hobbes and the Creation of Order*, Part I.
[111] *De Homine*, XI.14.
[112] *Leviathan*, XIII: 63.
[113] *Leviathan*, XIII: 63.
[114] Hobbes's puzzling assertion here reproduces, in essence, his response to Bramhall regarding the state of nature (*Questions Concerning Liberty, Necessity, and Chance*, EW, V: 183–84). Cf. *De Cive*, I.10, note to "In the meere state of Nature."
[115] For a survey and assessment of the voluminous literature that goes down this path, see Eggers, "Hobbes and Game Theory Revisited," although Eggers is overly optimistic regarding the utility of applying the perspective of game theory to Hobbes.

hesitant of individuals, in conditions of absolute equality, will sooner or later discern the benefits of collective action by focusing on a common enemy.[116]

Imagine, for instance, a scenario involving three effectively equal individuals – A, B, and C – in which C routinely attacks the others. Even if A were extremely diffident, the realization that C also attacks B would have a transformative effect on his calculus. Upon the occasion of a fight between B and C, A could also attack C, thereby putting an end to equality, and making clear the benefits of inequality to all. The hypothetical statement by every man to every man that results in the unity of the commonwealth demonstrates that third parties are crucial to the individual's calculus in the state of nature.[117] Every individual in that situation gives up the right to govern himself not in the abstract, but to a third party, and this is the reason why that hypothetical agreement is *not* a covenant of mutual trust.[118] The establishment of a lasting association that can provide reliable security frees individuals of the need to worry about their safety and the fruits of their labor. Their ability to engage in industry under the protection of the sovereign in turn allows the sovereign to grow. A greater sense of security will result in greater industry, and greater industry in greater strength.[119] Anarchy without equality means that bodies politic can become radically unequal, and therefore, the dynamics of international relations are not those of the state of nature writ small.[120]

The domain in which sovereigns assume the posture of gladiators and enable their subjects' pursuit of commodious living thus marks the boundary between the state of nature and civil society. Partaking of both, this example marks the culmination of Hobbes's attempt to persuade the reader of the "misery, which accompanies the Liberty of particular men," by portraying such a condition in a possible, probable, and memorable manner.[121] If a few of Hobbes's readers could relate to the uncertainties and liabilities of life in America, most could certainly understand the horrors of civil war, and all could grasp readily the difference between peace and war, in which force and fraud are the cardinal virtues.[122] Unlike the anodyne contrast between the mathematicians and dogmatists, and the blurry one between

---

[116] *The Elements of Law*, I.19.6; I.19.8. Cf. Evrigenis, *Fear of Enemies and Collective Action*, 120–26.

[117] *Leviathan*, XVII: 87.

[118] *Leviathan*, XIV: 68.

[119] In his introductory metaphor, Hobbes describes the "*Wealth* and *Riches* of all the particular members" as the "*Strength*" of the body politic (*Leviathan*, Introduction: 1).

[120] Certain conditions, however, remain the same. For instance, Hobbes argues that "every Soveraign hath the same Right, in procuring the safety of his People, that any particular man can have, in procuring his own safety," and adds that "the same Law, that dictateth to men that have no Civil Government, what they ought to do, and what to avoyd in regard of one another, dictateth the same to Common-wealths, that is to the Consciences of Soveraign Princes, and Soveraign Assemblies ..." (*Leviathan*, XXX: 185).

[121] *Leviathan*, XIII: 63.

[122] *Leviathan*, XIII: 63. Cf. *De Cive*, Pref., § 2.

reason and the passions, the contrast between peace and war appeals with urgency to the "Passions that encline men to Peace, ... Fear of Death; Desire of such things as are necessary to commodious living; and a Hope by their Industry to obtain them."[123] It is to the destinations set by these passions that reason charts the course, using means wherever they may be found.

EPIC POETRY

As Hobbes was writing *Leviathan*, a fellow exile, Sir William Davenant, was composing his epic poem, *Gondibert*. The two men were in close contact during this time, and Hobbes performed for Davenant that service that he himself valued greatly: he read and critiqued *Gondibert* "daylie," as Davenant was composing it.[124] Davenant valued Hobbes's assistance to such an extent that he effectively dedicated the work to him, by addressing its Preface to Hobbes. In return, Hobbes composed an answer to Davenant's Preface, in which he comments on *Gondibert*, but also sets forth his view of poetry.[125] Based on Hobbes's description of his own project and his conception of civil philosophy, one would expect to find nothing in Hobbes's view of poetry that might be relevant to *Leviathan*. Yet, Hobbes's answer to Davenant is striking for the degree to which it breaks down the barrier between the epic poem and the political treatise.[126] In his answer to Davenant, Hobbes confesses that *Gondibert* leaves him with the impression that the poet has seen "a curious kind of perspectiue, where, he that lookes through a short hollow pipe, vpon a picture conteyning diuerse figures, sees none of those that are there paynted, but some one person made vp of their partes."[127]

---

[123] *Leviathan*, XIII: 63; cf. *ibid.*, XIV: 70. See also Hobbes's definition of safety and, therefore, of the office of the sovereign (*ibid.*, XXX: 175).

[124] Davenant, *The Preface to Gondibert*, 1; cf., Martinich, *Hobbes: A Biography*, 210–12. Malcolm considers it probable that Hobbes's acquaintance with Davenant "dated back to the 1630s" (*Aspects of Hobbes*, 243).

[125] Davenant's Preface and Hobbes's answer to it were published together in 1650. *Gondibert* was published in 1651 (see Macdonald and Hargreaves, *Thomas Hobbes: A Bibliography*, nos. 38–40).

[126] Defining the epic tradition as "political theory which is inspired mainly by the hope of achieving a great and memorable deed through the medium of thought," Wolin classifies Hobbes as an epic political theorist, and thus characterizes not only *Leviathan*, but all of Hobbes's works as examples of epic political thought ("Hobbes and the Epic Tradition of Political Theory," 4). On *Leviathan* and Gondibert, in particular, see Miller's insightful examination focusing on audiences ("The Uniqueness of *Leviathan*," esp. 81–89). As we will see, there is a basis for considering *Leviathan* an epic work even on the much narrower definition that Hobbes offers in regard to poetry. As Hoekstra points out, Hobbes "thinks that the point of philosophy is to change people's opinions, and thus to change the world" ("The End of Philosophy," 31). Harrison includes Hobbes in a group of thinkers for whom "science and philosophy are still conceived to be one thing, and that thing not remote from poetry" ("Bacon, Hobbes, Boyle, and the Ancient Atomists," 192).

[127] *Answer to the Preface to Gondibert*, 159. On a possible inspiration behind Hobbes's description of this contraption, see Malcolm, *Aspects of Hobbes*, 201–02, 217, 222.

Hobbes admits to Davenant that *Gondibert* produced in his imagination "an effect not vnlike it."[128] That this perspective would have appealed to Hobbes, given his description of the union of a multitude as the institution of a body politic and its transformation into one person, is clear.[129] More interesting is the fact that at the time when he was setting down these reflections for Davenant, Hobbes was at work on his own version of this image, the body politic of *Leviathan*.

Faced with an innovative work, which defies classification according to strict criteria, Hobbes begins his answer to Davenant in a familiar way. Despite declaring himself an "incompetent" witness when it comes to poetry, he boldly breaks it down to "neither more nor lesse than six sorts," and argues that *Gondibert* is an epic poem, even though its form is that of a tragedy.[130] The poet's task, according to Hobbes, is "by imitating humane life, in delightfull and measur'd lines, to auert men from vice, and encline them to vertuous and honorable actions."[131] Still, one should not be fooled by the form in which something is written, for not all verse is poetry, just as not all poetry comes in verse. Lucretius was no poet, but a natural philosopher, Theognis a moralist, and Lucan a historian.[132]

Unsurprisingly, given his own aversion to authority for its own sake, Hobbes admires Davenant's irreverent procedure. Using his own reason, rather than following the "fashion of precedent times," Davenant avoids empty and possibly dangerous gestures, such as the invocation of a muse, and thus produces noble poetry, which seeks to "adorne vertue, and procure her Louers."[133] Hobbes notes that it made sense for the ancient poets – themselves divines and prophets, who exercised spiritual authority over the people – to invoke a muse, since that was consonant with their religion.[134] Even when they are made in the right context, however, such invocations can be dangerous in the hands of "unskillfull Coniurers," raising cruelty instead of zeal, discord instead of truth, fraud instead of wisdom, tumult instead of reformation, and controversy instead of religion.[135] Fully consonant with Hobbes's contrasts between reasonable, orderly procedure and self-interested, passionate preaching, this list of right and wrong outcomes is perhaps unsurprising in its emphasis on peace. What is arresting, however, is Hobbes's equation of truth with concord. That concord and truth are synonymous means not simply that when the truth is discovered there is no

---

[128] *Answer to the Preface to Gondibert*, 159.
[129] See, for example, *The Elements of Law*, II.1.2.
[130] *Answer to the Preface to Gondibert*, 130, 132.
[131] *Answer to the Preface to Gondibert*, 130.
[132] *Answer to the Preface to Gondibert*, 133. It is because verse has an advantage in "delightfulnesse" over prose that most poetry is in verse (133–34).
[133] *Answer to the Preface to Gondibert*, 139.
[134] *Answer to the Preface to Gondibert*, 139.
[135] *Answer to the Preface to Gondibert*, 139–40.

disagreement, but also that since truth is the aim of philosophy, the aim of
civil philosophy is concord.[136]

Far from inimical to the pursuit of everything good on that list, noble
poetry can come to the aid of truth, as it had when with allegories and verse
it protected civil philosophy from becoming defiled by *"the disputations of
private men."*[137] Consistently, from the translation of Thucydides, through
the *Elements*, *De Cive*, and *Leviathan*, Hobbes insists that experience is the
essential prerequisite to prudence. From the store of memory, which consists of one's experiences, arise judgment and fancy. The former provides the
strength and structure of a poem, and the latter its ornaments. This, according to Hobbes, is the reason why the ancients made memory the mother of
the Muses,

> For memory is the World (though not really, yet so as in a looking glasse) in which
> the Iudgment the seuerer Sister busieth her selfe in a graue and rigide examination
> of all the parts of Nature, and in registring by Letters, their order, causes, vses, dif-
> ferences and resemblances; Whereby the Fancy, when any worke of Art is to be
> performed, findeth her materials at hand and prepared for vse, and needes no more
> than a swift motion ouer them, that what she wants, and is there to be had, may not
> lye too long unespied.[138]

Fancy is able to "fly from one Indies to the other, and from Heauen to Earth,
and to penetrate into the hardest matter, and obscurest places," not because
of swiftness, but because of "copious Imagery discreetly ordered, and perfectly registred in the memory."[139]

The two processes are obviously not identical. Judgment works hard
and slowly, whereas fancy flies. The former yields philosophy, the latter
sometimes leads men to grossly mistake philosophy and "embrace contention in her place."[140] When, however, fancy has traced the "wayes of true
Philosophy, … it hath produced very maruellous effects to the benefit of
mankind."[141] To the reader acquainted with Hobbes's political treatises,
these are well known: "All that is bewtifull or defensible in buildinge; or

---

[136] Hoekstra rightly points out that if Hobbes takes peace to be the lowest common denomina-
tor among the multitude of conceptions of the *summum bonum*, then his desire for peace
could be "independent of, and perhaps even in tension with, a philosophy with truth as
its primary aim" ("The End of Philosophy," 32; cf. Keller, "In the Service of 'Truth' and
'Victory'"). It may be impossible to determine the precise relationship, for Hobbes, of
peace to the truth, but his statement to Davenant seems to suggest that he considers them
coterminous. Such a conclusion also accords well with Hobbes's reasons for thinking that
there is no *finis ultimus* nor *summum bonum*.
[137] *De Cive*, Pref., § 2.
[138] *Answer to the Preface to Gondibert*, 141–42; cf. Hesiod, *Theogony*, 53–55.
[139] *Answer to the Preface to Gondibert*, 142.
[140] *Answer to the Preface to Gondibert*, 142.
[141] *Answer to the Preface to Gondibert*, 143.

meruaylous in Engines and Instruments of motion; Whatsoeuer commodity men receaue from the obseruation of the Heauens, from the description of the Earth, from the account of Time, from walking on the Seas."[142] Returning to a familiar antithesis, Hobbes declares that everything that distinguishes the civility of Europe from the barbarity of America's savages is the result of fancy "guided by the Precepts of true Philosophy."[143] Yet in a move that confirms that what matters is the result rather than the medium, Hobbes takes one step further and proclaims, "where these precepts fayle, as they haue hetherto fayled in the doctrine of Morall vertue, there the Architect (*Fancy*) must take the Philosophers part vpon her selfe."[144]

The noble poet may assume the mantle of the philosopher, joining the ranks of the mathematician, the civil philosopher, the sovereign, and anyone who, by any means, contributes to order and thereby makes its fruits possible. Davenant's poem parallels Hobbes's *Leviathan* in this regard: just as a multitude of individuals – "this, or that particular man" – unite to form the Leviathan in the latter, the "actions of men, which singly are inconsiderable," in *Gondibert*, "grow at last either into one great protecting power, or into two destroying factions," and thus capture human life as peace or war.[145] "Poets are Paynters," declares Hobbes, and just as truth is the boundary of the historical, "so the Reseblance of truth is the vtmost limit of Poeticall Liberty."[146]

To succeed in his aim, the poet must first "*know well*, that is, ... haue images of nature in the memory distinct and cleare," and "*know much*."[147] Then, taking into account the needs, limitations, and diversity of his audience, he must address them in a manner that "delight[s] all sortes of men, either by instructing the ignorant, or soothing the learned in their knowledge."[148] Hobbes notes that novelty of expression achieves the latter. It is no accident, therefore, that he engages in redefinition as much as he does. That Hobbes's remark regarding the novelty of expression is related to his own project becomes clear in the two pages that follow, wherein he juxtaposes clarity of expression to the insignificant speech that abounds all around him and Davenant, the origin of which he locates in the schools.[149] Extending the principle of appropriateness, Hobbes notes that a poet should maintain proportion between his characters and their actions, refraining, for example,

---

[142] *Answer to the Preface to Gondibert*, 143.
[143] *Answer to the Preface to Gondibert*, 143.
[144] *Answer to the Preface to Gondibert*, 143.
[145] *Leviathan*, Introduction: 2; *Answer to the Preface to Gondibert*, 145.
[146] *Answer to the Preface to Gondibert*, 146–47.
[147] *Answer to the Preface to Gondibert*, 150.
[148] *Answer to the Preface to Gondibert*. 150.
[149] *Answer to the Preface to Gondibert*, 150–51.

from representing base and inhumane vices such as cruelty in great persons. Hobbes notes that the ancients reserved those not for "the persons of men, but of monsters and beastly Giants, such as *Polyphemus, Cacus,* and the *Centaurs.*"[150] A poet who knows much is able to produce metaphors and similitudes of "admirable variety and nouelty," allowing him to affect the reader without giving him more sense of their force than the flesh has "of the bones that susteine it."[151] Language makes this possible through its trans-formations, which allow the poet to translate words already received to his purpose, and put them to use in "farre fetch't (but withall, apt, instructive, and comely) similitudes."[152]

Hobbes's flexibility in drawing the boundary between poetry and phi-losophy invites us to consider what his description of Davenant's craft can tell us about his own project. The last set of observations, for instance, apply to Hobbes as much as they do to Davenant. First and foremost, is of course Hobbes's own monster and beastly giant.[153] Tasked with taking care of everything undesirable, Leviathan makes it possible to begin to imagine felicity and commodious living in a world in which there is no *summum bonum.* But the similarities do not end there: Hobbes's criticism of the schools' insignificant speech and painstaking redefinition of basic terms, and his numerous appeals to the reader's knowledge and ability to reason, con-form to the tasks he ascribes to the poets. No less important is the complex web of metaphors that opens *Leviathan* and operates across the entire book, and the multitude of Hobbes's allusions and images. Hobbes's own images encapsulate this function perfectly: they are the bones that sustain the flesh of *Leviathan* nearly imperceptibly.

Indeed, Hobbes's images and metaphors were so successful that Bramhall declared, "He scrupleth not *to remove the ancient land-marks which his fathers had set, nor to stumble from the ancient paths, to walk in a way that was never cast up,*" adding that it would be "meer folly to expect either a known ground, or a received term from him."[154] Although understandable,

---

[150] *Answer to the Preface to Gondibert,* 152–53; cf. *Leviathan,* II: 5–6; Hobbes's translation of the *Odyssey* (*Homer's Odysses,* 101).

[151] *Answer to the Preface to Gondibert,* 154–55.

[152] *Answer to the Preface to Gondibert,* 154.

[153] Alluding to the frontispiece, Cowley described *Leviathan* as follows: "His Monstrous Thoughts may well be call'd *Gigantick Sense,* / To Heaven they fain would offer *violence,* / Like those *Giants* of old / Of which the *Poets* told" (*The True Effigies of the Monster of Malmesbury,* B^r).

[154] Bramhall, *Castigations of Mr. Hobbes,* 70. This is a common complaint. Thus, for instance, Bramhall claims that "Mr. *Hobbes* consulted too few Authors, and made use of too few Books" (*A Brief View and Survey,* Pref.). For Cowley, when it comes to Hobbes,

> The Fields which answered well the Antients Plow,
> Spent and out-worn return no Harvest now (*The True Effigies of the Monster of Malmesbury,* 6).

Bramhall's reaction is perhaps a little too reverential of Hobbes's claims to novelty. Despite his repeated profession of openness and strict adherence to proper method, Hobbes in fact embedded a series of allusions and images in his works, which took advantage of the rich foundation already present in his readers' minds, in order to frame them to consider the state of nature a condition both possible and relevant to them, and to allow them to recall it readily, as they considered their next political move.

PART III

IMAGES "HISTORICAL OR FABULOUS"

But for other Sciences, they who have not been taught the beginnings, and some progresse in them, that they may see how they be acquired and generated, are in this point like children, that having no thought of generation, are made believe by the women, that their brothers and sisters are not born, but found in the garden.

– Hobbes, *Leviathan*

FIGURE 6. The Fall of Man.

Source: Thomas Hariot, *A Briefe and True Report of the New Found Land of Virginia* ... (Frankfurt, 1590). Courtesy of the John Carter Brown Library at Brown University.

6

Lapse and Relapse or the First Rebellion

[T]he authority of *interpreting the Holy Scriptures* consisted not in this, that the interpreter might without punishment, expound, and explicate his sentence & opinion taken thence, unto others, either by writing, or by his owne voice; but, that others have not a Right to doe, or teach ought contrary to his sentence; insomuch as *the interpretation* we speak of is the same with *the power* of defining in all manner of controversies to be determined by sacred Scriptures.

– Hobbes, *De Cive*

When Hobbes's contemporaries read his account of the state of nature, the first thing they thought of was Genesis.[1] Thus, for example, even though he concludes that *"no man ... hath so amply and judiciously handled"* the rights of sovereignty as Hobbes, Filmer nevertheless finds that he *"cannot agree to his meanes of* acquiring" them, and wishes that Hobbes would consider strengthening them by basing them on the principles of the patrimonial kingdom, which is according to "Scripture *and* Reason."[2] Similarly, Tenison faults Hobbes with having failed to consult "the History of *Moses*," or experience.[3] With the benefit of a certain amount of hindsight, and despite their

---

[1] See Luscombe, "The State of Nature and the Origin of the State." In Hill's terms, the Bible "was central to all intellectual as well as moral life in the sixteenth and seventeenth centuries" (*The English Bible and the Seventeenth Century Revolution*, 20). As Robertson notes, Hobbes lived "in an age when Scriptural warrant was demanded for every conclusion of the natural reason that in any way touched the fabric of religious doctrine" (*Hobbes*, 156). Cf. Reventlow, *The Authority of the Bible and the Rise of the Modern World*, esp. 208–14.

[2] [Robert Filmer], *Observations Concerning the Originall of Government, etc.*, A3ʳ; cf., for example, *Leviathan*, Review and Conclusion, 395. These, of course, are the very standards that Hobbes claims he consulted (see, for example, *Leviathan*, VIII: 38–39; Review and Conclusion: 394–95).

[3] Tenison, *The Creed of Mr. Hobbes Examined*, 139. Cf. Coke, *A Survey of the Politicks of Mr. Thomas White, Thomas Hobbes, and Hugo Grotius*, 24–36; Clarendon, *A Brief View*

divergent interpretations of Hobbes's thought, numerous more recent commentators make the same connection between Hobbes's state of nature and the Bible's account of the Fall.[4]

This impressive consensus is noteworthy because these commentators saw something in Hobbes's account of the state of nature that, at least on the surface, was not there. Whether they agreed or disagreed with him, then, and regardless of which aspect of the state of nature they focused on, commentators understood Hobbes as commenting on Genesis. This is not entirely surprising: his was a time in which it would have been inconceivable to address the question of the origin of mankind and of civil society without referring to the Bible. What is surprising, therefore, is that Hobbes did the one without the other.

In *The Elements of Law*, the two versions of *De Cive*, and the English *Leviathan*, Hobbes makes no reference to Genesis when he discusses the state of nature. It was not until the Latin *Leviathan* of 1668 that Hobbes made the connection explicit by adding the following passage to his list of examples of a war of all against all:

---

and Survey, 26–41, 63–79; [Parker], *A Discourse of Ecclesiastical Politie*, Chapter IV; Ward, *Vindiciæ Academiarum*, 54; Ward, *In Thomæ Hobbii philosophiam*, V.i.

[4] Notable examples are Sorell (*Hobbes*), Thornton (*State of Nature or Eden?*), and Williams ("Normatively Demanding Creatures"), but a broad range of commentators identifies the connection in one way or another. Goldsmith argues that "Hobbes's analysis of the state of nature inclines him toward St. Augustine's opinion that peace is difficult to maintain among fallen men" and suggests that "*Leviathan* describes the political organization necessary for peace among fallen men" (*Hobbes's Science of Politics*, 177). Thomas A. Spragens, Jr., sees Hobbes's account as having "much in common with the Augustinian tradition," in particular as regards their respective accounts of human nature and sinfulness (*The Politics of Motion*, 104). Bobbio, too, sees Hobbes as providing a secular solution to man's sinfulness that is inspired by the "Augustinian-Lutheran conception of the state" (*Thomas Hobbes and the Natural Law Tradition*, 68). According to Sommerville, Hobbes's "state of nature in some ways resembles the traditional notion that coercive power is made necessary by the Fall" (*Thomas Hobbes*, 41). Harrison sees Hobbes as "reluctant to draw explicitly upon scripture to support his philosophical views," but nevertheless finds it "difficult not to see in aspects of Hobbes's political philosophy a Protestant emphasis on the corruption of human nature" (*The Fall of Man and the Foundations of Modern Science*, 160). Condren finds Hobbes's description of the state of nature ambivalent and, hence, as unsatisfactory as "more established Edenic myths of social formation," and sees a family resemblance between the two conditions (*Thomas Hobbes*, 41; cf. *ibid.*, 49). Oakeshott considers *Leviathan* "the first great achievement in the long-projected attempt of European thought to re-embody in a new myth the Augustinian epic of the Fall and Salvation of mankind" (Introduction to *Leviathan*, liii–lv). Malcolm concurs with the view that some of Hobbes's positions were similar to or compatible with the tradition originating with Saint Augustine, according to which man's fallen nature provided "justification for coercive rule" (*Aspects of Hobbes*, 504–05; *Reason of State, Propaganda, and the Thirty Years' War*, 95). Cf. Cook, *Hobbes and Christianity*, 8; Harvey, "The Israelite Kingdom of God in Hobbes' Political Thought," 316, 323–27. Ashcraft offers a concise account of Calvinist commentary on man's wickedness and of its relationship to Hobbes's writings ("*Leviathan* Triumphant," 145–46).

But (someone will say) there never was a war of all against all. What? Did not Cain kill his own brother Abel out of envy – a misdeed so great that he would not have dared to commit it if there had then existed a common power capable of avenging it?[5]

The addition of Cain's crime to the examples was meant to demonstrate the existence of the state of nature and appears to validate those who saw a connection between Genesis and Hobbes's account of the natural condition, but it does little to indicate what Hobbes thought of that connection. If the complete absence of Genesis from an account of the natural condition of mankind is curious, the assertion that there was no common power over Cain and Abel that could have punished the fratricide is both puzzling and downright blasphemous.[6] Leibniz was certainly perplexed by the suggestion, doubting that Hobbes would deny that men could ever be in a pure state of nature, given the existence of God, the common Monarch of men.[7] Hobbes's choice of this episode is all the more puzzling, given that from the story of Adam's rebellion to the attempt to scale the heavens by building the Tower of Babel, Genesis contains other examples that he could have selected.

---

[5] Hobbes, *Leviathan*, ed. Malcolm, XIII, 194, note 38.

[6] Curley suggests that "[t]he Biblically alert reader might object that Cain *was* living under a power able to punish his misdeeds. (Genesis 4: 6–16 relates that God punished him immediately)" (*Leviathan*, ed. Curley, XIII, note 7). The Biblically alert reader would have also noticed, however, that after listening to Cain's entreaty (4:13–14), God tells him that if anyone dare kill Cain, "vengeance shall be taken on him sevenfold," and proceeded to "set a mark upon Cain, lest any finding him should kill him" (4:15, KJV).

[7] Gottfried Wilhelm Leibniz to Thomas Hobbes, Mainz, July 13/23, 1670 (British Library Add. MS 4294, fol. 64ᵛ): "neque diffiteris supposito mundi Rectore nullum esse posse hominum statum pure naturalem extra omnem Rempublicam cum Deus sit omnium Monarcha communis." We have already noted that Grotius had made the same suggestion before Hobbes. It is worth noting that the word "*pure*" in Leibniz's letter is interlined. This suggests that Leibniz attempted to make sense of Hobbes's perplexing example by distinguishing between a pure state of nature and a state of nature in which God's sovereignty, but no human sovereignty, existed. As we will see, Leibniz's later correspondence shows that the matter continued to interest him (see Landucci, *I filosofi e i selvaggi*, 142–43; Leibniz, *Die Philosophischen Schriften*, III: 424).
   Templer noted that Hobbes's inclusion of Cain as an example of the state of nature disregarded Adam's "jure paterno" (1679: 60). Bramhall, however, understood Hobbes as having granted that "*fatherly Empire or Power was instituted by God in the Creation, and was Monarchical*" (*Castigations of Mr. Hobbes*, 519; cf. 182–83). Bramhall based this claim on *De Cive* X.3, but earlier in that work, Hobbes had declared that "*a Sonne cannot be understood to be at any time in the State of Nature, as being under the power and command of them to whom he owes his protection as soon as ever he is born, namely either his Fathers, or his Mothers, or his that nourisht him*" (I.10, note to "In the meere state of Nature"). In his response to Bramhall, on liberty and necessity, Hobbes described the recognition of Adam's dominion as "no deep consideration" (*EW*, V: 184), indicating that the important part of the story was that whatever his de jure authority might have been, Adam did nothing either to prevent the crime or to punish the offender (Genesis 4).

As we have noted, Hobbes's earlier attempts to depict the natural condition of mankind are strikingly different. In *The Elements of Law*, Hobbes prepares the ground for the state of nature in Chapter 13 of Part I, before discussing it explicitly in the next chapter, where he offers a rather insipid account of it. By contrast, *De Cive* opens with the state of nature, and the provocative suggestion that the origin of large and lasting societies lay in mutual fear. For all their differences, however, these accounts also have certain important features in common. Perhaps the most striking of these is their distance from Genesis. Neither mentions God, and neither contains any explicit reference to the Bible. What the reader finds instead points to a purposeful attempt to steer clear of theology. Thus, Hobbes depicts the state of nature as the condition of the Indians of America, refers to Aristotle's contention that man is a πολιτικόν ζῷον, and has plenty to say about human nature, natural law, and natural right, but nothing about Creation or the Fall.[8]

Already puzzling, this absence becomes even more challenging when one considers that despite citing other sources only very rarely, Hobbes regards Scripture as an authoritative source. For instance, when he explains his aims in *De Cive*, he claims that he added the last part of that work (*religio*) in order "to show that the right of Sovereigns over citizens," which in the previous two parts (*libertas, imperium*) he had proved by reason, "is not in conflict with the holy Scriptures."[9] Similarly, in the Review and Conclusion of *Leviathan*, he declares, "all Truth of Doctrine dependeth either upon *Reason*, or upon *Scripture*; both which give credit to many, but never receive it from any Writer."[10] Finally, consider that Hobbes's own account of the rise of sovereignty – man's passage from the state of nature to civil society – contains no reference to Scripture, as many contemporary readers thought it should.[11]

This cannot be because Hobbes thought Scripture irrelevant on this point, since in a subsequent chapter in which he considers dominions "Paternal and Despoticall," he supplements his argument from reason by considering

---

[8] Nearly every commentator ignores this striking fact. One exception is Thornton (*State of Nature or Eden?* 166–67), but the hypotheses she lists indicate that the question is not central to her inquiry. This is not surprising in light of the fact that she finds "Hobbes's use of scripture ... by no means essential to the argument of the first half of *Leviathan*, or what we might call the specifically political part" (*ibid.*, 13). On the relationship between politics and theology, see Goldie, "The Reception of Hobbes," 590.

[9] *De Cive*, Pref. § 16. Hobbes's tactic here is reminiscent of the relationship between Marsilius's first and second discourses, aimed at addressing what Brett refers to as "different cognitive procedures" (Introduction to *The Defender of the Peace*, xv).

[10] *Leviathan*, Review and Conclusion: 395; cf. *ibid.*, VIII: 38–39.

[11] See, for example, [Filmer], *Observations Concerning the Originall of Government*, A3^r; Ward, *Vindiciæ Academiarum*, V.i; [Parker], *A Discourse of Ecclesiastical Politie*, Chapter IV; Tenison, *The Creed of Mr. Hobbes Examined*, 139; Clarendon, *A Brief View and Survey*, 26–41, 63–79.

a number of relevant Scriptural passages, including Genesis 3:5.[12] Nor can it be because Hobbes thought Genesis, in particular, irrelevant. *Leviathan* contains no fewer than forty-nine references to it.[13] Furthermore, when at the end of the Latin edition of that work Hobbes called attention to sixteen especially important Biblical passages that occur twenty times in the text, he included three passages from Genesis.[14] But even in the early, allegedly "political" part of *Leviathan*, one finds plenty of material that evokes Genesis.[15] In the Introduction, Hobbes likens man's creation of the commonwealth to God's creation of man, and in Chapter IV, in examining the origin of speech, he locates it in God, "that instructed *Adam* how to name such creatures as he presented to his sight."[16] It is also worth noting that in Hobbes's introductory account of human nature, the chapter on the state of nature is preceded by a chapter on religion.[17] And yet, as we have seen, it was not until the Latin edition of *Leviathan* that Hobbes drew an explicit connection between the state of nature and Genesis.

Peculiar though it may be, Hobbes's treatment of Genesis in connection with the state of nature is broadly consistent with a notable increase of interest in religious matters in his political treatises. Having avoided it almost entirely in 1640, by 1651 Hobbes had come to consider religion the dominant political problem.[18] Similarly, Hobbes's peculiar approach to Genesis is consistent with his overall use of the Bible, which, to put it simply, is strange.[19] These reasons, coupled with Hobbes's unorthodox theological

---

[12] *Leviathan*, XX: 106.

[13] According to Curley's index of Biblical references, excluding references to the Appendix.

[14] Thomas Hobbes, *Leviathan* (Latin ed., 1678), Bbb2ʳ. The passages in question are Gen. 1:2 (occurs in Ch. XXXIV), Gen. 2:18 (Ch. XXXVIII; recurs in the Latin Appendix, p. 336), Gen. 3:5 (Ch. XXI).

[15] The characterization is Thornton's (*State of Nature or Eden?* 13); cf. Martinich, *The Two Gods of Leviathan*, 50.

[16] *Leviathan*, IV: 12.

[17] Chapters XII and XIII, respectively.

[18] See Goldsmith's introduction to *The Elements of Law*, ix. For instance, *The Elements of Law* differs in many ways from its successors, but one of the more striking is that unlike *De Cive* and *Leviathan*, this work does not contain a section devoted to religion. In the *Elements*, one finds only a single chapter whose title promises theology, Chapter XVIII of Part I, which is devoted to demonstrating that Hobbes's exposition of the laws of nature can be confirmed by reference to the Holy Scripture. By contrast, one of the three sections of *De Cive* is devoted specifically to religion. As its title and frontispiece announce, *Leviathan* goes several steps further. It consists of four parts, the first two of which deal with man and commonwealth, while the other two treat "OF A CHRISTIAN COMMON-WEALTH" and "OF THE KINGDOME OF DARKNESSE," respectively. Thus, excluding the Introduction and Review and Conclusion, the book is divided into two roughly equal halves, of which the second is devoted to religion. In addition to focusing increasingly on religious matters in his political treatises, in his later years, Hobbes also composed works in which he explores religious questions directly, among which *An Historical Narration concerning Heresie, and the Punishment Thereof*, and *Historia Ecclesiastica* stand out.

[19] On Hobbes's use of the Bible, see, for example, Somos, "Hobbes's use of the Authorised Version, the Geneva and other Bibles in *Leviathan*, Part III."

positions and his openly combative attitude toward the clergy, led many of his contemporaries to accuse him of atheism.[20] Several more recent commentators have explained Hobbes's curious treatment of Scripture as an attempt, on his part, to subvert the authority of the Bible.[21] It is clear that Hobbes's state of nature differs from Genesis in important ways – the most obvious of which is the fact that it largely ignores it – but I think that it is potentially misleading to describe it as an attempt to subvert Genesis and leave it at that.

The first, and most serious, problem with such a claim is that it gives a mistaken impression of the status of Genesis by implying that its meaning was clear and uncontested. While it is true that several of those who took it upon themselves to attack Hobbes in print claimed that his account of the state of nature contradicted Genesis, one should not conclude thereby that their claims were either uncontroversial or representative of an established view of the matter. When Hobbes's contemporary critics and many subsequent commentators contrast his account of the natural condition of mankind to that of Genesis, they tend to focus on life in the Garden of Eden. The contrast could not be clearer: while in Hobbes's version life is "solitary, poore, nasty, brutish, and short," in the latter it is social, rich, tranquil, and eternal. This picture, however, is incomplete, for it leaves out the most important part of the story, one that plays a central role in nearly every commentary on Genesis from Augustine to Hobbes, and one that Hobbes identifies as such: Eden was the site of the first and most striking rebellion.

To evaluate the suggestion that the state of nature constitutes a subversion of Genesis in particular, one would have to ask what the reason behind such a subversion would have been and how the alleged subversion would have served Hobbes's purpose. As we have seen, Hobbes is quite clear about the latter: to promote peace by eliminating political conflict stemming from disagreement. Thus, it is important to add that Hobbes's reason for undermining the authority of Scripture could only have been "to subordinate belief in Scripture to belief in the state" and that to promote agreement, Hobbes had to "find a way to reconcile competing transcendent interests."[22]

---

[20] See, for example, *EW*, IV: 291–92; cf. Parkin, *Taming the Leviathan*, 15–16, 133–35.

[21] For instance, Strauss argues that "Hobbes with double intention becomes an interpreter of the Bible, in the first place in order to make use of the authority of the Scriptures for his own theory, and next and particularly in order to shake the authority of the Scriptures themselves" (*The Political Philosophy of Hobbes*, 71). Similarly, Moloney claims that "Hobbes came to realize that the viability of his own narrative of political creation required the subversion of traditional glosses on *Genesis*" ("Leaving the Garden of Eden," 243). See, however, Lessay's salient warning ("Hobbes's Covenant Theology," 265).

[22] Kahn, *Rhetoric, Prudence, and Skepticism*, 172; Lloyd, *Ideals as Interests*, 44. Similarly, Milner suggests that "Hobbes wants his teaching to be accessible to men of every persuasion and every intellectual capacity" ("Hobbes on Religion," 418); cf. Collins, *The Allegiance of Thomas Hobbes*, 33. See also Fawne, et al., *A Beacon Set on Fire*, 14–15; Glover, "God and Thomas Hobbes," esp. 157; Pangle, "A Critique of Hobbes's Critique of Biblical and Natural

By virtue of its authority, richness, and indeterminacy, the Bible was an important tool for the warring parties in the conflict that had prompted Hobbes's account of the state of nature. The first characteristic rendered it the ultimate source of justification and, as we have seen, Hobbes accepted this fact.[23] The second and third allowed individuals with wildly divergent views to find something in the Bible that they could use to justify their arguments.[24] An attentive observer might point out here that the third characteristic ultimately undermines the first: if the Bible can be made to justify any view, then perhaps its authority should be questioned. Hobbes saw that each of these unavoidable characteristics could help him advance his project. His approach to the Bible thus constituted a careful balancing act, intended to reap the benefits of its authority, richness, and indeterminacy, while steering clear of the potential pitfalls involved in detailed Biblical exegesis.[25] In the conclusion of the third part of *Leviathan*, Hobbes explains, "in the allegation of Scripture, I have endeavoured to avoid such texts as are of obscure, or controverted Interpretations; and to alledge none, but in such sense as is most plain, and agreeable to the harmony and scope of the whole Bible," and warned, famously, that

they that insist upon single Texts, without considering the main Designe, can derive no thing from them cleerly; but rather by casting atomes of Scripture, as dust before mens eyes, make every thing more obscure than it is; an ordinary artifice of those that seek not the truth, but their own advantage.[26]

But what was "the scope of the whole Bible," and what "plain" and "obscure" passages? For Hobbes, the obscure Biblical passages that had

Religion in *Leviathan*," 34. Several commentators interpret such a subordination as a sign of atheism, but it need not be, since it can be animated by the pursuit of peace and order, which may be given priority over the truth and which, as Augustine argues most prominently, are fully consistent with Christianity (*Concerning the City of God*, V, XIX.13). As Hobbes himself states in *Leviathan*, "Doctrine repugnant to Peace, can no more be True, than Peace and Concord can be against the Law of Nature" (XVIII: 91). Cf. Malcolm, *Aspects of Hobbes*, 428–29; Somos, *Secularisation and the Leiden Circle*.

[23] For Glover, there is thus "no question but that Hobbes did appeal to the religious beliefs of his readers in support of his political theory" ("God and Thomas Hobbes," 147). The reason, in Farr's terms, is that "[f]or Hobbes's Christian audience, [Scripture] is that final invocation to which nothing else can or should be said" ("Atomes of Scripture," 178).

[24] See Thornton's survey of some of these positions (*State of Nature or Eden?*).

[25] The interpretation of an author's use of the Bible is an exceedingly complicated matter, since techniques such as the use of commonplaces and omission could be evidence of an attempt to subvert its authority, but could also result from other motives or even accidentally. On this matter more generally, see Somos, *Secularisation and the Leiden Circle*. Where Hobbes is concerned, and using his own principle of Biblical interpretation (*Leviathan*, XLIII: 331), one ought to look for the spirit of the Bible without becoming entangled in "atomes of Scripture" (cf. "An Answer to Bishop Bramhall's Book, called, *The Catching of the Leviathan*, *EW*, IV: 285). On the question of the relationship between an author's claim and his readers' view of the facts that pertain to it, see Martinich, "The Interpretation of Covenants in *Leviathan*," esp. 229–33.

[26] *Leviathan*, XLIII: 331; cf. "An Answer to Bishop Bramhall," *EW*, IV: 285.

become the centers of controversy were the ones concerning "the Mysteries of Religion," and the plain ones were the ones that teach men "their Duty."[27] The significance of the Bible for Hobbes's readers meant that ignoring it was not an option. The task was, therefore, to show that his project of peace was consistent with the main design of the Bible, without entering into the exegetical fights that fuel political disagreement and that had helped perpetuate the English Civil War.[28]

WHAT HOBBES SAID ABOUT GENESIS

With the exception of an allusion to Adam and Eve toward the end of *The Elements of Law* and in the context of a discussion of procreation, Hobbes makes no reference to Genesis in his earliest political treatise.[29] We have seen, by contrast, that in considering the causes of the dissolution of commonwealths in *De Cive*, Hobbes proclaims that "[o]f doctrines that dispose men to sedition, the first, without question, is: *that knowledge of good and evil is a matter for individuals.*"[30] For Hobbes, this is the litmus test of sovereignty because this doctrine is true in the natural state and false in the civil state, wherein men have "submitted by their own agreement to other men's power."[31] If the language that Hobbes uses to describe this transgression calls to mind Genesis, the association is not accidental. Hobbes argues that "[w]hen private men claim for themselves a knowledge of *good* and *evil*, they are aspiring to be as Kings," and adds that "[w]hen this happens, the commonwealth cannot stand."[32] The example he uses, as we have seen, is telling:

The most ancient of all Gods commands is, *Gen.* 2.15. *Thou shalt not eat of the tree of knowledge of good and evill*; and the most ancient of all diaboliçall tentations, Chap. 3. vers. 5. *Yee shall be as Gods, knowing good and evill*; and Gods first

---

[27] That duty is "Beleefe in Christ, Loue towards God, Obedience to the King, and Sobriety of behauiour" (*Behemoth*, 177–79). For an excellent discussion of how these two categories of Biblical passages, as well as metaphorical ones, are to be treated, see Farr, "Atomes of Scripture," 178–88.

[28] Lloyd is thus exactly right when she suggests that the task of the second half of *Leviathan* is

> to reconcile competing religious interests through an elaborate process of rediscription. Hobbes aims to redescribe competing substantive descriptions of men's transcendent interest in fulfilling their duties to God in such a way that each former faction can affirm the redescription as accurately capturing its interest, while all will be affirming the very same description (*Ideals as Interests in Hobbes's Leviathan*, 44–45).

[29] *The Elements of Law*, II.9.3.

[30] *De Cive*, XII.1, emphasis in the original.

[31] *De Cive*, XII.1. Hobbes claims that he has proven the status of the claim in each condition, in *De Cive* I.9 and V.9, respectively.

[32] *De Cive*, XII.1.

expostulation with man, vers. 11. *Who told thee that thou wert naked? Hast thou eaten of the tree, whereof I commanded thee that thou shouldest not eat?* As if he had said, how comest thou to judge that nakedness, wherein it seemed good to me to create thee, to be shameful, except thou have arrogated to thy selfe the *knowledge of good and evill?*[33]

Hobbes's description of this story gives us some crucial clues regarding his conception of the state of nature. Leibniz may have been correct when he doubted that Hobbes would deny God's sovereignty over man, but Hobbes points out that God's sovereignty over man began when God issued His first command.[34] Prior to that moment, the condition of Adam was "peculiar" insofar as he was under God's authority, but at liberty with regard to actions not proscribed by God.[35] Thus, in *Leviathan*, Hobbes argues that "[i]n cases where the Soveraign has prescribed no rule, there the Subject hath the Liberty to do, or forbeare, according to his own discretion."[36] Until God had spoken to him, commanding him not to eat from the tree, Adam had been completely – and uniquely – free.[37]

The distinctiveness of Adam's condition is captured in Hobbes's observation that "[f]rom the very Creation, God not only reigned over all men *naturally* by his might; but also had *peculiar* Subjects, whom he commanded by a Voice, as one man speaketh to another."[38] It is also evident in Hobbes's judgment that the "origin of the *Kingdom of God*" lies with Abraham, rather than Adam.[39] According to Hobbes, in addition to being natural, in the beginning God's rule over Adam and Eve was also *"by way of Covenant ...*

---

[33] *De Cive*, XII.1. In the following paragraph, Hobbes adds that because of Adam's original sin, "by judging of good and evil for ourselves we ensure that we commit a sin whether we obey or disobey" (XII.2).

[34] Gottfried Wilhelm Leibniz to Thomas Hobbes, Mainz, July 13/23, 1670, British Library Add. MS 4294. According to Genesis 2:15, "the LORD God took the man, and put him into the garden of Ē'-děn to dress it and to keep it" (KJV). This appears to describe an intention rather than a command. Hobbes, in any case, sees the first command as occurring at 2:17.

[35] Hobbes uses the term to describe one aspect of Adam's condition in *Leviathan* (XXXV: 216).

[36] *Leviathan*, XXI: 113.

[37] Contemporary readers eager to see this period in Eden behind Hobbes's description of the state of nature as one in which there is "no Law, no Injustice" (*Leviathan*, XIII: 63) rushed to counter that Adam was endowed with an understanding of natural law since his creation (see, for example, Andrewes, Ἀποσπασμάτια *Sacra*, 183; Babington, *Certaine Plaine, Briefe, and Comfortable Notes upon Euerie Chapter of Genesis*, Fol. 10, C2ʳ; Ainsworth, *Annotations upon the First Book of Moses Called Genesis*, 2:15, p. 11; Jackson, *A Help for the Understanding of the Holy Scripture*, 10). Hobbes's catalogue of the Hardwick library contains entries for a copy of Ainsworth's commentary, as well as for an edition of Babington's works (Devonshire Mss., Chatsworth HS/E/1A).

[38] *Leviathan*, XXXV: 216.

[39] *De Cive*, XVI.2; cf. *Questions concerning Liberty, Necessity, and Chance*, EW, V: 101–03. Hobbes considers the survivors of the Flood "the then *Kingdom of God*," which was replaced by the covenant with Abraham (*Leviathan*, XXXV: 216; *De Cive*, XVI.3).

so as it seems he would have no obedience yeelded to him, beside that which naturall Reason should dictate, but *by the way of Covenant*, that is to say, by the consent of men themselves."[40] The distinction is important, because a few pages earlier Hobbes had argued that God has the right to reign because of his omnipotence, whence it follows that men yield to Him because of their weakness and proceeded to add that the "*obligation* which rises from Contract, of which we have spoken in the second Chapter, can have no place here, where the Right of Ruling ... rises from nature."[41] This obligation, however, is of the kind required by reason, which dictates "to all, acknowledging the divine power and providence, *that there is no kicking against the pricks*."[42] Hobbes is not alone in interpreting Adam's apparent acquiescence to God's first command as a sign of agreement. Although there is disagreement among translators as to the precise meaning of "Adam" in Hosea 6:7, some take it to refer to Adam's transgression of his covenant with God.[43] In *De Cive* itself, a marginal note to the paragraph in question encapsulates Hobbes's conception of this covenant well: "*Pacto inter Deum & Adamum, prohibita est disputatio de mandatis superiorum*."[44] One might nevertheless wonder here why this relationship could be described as a "covenant." Already prominent in earlier sixteenth-century commentaries, by Hobbes's

---

[40] *De Cive*, XVI.2.

[41] *De Cive*, XV.7.

[42] *De Cive*, XV.7. In the note added to this paragraph for the 1647 edition, Hobbes explains,

> If anyone thinks this harsh, I ask him to reflect quietly, if there were two who were omnipotent, which one would be obligated to obey the other. It will be admitted, I believe, that neither is obligated to the other. If this is true, my point is also true, that men are subject to God primarily because they are not omnipotent. For when our Saviour warned Paul (who was at that time an enemy of the church) not to kick against the pricks, He seems to have required obedience from him on the ground that he did not have strength to resist (Silverthorne, trans.; cf. "Of Liberty and Necessity," § 12).

[43] For example, in the Vulgate, which Hobbes uses often. Other versions, such as the 1560 Geneva Bible, take it to refer to men in general: "But thei like men haue transgressed yᵉ couenant: there haue they tresspaced against me" (*The Bible and Holy Scriptures Conteyned in the Old and Newe Testament, etc.* [Geneva: Rovland Hall, 1560]). Others, still, take it to refer to an unknown location.

[44] *De Cive, The Latin Version*, ed. Warrender, XVI § 2. *Pace* Curley ("The Covenant with God in Hobbes's *Leviathan*," 209) and Lessay, whose analysis is admittedly focused on *Leviathan* ("Hobbes's Covenant Theology and Its Political Implications," 248), Hobbes states explicitly here that a covenant centered specifically on obedience has taken place between God and Adam. In his response to Curley, Martinich points to the important distinction between rights and power ("The Interpretation of Covenants in *Leviathan*," 239). Sovereigns grant rights to subjects regularly, even though they possess the power to act against them. In the case at hand, God's permission to Adam to use the trees of the Garden of Eden constitutes such a grant. Once Adam has consumed a fruit from one of the trees that he was given access to, he has exercised a right to it that God granted him. God's omnipotence – for example, His ability to bring the fruit back or kill Adam – has no bearing on the covenant, until God, in His omnipotence, decides otherwise. Cf. *Leviathan*, XIV: 66.

time the concept of a covenant began to be applied to the "covenant of works" between God and Adam.[45]

Hobbes's own analysis of paternal dominion is instructive in this regard as well. Therein, Hobbes explains that mothers have dominion over their children because they possess the power to destroy them when they are infants. If they choose not to do so, we can presume that they expect that, once grown, the child will not become the mother's enemy. On the other side, the child owes "everything" to the one who preserves him. Since covenants entail promises of future performance for Hobbes, we may conclude that a covenant exists between the mother and her child insofar as each expects that the other will assist or, at least, not hinder his or her preservation.[46] In this case, therefore, God's permission to Adam to eat freely of every tree of the garden is the first reason to conclude that a covenant had taken place.[47] God's omnipotence, and the command to Adam to abstain from eating from the tree of the knowledge of good and evil at pain of death, add further reasons for Hobbes, "because preservation of life being the end, for which one man becomes subject to another, every man is supposed to promise obedience, to him, in whose power it is to save, or destroy him."[48] Hobbes notes that the generation of paternal dominion occurs from the child's consent, "either expresse, or by other sufficient arguments declared."[49] Having given no sign of disagreement with God's command, Adam can be presumed to have entered into a covenant of obedience.

If the terms "kingdom," "command," "pact," "obedience," and "disobedience" suffice to render the simplest version of this story ideally suited to Hobbes's attempt to promote peace, its details conceal all sorts of further

[45] Martinich lists examples of general uses of the term (*The Two Gods of Leviathan*, 147). McGiffert argues that the specific idea of a "covenant of works" between God and Adam appears to have emerged in the 1580s and was "well defined by 1600" ("From Moses to Adam," 132–33). Cf. Krause, "Der Bund im Alten Testament und bei Hobbes."

[46] See, for example, *De Cive*, IX §§ 3–4; *Leviathan*, XX: 103. Hobbes therefore insists that "in the condition of meer Nature," it is not the generation, but the preservation that renders the mother *domina*. He also points out that the dominion would in fact be transferred to another, if the mother were to abandon her child and that other found it and nourished it, because "the Dominion is in him that nourisheth it" (*Leviathan*, XX: 103).

[47] Thus, Andrewes argues, "As therefore hitherto *God hath opened only his hand to fill Adams hands with his blessings, his mouth with laughter, and his heart with joy*; So now God openeth his mouth to shew what shall be his reciprocall duty for all his benefits, and what duty he requireth of him." Andrewes also invokes the authority of the "ancient Writers" to argue that in Genesis 2:16–17, "first of all God and Man doe enter into a league, obligation, and covenant one to the other, by which they prove, that *Ecclesia & vinculum Ecclesiæ* is more ancient than the state Politique, that is, that the bond ecclesiasticall is of greater antiquity than the bond of Commonweals Politicall or œconomicall" (Ἀποσπασμάτια *Sacra*, 183, 187).

[48] *Leviathan*, XX: 103.

[49] *Leviathan*, XX: 102.

riches. Some are especially relevant to Hobbes's vocabulary and to his description of the relationship between the state of nature and civil society. The first of these has to do with God's command. What exactly did God demand of Adam, and why? It is not unusual for commentators to focus on the precise meaning of the terms "good and evil," with some noting the obvious moral implications of this knowledge, and others pointing out that in Hebrew the phrase can be taken to mean knowledge of everything.[50] God's omniscience makes the appeal of this line of interpretation obvious, since Adam's rebellion could be construed as an attempt to come to know what God knows and, hence, as an attempt to usurp His authority. After all, having been given access to every other tree in the Garden, Adam did not *need* to eat from the tree of the knowledge of good and evil, so his disobedience has to be explained in another way.[51] Was he intrigued by the prohibition? According to Genesis, Adam and Eve appear to have been uninterested in the prospect of becoming "as gods, knowing good and evil," until the subtle serpent put the thought into Eve's head.[52] The instigation for this rebellion came in the form of speech.[53]

An incidental remark in *De Cive* confirms that Hobbes is fully aware of the significance of these details. He notes "*in passing*" that

by that precept of not eating of the tree of *the knowledge of good and evil* (whether the judicature of good and evill, or the eating of the fruit of some tree were forbidden) God did require a most simple obedience to his commands, without dispute whether that were *good*, or *evill*, which was commanded; for the fruit of the tree, if the Command be wanting, hath nothing in its own nature, whereby the eating of it could be morally *evill*, that is to say, *a sinne*.[54]

For Hobbes, then, as for many commentators before him, the simplicity of the offense is an essential part of the story. The motive proposed by the serpent goes too far, and is thus unnecessary.[55] Absolute sovereignty demands absolute obedience, and the best test of it is a simple command that is easy to remember and simple to observe. Knowledge of good and evil here is no knowledge of the laws of creation or some complicated moral code, but is centered on the simple principle that follows from God's command, namely that we obey what God commands "without argument as to whether the

---

[50] See, for example, Davidson, *The Cambridge Bible Commentary: Genesis 1–11*, 35; West, *Introduction to the Old Testament*, 89. Clark considers von Rad's commentary largely responsible for the uncritical acceptance of this interpretation ("A Legal Background to the Yahwist's Use of 'Good and Evil' in Genesis 2–3," 278). Cf. von Rad, *Genesis*, 80–82.

[51] See, for example, Andrewes, Ἀποσπασμάτια *Sacra*, 186–87.

[52] Genesis, 3:5.

[53] In *The Elements of Law*, Hobbes argues, "there can be no author of rebellion, that is not an eloquent and powerful speaker" (II.8.14).

[54] *De Cive*, XVI.2.

[55] It is interesting, in this regard, that Hobbes makes no explicit use of the serpent in his numerous attacks on instigators of rebellion and disobedience.

precept was *Good* or *Bad.*"[56] It is not an accident that Hobbes chose as the ultimate symbol of his political theory the story that teaches this lesson as no other does: that of Job.

If Hobbes's interpretation of Genesis 2:17 sounds somewhat presumptuous, it is nevertheless far from eccentric. For instance, in a sermon on Genesis 2:17, Bishop Andrewes – who in 1604 headed the Westminster company charged by King James with the task of producing an authorized version of the Pentateuch – notes that the fruits of the tree of knowledge were "without question no more evill than the other trees," and adds,

> if this restraint had fallen on any other tree in the Garden as it did on this, it had been as unlawfull to eat as this: So that it is not the nature of the tree, but of Gods word which made it evill to eat, for there was no difference between them but in respect of Gods word and charge, which said, *Thou shalt not eat thereof.* In which respect it is called *the tree of knowledge of good and evill.* We must understand that this tree hath not his name of every quality in it, but of the event and effect which should come by it, *Exod.* 15.25.[57]

Indeed, Andrewes's interpretation has a very long and distinguished lineage. Commentators from Augustine, to Bede, to Calvin note that there was nothing inherent in the nature of the tree of the knowledge of good and evil that rendered it deadly, and point out that this rather small detail has enormous consequences.[58] What is striking in these commentaries is the degree to which these consequences are described in political terms. Thus, in *The Literal Meaning of Genesis*, Augustine notes that man "was forbidden to touch that tree, which was not evil, so that the observance of the command in itself would be a good for him and its violation an evil."[59] Augustine insists that it was the prohibition that rendered the tree special, and that the objective of God's command was to teach Adam obedience, and concludes,

> … nothing else is sought by the sinner except to be free of the sovereignty of God when he does a deed that is sinful only in so far as God forbids it. If this alone were attended to, what else but the will of God would be attended to? What else but the will of God would be loved? What else but the will of God would be preferred to

---

[56] *De Cive*, XVI.2. For an excellent discussion of the consequences of this realization, see Williams, "Normatively Demanding Creatures."

[57] Andrewes, Ἀποσπασμάτια *Sacra*, 188. See McCullough, "Andrewes, Lancelot (1555–1626)"; *Lancelot Andrewes: Selected Sermons and Lectures*; Norton, *The King James Bible*, 55. Hobbes's catalogue of the Hardwick library lists a copy of Andrewes's sermons (Devonshire Mss., Chatsworth HS/E/1A).

[58] A notable exception is Lactantius, *Divine Institutes*, II.12.16. Almond notes that "[g]enerally, seventeenth-century commentators believed that, had Adam not sinned, he would have been immortal," a view that had been central since the Council of Carthage in 417 (*Adam and Eve in Seventeenth-Century Thought*, 190). All four authors are represented in Hobbes's catalogue of the Hardwick library (Devonshire Mss., Chatsworth HS/E/1A); cf. *Leviathan*, XLVI: 379.

[59] Saint Augustine, *The Literal Meaning of Genesis*, VIII.13 § 28.

man's will? Leave the reason for the command in the Lord's hands. He who is His servant must do His bidding, and then perhaps by the merit of his obedience he will have grounds for seeing the reason of God's command.

But we need not prolong our enquiry into the reason for this command. If the service of God is a great good for man, God by His command makes useful whatever He wishes to command, and we must not fear that He could command what is not for our good.[60]

The political language of Adam's relationship to God in Augustine's description is hard to miss, and subsequent commentators did not miss it. In his own commentary, which is heavily indebted to Augustine's, Bede paraphrases Augustine's account by describing God as "Governor" and Adam's desire as "not to be under the governance of God."[61] By the end of the sixteenth century, political language had taken over the narrative completely.[62] According to a 1578 translation of Calvin's commentary on Genesis,

> Moses now teacheth that man was made ruler of the earth, with this exception, that he shoulde nevertheless be subject unto God. A lawe is given unto him in token of subiection. For it made no matter to God, if he had eaten of all y[e] fruits of the garden without exception. Therefore the forbidding of one tree, was a proofe and triall of obedience. And by this meanes God would haue all mankind to be enured, even from the beginning, with the reuerence of his Maiestie: euen as it was needefull, he beeing Adorned and inriched with so many excellent giftes, shoulde be kept in awe and obedience, least he shoulde burst foorth into wantonnes and rebellion. There was an other special reason which we touched before: namely, that Adam shoulde not desire to be more wise then was conuenient. But this generall purpose of God is to be obserued, whereby he would make man subiect to his gouernment. Therfore the absteining frō the fruite of one tree, was a certaine leading to obedience: to the end man might knowe that he had a Guider and Lorde of his life, upon whome he ought to depend, and whose hestes it behoued him to obey.[63]

A survey of near-contemporary English commentaries reveals the extent to which this type of interpretation was accepted. Thus, Babington describes Adam's conduct as "contempt of God's commaundement by disobedience," and argues that God sought to have Adam and Eve "knowe what awe was to theyr superiour."[64] Ainsworth considers God's command "a significative

[60] Saint Augustine, *The Literal Meaning of Genesis*, VIII.13 § 30.

[61] Bede, *On Genesis*, 118; cf. *ibid.*, 112–13; "dominantis" and "dominatione," respectively, in the original (Migne, *Patrologia Latina*).

[62] Almond argues, "[t]here was virtual unanimity in the belief that the prohibition against eating the fruit of the Tree of the Knowledge of Good and Evil was to test the obedience of Adam and Eve" (*Adam and Eve in Seventeenth-Century Thought*, 193).

[63] *A Commentarie of John Caluine, upon the First Booke of Moses Called Genesis*, 69. Hobbes's catalogue of the Hardwick library contains numerous Biblical commentaries, including several of Calvin's (Devonshire Mss., Chatsworth HS/E/1A).

[64] Babington, *Certaine Plaine, Briefe, and Comfortable Notes upon Euerie Chapter of Genesis, etc.*, Ch. II, Fol. 10, § 7 (C2).

law, concerning a thing of it selfe indifferent, but at the pleasure of God made unlawfull and evill for man to doe; that by observing this outward rite, hee might testifie his willing obedience unto the Lord."[65] Similarly, Ross argues that God issued his command to Adam "[n]ot because [the tree] was euill in it selfe, or hurtfull to man: but because by this command, God would try mans obedience."[66] In his own commentary on Genesis, Andrew Willet concurs with this assessment of the tree, and siding with Tertullian and Augustine argues that God's "precept, though in shew but easie and light, yet containeth the very foundation of all precepts, and of the whole morall law."[67] In his *Help for the Understanding of the Holy Scripture*, published ten years later, Arthur Jackson also finds that "the Lord gave [Adam] also this positive and particular commandment concerning a thing of it self indifferent, but by Gods command made unlawfull, that the Lords absolute Dominion over him might be hereby made known, and his disobedience might become the more manifest."[68]

For theologians, this reading was necessitated by Genesis 1:12, according to which the trees were good, and by 1:31, according to which when God beheld everything He had made, it was good. Augustine emphasizes these facts in his interpretation, and, as we have seen, many commentators followed his lead.[69] Augustine also draws our attention repeatedly to the significance of the fact that the "injunction forbidding the eating of one kind of food ... was so easy to observe, so brief to remember."[70] The upshot of these observations is that the tree's special status derives not from any inherent quality that it had, but from the fact that God chose to place it beyond Adam's reach. Using a term that is closer to Hobbes's concerns, but which nevertheless captures the tenor of these interpretations, we might describe the choice as "arbitrary," the kind that an all-powerful sovereign would make.[71]

WHAT HOBBES DID NOT SAY ABOUT GENESIS

In *Leviathan*, Hobbes put such a sovereign on the frontispiece and reinforced the message by crowning the image with a quotation from Job, reminding

---

[65] Ainsworth, *Annotations upon the First Book of Moses Called Genesis, etc.*, 2:16, p. 11.

[66] Ross, *The First Booke of Questions and Answers upon Genesis, etc.*, 42.

[67] Willet, *Hexapla in Genesin & Exodum*, 27.

[68] Jackson, *A Help for the Understanding of the Holy Scripture, etc.*, 10. The formulaic nature of the claim is illustrated, for instance, by the degree to which Jackson's expression follows Ainsworth's. For several other examples, see Almond, *Adam and Eve in Seventeenth-Century Thought*, 193–94.

[69] Augustine, *The Literal Meaning of Genesis*, VIII.13 § 28.

[70] Augustine, *Concerning the City of God against the Pagans*, XIV.12. Thereby, he argues, God sought to "impress upon this created being that he was the Lord; and that free service was in that creature's own interest" (*ibid.*, XIV.15).

[71] See, for example, the marginal notes to Hobbes's discussion of the initial distribution of rewards, punishments, and property in *Leviathan*, XVIII: 92 and XXIV: 128.

the reader that there is no power on earth that compares to him. Inside the
work, Hobbes argues that "[t]o those therefore whose Power is irresistible,
the dominion of all men adhaereth naturally by their excellence of Power;
and consequently it is from that Power, that the Kingdome over men, and the
Right of Afflicting men at his pleasure, belongeth Naturally to God Almighty;
not as Creator, and Gracious; but as Omnipotent."[72] He then goes on to discuss the cases of Job and Adam, both of which center on omnipotence. In
the former, despite Job's earnest expostulations "for the many Afflictions he
suffered, notwithstanding his Righteousnesse," the matter "is decided by God
himselfe, not by arguments derived from *Job's* Sinne, but his own Power."[73]
Similarly, Hobbes points out that God could have decided to render Adam
mortal justly even if the latter had not sinned.[74] Perhaps less prominent than
the opening sections of Genesis, the Book of Job nevertheless has several
attributes that would recommend it to Hobbes. It occupies far more space
than Adam's disobedience, conveying the centrality of omnipotence in no
uncertain terms, and making it clear that agency on the part of the subject
is simply irrelevant. What is more, its explicit emphasis on pride makes it
a natural example of vainglory. Perhaps most importantly, given Hobbes's
criteria for the selection of Biblical passages, its meaning and significance
appear to have been less contentious than those of Genesis.[75]

As we have noted, in the introduction to *Leviathan*, Hobbes draws an
analogy between God's creation of man and man's creation of the artificial man that is the commonwealth.[76] These unmistakable signs prepare the
reader's mind for a discussion steeped in religion, yet what follows is somewhat surprising. The introductory chapters are devoted to man, but the only
mention of man's creation comes in Chapter IV, wherein Hobbes declares,

the most noble and profitable invention of all other, was that of SPEECH, consisting of *Names* or *Appellations*, and their Connexion; whereby men register their
Thoughts; recall them when they are past; and also declare them one to another for
mutual utility and conversation; without which, there had been amongst men, neither Common-wealth, nor Society, nor Contract, nor Peace, no more than amongst
Lyons, Bears, and Wolves. The first author of Speech was *God* himself, that instructed
Adam how to name such creatures as he presented to his sight; For Scripture goeth
no further in this matter.[77]

[72] *Leviathan*, XXXI: 187.
[73] *Leviathan*, XXXI: 188. Cf. "Of Liberty and Necessity," § 12.
[74] *Leviathan*, XXXI: 188.
[75] *Leviathan*, XLIII: 331. Citing a series of examples, Greenleaf argues that Job's "symbolic or
allegorical value for … political consideration seems very substantial and was, in fact, clearly
recognized in Hobbes's day" ("A Note on Hobbes and the Book of Job," 14); cf. Mintz,
"Leviathan as Metaphor"; Hull, "'Against this *Empusa*.'" Greenleaf draws an interesting
parallel between Job's condition and Hobbes's state of nature (*ibid.*, 28–31).
[76] *Leviathan*, Introduction: 1.
[77] *Leviathan*, IV: 12; cf. *De Corpore*, I.6.11.

Whatever language Adam and his children developed, however, was "lost at the tower of *Babel*, when by the hand of God, every man was stricken for his rebellion, with an oblivion of his former language."[78] Hobbes does not mention Genesis explicitly again in Part I of the book, even though therein he discusses the role of religion in man's nature, noting that it, too – much like speech – distinguishes man from the animals.[79] Nor does Hobbes cite Genesis in the following chapter, which treats "*Of the* NATURALL CONDITION *of Mankind, as concerning their Felicity, and Misery,*" until the final version, the Latin edition of 1668.[80] More importantly, nothing in Hobbes's description in *Leviathan* XIII bears even the slightest resemblance to prelapsarian Eden; everything points to the Fall and its aftermath.

As we have seen, however, the absence of such references did not prevent readers from making the obvious connection. Just as Hobbes had seen the political implications of the Augustinian interpretation of God's command and Adam's disobedience, his readers saw that his seemingly secular version of the state of nature was in fact directly anchored in Genesis. From his earliest political writings, Hobbes had made it clear that where the sovereign determines what is good and evil; private judgment has no place. The suggestion that it does is the fundamental cause of the demise of commonwealths, and a relapse into the state of nature.[81] That his choice of language was not accidental is evident from his own invocation of Adam's sin as the quintessential example of rebellion.[82]

But as even the brief survey of the aforementioned commentaries shows, the reader familiar with Genesis would have found plenty of other reminders, in the Introduction and Part I of *Leviathan*, of the opening episodes of the Bible. Certain terms and concepts such as creation, dominion, kingdom, obedience, rebellion, naming, language, command, covenant, good and evil, natural condition, and pride, which describe much of what takes place in Genesis 1–4, are scattered throughout the foundational elements of Hobbes's political edifice – from the state of nature, to the social pact, to life under a sovereign ruling over the children of pride – by keeping them "all in awe."[83]

---

[78] *Leviathan*, IV: 12.
[79] *Leviathan*, XII: 52.
[80] *Leviathan*, XIII: 60.
[81] See, for example, *The Elements of Law*, II.10.8; *De Cive*, V.6, VI.9, XII.1; *Leviathan*, XIV: 64, XVII: 87; XVIII: 91; XLV: 356–57.
[82] *De Cive*, XII.1.
[83] *Leviathan*, XIII: 62. Perceptively, Lucy criticized Hobbes for trying, "like another *Adam*, [to] impose Names upon every thing" in the opening sections of *Leviathan* (*Observations, Censures and Confutations of Notorious Errours in Mr. Hobbes His Leviathan*, 46). On the connection between Hobbes's emphasis on linguistic authority and Genesis, see Moloney, "Leaving the Garden of Eden." Milner ponders the possibility that Hobbes may have composed certain passages in his works so that they would be "reminiscent of Biblical language" ("Hobbes on Religion," 412). Thornton argues that Hobbes's natural condition of mankind

Much later, in Chapter XX, Hobbes considers passages from Scripture that support the rights of sovereignty. He returns to Genesis 3, and expands on the passage that he had discussed in *De Cive* XII, adding,

And whereas it is sayd, that having eaten, they saw they were naked; no man hath so interpreted that place, as if they had been formerly blind, and saw not their own skins: the meaning is plain, that it was then they first judged their nakednesse (wherein it was Gods will to create them) to be uncomely; and by being ashamed, did tacitely censure God himselfe. And thereupon God saith, *Hast thou eaten, &c.* as if he should say, doest thou that owest me obedience, take upon thee to judge of my Commandments? Whereby it is cleerly, (though Allegorically,) signified, that the Commands of them that have the right to command, are not by their subjects to be censured, nor disputed.[84]

The greatest objection to this argument, Hobbes goes on to state, comes from those who ask where and when subjects have ever acknowledged such power over themselves, to which one should respond by asking, "when, or where has there been a Kingdome long free from Sedition and Civill Warre[?]"[85] The reply to Leibniz's question, therefore, appears to be that there is never any power able to keep all men in awe, and this is illustrated most aptly by Adam's disobedience. Even in a condition without need, where a single man had been appointed viceroy over the rest of creation by his omnipotent sovereign, the explosive mix of a single curb with free will was sufficient to give rise to rebellion.

Having implied that at least one manifestation of the state of nature was the pre-political condition of mankind, Hobbes had stepped into the territory of Genesis. While this was unavoidable, given his audience's conception of history and religious beliefs, it was also very problematic since it entailed taking a position on issues that were highly controversial. Indeed, one could argue that they were at the heart of the disorder that had occasioned Hobbes's efforts to bring about peace. If talk of the natural condition of mankind was likely to cause readers to think of the story of Creation, how could Hobbes simultaneously convince them that there was nothing in his account that was essentially incompatible with their understanding of Genesis *and* avoid entering into the particulars of whether natural man was pre- or postlapsarian, ante- or postdiluvian, good or bad?[86] Was Eden the state of nature, or the condition that had preceded it?

---

was "recognizable to his readers, because it could be understood to have been built from fragments of" the three different conditions of Eden, the fall, and the fallen condition (*State of Nature or Eden?* 69); cf. Martinich, *The Two Gods of Leviathan*, 138.

[84] *Leviathan*, XX: 107.

[85] *Leviathan*, XX: 107.

[86] For the most part, commentators do not use these terms, but rather contrast one condition with the other, as nearly all of Hobbes's contemporary critics do. When they do, they refer to the two conditions as "supralapsarian" and "sublapsarian" (see, for example, [Parker], *A Reproof to the Rehearsal Transposed*, 381).

By using the vocabulary of Genesis, but steering clear of biblical exegesis, Hobbes was able to signal that his account of the state of nature was far from irrelevant to his readers' conceptions of their origins. At the same time, he was able to avoid becoming entangled in theological debates that would have diverted him from his goal.[87] Andrewes's sermons offer a glimpse of just how difficult some of those questions were. To cite but one example, in an attempt to locate Adam, Andrewes argues that when he was placed in Eden, "he was taken out of the common of the World, as when he had transgressed the commandment, he was cast out into the wide world again," whence Andrewes concludes, "[t]his then kindly worketh in us the conceit of humility to consider and remember that first man was a companion to Beasts, both in the same common matter and place, untill God took and brought him into a more excellent place."[88] More importantly, perhaps, by focusing simply on the issue of sovereignty in Genesis, Hobbes was able to adhere to his position that the authority to interpret Scripture was part and parcel of the authority of the sovereign.[89]

Genesis was a frame of reference that Hobbes could afford neither to ignore nor to engage outright. In this sense, it was indispensable, just as it was challenging, though by no means simply a hindrance, since, as we have seen, Hobbes's interpretation of Adam's place in Eden and of his disobedience was consistent with one of the most prominent exegetical traditions.[90] Far from simply subverting traditional glosses on Genesis, Hobbes seems to have relied on them to render his account plausible.

But even if we were to grant that Hobbes's rhetorical strategy allowed him to deal with the inescapable specter of Genesis in the least messy manner, we are still left with an important, perhaps the most crucial, difficulty: If the state of nature is a condition of anarchy, in which there is no power to keep all in awe, how could one imply that God's direct dominion over man was akin to the state of nature? The answer is that if rebellion was possible even for Adam, who not only lived under the best of conditions, but was also in direct communication with and under the reign of God, then rebellion is possible anywhere, even under the most powerful of earthly sovereigns.[91] In this light, it is not hard to see why Hobbes opted for Cain and Abel over Adam, when he decided to tie the state of nature to Genesis

---

[87] Strong argues that Hobbes refuses to interpret the Bible for his reader because "*each* must find him- or herself in Scripture" ("How to Write Scripture," 153–54).

[88] Andrewes, Ἀποσπασμάτια Sacra, 177–78.

[89] See, for example, *De Cive*, XIII.9; *Leviathan*, XXXIII: 206; *ibid.*, XLII: 300. "It is the Civill Soveraign, that is to appoint Judges, and Interpreters of the Canonicall Scriptures; for it is he that maketh them Laws." Cf. Malcolm, *Aspects of Hobbes*, 422–26.

[90] I thus disagree with Moloney, who argues that after his "re-reading of *Genesis*," Hobbes had "no need of the story of Paradise" ("Leaving the Garden of Eden," 266).

[91] See *Leviathan*, XXXV: 216. Cf. Slomp, *Thomas Hobbes and the Political Philosophy of Glory*, 47; Thornton, *State of Nature or Eden?* 41–45.

explicitly. Whereas Adam had enjoyed his peculiar moment of absolute freedom, Cain and Abel were always both under God's explicit sovereignty and
under Adam's sovereignty by *jure paterno*. As the paradigmatic fratricide,
Cain's challenge to that sovereignty was thus the best possible metaphor for
the fratricide that had plunged Hobbes's world into the state of nature.

Hobbes knew well that no amount of supervision, coercion, and civic
education was sufficient to persuade everyone to submit and obey. Necessary
though they were, these measures would always have to be supplemented
by the threat of a relapse into the state of nature, a condition so undesirable
as to be avoided at almost any cost. It is not uncommon to present the state
of nature as the antithesis of civil society, but this simple opposition misses
an important aspect of the state of nature, which is that it is never too far
away. As Hobbes reminded his readers in *Leviathan*, even in the best-run
commonwealths, one locks one's door at night.[92] The state of nature can
never be eliminated, not even in the ideal commonwealth, instituted according to Hobbes's prescriptions, since in reading *Leviathan*, its subjects would
encounter it in Chapter XIII.[93] By framing the minds of his readers with the
language and imagery of Genesis, Hobbes ultimately reminded them that
the threat of a perpetual relapse into a condition of anarchy and equality
that is "solitary, poore, nasty, brutish, and short" is mankind's inheritance
from Adam's lapse.[94]

92 *Leviathan*, XIII: 62; cf. *De Cive*, Pref., § 11.
93 In the Review and Conclusion to *Leviathan*, Hobbes urges the powers that be to make the
   book mandatory reading (395); cf. *ibid.*, XXXI: 193.
94 *Leviathan*, XIII: 62. The connection is captured by several commentators. Hood notes that
   every time a subject disobeys his sovereign, he "repeats the sin of Adam, for he disobeys God"
   (*The Divine Politics of Thomas Hobbes*, 175–76). According to Sorell, "Adam's descendants,
   the rest of humanity, inherit from him not only their mortality but also life outside Paradise"
   (*Hobbes*, 34). For Wolin, "far from marking the literal origins of political society, the state
   of nature denoted a relapse, a reversal of time," and adds that it was "a kind of political version of Genesis, without sacral overtones and without sin, but a fall, nevertheless, from the
   highest level of human achievement, life in a civilized society" (*Politics and Vision*, 237).

7

Another Scripture

> In the state of nature, where every man is his own judge, and differeth
> from other concerning the names and appellations of things ... it was
> necessary there should be a common measure of all things that might
> fall into controversy.... This common measure, some say, is right rea-
> son: with whom I should consent, if there were any such thing to be
> found or known *in rerum naturâ*.
>
>   – Hobbes, *The Elements of Law*

Of the several meanings that one could ascribe to it, many of Hobbes's
readers treated the state of nature first and foremost as the condition *prior
to* the establishment of civil society rather than "outside" or "without" civil
society.[1] They had several good reasons for doing so. Not only had Hobbes
referred to the state of nature as the "naturall condition of mankind,"
thereby prompting his readers to think of the opening chapters of Genesis,
but he also posited that the founding of the commonwealth constituted the
way out of that miserable condition. Hobbes's two explicit examples, in the
Elements and *De Cive*, reinforced the impression that his was an account
of man's pre-political condition. The first, that of the Indians of America,
represented savage contemporaries who had not made the transition from
small families to large and lasting societies. Suggestively vaguer, the second –
the savage ancestors of civilized nations – merely solidified the sense that
Hobbes had ancient history in mind. None of this would have seemed strange
to readers who, in addition to being intimately familiar with Genesis, might
have encountered this sort of exercise in the pages of Plato, Polybius, Ovid,
or Cicero. Hobbes does not name any literary sources in connection with
the state of nature.[2] A sufficient number of his contemporaries, however,

---

[1] Notable examples are Pufendorf and Barbeyrac (see the annotation in Pufendorf, *De Jure
Naturæ et Gentium Libri Octo*, II.ii.2).

[2] The closest to an exception to this practice is the reference to Cain and Abel, in the Latin
Leviathan. It should be borne in mind, however, that for all his innovations and departures

believed that they detected vestiges of Epicureanism in Hobbes's doctrine, to give rise to the widespread impression that Hobbes's state of nature was but a modern version of Lucretius's description of primitive man, in Book V of *De rerum natura*.[3]

The characterization of Hobbes as an Epicurean was more often than not superficial and disingenuous.[4] Even though it was fueled mainly by disagreement with Hobbes and a desire to discredit him, it was doubtless facilitated by Hobbes's association with Gassendi, who was widely considered an Epicurean. Even if Hobbes's view of man and interest in utility were in part the result of a certain Epicurean influence, however, they were already

---

from custom in regard to Scripture, Hobbes treats Biblical history as history, even when he questions the authority or antiquity of the sources.

[3] Harrison ventures to describe Hobbes as "the central English figure in what was termed the 'Epicurean revival,'" although Hobbes certainly never considered himself an Epicurean in any sense" ("The Ancient Atomists and English Literature of the Seventeenth Century," 3); cf. Westfall, *Science and Religion in Seventeenth-Century England*, 109; Kargon, *Atomism in England from Hariot to Newton*, 62; Pacchi, *Scritti Hobbesiani*, 43; Sarasohn, *Gassendi's Ethics*, 149; Glover, "God and Thomas Hobbes," 143–44. On the connection between Epicurean theories of the origin of society and Hobbes's account of the transition from the state of nature to civil society, see, for example, Creech's comments in Lucretius, *T. Lucretius Carus the Epicurean Philosopher, His Six Books De Natura Rerum*, ed. Creech (Preface, b3ᵛ; notes: pp. 39–41); Clarendon, *The Miscellaneous Works*, 143–44; Cumberland, *A Treatise of the Laws of Nature*, V: 590; Parker, *Disputationes de Deo et Providentia Divina*, xii, 86–97, 101–02; Tyrrell's comment to Locke (James Tyrrell to John Locke, Oxford, August 9, 1692, in de Beer, ed., *The Correspondence of John Locke*, IV: 495); Hume (*An Enquiry concerning the Principles of Morals*, App. 2, § 4), and Pufendorf (*De Jure Naturae et Gentium Libri Octo*, II.2).

[4] This is in part the result of the fact that for much of the seventeenth century, the term "Epicurean" did not have a precise meaning. Although it was used to designate an adherent to the views of Epicurus or his followers, it was mainly used as a rather loose synonym for atheism, or to describe an even looser set of pagan views. There were, however, as we shall see, commentators who used it in reference to Hobbes and attempted to draw parallels between his views and those of Lucretius, or those ascribed to Epicurus. Its vagueness is also evident in the fact that some of Hobbes's noted opponents, such as Boyle and White, were also considered Epicureans.

Perhaps aware of these difficulties and equipped with a better knowledge of Epicurus, recent commentators have been more cautious in their descriptions of Hobbes's relationship to Epicureanism. Thus, Harrison points out that "the broad parallelism between Hobbes and Epicurus is striking," and that "[w]hether Hobbes was actually an Epicurean or not, his opponents were justified in thinking that he was very like one" ("Bacon, Hobbes, Boyle, and the Ancient Atomists," 200, 192). As Mayo observes, "[o]ne thing, at any rate, Hobbism had in common in the public mind with seventeenth century Epicureanism – the taint of heresy" (*Epicurus in England*, 115). Mayo surveys some of the affinities, paying particular attention to the ones noted by Creech, and concludes that Hobbes's physics and philosophy are "in no exact sense 'Epicurean,'" but adds rightly that "the flavor of his thought was sufficiently similar to that of Epicureanism to make natural and indeed inevitable the popular association of the two philosophies" (*ibid.*, 124); cf. Goldschmidt, *La doctrine d'Épicure et le droit*, 245–46.

well established from the outset of his literary career, and certainly predate Hobbes's reading of Gassendi's work on Epicurus, which did not take place until October 1644.[5] That their friendship might have left its mark in certain expressions or images in their respective works is highly probable, but that it shaped Hobbes's outlook in any fundamental sense is doubtful.[6]

That Epicurus's doctrine survives at second hand and that Lucretius's poem was a relative latecomer in England, where no Latin edition was published until 1675 and no full English edition until Creech's of 1682, certainly did not help.[7] Hobbes himself, however, did not need to rely on these editions, nor on Evelyn's 1656 translation of Book I, in order to study *De rerum natura*.[8] Hobbes mentions Lucretius and Epicurus only very rarely, but some of the occasions on which he does so allow us to conclude that he was most likely familiar with Lucretius's poem since at least the late 1630s.[9] Working in reverse chronological order, Hobbes invokes Epicurus and Lucretius in his disagreement with Boyle, and, as we have seen, he uses Lucretius in the *Answer to the Preface to Gondibert* as an example of one who, even though he wrote in verse, was no poet, but rather a natural philosopher.[10] Hobbes had, in fact, treated him as one for the preceding decade. In addition to his extensive refutation of Lucretius's arguments in

---

[5] See Schuhmann, "Hobbes und Gassendi," 165; Tuck, *Philosophy and Government*, 288.

[6] Schuhmann in fact argues that if there were any influence, its direction was from Hobbes to Gassendi, rather than the other way around ("Hobbes und Gassendi," 168). Cf. Funkenstein, *Theology and the Scientific Imagination from the Middle Ages to the Seventeenth Century*, 328–31.

[7] *Titi Lucretii Cari De Rerum Natura Libri Sex., etc.*, edited by Tanaquil Lefebvre (Cambridge: John Hayes for W. Morden, 1675); *T. Lucretius Carus the Epicurean Philosopher, His Six Books De Natura Rerum, etc.*, translated by Thomas Creech (Oxford: L. Lichfield for Anthony Stephens, 1682). Mayo notes, however, that "at least twenty-six Latin editions of all or parts of the poem" were available in Europe since 1473 (*Epicurus in England*, 58).

On Gassendi, see, for example, Cowley, *The True Effigies of the Monster of Malmesbury*, Pref.; Cudworth, *The True Intellectual System of the Universe*, 462, 675, 697. Gassendi's reputation as an interpreter of Epicurus was such that he was referred to as an "incomparable man" in the preface to the Lefebvre edition (Lucretius, *Titi Lucretii Cari De Rerum Natura Libri Sex*, ed. Lefebvre, A5ᵛ; cf. Jones, *Pierre Gassendi*, 25–26, 205–06, 225–42).

[8] Evelyn, *An Essay on the First Book of T. Lucretius Carus De Rerum Natura*. On the availability of Epicurean works in the 1630s, see Barbour, *English Epicures and Stoics*, 25–26.

[9] Indeed, Lucretius's connection to Thucydides, which we will examine briefly, suggests the possibility that Hobbes had studied Lucretius in the 1620s during his translation of the history of the Peloponnesian War, although Hobbes's catalogue of the Hardwick Library contains no entry for *De rerum natura* (Devonshire Mss., Chatsworth HS/E/1A). Hobbes's aversion to arguments from authority perhaps accounts for the relative paucity of direct references to Lucretius in his works. Nevertheless, Hobbes includes Epicurus among the "men worthy of praise," the list of ancient philosophers whose wisdom was their own and benefited the human race (*Historia Ecclesiastica*, 407–08), a list that includes Aristotle (cf. *OL*, III: 540; *EW*, VII: 76).

[10] *Dialogus Physicus* (*OL*, IV: 277–83); *Answer to the Preface to Gondibert*, 133.

favor of the vacuum in *De Corpore*, which predated the publication of any English edition of *De rerum natura*, Hobbes had addressed a central tenet of Lucretius's philosophy in his critique of Thomas White's *De Mundo*.[11] More importantly, for the present purposes, apart from its title, which already implies a connection to Lucretius, Hobbes's *Elements* also contains a telling allusion to *De rerum natura*, to which we will turn later in this chapter, and which shows that Hobbes's encounter with Lucretius precedes his association with Gassendi.[12]

But even aside from these references, there appears to be ample prima facie justification for detecting Epicureanism in Hobbes's views. The reader who is only vaguely familiar with or perhaps not very interested in Epicureanism and knows it as a materialist philosophy that prizes utility, in which egoism and the pursuit of pleasure occupy central places, will find sufficient echoes in Hobbes's writings to justify the connection.[13] The case is stronger,

---

[11] *De Corpore*, IV.26.3; *Thomas White's De Mundo Examined*, 439ᵛ–440ʳ.

[12] Robertson's view that "it is a mistake to suppose that the reviver of the Epicurean philosophy can have exercised any special influence on Hobbes" (*Hobbes*, 64, n. 1) is, in essence, correct. The question of Gassendi's role in relation to Hobbes's Epicureanism has received a considerable amount of attention in recent decades. Ludwig argues that a political Epicureanism distinguishes *Leviathan* from *De Cive*, and that this Epicureanism can be traced to Hobbes's Parisian exile in general, and his association with Gassendi in particular (*Die Wiederentdeckung des epikureischen Naturrechts*, esp. 401–54; "Cicero oder Epikur? Über einen 'Paradigmenwechsel' in Hobbes' politischer Philosophie," esp. 161–62, 171–79), but the scope of his study does not allow him to consider the question of affinity between Hobbes and Epicureanism in *The Elements of Law*, which is in this sense, as in many others, quite similar to *Leviathan*. Hobbes's allusion to Lucretius in *The Elements of Law*, II.10.8, and the paragraph summary of I.5.6 are but the most obvious indications of an earlier interest in Epicurean themes. Paganini agrees that Gassendi is important, but disagrees with Ludwig's dating of Hobbes's Epicureanism, arguing that it predates *Leviathan* ("Hobbes, Gassendi and the Tradition of Political Epicureanism," 21–24). He argues that there is evidence of mutual influence, citing certain common themes and expressions, such as Hobbes and Gassendi's distillation of natural law into the Golden Rule (*ibid.*, 20–21), and the fact that both make use of some version of the "homo homini lupus" formula (*ibid.*, 15–17; "Hobbes, Gassendi et le *De Cive*," 183–93).

For a comparison of their respective systems, see Sorell, "Hobbes and Gassendi." On the relationship of Gassendi's conception of the state of nature and natural right to Hobbes's, see Sarasohn, *Gassendi's Ethics*, 142–54, although Sarasohn's distinction between Gassendi's emphasis on rationality and Hobbes's on fear (143) should be treated with caution. On their respective views of the will, see Sarasohn, "Motion and Morality." It is important to note that whereas Gassendi's name was closely tied to Epicurus, his version of Epicureanism was considered "innocuous" (Wilson, *Epicureanism at the Origins of Modernity*, 2; cf. *ibid.*, 27; Osler, "Ancients, Moderns, and the History of Philosophy," 129), whereas for Hobbes the association was almost entirely negative (cf. Goodrum, "Atomism, Atheism, and the Spontaneous Generation of Human Beings," 212–13).

[13] See, for example, Leibniz, *Die Philosophischen Schriften*, III: 68. Brandt had expressed great interest in the possible connection between the "Short Tract on First Principles," which Tönnies had attributed to Hobbes, and "antique atomism" (*Thomas Hobbes' Mechanical Conception of Nature*, 73), but declared his investigation inconclusive. Malcolm affirms the

if anything, when it comes to Lucretius's *De rerum natura*.[14] Although there are important differences in their respective treatments of the subject, both Lucretius and Hobbes are centrally preoccupied with fear, especially as it relates to religion. Lucretius declares that his mission is to rid mankind of the consequences of superstition.[15] The parallel here is so compelling that verses from *De rerum natura* adorned the early, unauthorized, editions of *Behemoth*.[16] This matter, more than any other, appealed to Hobbes's contemporaries, for it presented interested critics with an opportunity to paint Hobbes as an atheist.[17] Among the many elements of *De rerum natura* that could challenge the sensibilities of the pious, one of the more notorious was Lucretius's argument that religion arose from fear.[18] In his own preliminary discussion of religion, in Chapter XII of *Leviathan*, Hobbes writes of man's "perpetuall feare" and "ignorance of causes," and points to "some of the old Poets [who] said, that the Gods were at first created by humane Feare."[19] Hobbes hastens to add that this describes the Gods of the Gentiles, rather than the "one God, Eternal, Infinite, and Omnipotent," who is discoverable "from the desire men have to know the causes of naturall bodies, and their

Epicurean elements of the tract, but also lists a series of reasons for attributing it to Payne (*Aspects of Hobbes*, 113–39).

[14] The list of affinities is quite long. Examples in *De rerum natura* include a challenge to prevailing notions regarding life after death (I.102ff.), the importance of sense (I.699–700), but also the dangers inherent in the deceptions of sense and the need to engage in reasoning (I.127ff.; II.308ff.; III.379ff.), the rejection of incorporeal beings (I.146ff.; I.265ff.), the centrality of motion (I.995), the relationship between free will and necessity (II.251–93), the observation that human life is restless (III.1053–94), and a mechanical conception of the will (IV.877–906).

[15] The authorities are divided on Lucretius's term, "religio." Evelyn and Creech render it "religion," as does Bailey, whereas Hutchinson and Rouse translate it as "superstition."

[16] See items 86, 87, 87a, and 89 in Macdonald and Hargreaves, *Hobbes: A Bibliography*; cf. Seaward's introduction to *Behemoth*, 84–85. The lines in question are: I.83, "religio peperit scelerosa atque impia facta," and I.101, "tantum religio potuit suadere malorum," which Rouse translates as "[s]uperstition has brought forth criminal and impious deeds" and "so potent was Superstition in persuading to evil deeds," respectively. Hobbes commented on the unauthorized publication in a letter to Aubrey (August 18/28, 1679, *The Correspondence of Thomas Hobbes*, II: 772–73); cf. Seaward's introduction to *Behemoth*, esp. 14–15, 53.

[17] The characterization of Epicureanism as a form of atheism is already evident in the early part of the seventeenth century, long before the advent of the English editions of Lucretius (see, for example, Andrewes, *A Patterne of Catechisticall Doctrine*, esp. 15–16), but a much more frequent phenomenon in the latter half of that century and the early part of the next (see, for example, Bentley, *The Folly and Unreasonableness of Atheism Demonstrated*, 31; Cudworth, *The True Intellectual System of the Universe*, 656; Edwards, *The Eternal and Intrinsick Reasons of Good and Evil*, 20; Parker, *A Demonstration of the Divine Authority of the Law of Nature, and of the Christian Religion*, 88–13; Wolseley, *The Unreasonablenesse of Atheism*, 77; Tate's preface to Davies, *The Original, Nature, and Immortality of the Soul*, A7ᵛ–A8ʳ).

[18] See, for example, *De rerum natura*, I.102–58; V.1161–68.

[19] *Leviathan*, XII: 52.

severall vertues, and operations; than from the feare of what was to befall them in time to come."[20] Nevertheless, critics saw this as a veiled reference to and sign of agreement with Lucretius.[21]

Perhaps the best example of how easy it was to associate Hobbes with Lucretius, however, was Creech's preface to his celebrated translation. In introducing Lucretius to his countrymen, Creech was in a position somewhat similar to that of Hobbes vis-à-vis Thucydides, half a century earlier. He had to give them a reason to want to read an author who had not received much attention in England before. Yet, whereas defending Thucydides from the charge of atheism was but a small part of Hobbes's task, Creech had to confront his author's reputation head on. Far from shying away from that reputation, Creech rather makes the case that the best way to combat atheism is to expose it to public view.[22] But there are other reasons that justify his labor and render it appealing to his contemporaries, not the least of which is that *"the admirers of Mr.* Hobbes *may easily discern that his* Politicks *are but* Lucretius *enlarg'd; His state of* Nature *is sung by our* Poet; *the rise of* Laws; *the beginning of* Societies; *the* Criteria *of* Just *and* Unjust *exactly the same, and natural* Consequents *of the Epicurean Origine of Man; no new Adventures."*[23] Creech's sales pitch is not as unfair as one might think, for Book V of *De rerum natura* is replete with language and imagery that transport the reader not back to the golden age, but to a condition every bit as miserable as *Leviathan*'s state of nature.

Evidence of this affinity is already present at the opening of Book V, in Lucretius's praise of Epicurus. Therein, the poet enumerates the beasts and monsters mythical and real that roam the world, only to declare that the worst of them are unlikely to harm us and that the threat they represent pales, in any case, when compared with the fears that ravage our troubled minds.[24] Epicurus's great achievement lay in having vanquished these, and Lucretius's own task is to follow in his footsteps and produce an account of the laws of nature in the generation and death of all things. Lucretius insists that the universe is not centered on man, and thus argues that the vision of the Gods as anthropomorphic beings who are continuously directing man's fortune is mistaken.[25] This realization is a crucial step toward

---

[20] *Leviathan*, XII: 52–53.

[21] See, for example, Cudworth, *The True Intellectual System of the Universe*, 656, 730; Tate's preface to Davies, *The Original, Nature, and Immortality of the Soul*, A7ᵛ–A8ʳ; Edwards, *The Eternal and Intrinsick Reasons of Good and Evil*, 12, 20, 23–24; Wolseley, *The Unreasonablenesse of Atheism*, 17–18, 77–78.

[22] Lucretius, *T. Lucretius Carus the Epicurean Philosopher, His Six Books De Natura Rerum*, Preface, b2ʳ; cf. Mayo, *Epicurus in England*, 65–76, on Creech's detailed refutation in the notes, as well as on the inadvertent association of his name with Hobbes's.

[23] Lucretius, *T. Lucretius Carus the Epicurean Philosopher, His Six Books De Natura Rerum*, Preface, b3ᵛ.

[24] *De rerum natura*, V.22–48.

[25] *De rerum natura*, V.76–90; cf. I.44–49; II.177–81, 646–51.

understanding why the world around us is not entirely hospitable.[26] A "greedy" part of the world is "possessed by mountains and forests full of wild beasts, part rocks and vasty marshes hold, and the sea that keeps the shores of lands far apart," of which nearly "two parts ... are robbed from mortals by scorching heat, and constantly falling frost."[27] With "great labour," human beings are able to extract something from the plants and trees, which, however, are "either scorched up by the sun in heaven with too great heat, or cut off by sudden rains and chilly frost, and the blasts of the bitter wind batter them with violent storms."[28] "Besides," wonders Lucretius, "why does nature feed and increase the frightful tribes of wild beasts, enemies of the human race, by land and sea? Why do the seasons of the year bring disease? Why does untimely death stalk abroad?"[29] And all this is but the environment in which human beings, themselves frail and needy, are born.

In a famous passage, Lucretius contrasts the helpless infant with the other animals:

Then further the child, like a sailor cast forth by the cruel waves, lies naked upon the ground, speechless, in need of every kind of vital support, as soon as nature has split him forth with throes from his mother's womb into the regions of light, and he fills all around with doleful wailings – as is but just, seeing that so much trouble awaits him in life to pass through. But the diverse flocks and herds grow, and wild creatures; they need no rattles, none of them wants to hear the coaxing and broken baby-talk of their foster-nurse, they seek no change of raiment according to the temperature of the season, lastly they need no weapons, no lofty walls to protect their own, since for them all the earth herself brings forth all they want in abundance, and nature the cunning fashioner of things.[30]

This account, which is offered in the service of arguments that are more central to Lucretius's purpose, is not yet that of a primitive condition. That account is to come later.[31] Here, Lucretius is describing the world as it was

[26] *De rerum natura*, V.156–80, 195–99.
[27] *De rerum natura*, V.201–05 (Rouse translation).
[28] *De rerum natura*, V.213–17 (Rouse translation).
[29] *De rerum natura*, V.218–21 (Rouse translation).
[30] *De rerum natura*, V.222–34 (Rouse translation).
[31] *De rerum natura*, V.925f. On the relationship between Lucretius's stages to the accounts of his predecessors, see Campbell, *Lucretius on Creation and Evolution*, 10–12. On the relationship to other Epicurean accounts of the rise of society, see Fowler, "Lucretius and Politics," 422–31. The chronological and dramatic sequences in which Lucretius presents the stages of human development have been the subjects of considerable debate. As Campbell notes, Lucretius is clearly relying on the "very many topoi available to him, ready to be turned to his own devices" (*ibid.*, 10). Hence, both the original state of man and that of his contemporaries bring their respective advantages and disadvantages, prompting Campbell to reject the terms "progressivism" and "primitivism" employed, among others, by Lovejoy and Boas (*ibid.*, 11–12, and note 38). Cf. Segal, *Lucretius on Death and Anxiety*, esp. 214–27; Gale, *Myth and Poetry in Lucretius*, 174–77.

and is, to show that its faults and hostility to man belie the divine providence that others associate with life on Earth.[32]

It was into an environment of this sort that man was born. The first men
sprang from the earth, and were thus hardier than their descendants, living
a life similar to that of the beasts.[33] Lacking the necessary implements to cultivate the earth, they confined themselves to what they could procure from
nature's labors.[34] Driven by the elements into places of refuge rendered temporary by the invasions of the wild beasts that deposed them, and lacking
the knowledge to make fire and skin animals, they had none of the makings
of commodious living.[35] In such conditions, there was but little association,
and that fleeting. Intercourse between the sexes was as likely the result of
mutual attraction as of bribes or violent lust.[36] Beyond that, there was no
sense of a common good or law.[37]

Although in some ways not as undesirable as life in civilization, with its
wars and other miseries, this existence was sufficiently miserable to drive
individuals "by voice and gesture with stammering tongue" to signify that
"it was right for all to pity the weak."[38] This gave rise to no concord, but
many did uphold the covenant, thereby preventing the annihilation of the
human race.[39] The development of language facilitated society further, and
eventually men learned how to make fire and use it to cook.[40] Lucretius may
reject the theory that a wise man gave mankind language, but he credits the
genius of preeminent men with having illuminated the path toward society

---

[32] Lucretius's initial formulation, at 195, is his *etiamsi daremus*: as Bailey notes, the "si …
ignorem" is an "idiomatic Lucretian" formulation, whose result is "'suppose I were to be
ignorant' (as I am not)" of the first beginnings of things (*De rerum natura*, ed. Bailey, III:
p. 1352). A comparison with the description at 925–87 reinforces the sense that the earlier
account is of the world as it is, rather than as it was. Compare, for instance, V.206–12 to
V.933–36.

[33] *De rerum natura*, V.925–32, 966–69; cf. *De Cive*, VIII.1; *The Elements of Law*, I.14.12; *De
Cive*, I; *Leviathan*, XIII.

[34] *De rerum natura*, V.933–57. In contrast with the earlier account, Lucretius here writes of
abundance (V.937–44), despite the physical difficulties involved in securing food (V.933–36,
945–57).

[35] *De rerum natura*, V.953–57, 970–87; 988–98.

[36] *De rerum natura*, V. 962–65.

[37] *De rerum natura*, V. 958–61.

[38] *De rerum natura*, V.1019–23. On Lucretius's balancing act between these two conditions, see
Blickman, "Lucretius, Epicurus, and Prehistory," 161–63, 178–88.

[39] *De rerum natura*, V.1024–27. The relevant terms are "concordia" and "foedera." This
language caused Creech to associate the poem with Hobbes's covenant (cf., Lucretius,
T. Lucretius Carus the Epicurean Philosopher, His Six Books De Natura Rerum, ed. Creech,
Preface, b3ᵛ; cf. notes: pp. 39–41).

[40] Lucretius devotes several lines to disproving the suggestion that language was bestowed on
mankind by some wise man. He lists several difficulties in that scenario, and points to the
fact that even the animals produce different sounds in different circumstances, and thus concludes that the names of things are no arbitrary imposition, but the products of the evolution
of natural sounds (V.1028–90).

and civilization.[41] Those men, whom he calls "kings," gathered their people in cities, distributed property and honors to them, and built forts "for their own protection and refuge," from their subjects.[42] The kings' anticipation of rebellion was justified, as it turns out. Disparities in wealth, titles, and power gave rise to envy and vanity, which in turn led to revolution. Kings were put to death by their subjects. Each man sought power for himself, so anarchy reigned, until some men intervened once again and proposed that magistrates be appointed. Renewed weariness from the chaotic violence and fear at the prospect of every man exacting his own revenge had readied men for submission to the rule of law, and fear of punishment both temporal and divine consolidated the new state of affairs.[43]

After a long section on the origin of religion, Lucretius devotes the rest of Book V to the rise of the arts and crafts.[44] The common thread that runs through Lucretius's description of these activities is that by observing nature, men were able to invent ways of imitating it. Thus, for example, men discovered metals by chance when an accidental fire had melted them, or they learned how to cultivate the earth by observing the natural generation and regeneration of plants. They invented ways of entertaining themselves by imitating the sounds of nature, and learned to account for the passage of time and of the seasons by observing the sun and moon.[45] These developments were fueled by man's appetite: "For what is ready to hand, unless we have known something more lovely before, gives preeminent delight and seems to hold the field, until something found afterwards to be better usually changes our taste for anything ancient."[46] The results were not always beneficial, for the discovery of precious metals eventually led to competition, just as that of iron brought about more efficient warfare.

Nevertheless, human beings were able to escape the primitive conditions that had rendered their life so miserable in the beginning and progressed toward a daily existence of the kind that Hobbes would describe as commodious. Men lived protected inside fortifications, property existed because the land had been divided and was being cultivated, the seas were strewn with the colorful sails of ships transporting goods and knowledge, and

---

[41] *De rerum natura*, V.1105–07.

[42] *De rerum natura*, V.1108–16. As Bailey notes, the kings were "careful to provide a citadel for themselves, in which to protect themselves against revolt" (*De rerum natura*, ed. Bailey, III: p. 1499), an interpretation that is justified by the rebellions that Lucretius begins to describe at V.1136.

[43] *De rerum natura*, V.1136–240.

[44] *De rerum natura*, V.1161–240 for the former, 1241–1457 for the latter. Bailey concurs with Giussani's view (Lucretius, *T. Lucreti Cari De rerum natura libri sex*, ed. Giussani, IV: 148–49) that the section on the arts and crafts is intended to show that these developments were possible without the intervention of the Gods (*De rerum natura*, ed. Bailey, III: p. 1520). The placement and contents of these sections justify this view.

[45] *De rerum natura*, V.1241–96, 1361–78, 1379–411, 1436–39.

[46] *De rerum natura*, V.1412–15.

letters allowed poets to record great exploits.⁴⁷ The result is reminiscent of Hobbes's lists:

Ships and agriculture, fortifications and laws, arms, roads, clothing and all else of this kind, all life's prizes its luxuries also from first to last, poetry and pictures, artfully wrought polished statues, all these as men progressed gradually step by step were taught by practice and experiments of the active mind. So by degrees time brings up before us every single thing, and reason lifts it into the precincts of light. For they saw one thing after another grow clear in their minds, until they attained the highest pinnacle of the arts.⁴⁸

We have seen that in his own earliest such list, in the *Elements,* Hobbes focuses on the mathematicians and thus does not name such benefits as poetry and pictures, although he does imply that *every* benefit ultimately stems from the comforts made possible thereby, in the same manner as Lucretius does here: namely, illumination through reasoning.

The most compelling reason to think of Lucretius in connection with Hobbes's account of the state of nature in the *Elements,* however, comes first in the paragraph heading of I.5.6, which reads "Universalls not in Rerum natura," a claim to which Hobbes returns toward the end of that work, in a chapter that the table of contents describes as treating "Of the causes of rebellion."⁴⁹ There, Hobbes considers one of his most controversial suggestions, namely that civil laws are the measure of right and wrong. He points out that in the state of nature, where each man is his own judge, and disagreements over what is one's own and what belongs to another lead to conflict, it is necessary that there be a common measure for settling disputes. Some have suggested that right reason could provide such a standard, but Hobbes argues that no such thing is "to be found or known *in rerum naturâ,*" for those who invoke it usually mean their own.⁵⁰ The absence of such a universal standard is the reason why Hobbes believes that "the reason of some man, or men, must supply the place thereof," and why the civil law, rather than anything else, will determine what is right or wrong.⁵¹

The dutiful adherence to categories perhaps makes it difficult to see how a poem such as *De rerum natura* could have been a possible source for the state of nature in a work of science, such as *The Elements of Law.* As we have seen, however, Hobbes had a peculiar understanding of poetry and considered Lucretius not a poet, but a natural philosopher. Hobbes's

---

⁴⁷ *De rerum natura,* V.1440–47.
⁴⁸ *De rerum natura,* V.1448–57; cf., in particular, *The Elements of Law,* I.13.3, but also *Leviathan,* XIII: 62. For a comparison of various ancient accounts of the rise of civilization, including Lucretius's, see Cole, *Democritus and the Sources of Greek Anthropology,* Chapter 2.
⁴⁹ *The Elements of Law,* I.5.6. Cf. Devonshire Mss., Chatsworth HS/A/2A, HS/A/2B, HS/A/2C; London Mss., British Library Harl. 4235.
⁵⁰ *The Elements of Law,* II.10.8. Cf. *De Cive,* XIII.9.
⁵¹ *The Elements of Law,* II.10.8.

concluding description of the state of nature in his earliest political treatise shows not only that Hobbes was familiar with Lucretius long before his encounter with Gassendi, but also that Lucretius's account of man's rise in Book V of *De rerum natura* had informed Hobbes's conception of the state of nature from the start.

Two further considerations render the connection between the two even likelier. The first concerns Lucretius's most notorious and shocking teaching. In a passage at the start of Book II that inspired the promontories of the modern world and became emblematic of Epicureanism everywhere, Lucretius declares,

PLEASANT it is, when on the great sea the winds trouble the waters, to gaze from shore upon another's great tribulation: not because any man's troubles are a delectable joy, but because to perceive what ills you are free from yourself is pleasant. Pleasant is it also to behold great encounters of warfare arrayed over the plains, with no part of yours in the peril.[52]

For the poet, this is but the prelude to an appreciation of the sanctuaries and fortifications of philosophy, yet it also beautifully captures Hobbes's eirenic plan, as he described it in the Preface to *De Cive*. There, true to his claim to novelty, he promised no panacea for the reader's troubles, but only held up the prospect of uncertainty, misery, and a violent death as the alternative to a commodious, if imperfect, life.[53] Emphasizing the didactic value of such an observation, Hobbes would open his history of the English civil war with the following exchange:

A: For he that thence, as from the diuells mountain, should haue looked vpon the world, and obserued the actions of men, especially in England, might haue had a prospect of all kinds of Iniustice, and of all kinds of Folly that the world could afford, and how they were produced by their dams *hypocrisy* and *self-conceit*; whereof the one is double iniquity, and the other double folly.

B: I should be glad to behold that prospect. You that haue liued in that time, and in that part of your age wherein men vse to see best into *good* and *euill*, I pray you set me (that could not then see so well) vpon the same mountaine by the relation of the actions you then saw, and of their causes, pretensions, iustice, order, artifice, and euent.[54]

---

[52] *De rerum natura*, II.1–6 (Rouse translation). Creech translates these verses as follows:

Tis pleasant, when the Seas are rough, to stand
And view another's danger safe at Land;
Not 'cause he's troubled, but tis sweet to see
Those cares and Fears, from which ourselves are free:
Tis also pleasant to behold from far,
How Troops engage; secure our selves from war
 (Lucretius, *T. Lucretius Carus the Epicurean Philosopher, His Six Books De Natura Rerum*, 35).

[53] *De Cive*, Pref., §§ 20–21.
[54] *Behemoth*, 107. Cf. Lund, "Hobbes on Opinion, Private Judgment and Civil War," 71–72.

As B's reaction shows, Hobbes's hope is that his state of nature will be for his readers what tragedy in the stormy sea is to Lucretius's grateful onlooker.

THUCYDIDES, ANEW

The second is the strong connection between Lucretius and Thucydides. The most compelling evidence for that is, of course, Lucretius's discussion of the plague of Athens, which ends *De rerum natura* as it survives.[55] Hobbes, the translator of Thucydides' history, would have been intimately familiar with that episode from the second year of the Peloponnesian War. The plague is not just another instance of anarchy in Thucydides' history, but rather, one of a handful of truly memorable episodes from it. We know this not simply through the benefit of centuries' worth of hindsight that tells us that readers of Thucydides remember his account of the plague in the same way that readers of Hobbes's *Leviathan* remember his description of man's "solitary, poore, nasty, brutish, and short" life in the state of nature, but also because the textual evidence tells us that Thucydides meant for it to stand out. Its horrific description of the effects of this mysterious illness on its victims, coupled with its consequences for the city, capture the reader's attention. Then, as commentators have noted repeatedly, there is the matter of the way in which the tone, language, and imagery of that episode relates to Thucydides' statement of method in Book I.[56] The most conspicuous evidence of its special significance, however, is its location in Book II, where it sits between Pericles' most famous speech – the funeral oration – and his final speech to the Athenians. The contrast between the Athens that Pericles describes in the funeral oration and the Athens that Thucydides describes during the plague could not be sharper.[57] The former is a picture of Hobbes's commonwealth, a realm of reason in which man thrives and commodious living is at its apex. The latter is a place of unimaginable suffering, a hellish state of nature.

---

[55] Scholars have suggested that the poem is incomplete as it stands, and have advanced theories regarding Lucretius's intentions. Bailey discusses Bignone's theory, according to which the description of the plague was to be followed by a description of "the life and imperturbability of the gods" (*De rerum natura*, ed. Bailey, III: p. 1759), but Commager dismisses the idea ("Lucretius' Interpretation of the Plague," 114, 118). In addition to Commager (ibid.) and Bailey (*De rerum natura*, III: pp. 1723–44), see Fowler, "Lucretian Conclusions." On the relationship between Thucydides' account and Lucretius's, see also Foster, "The Rhetoric of Materials," esp. 388–96.

[56] See, for example, Gomme, *A Historical Commentary on Thucydides*, II, 147–62, for a discussion of the difficulties involved in composing an account of this situation that conforms to the standards that Thucydides sets for himself in Book I. Cf. Hornblower, *A Commentary on Thucydides*, I: 316–18.

[57] Connor delineates the contrast very well (*Thucydides*, 63–64). See also Saxonhouse, "Nature & Convention in Thucydides' History."

Backed by his assertion – offered to bolster its credibility – that he himself contracted the disease but survived it, Thucydides' detailed description of its effects on its victims conveys the magnitude of personal suffering in a manner that allows the reader to grasp it fully and vividly.[58] Preceding, as it does, the account of the disease's social effects, this description emphasizes the individual nature of this source of upheaval, and allows the reader to see that even in the midst of social unrest at the heart of the world's most illustrious city, an affliction such as this can result in a war of every man against every man.[59] This was a condition of radical equality: no one, no matter how rich or poor, strong or weak, was safe from it.[60] It was also a condition of anarchy, for the fear of the Gods and of the laws that normally restrain human beings were lifted, and with it shame and honor disappeared.[61] The inevitability and proximity of the horrific fate that awaited them transformed the calculus of the Athenians radically.[62] Foresight no longer made any sense. The commodious living that had made Athens the envy of the whole world in Pericles' assessment gave way to a breakdown of commitments so fundamental that individuals began to live as though they were alone in a universe that was about to come to an end.[63]

Violence and mayhem are the stuff of war, and Thucydides' history is filled with examples of its horrors. As we have seen, however, certain devices alert the reader that he has reached an episode in which the protagonists' excesses are so nasty as to require a reconsideration of the depths to which human beings can sink.[64] Thucydides uses several techniques in order to signal that we have arrived at such an episode. One with a long history, and thus likely to be familiar to Thucydides' readers, is to indicate that things

---

[58] Thucydides' self reference is at 2.48. His description of the possible origin and symptoms is extensive, and occurs at 2.47–51. The terminology and structure of these passages have been the subjects of endless debate, and disagreement remains strong. For a small sample, see Hornblower, *A Commentary on Thucydides*, I: 316–22 and note Hornblower's distinction between the tone of 2.49 and the rest (*ibid.*, I: 317–18). Foster offers the interesting suggestion that the force of Thucydides' account of the symptoms at 2.49.2–4 "is achieved through an easily discernible arrangement that deploys each familiar part of the body as a station along the way to destruction" ("The Rhetoric of Materials," 379–80).

[59] As Connor notes, the change that has taken place between Pericles' funeral oration and final speech to the Athenians is striking: "'We' disappears: 'I' and 'you' become the means of discourse" (*Thucydides*, 65).

[60] The extent of equalization that occurred is evident mainly at 2.51, but also in 2.52.

[61] Thucydides, 2.52–53.

[62] Thucydides, 2.53. At every opportunity, Thucydides emphasizes the magnitude of the disease, claiming, among other things, that it was the greatest (2.47; cf. 1.23), and that it was "a kind of sickness which far surmounted all expression of words, and both exceeded human nature in the cruelty wherewith it handled each one; and appeared also otherwise to be none of those diseases that are bred amongst us, and that especially by this" (2.50, Hobbes translation).

[63] In particular, in 2.53–54.

[64] See Orwin, "Stasis and Plague," 839–40, 846.

have deteriorated to such an extent that even the most fundamental elements of human life can no longer be taken for granted.[65] As we have seen,
Hobbes considered this quality of Thucydides' history one of its greatest
advantages. No reader will fail to understand that one can no longer rely
on anything for safety when even the simplest words have lost their meaning, and the most basic moral points of reference – pleas for mercy, and the
Gods and their temples – have ceased to command any respect. Thucydides'
account of the plague contains several such signs. In desperation, "what any
man knew to be delightful and to be profitable to pleasure, that was made
both profitable and honorable."[66] Temples became morgues, and the funeral
pyres prepared by friends for their own relatives, an opportunity for others
to dispose of their dead.[67]

Thucydides returns to these signals in Book III, when he recounts the
events that took place in Corcyra, in the fifth year of the war.[68] If the plague
marked the dissolution of society through its "depoliticization," the civil
war in Corcyra signaled its end through "radical politicization."[69] If this
language puts the plague and civil war at opposite ends of the spectrum of
politics, it is doubly useful in interpreting Hobbes because it points out that
normal political life is a mean flanked by extreme states of nature. At the
one end, the disintegration of civil society through radical individualism can
be perceived as a regression to a time when it was every man for himself. At
the other end, the move away from individualism that is represented in the

[65] Edmunds demonstrates the long lineage of this technique, focusing mainly on Hesiod, and
concludes that Thucydides' use of it constitutes evidence of his traditional, indeed conservative, ethics ("Thucydides' Ethics as Reflected in the Description of Stasis"). We will return to
the connection with Hesiod below; cf. Williams, "Two Traditional Elements in Thucydides'
Corcyrean Excursus." Hornblower considers the first sentence of 3.83 "the most straightforward authorial expression of conservative, nonsophistical morality in all Th[ucydides]"
(A Commentary on Thucydides, I: 478).
[66] Thucydides, 2.53 (Hobbes's translation).
[67] Thucydides, 2.52.
[68] Commentators point to a variety of evidence that links the two passages, including common
expressions and Thucydides' tone, which differs therein from much of the rest of his narrative, especially insofar as it includes his judgment, in addition to the events themselves (see
Hornblower, A Commentary on Thucydides, I: 477–79).
[69] The terms and illuminating contrast are Orwin's ("Stasis and Plague," 843; cf. Slomp,
"Hobbes, Thucydides, and the Three Greatest Things," 572). Thucydides uses the word
"στάσις" to describe this type of conflict. Translators use such terms as "revolution," "strife,"
"commotion," and "sedition." Edmunds ("Thucydides' Ethics as Reflected in the Description
of Stasis," 88) draws attention to a dictum of Solon's, "στάσιν ἔμφυλον πόλεμόν θ' εὕδοντ'
ἐπεγείρει" (Demosthenes, Περὶ τῆς Παραπρεσβείας, 255.21), according to which stasis awak-
ens dormant civil war. Some translators, Hobbes included, use different terms to translate
"στάσις," depending on the context (for example, at 3.82, Hobbes translates στάσις as "commotion," whereas at 3.83 as "sedition"). Uncomfortable with these options, some commentators leave the term untranslated. "Sedition" and "faction" are accurate translations, but I
have opted here for "civil war," which is the outcome in this particular case, and the subject
that most approximates Hobbes's war of all against all.

radical pursuit of faction has the paradoxical effect of bringing about the implosion of the larger group of which the faction is a subset. Either tendency, however, results in a state of nature, and the signs point to a certain common ground, although a comparison of the two conditions shows that the state of nature that results from the excessive pursuit of politics is the nastier of the two.

In his translation, Hobbes has Thucydides attribute the difference to the fact that "war, taking away the affluence of daily necessaries, is a most violent master and conformeth most men's passions to the present occasion."[70] Using language that would be granted an important role in *The Elements of Law* and *Leviathan* a few years later, Hobbes's Thucydides describes the extent of the disorder by reverting to a familiar trope: "The received value of names imposed for signification of things was changed into arbitrary."[71] Hobbes's translation of this passage is more felicitous than most, because it draws attention to the fact that what changed was not the meaning of words, but the way in which these words were applied. Thus, "true-hearted manliness" and "modesty" remained terms of approbation, but were now applied to "inconsiderate boldness" and "handsome fear."[72] A few years later, in discussing the dangers inherent in the abuse of speech, Hobbes would warn the reader to pay attention not just to the meaning of words, but also to the "nature, disposition, and interest of the speaker," especially when it comes to virtues and vices, "[f]or one man calleth *Wisdome*, what another calleth *feare*; one *cruelty*, what another *justice*; one *prodigality*, what another *magnanimity*; and one *gravity*, what another *stupidity*, &c."[73]

[70] Thucydides, 3.82.
[71] Thucydides, 3.82. The signification of words is, of course, central to Hobbes's political theory: when it is inconstant, it is the prelude to conflict, whereas when it is established and fixed, it is a sign of sovereignty (see, for example, *The Elements of Law*, I.5.7, II.2.11, II.10.5, II.10.8; *De Cive*, XVII.27; *Leviathan*, IV, XXVI).
[72] Thucydides, 3.82. On the translation of the passage in question, see Wilson, "'The Customary Meanings of Words Were Changed' – Or Were They?" Müri ("Politische Metonomasie," 72–77) and Macleod ("Thucydides on Faction," 54) consider the abuse of terms in the context of sophistic rhetorical practices. Apparently following Peacham's compendia (*The Garden of Eloquence* [1577], niii^v; *The Garden of Eloquence* [1593], 168), Skinner refers to this technique as "paradiastole" (*Reason and Rhetoric in the Philosophy of Hobbes*, esp. 175–80). It should be noted, however, that in addition to being very rare, that term was mainly used in sixteenth- and seventeenth-century compendia to denote a much broader opposition and enlargement of terms. Thus, for example, in his 1538 dictionary, Elyot defines it as "a dilatinge of a matter by an interpretation (*The Dictionary of Syr Thomas Eliot Knyght*), while in his own, of 1677, Coles defines it as "a distinction, an enlarging by interpretation" (*An English Dictionary, etc.*); see Martinich's review of *Reason and Rhetoric in the Philosophy of Hobbes*, 150. Müri and Macleod rightly identify the sophistic abuse of terms as the most appropriate context for Thucydides.
[73] *Leviathan*, IV: 17; cf. XV: 79; XVII: 87. The inclusion of prodigality and magnanimity on this list also calls to mind Machiavelli's questioning of the application of terms of approbation and disapprobation, in *The Prince* (esp. Chapter XVI). Cf. Skinner, *Reason and Rhetoric in the Philosophy of Hobbes*, 170–71.

If the subjective use of terms of approbation and disapprobation is part and parcel of politics and, hence, to be expected in a more aggravated form in a state of war, a clearer sign of the collapse of common standards was the violence that was, paradoxically, directed and indiscriminate at the same time. Directed, because specific individuals were targeted, hunted down, and killed in the most atrocious ways, and indiscriminate, because it did not matter that the victim was the killer's son or brother, nor that the murder took place inside or right in front of a temple.[74] Bands and factions existed, but their composition varied by the minute and was determined by the proximate goal, rather than long-term interest or any sense of the common good.[75] What is more, the existence of groups did not alter the underlying effective equality that characterized the civil war: everyone was equally vulnerable to the whims of nearly everyone else, and for any reason. Former friends turned into enemies and vice-versa, and any pretext was good enough.[76] Force and fraud, the furies that Hobbes had dubbed the "virtues of war" in *De Cive*, ruled Corcyra.[77] "All forms of death were then seen," writes Hobbes's Thucydides, leaving no doubt that this was, in the fullest sense, a war of all against all, a state of nature.[78]

However, if Thucydides' descriptions of the consequences of anarchy during the plague and the Corcyrean civil war are clearly apt examples of Hobbes's state of nature, why did Hobbes make so little use of them in his political treatises? As we have seen, the earlier *Elements* and *De Cive* contain faint traces of the language and imagery of these two episodes, but little more beyond that, and Hobbes did not link civil war with the state of nature explicitly until the English *Leviathan*.[79] It may be tempting to explain the evolution of Thucydidean language and imagery in Hobbes's political treatises as a consequence of timing: by 1651, civil war was a much more pertinent and persuasive example than it would have been in 1640. There can be little doubt that there is some truth to this, but between the early events

---

[74] Thucydides, 3.81. Macleod thus points out that this phenomenon is an extension of the abuse of terms: "[j]ust as the *stasiotai* perverted the 'traditional value' ... of words, so also they undid traditional ties and restraints" ("Thucydides on Faction," 57).

[75] Thucydides, 3.82–83.

[76] Thucydides points out that the civil war afforded the opportunity to settle old scores: "some were slain upon private hatred and some by their debtors for the money which they had lent them" (3.81).

[77] *De Cive*, Ep. Ded., § 2. This designation, too, cannot fail to evoke Machiavelli's *The Prince* (XVIII).

[78] Thucydides, 3.81. Hobbes's rendering of 3.81–83 in particular is replete with words and concepts that would recur in the *Elements*, *De Cive*, and *Leviathan*. In addition to repeated references to force and fraud, as well as to temporary alliances that would re-form at the first opportunity, Hobbes uses such terms as "dissolver of society" (3.82), "rapine" (3.82), "diffidently" (3.83), and "great fear" (3.83).

[79] The closest thing to an exception occurs in *De Cive*, long after Chapter 1, when Hobbes argues that one should not assume from the absence of a monarch's designation of a successor that he wished that his "commonwealth return to Anarchy, that is, civil war" (IX.14).

in England and the ongoing Thirty Years War on the continent, Hobbes already had sufficient grounds for invoking the specter of civil war even as early as 1642, but certainly by the publication of *De Cive*, in 1647. A more important consideration has to do with Thucydides' examples themselves, which are, in some sense, too good.

Thucydides' accounts of the plague and *stasis* are examples of the perils of anarchy *in extremis*. They are iconic illustrations of how far disorder can extend when the norms and rules break down, and are treated as such: time and again, they are invoked to establish boundaries in the way we think about human behavior. In following Thucydides' narration, the reader focuses less on the diffidence that underlies the build-up to these conditions and more on the aberrant events that mark the culmination of chaos. Hobbes was aware of this danger, for he warns the reader of his translation that "for the greatest part, men came to the reading of history with an affection much like that of the people in Rome: who came to the spectacle of the gladiators with more delight to behold their blood, than their skill in fencing," knowing that "they be far more in number that love to read of great armies, bloody battles, and many thousands slain at once, than that mind the art by which the affairs both of armies and cities be conducted to their ends."[80] Hobbes considered these tendencies so problematic that he set aside his translation after he had finished it, fearing that his readers would not find it sufficiently exciting.[81] Thucydides is more sober than most historians in this respect, but even his history contains such distractions, and the descriptions of the plague and stasis in particular are of this sort.[82]

For Hobbes's purposes, however, these passages are problematic for a further reason. They portray individuals who are, psychologically, too close to a point of no return. The actors who are driven mad by the sickness and surrounded by a collapsing moral order and anarchy are individuals who have nothing to lose and hence operate on a different calculus; what appears as irrational to an outside observer makes sense to them.[83] Hobbes is hoping to

---

[80] *EW*, VIII: ix.

[81] *EW*, VIII: ix. "After I had finished [the translation], it lay long by me: and other reasons taking place, my desire to communicate it ceased." There has been some speculation as to whether those "other reasons" might involve a particular event or political development, but the very next sentence – which initiates the section on readers' tendencies quoted earlier – explains: "For I saw that, ..." (*ibid.*).

[82] Commentators note that Thucydides' tone changes in both passages. Hornblower, for instance, suggests, "[o]ne can agree that these final chapters of the plague description, including those on moral degeneration (53–4) are in Th.'s richest and most generalizing manner, and look forward to the Corcyrean *stasis* description" (*A Commentary on Thucydides*, I: 317). No longer merely the historian who is reporting facts, the author of the plague and civil war passages is described as "rhetorically-minded" (*ibid.*), and as expressing his own opinions (*ibid.*, p. 478).

[83] Ahrensdorf thus rightly identifies the danger inherent in taking fear too far and thereby rendering human beings desperate and unable to "truly recognize or accept" their condition

catch his readers before they reach that point. On the one hand, therefore, there is a certain appeal to holding up the examples of the Athenians during the plague and of the Corcyreans during civil war as ones to be avoided at all cost. On the other hand, doing so entails the possibility that those who have already begun to feel boxed in may find in them a vindication of their point of view, and thus be driven not toward peace, but toward perpetual conflict.[84]

Hobbes's critics often complain that his focus on the fear of violent death is excessive, resulting in a caricature of human nature, with beings overly frightful and willing to submit to any conditions so long as their sovereign guarantees their lives.[85] Hobbes's description of the state of nature, however, shows that this criticism is exaggerated. The first piece of evidence, as we have seen, is direct: when he enumerates the passions that incline men toward peace, Hobbes lists not simply the fear of violent death, but also the "[d]esire of such things as are necessary to commodious living; and a Hope by their Industry to obtain them."[86] Whereas Thucydides' plague and civil war episodes leave little room for commodious living, Hobbes's accounts put it at the center.[87] Recall that Hobbes's first contrast between the state of nature and civil society consisted of a juxtaposition of the benefits derived from mathematics to the brutish life of the savages of America.[88] The list of civilization's benefits formed the basis of Hobbes's subsequent contrasts, and explains why, in addition to being short, life in the state of nature was also solitary, poor, nasty, and brutish.[89] The fullest and most detailed version of Hobbes's state of nature confirms this sense. In it, death plays but a very small part, whereas uncertainty and inconvenience reign supreme, leaving little doubt about the relative balance between felicity and misery promised by the chapter's title.[90]

---

and deal with it rationally ("The Fear of Death and the Longing for Immortality," 588). Cf. Cogan, *The Human Thing*, 152–54; Brown, "Thucydides, Hobbes, and the Derivation of Anarchy," 60.

[84] The perils of desperation figure prominently in Diodotus's argument regarding the Mytileneans (3.46) and the Melians' response to the Athenians (5.98), in Thucydides' history, as well as in Josephus's description of the siege of Jerusalem (see, e.g., VI.199–219).

[85] See, for example, [Eachard], *Mr. Hobbs's State of Nature Considered.*

[86] *Leviathan*, XIII: 63.

[87] The radical dissolution of social ties is perhaps the most obvious way in which Thucydides' episodes approach the issue of commodious living. The only reference to material goods is to the mindless spending that resulted from the loss of all forethought at the prospect of certain death (2.53).

[88] *The Elements of Law*, I.13.3.

[89] *Leviathan*, XIII: 62; OL, III: 100; *Answer to the Preface to Gondibert*, 143. Thus, Macpherson is in essence correct when he emphasizes the significance, for Hobbes's argument, of his readers' desire for commodious living (see, for example, *The Political Theory of Possessive Individualism*, 17–29). Cf. Landucci, who sees grounds for considering Hobbes's state of nature in *Leviathan* merely a projection, to the limit, of the English mercantile society of the seventeenth century (*I filosofi e i selvaggi*, 127–28).

[90] "*Of the* NATURALL CONDITION *of Mankind, as concerning their Felicity and Misery*" (*Leviathan*, XIII: 60). In *Leviathan* XIII, Hobbes refers twice to the fear of death – once as

For Hobbes, who wished to conjure an image of this condition that would ring true to his readers, the decision to link the state of nature to the savage ancestors of civilized nations must have been an easy one. Looking beyond the Bible, one could find a wealth of well-known histories, myths, and speculative accounts of man's pre-social condition, filled with images and catchwords that Hobbes's contemporaries would have come across in one form or another. These accounts were no less problematic than Genesis. In many of them, primitive life was idyllic and peaceful, the very antithesis of Hobbes's war of all against all – a golden age. But the ancient poets' and historians' accounts of the natural condition of mankind were no less controversial or problematic than that of Genesis. Many of these stories describe man either as created by the Gods or as born into a world already ordered and governed, prompting the type of objection that Leibniz raised to Hobbes. Nevertheless, even in stories in which the role of the Gods was less central, as in *De rerum natura*, it was not always clear whether the very first stage of man or a subsequent one was to be taken as his natural condition. In any case, the transition to a civil society that would have been familiar to Hobbes's readers involved several intermediary steps during which life was precarious and brutish. In short, there was ample material from which to draw.[91]

For Hobbes's contemporaries, such material might have come from Hesiod, who is credited with having introduced the metallic paradigm into Greek literature, or Ovid, whose account of the golden age became emblematic.[92] In *Works and Days*, the former never refers to a "golden

---

the means by which man leaves the state of nature – but twice as many times to diffidence. The content of the chapter is devoted mainly to the circumstances that render the natural condition of mankind such a miserable place beset with danger.

[91] Indeed, Hobbes was not alone in this. Bodin describes the golden and silver ages as times "in which men were scattered like beasts in the fields and the woods and had as much as they could keep by means of force and crime, until gradually they were reclaimed from that ferocity and barbarity to the refinement of customs and the law-abiding society which we see about us" (*Method for the Easy Comprehension of History*, 298).

[92] It is worth noting that in Hesiod's account, the Gods created a race of heroes (*Works and Days*, 156–73) between the penultimate (bronze) race and final (iron) race. Given that Hesiod uses the term "race" (γένος) rather than "age," for each of these stages, and considers himself one of the iron race (174–75), it is possible to see the development not of a single genus, but rather the distinct evolutions of separate ones. This in turn would mean that the natural condition of mankind as we know it is not to be found in the golden age, but in lines 182–201.

West lists possible antecedents (Hesiod, *Works & Days*, 199), and Norlin offers a valuable survey of Greek descriptions of man's primitive condition in general ("Ethnology and the Golden Age"). For a schematic account of the golden age, see Levin, *The Myth of the Golden Age in the Renaissance*, 3–31. On the issues surrounding the origins of the story, see Baldry, "Who Invented the Golden Age?" as well as the subsequent exchange between Baldry and Griffiths; cf. Cole, *Democritus and the Sources of Greek Anthropology*. There are several other well-known examples, including Virgil's different versions in the *Georgics*

age," but he describes the first *race* of "speech-endowed human beings" as golden.[93] Although mortal, these beings lived like gods, without a care for sickness or old age, and with ready access to "all good things."[94] Ovid's account, in which he describes the age itself as golden, is similar in structure, but differs in one important respect for the present purposes: Whereas Hesiod describes the life of the golden race by listing the benefits it enjoyed, Ovid does so by contrasting the benefits that flowed directly from nature to the human inventions that would come to characterize civilized life. Thus,

There was no fear of punishment, no threatening words were to be read on brazen tablets; no suppliant throng gazed fearfully upon its judge's face; but without defenders lived secure. Not yet had the pine-tree, felled on its native mountains, descended thence into the watery plain to visit other lands; men knew no shores except their own. Not yet were cities begirt with steep moats; there were no trumpets of straight, no horns of curving brass, no swords or helmets. There was no need at all of armed men, for nations, secure from war's alarms, passed the years in gentle ease. The earth herself, without compulsion, untouched by hoe or ploughshare, of herself gave all things needful.[95]

This was the age of Saturn's rule, which Hobbes admired because in it rebellion and regicide were inconceivable.[96] Alas, it was not meant to last. Both Hesiod and Ovid speak of a gradual deterioration, during which the golden race was succeeded by silver, bronze, and iron races, each worse than the one before.[97] The worst of these, the iron age, was the time when "all evil burst forth."[98] As in Corcyra during the civil war, when

baneful iron had come, and gold more baneful than iron; war came, which fights with both, and brandished in its bloody hands the clashing arms. Men lived on plunder. Guest was not safe from host, nor father-in-law from son-in-law; even among brothers 'twas rare to find affection. The husband longed for the death of his wife, she of her husband; murderous stepmothers brewed deadly poisons, and sons inquired into their fathers' years before time. Piety lay vanquished, and the maiden Astraea, last of the immortals, abandoned the blood-soaked earth.[99]

(I.121–75) that correspond to Hesiod's model and ascribe the deterioration to the transition from Saturn to Jupiter, and in the *Eclogues* (IV) where Virgil posits a new golden age that will succeed the iron age, and thus departs from the usual trend of deterioration (see Johnston, *Vergil's Agricultural Golden Age*).

[93] Hesiod, *Works and Days*, 89.
[94] Hesiod, *Works and Days*, 109–20.
[95] Ovid, *Metamorphoses*, I.89–102.
[96] *De Cive*, Pref., § 6.
[97] Whereas Hesiod's golden race was covered by the earth (*Works and Days*, 121), Ovid ties the shift to silver to the transition from the rule of Saturn to that of Jupiter (*Metamorphoses*, I.113–18).
[98] Ovid, *Metamorphoses*, I.128–29.
[99] Ovid, *Metamorphoses*, I.142–50. Hesiod's version is equally powerful:

Father will not be like-minded with sons, nor sons at all, nor guest with host, nor comrade with comrade, nor will the brother be dear as he once was. They will dishonor

But here, too, Hobbes already had a precedent in Thucydides, whose account of the earliest conditions in Hellas offers a vivid and memorable picture of how uncertain and uncomfortable life without adequate security can be. Lacking any established authority capable of enforcing rules, the earliest Hellenes experienced great upheaval and diffidence. As translated by Hobbes, Thucydides describes that period as a time of "everyone easily leaving the place of his abode to the violence always of some greater number."[100]

This is precisely the image that Hobbes uses in *Leviathan* when he seeks to persuade the reader that effective equality will result in pervasive diffidence in the state of nature, where, "if one plant, sow, build, or possesse a convenient Seat, others may probably be expected to come prepared with forces united, to dispossesse, and deprive him, not only of the fruit of his labour, bur also of his life and liberty," adding that "the Invader again is in the like danger of another."[101] Amid such uncertainty, Thucydides continues, there was no commerce, no travel by land or sea without fear, no contact, and no accumulation of wealth, because foresight made no sense since there were no fortifications.[102] The absence of reliable security and the concern with immediate survival meant that no cities of any note could flourish. Such as emerged, were thus constantly at the mercy of pirates and

their aging parents at once; they will reproach them, addressing them with grievous words – cruel men, who do not know the gods' retribution! – nor would they repay their aged parents for their rearing. Their hands will be their justice, and one man will destroy the other's city. Nor will there be any grace for the man who keeps his oath, nor for the just man or the good one, but they will give more honor to the doer of evil and the outrage [sic] man. Justice will be in their hands, and reverence will not exist, but the bad man will harm the superior one, speaking with crooked discourses, and he will swear an oath upon them. And Envy, evil-sounding, gloating, loathsome-faced, will accompany all wretched human beings. Then indeed will Reverence and Indignation cover their beautiful skin with white mantles, leave human beings behind and go from the broad-pathed earth to the race of the immortals, to Olympus. Baleful pains will be left for mortal human beings, and there will be no safeguard against evil (*Works and Days*, 182–201).

Edmunds notes the similarities between Hesiod's account of the iron race and Thucydides' description of the civil war, focusing in particular on the inversion of values ("Thucydides' Ethics as Reflected in the Description of Stasis," esp. 83–92). Cf. Statius, *Silvae*, I.6.39–45.

[100] Thucydides, 1.2.1; cf. 1.2.2, 1.2.3–6; cf. Cicero, *De officiis*, II.iii, § 12.
[101] *Leviathan*, XIII: 61.
[102] Thucydides, 1.2.2. Klosko and Rice point out the remarkable similarities between Hobbes's notorious list in *Leviathan*, XIII (62) and Thucydides' 1.2, and deem it reasonable to conclude that the former was based on the latter ("Thucydides and Hobbes's State of Nature," 408; cf. Malcolm's introduction to his edition of *Leviathan*, I: 325). Gomme notes that "inter-state commerce is the first sign, for Thucydides, of a settled life and higher standards of living" (*A Historical Commentary on Thucydides*, I: 92). Orwin observes that in the "archaeology," Thucydides remains "silent as to the rights and wrongs of the wars ascribed to those times" (*The Humanity of Thucydides*, 30).

plunderers, whose exploits, amid such lawlessness, were not only "nowhere in disgrace," but even had "something of glory."[103]

Professing to write history in a methodical manner, Thucydides knows that even though it is necessary because it will explain how the events he is principally interested in came to take place, his "archeology" of Hellas is also problematic. For the very reasons that made life primitive, those early times have left no reliable records, such as would allow us to reconstruct them.[104] One of the ways in which Thucydides compensates for this lack of evidence is by a conjecture based on the hypothesis that they would be similar to the conditions of the barbarians of his day, precisely the formula Hobbes relies on in the *Elements* and *De Cive*.[105] Equally importantly, while the various accounts of primitive life that were available to Hobbes's contemporaries contained ample material that one could mine in order to construct an unappealing image of the pre-social condition, the trajectory of most of these stories was one of deterioration rather than improvement. Theirs was the opposite of the story that Hobbes was looking to tell because the further away one moved from those early times, the worse the life of man looked.[106] By the time Hobbes came to his own "archeology," however, a solution to both of these problems had presented itself in the form of the New World.

---

[103] Thucydides, 1.5. As we have seen, Hobbes refers to this fact in similar terms, in *De Cive* (V.2).

[104] See, for example, Thucydides, 1.1.3; 1.3.1. Romilly notes the difficulty that the conjectural history of the opening chapters poses for Thucydides' statement of method (*Histoire et raison chez Thucydide*, 240–44); cf. Forbes, *Thucydides Book I*, Notes: pp. 5–8.

[105] Thucydides, 1.6: "And the nations of Greece that live so yet, do testify that the same manner of life was anciently universal to all the rest."

[106] This is from the point of view of the author and reader, and so it does not apply to those cases in which a better state has yet to happen, such as Virgil's second golden age, or Christ's Second Coming.

A weroan or great Lorde of Virginia. III.

He Princes of Virginia are attyred in fuche manner as is expreſſed in this figure. They weare the haire of their heades long and bynde opp the ende of thefame in a knot vnder thier eares. Yet they cutt the topp of their heades from the forehead to the nape of the necke in manner of a cokſcombe, ſtirkinge a faier lōge pecher of ſome berd att the Begininge of the creſte vppun their foreheads, and another ſhort one on bothe ſeides about their eares. They hange at their eares ether thicke pearles, or ſomwhat els, as the clawe of ſome great birde, as cometh in to their fanſye. Moreouer They ether pownes, or paynt their forehead,cheeks,chynne,bodye, armes,and leggs, yet in another ſorte then the inhabitantz of Florida. They weare a chaine about their necks of pearles or beades of copper, wich they muche eſteeme, and ther of wear they alſo braſelets ohn their armes. Vnder their breſts about their bellyes appeir certayne ſpotts,whear they vſe to lett them ſelues bloode,when they are ſicke. They hange before thē the ſkinne of ſome beaſte verye feinelye dreſſet in fuche ſorte, that the tayle hangēth downe behynde. They carye a quiuer made of ſmall ruſhes holding their bowe readie bent in on hand,and an arrowe in the other,radie to defend themſelues. In this manner they goe to warr, or tho their ſolemne feaſts and banquetts. They take muche pleaſure in huntinge of deer wher of theris great ſtore in the contrye,for yt is fruitfull,pleaſant,and full of Goodly woods.Yt hathe alſo ſtore of riuers full of diuers ſorts of fiſhe. When they go to battel they paynt their bodyes in the moſt terible manner that thei can deuiſe.

FIGURE 7. A weroan or great Lorde of Virginia.
Source: Thomas Hariot, *A Briefe and True Report of the New Found Land of Virginia* ... (Frankfurt, 1590). Courtesy of the John Carter Brown Library at Brown University.

8

America

[W]hatsoeuer distinguisheth the ciuility of *Europe*, from the Barbarity of the *American* sauuages, is the workemanship of Fancy, but guided by the Precepts of true Philosophy.
– Hobbes, *Answer to the Preface to Gondibert*

It is impossible to comprehend and describe fully the magnitude of the challenge that the New World posed for Europeans in the fifteenth, sixteenth, and seventeenth centuries. It is clear, however, that any event that is in contention for the title of most significant in the history of the world will have fundamental consequences for the way in which human beings understand and describe their universe.[1] The extent of the difficulty is evident both in the relative paucity of early commentary, which has been attributed to the shock of the discovery, and in the fact that the questions it raised continued to be debated well into the seventeenth century.[2] Neither the categories nor the language to describe some of the new discoveries existed; Europeans sometimes had to adjust their cosmology to the new facts, and sometimes attempted to fit the new into the old.[3] A wealth of evidence demonstrates

[1] See the examples of such declarations cited in Elliott, *The Old World and the New*, 9–10, and Burke, "America and the Rewriting of World History," 40–41; cf. Campanella's assessment near the end of the sixteenth century: "about our present century, which has produced more history in a hundred years than the whole world did in the preceding four thousand" (*La città del sole*, 121), and Smith's, nearly two hundred years later (*An Inquiry into the Nature and Causes of the Wealth of Nations*, IV.vii.c.80), which, as the editors point out, has an exact precedent in Raynal's *Histoire philosophique*.
[2] Elliott, *The Old World and the New*, Chapter 1.
[3] Pagden discusses examples of both tendencies (*The Fall of Natural Man*, 11–13). As Rubiés points out, where cosmologies had made allowances for terræ incognitæ, any discovery could be fitted into an existing scheme without great difficulty. This was not the case with an entire continent, whose existence and population required an explanation ("Hugo Grotius's Dissertation on the Origin of the American Peoples and the Use of Comparative Methods," 227–28). Wey Gómez relates the astonishing example of Columbus's attempt to explain the

how complicated this task was. Records from the earliest chroniclers and commentators employ language ranging from heaven to hell.[4] In the years following the discovery, it was not uncommon for explorers to liken America to Eden and the golden age, or to depict it as a land inhabited by monsters and savages.[5]

This uncertainty about the nature of America and its inhabitants was exacerbated by the fact that the New World became the battleground on which a new range of lucrative commercial wars would be fought. To secure royal and papal permission, as well as financial backing for the expeditions they proposed to carry out, explorers had to persuade sovereigns and investors alike that they could expect rich returns on their investments. Natural resources and land were obvious rewards, and pleas, advertisements, and eye-witness reports from the end of the fifteenth century until Hobbes's time are replete with promises of gold, precious stones, spices, and other valuable commodities in immeasurable quantities.[6] But who owned these resources

---

temperate climate that he encountered by dismissing the ancient theory that the Earth was round, and in favor of the "form of a pear that is all very round, except for where it has the bump [peçon] that makes it taller" (*The Tropics of Empire*, 431).

[4] For some earlier cosmologies, beyond the Pillars of Hercules lay the Hesperides whereas for others it was the locus of the earthly paradise. Columbus and Raleigh are among those who made the latter claim (see Wey Gómez, *The Tropics of Empire*, 234, 398, 433). Although problematic in that regard, the location of these newly discovered lands was also promising, however, because it placed them outside the sphere that had been assigned exclusively to the Portuguese (see Pagden, *The Fall of Natural Man*, 33–34). Richard Eden's explanation for why they were discovered so late is particularly entertaining in the present context: Christ, he claims,

> hath suffered the greate serpente of the sea Leuiathan, to haue suche dominion in the Ocean and to caste such mustes in the eyes of men, that sense the creation of the worlde untyll the yeare before named [1492], there hath byn no passage from owr knowen partes of the world to these newe landes, wheras nowe the same are moste certeynely knowen to be not past xxx. dayes saylynge from Spayne (Anghiera, *The Decades of the Newe Worlde or West India*, a.iiiᵛ).

[5] In Hariot's *Briefe and True Report*, the section devoted to John White's depictions of Virginia is preceded by Theodor De Bry's depiction of the Fall (see image 6). For an example of this association, see Hakluyt, *The Principal Navigations*, III: 249; cf. Elliott, *The Old World and the New*, 20–21, 24–25; Sloan, *A New World*, 14–16. As Pagden points out, citing the example of Peter Martyr, this terminology was often invoked in contexts that were, prima facie, problematic, although nevertheless acceptable (*The Fall of Natural Man*, 24). Despite important differences, various ancient and medieval cosmologies held that terræ incognitæ were inhabited by monsters (see, for example, Friedman, *The Monstrous Races in Medieval Art and Thought*, esp. 198–207; Wittkower, "Marvels of the East"). One finds traces of this expectation in several early accounts of the discovery of America (see, for example, Columbus's letter to the Sovereigns during his first voyage, in Morison, ed., *Journals and Other Documents on the Life and Voyages of Christopher Columbus*, 184; Raleigh, *The Discovery of the Large, Rich, and Beautiful Empire of Guiana*, 85; cf. Mason, *Deconstructing America*, 97–115).

[6] See, for example, Eden's preface to his translation of part of Peter Martyr's *De Orbo Nove* (Pietro Martire d'Anghiera, *The Decades of the Newe Worlde or West India*); Whitaker,

and the lands in which they were found? This question was inextricably intertwined with that of the status of the natives. Were they human beings and hence the owners with whom one had to negotiate or trade, or something less and, therefore, no obstacle to appropriation by conquest? The answer to this question would determine not only whether the natives could be deprived of the land and natural wealth, but also whether they themselves could be enslaved and traded.[7]

Arguments on either side required some justification. Attempts to provide such justification had been made before, whenever abductions and enslavement had been carried out, so there was some precedent for the positions that began to develop at the end of the fifteenth century.[8] These rested on a variety of sources and reasons, ranging from Aristotle's theory that certain latitudes generated people naturally fit to be slaves to Scriptural passages that appeared to present slavery as the penalty for ancestral sin. No less important was the determination of where the Indians had come from, a problem whose implications extended well beyond the question of dominion and into the question of the very authority of the Bible and of the ancient historians.[9] Ultimately, these sources were tied to accounts of the order of nature that classified the natives as inferior beings, and thus justified their subjection by natural law.[10] Lying to the west of Europe, rather than to the north or the south, the American natives did not fit neatly into the established paradigm that held that only the inhabitants of the temperate middle zone of the Earth were fit for freedom, one that had been invoked time and again to justify the enslavement of Africans.[11] What is more, the Indians

---

Good Newes from Virginia, 41–44; Raleigh, *The Discovery of the Large, Rich, and Beautiful Empire of Guiana*, 109, whose title is telling. Also instructive are the letters of Columbus and de Cuneo (Morison, ed., *Journals and Other Documents on the Life and Voyages of Christopher Columbus*), as well as the accounts of Best, Keymis, and Parkhurst, among others (Hakluyt, *The Principal Navigations, Voyages, Traffiqves and Discoveries of the English Nation, etc.*). Cf. the more measured and detailed lists in Hariot (*A Briefe and True Report*, 7–24); Elliott, *The Old World and the New 1492–1650*, 11–12.

[7] The centrality and persistence of the question of the natives in particular is illustrated by Las Casas' continued involvement in disputes from the first and until his debates with Sepúlveda in 1550 (see Pagden, *The Fall of Natural Man*; Wey Gómez, *The Tropics of Empire*, 104–05). Cf. Vitoria, *On the American Indians*.

[8] See, for example, Pagden, *The Fall of Natural Man*, Chapter 3.

[9] See Grotius, *On the Origin of the Native Races of America*. As Rubiés notes, "Indians derived from European Norse, civilized Chinese, and Christian Ethiopians would have had to be treated with more respect than barbarians whose ancestry could be traced back to infidel Tartars and lost Jews" ("Hugo Grotius's Dissertation on the Origin of the American Peoples and the Use of Comparative Methods," 234).

[10] See the examples discussed in Wey Gómez, *The Tropics of Empire*, Chapter 1; cf. Pagden, *The Fall of Natural Man*, Chapter 3.

[11] For examples of *mappæmundi* based on this model, see Wey Gómez, *The Tropics of Empire*, Chapter 1. Wey Gómez argues that this difficulty explains why Columbus sailed not simply west, but also south, to the Indies (*ibid.*, 40–56). Cf. Williams, *The American Indian in Western Legal Thought*, Chapter 2.

were not Christians and they did not make good use of the resources that God had placed before them.[12]

This mix of self-interest, partial information, and uncharted intellectual territory is an apt illustration of what Hobbes had in mind when he warned of the dangers inherent in the inconstant signification of terms. The difficulties involved in saying something about America and their attendant consequences are evident in Montaigne's famous essay "*Of the Cannibales.*"[13] This work is instructive for the present purposes not because there is any evidence that it served as a source for Hobbes, but rather because it shows that even though Montaigne was never considered an authority on America, his descriptions and language gripped the minds of his English readers and became a part of the folklore surrounding the New World.[14]

Although very short and composed with the benefit of some eighty years' worth of information about America, this essay displays all of the hesitations and cautions of the age.[15] First, of course, is the title itself, which warns the reader that the subject is not merely other, but also, perhaps, dangerous. The contents in fact reveal that there can be such a thing as too much caution since in many ways, the "*Cannibales'*" condition is preferable to that of the civilized nations of Montaigne's day. Invoking the type of list that the ancient ethnographers had used to trace the emergence of civilization and that would reappear in Hobbes's work, Montaigne's description of America challenges not merely accounts of the golden age, but also the perfect commonwealth envisioned by Plato. "Those nations," declares Montaigne, "seeme ... so barbarous vnto mee, because they have received very little fashion from humane wit, and are yet neere their originall naturalitie."[16]

---

[12] These arguments were used from the start. For a particularly prominent example, see Eden's preface to Peter Martyr's account (*The Decades of the Newe Worlde or West India*, esp. a.ii^v). For other examples, see Landucci, *I filosofi e i selvaggi*, 94–100; Malcolm, *Aspects of Hobbes*, 59–62; Fitzmaurice, *Humanism and America*, 140–46.

[13] In Lovejoy's view, this essay contains "the *locus classicus* of primitivism in modern literature" (*Essays in the History of Ideas*, 238), but cf. Hamlin, *The Image of America in Montaigne, Spencer, and Shakespeare*, 46–55. In what follows, I quote from Florio's celebrated translation of 1603, which was the "[f]irst English version, often reprinted" (Frame, Introduction to *The Complete Essays of Montaigne*, xvii), and thus likely to have been the one that most of Hobbes's contemporaries would have read (see Hamlin, "Florio's Montaigne and the Tyranny of 'Custome'"). In the Florio edition, "*Of the Caniballes*" is Chapter 30 of Book I (due to the absence of I.14), whereas in complete editions, such as Frame's, it is I.31. Citing Talaska's research, Malcolm claims that Montaigne was among the authors included in the Hardwick library (*Aspects of Hobbes*, 458), but I have not been able to find such an entry in Hobbes's catalogue (Devonshire Mss., Chatsworth HS/E/1A).

[14] The most famous example of this influence is Shakespeare's appropriation of elements of the essay for *The Tempest* (II.i: 147–68), but Hamlin lists several other playwrights who borrowed from Montaigne ("Florio's Montaigne and the Tyranny of 'Custome,'" 511–12).

[15] On the essay's ambiguity and ambivalence, see Hamlin, *The Image of America in Montaigne, Spencer, and Shakespeare*, Chapter 2, which also contains a valuable discussion of Montaigne's sources; cf. Hoffmann, "Anatomy of the Mass."

[16] Montaigne, *The Complete Essayes*, 102.

Driven only by the laws of nature, and uncorrupted by human convention, the savages have

> no kinde of traffike, no knowledge of Letters, no intelligence of numbers, no name of magistrate, nor of politike superioritie; no vse of service, or riches, or of poverty; no contracts, no successions, no dividences, no occupation but idle; no respect of kindred, but common, no apparrell but naturall, no manuring of lands, no vse of wine, corne, or mettle.[17]

Yet, alongside these trappings of civilization, they also lack the "very words that import lying, falshood, treason, dissimulation, covetousnes, envie, detraction, and pardon."[18] Montaigne's description of the Cannibals makes clear the extent to which the discovery of America challenged even the boundaries between terms of approbation and disapprobation. By pointing to the fact that his contemporaries attached both terms such as "natural" and "savage" to the American natives, Montaigne invites the reader to engage in reevaluation by association. If "natural" is a term of approbation, then perhaps "savage" ought not to be a term of disapprobation, except insofar as "men call that barbarisme, which is not common to them."[19] Montaigne appears willing to push his challenge quite far: using the most extreme trait associated with the Americans – the fact that they are Cannibals – he declares his grief that in "prying so narrowly into their faults, we are so blinded in ours."[20] Europeans were appalled at finding savages who eat corpses, but Montaigne thinks "there is more barbarisme" in the manner in which those around him treat one another.[21] He thus concludes, "[w]e may then well call them barbarous, in regarde of reasons rules, but not in respect of vs that exceede them in all kinde of barbarisme."[22]

Aware of the difficulties involved in discussing the Cannibals, Montaigne makes all the necessary stops. He opens his essay by reminding the reader to be wary of popular opinions regarding the other side. Things look different on one side of the ocean than they do on the other, and the significance of America means that the consequences of misunderstanding what it can teach us could be devastating. How momentous the discovery of America is can be seen by a quick glance at the history of speculation about what lay on the other end of the sea, and this history is most instructive. It shows that the wisest of men were ignorant and wrong. Montaigne's most important

[17] Montaigne, *The Complete Essayes*, 102.
[18] Montaigne, *The Complete Essayes*, 102.
[19] Montaigne, *The Complete Essayes*, 101. On Montaigne's use of positive and negative terms, see Levine, *Sensual Philosophy*, 98–102, esp. 101. Levine notes rightly (*ibid.*, 117) that an assessment of what Montaigne is up to in this essay needs to be supplemented by his judgment of the Indians' "horrible cruelty" in the preceding one, "Of Moderation" (*The Complete Essayes*, 99).
[20] Montaigne, *The Complete Essayes*, 104.
[21] Montaigne, *The Complete Essayes*, 104.
[22] Montaigne, *The Complete Essayes*, 104.

source is a man whose simple mind renders him unlikely to embellish his accounts of his first-hand experience of several years in America. As a result, Montaigne trusts his information more than the cosmographers'.[23] It bears noting, however, that the picture of life in America that allows Montaigne to engage in his contrast is not based solely on that information, but is corroborated by information from other eyewitnesses, by artifacts, and, most importantly, backed by evidence from the historians and ethnographers of antiquity.[24] Montaigne's cautionary remarks about comparisons give the impression that the proper assessment of the respective virtues and vices of the Americans and Europeans should be performed as though they were parallel, yet distinct, species. In one of the most striking moments of the essay, Montaigne abandons that parallel examination and points to something that the two species share: the ancient historians tell us that when they were besieged by Caesar in Alesia, his ancestors ate the old men, the women, and those who could not assist with the fighting.[25]

The passage of time and accumulation of further information did not have a singular or simple effect on the image of the Indians in Europe. Gradually, however, depictions at both extremes began to crumble under the weight of the evidence. Increased contact and greater numbers of eyewitnesses made it clear that this rich, promising, and dangerous place was neither utopia nor the island of the Cyclopes.[26] Moving away from these extremes and toward the mean meant that one had to come to terms with the notion that the Indians were human, and attempt to determine their place within humanity. Commentators often describe such endeavors as the birth of anthropology or of ethnography, but one of the noticeable features of this corpus is its reliance on the ancient ethnographers.[27] Travelers and cosmographers

---

[23] Montaigne, *The Complete Essayes*, 100–01. Cf. De Lutri, "Montaigne's 'Des Cannibales'," 78. For a brief discussion of Montaigne's possible sources, see Cro, *The Noble Savage*, 14–15. Hodgen points out the similarity between Montaigne and Peter Martyr, and of both to ancient sources (*Early Anthropology in the Sixteenth and Seventeenth Centuries*, 372; cf. 373), and Cro examines it (*The Noble Savage*, 13–34). On the respective quality of first-hand and second-hand accounts, see Dunn, "Seventeenth-Century English Historians of America," esp. 195–96; cf. Hartog, *The Mirror of Herodotus*, Chapter 7.

[24] On artifacts, see Montaigne, *The Complete Essayes*, 102–03; on other eyewitnesses, *ibid.*, 101. Montaigne ends the essay by relating his own encounters with Americans (*ibid.*, 106–07).

[25] Montaigne, *The Complete Essayes*, 104.

[26] See Hodgen, *Early Anthropology in the Sixteenth and Seventeenth Centuries*, 375–82. Elliott notes that "[b]y the middle of the sixteenth century the discrepancies between the image and the reality could no longer be systematically ignored" (*The Old World and the New*, 28).

[27] Thus, for example, Gliozzi's subtitle speaks of the birth of anthropology as colonial ideology, whereas Pagden's ties the origins of comparative ethnology to the American Indian, although Pagden acknowledges that the early chroniclers and natural historians "were attempting to bring within their intellectual grasp phenomena which they recognised as new and which they could only make familiar, and hence intelligible, in the terms of an anthropology made authoritative precisely by the fact that its sources ran back to the Greeks" (*The Fall of Natural Man*, 6).

alike furnished lists of the basic traits of the natives and often juxtaposed their habits to those of civilized Europeans or to their ancient ancestors, frequently invoking the example of Tacitus's account of the ancient Germanic tribes.[28] Tacitus's model was doubly appropriate because its description of the ancient Germans takes place in the context of a contrast with Rome, in which the two represent the extremes.[29]

By the end of the sixteenth century, this practice was so well established that when Theodor De Bry published Hariot's *Briefe and True Report of the New Found Land of Virginia* (1590), which contained John White's famous images of America, he appended to it a set of pictures of the Picts, who "in the Olde tyme dyd habite one part of the great Bretainne," explaining that he offered them alongside those of the Indians *"for to showe how that the Inhabitants of the great Bretannie haue bin in times past as sauuage as those*

---

[28] According to Rives,

> After its rediscovery in the early modern period, [the *Germania*] quickly became established as an authoritative account of the ancestors of *die Deutschen,* those peoples whom modern English speakers, adopting the name that Tacitus used for the inhabitants of northern Europe, call "Germans." (*"Germania,"* 45; cf. *ibid.,* 56–57)

Grotius (*On the Origin of the Native Races of America*) and Waterhouse (*A Declaration of the State of the Colony and Affaires in Virginia*) are among those who invoke Tacitus. On this practice more generally, see Hodgen, *Early Anthropology in the Sixteenth and Seventeenth Centuries,* 370; Mason, "Classical Ethnography and Its Influence on the European Perception of the Peoples of the New World."

For examples of lists, see those of Oviedo and Bembo (Cro, *The Noble Savage,* 23); Horn, *Arca Noæ,* 457–58; Arnauld (quoted in Landucci, *I filosofi e i selvaggi,* 117–18); Acosta and de la Vega (Ashcraft, "Hobbes's Natural Man," 1084–85). Cf. Hodgen, *ibid.,* 197–201; cf. *Leviathan,* ed. Malcolm, XIII, 195, note g.

Hakluyt's collection contains numerous examples of such descriptions of the natives. Dionise Settle's account of Frobisher's second voyage is indicative:

> They eate their meat all raw, both flesh, fish, and foule, or something perboyled with blood and a little water which they drinke. For lacke of water they will eate yce, that is hard frosen, as pleasantly as we will do Sugar Candie, or other Sugar.

> If they for necessities sake stand in need of the premisses, such grasse as the Countrey yeeldeth they plucke vp and eate, not deintily, or salletwise to allure their stomacks to appetite: but for necessities sake without either salt, oyles, or washing, like brute beasts deuouring the same. They neither vse table, stoole, or table cloth for comlines: but when they are imbrued with blood knuckle deepe, and their kniues in like sort, they vse their tongues as apt instruments to lick them cleane: in doing whereof they are assured to loose none of their victuals (Hakluyt, *Principal Navigations,* III: 37).

The documents discussed in Pope, "*A True and Faithful Account,*" show that this way of describing the natives was alive and well in the late seventeenth century. For examples, see Lescarbot, *Nova Francia,* 176, 178, 184, 276, 287–88, 293, 302; Bodin, *Method for the Easy Comprehension of History,* 298.

[29] There is widespread agreement regarding this characteristic of the *Germania,* even though there is notorious disagreement as to its purpose. See Syme, *Tacitus,* 46–48, 126–29; Rives, "*Germania,*" 50–53.

of Virginia."[30] Neat and elegant, White's depictions of the way of life of both Indians and Picts show conditions that are primitive by the European standards of his age, but far from nasty or poor. There are several scenes of industry, evidence of agriculture, and one of the towns depicted is very well fortified.[31] All this appears possible because there is no evidence of anything like a war of all against all. In the case of the Indians, the closest thing to violence depicted is a stag hunt behind the fierce "weroan or great Lorde of Virginia," whereas the first plate of a Pict shows him carrying the head of a vanquished enemy, with another at his feet, but with no other sign of the struggle that led to that outcome (see Figures 7, 8).[32]

In his preface to the reader, De Bry navigates the difficulties discussed earlier in a confident and skillful manner. He observes that despite having "noe true knoledge of God nor of his holye worde and are destituted of all learning," the Indians excel the Europeans in many things.[33] As the allegory of the Fall

[30] Hariot, *A Briefe and True Report*, E[r]. Hariot's report had been published on its own in 1588. For a slightly later example, see Johnson's *Nova Britannia*, where in language anticipating Hobbes's he compares "our present happinesse with our former auncient miseries, wherein wee had continued brutish poore and naked Brittans to this day, if Iulius Cæsar with his Romaine Legions, (or some other) had not laid the ground to make us tame and ciuill" (C2[r]). Kendrick notes that the exact way in which the Indians became associated with the Picts is not known, but adds that "the important links were the pictures of the tatoo'd Indians, and the idea that an ancient Pict, a painted man, must have looked very much like such an Indian" (*British Antiquity*, 123). On the significance of the images of the Picts for an English audience, see Smiles, "John White and British Antiquity." According to van Groesen, this was the only volume of the De Bry collection of voyages that was published in four languages (English, French, German, and Latin). The subsequent volumes were published only in German and Latin (*The Representations of the Overseas World in the De Bry Collection of Voyages*, 2, 390–91).

[31] See, for example, Hariot, *A Briefe and True Report*, Plates XII–XV, XIX–XX. The plates also contain abundant evidence of social and political hierarchies, which also contradicted the notion that the Indians largely lacked such distinctions (see, for example, Montaigne, *The Complete Essayes*, 104).

[32] Hariot, *A Briefe and True Report*, Plates III and Picte I, respectively. It is important to note that the backgrounds are not in White's drawings; they were added by De Bry, who also altered some of the other details in the originals. For example, in White's version, the Pict warrior is much more fearsome, but carries only one head, has no spear, and there is no second head at his feet (Hulton, *America 1585*, 91). Kupperman finds other differences as well, including changes to the faces, which were "sweetened, softened, and Europeanized" (*Indians & English*, 42; "Roanoke's Achievement," 8; cf. Pratt, "Truth and Artifice in the Visualization of Native Peoples"; Rubiés, "Texts, Images, and the Perception of 'Savages' in Early Modern Europe," 125–29). There is widespread consensus that publications of this sort in general, and De Bry's in particular, had propagandistic elements, something that is captured well by the title page of the first edition of Hariot's *Briefe and True Report* (1588). Thus, for example, Kuhlemann detects a "propagandistic message" ("Between Reproduction, Invention and Propaganda," 86–89) and van Groesen a marketing strategy, intended to "praise the fertility of the American province" (*The Representations of the Overseas World in the De Bry Collection of Voyages*, 175). Cf. Hodgen, *Early Anthropology in the Sixteenth and Seventeenth Centuries*, 369–70; Armitage, "The New World and British Political Thought," 59–60; Rubiés, "Texts, Images, and the Perception of 'Savages' in Early Modern Europe," 125–27.

[33] Hariot, *A Briefe and True Report*, "To the gentle Reader."

FIGURE 8. The trvve picture of a man of nation neighbour vnto the Picte.
Source: Thomas Hariot, *A Briefe and True Report of the New Found Land of Virginia* ... (Frankfurt, 1590). Courtesy of the John Carter Brown Library at Brown University.

with which he prefaced the entire exercise ought to remind those who might wonder, man's disobedience stripped him of all the gifts bestowed on him at the Creation, but not of "wit to prouyde for hym selfe, nor discretion to deuise things necessarie for his vse" (see Figure 6).[34] The reader who becomes acquainted with the Indians through the pictures that follow could easily conclude that their life was one of "a peaceful coexistence in balance with nature," and many readers received that message; White's pictures of the Indians in Hariot's *Briefe and True Report* was Europe's "first comprehensive iconographic representation of the overseas world and its inhabitants," and became "widely known and copied throughout Europe" (see Figure 9).[35] The extent to which both these depictions and the association between the natives and the savage ancestors of civilized nations became influential is evident in popular histories that were published in the first two decades of the seventeenth century and reprinted several times. In England, John Speed's *Theatre of the Empire of Great Britaine* and *History of Great Britaine* carry a frontispiece clearly influenced by Hariot's, which features the peoples that had shaped the history of Britain. If the "Britaine" at its center shows certain traces of De Bry's engravings, the portraits of the "ancient Britaines" contained in the *History* are unmistakable imitations (see Figure 10).[36] The same tendencies are evident in Philip Clüver's massive and exhaustive *Germania Antiqua*, a work which Hobbes knew.[37] Clüver's ancient Germans are clearly drawn after the manner of De Bry's Indians (see Figures 11, 12). In the only instance in which Hobbes

[34] Hariot, *A Briefe and True Report*, "To the gentle Reader."
[35] Kuhlemann, "Between Reproduction, Invention and Propaganda," 86; van Groesen, *The Representations of the Overseas World in the De Bry Collection of Voyages*, 3; cf. *ibid.*, 370; Kuhlemann, op. cit., 79; cf. *ibid.*, 87–92. For examples of the *Briefe and True Report*'s influence, see van Groesen, op. cit., 360–67. According to Pratt, these designs "took on an iconic authority that dictated the terms for representing American Indians for over a century" ("Truth and Artifice in the Visualization of Native Peoples," 38). As Vaughan observes, "adaptations of illustrations by John White and others proliferated for centuries without the artists seeing an Indian" (*Transatlantic Encounters*, 53). In Kupperman's words, the volume constitutes an "unparalleled American record" ("Roanoke's Achievement," 5).
[36] Speed, *The Theatre of the Empire of Great Britaine*, frontispiece; *The History of Great Britaine*, frontispiece, p. 180.
[37] The Hardwick library catalogue in Hobbes's hand contains entries for Clüver's *Germaniæ* (2 volume folio), *Sicilia* (folio), and *Italia* (2 volume folio) (Devonshire Mss., Chatsworth HS E/1A). More importantly, the surviving manuscript copy of *Leviathan* contains a reference to Clüver's *Germaniæ Antiquæ* (British Library Egerton 1910, 30ʳ). In Chapter X, the paragraph devoted to German titles of honor has a different ending than in the printed version. It reads: "The places of antient History out of wᶜʰ this that I haue sayd may be gathered, are at lardge collected by Philip Cluuerius in his *Germania antiqua*." Malcolm suggests two possible reasons for the change: Hobbes's "general policy throughout the book was not to give source references, and he may have preferred to be thought of as a person who had read widely for himself among the ancient sources, rather than as someone dependent on a secondary work" (*Leviathan*, I: 204). Hobbes used Clüver's map of Sicily from *Sicilia Antiqua* for his edition of Thucydides (*EW*, VIII: x). On Clüver's use of Tacitus and his depiction of the ancient Germans, see Egmond and Mason, *The Mammoth and the Mouse*, 160–84.

FIGURE 9. Title page of Hariot's *Briefe and True Report.*
Source: Thomas Hariot, *A Briefe and True Report of the New Found Land of Virginia* ... (Frankfurt, 1590). Courtesy of the John Carter Brown Library at Brown University.

themselues voluntarily depriue their Bodies of this Protection against the Aires offence, to procure pittie of others. And what speake we of these? seeing euen children for Custome, and Women for pride, wil suffer their Breasts, and most tender parts of their Body, to be exposed not only to offence of weather, but of modesty also? yea generally, the handes, and faces, being of most subtilest sence, yet by custome are enabled now to endure that, which by the like custome the olde *Britaines* endured in their whole Bodies; whereby *Plutarch* thinks they *vsually liued so long euen to the age of sixescore, the externe cold keeping-in and augmenting their internall heate.*

(6) As abilitie to endure colde, so *ignorance* (in many) of meanes to preuent it, may seeme another occasion of these *Britaines* nakednes. The *Romans* (it seemes) in their old *Consuls* times, and after, had not the skill nor vse of *Hats, Breeches, &c.* That *Britaine* abounded with *wooll* and other materials for cloathing, is past all doubt, for which cause, by one *Panegyrick*, it is named *Riche in Pasturage,* which by another is thus explicated, *that therein was an infinite multitude of tame cattell both with Vdders full of milke, and loaden with Fleeces to the ground.* So then *Woll* was not wanting, but *Will,* or *Skill*; the latter in most likelihood: for, as *Strabo* saith, that though those strutting *Vdders* yeelded great store of milk, yet some of them had not skill to make cheese, and hauing so rich grounds, yet had not the art of tillage, so their sheepe might haue such heauy fleeces, yet some of their Owners no cunning to keepe themselues warme therewith. Some of them, I say; for otherwise, as *Pliny,* touching *Tillage,* giues light to *Strabo,* witnessing, that others of them were so good *Husbands as to manure their grounds with Marle,* as likewise doth *Dioscorides,* saying *they had skill to make drinke of Barley*: so probable is it, that those other who were by *Cæsar* and *Tacitus* said to be so *like the French* in conditions, had also some part of their Art in fitting the Burthen of their Sheepes backes to couer their owne.

Plutarch.

2. Ignorance.

Paneg.ad Constan. Paneg ad Constan.

Strabo.

Pliny. Dioscorides.

Cæsar. Tacitus.

(7) The last reason of such their going *naked* sometimes, was out of an opinion that no cloathing so adorned them, as their painting and damasking of their Bodies, for which cause (saith *Herodian*) *they would not couer themselues, lest then their gay painting should not be seene*: but *Pomponius Mela* makes doubt, whether their thus painting themselues were for *ornament* or for *some other vse*; which doubt *Cæsar* seemes to resolue, as if the men did it; because it made them looke more terrible in warre.

(8) And thus we are now orderly fallen on the second of those three notes appropriated by *Authors* to our *Britaines,* which is their *painting* and *staining of their Bodies,* which appeares by *Cæsar* to haue beene more vniuersally vsed, then going *naked,* for all the *Britaines* (saith he) *die their bodies with staining.* As Authours differ in the reason of this their *painting,* (as we shewed) so in the *name,* perchance also in the *substance* of that wherewith they stained themselues, and somewhat also in the *colour* it selfe. The *substance Cæsar* calles *luteum,* which yet in vulgar acception is thought to be some *yellow* substance, as *Pliny* cals *luteum oui,* the yolke of the Egge; *Pliny* himselfe saith the *Frenchmen* call it *glastum,* describing it to be an herbe like *Plantayne,* which *Oribasius* (as learned *Cambden* sheweth) doth terme *Vitrum,* in which sense *Mela* is vnderstood, to say, that they were stained *Vitro* (and not *Vitrò,*) it being generally taken to be *Woad,* from those ancient times hitherto vsed for the surest staine. But for the *colour* which is made, *Cæsar* and the rest agree, it was *Cæruleus, blewish* or *azure,* which colour the *Cambro-Brytannes* doe yet call *glace,* whence our *glasse* for windowes (called also *vitrum*) seemeth by reason of the *colour,* to haue taken name. Onely *Pliny* leaueth no scruple in saying, that *the naked painted women imitated the Æthiopian colour;* which must be vnderstood either *comparatiuely,* in respect of People white and vnpainted, or because *blew* a farre-of hath the appearance of *blacke.*

(9) That the *Britaines* tooke their *Name* from this

3. Pride.

Herodian.

Mela.

Cæsar.

2. The second note of the Britaines, their painting. Cæsar.

Cæsar. Pliny.

Cambd. in Brit. p. 14. Mela.

Pliny.

See Chap.2 §.7

FIGURE 10. Ancient Britons.

Source: John Speed, *The History of Great Britaine,* ... (London, 1611), pf STC 23045, Houghton Library, Harvard University.

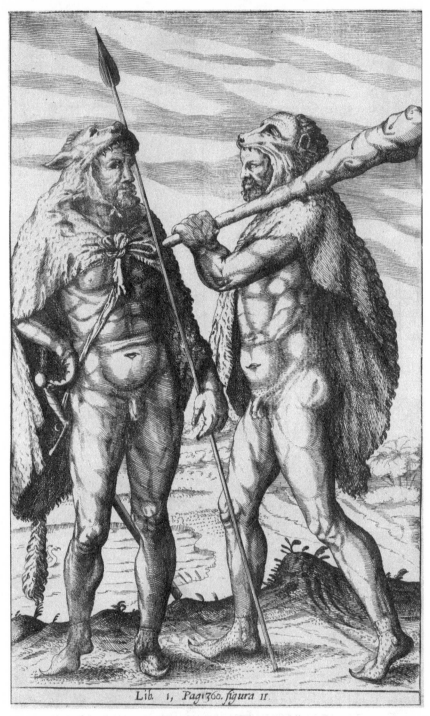

Lib. 1, Pag. 760. figura II.

FIGURE 11. Ancient Germans, I.ii.
Source: Philip Clüver, *Germaniæ Antiquæ Libri Tres* (Leiden: Elzevir, 1616), f GC6
C6275 616g, Houghton Library, Harvard University.

FIGURE 12. Ancient Germans, I.iii.
Source: Philip Clüver, *Germaniæ Antiquæ Libri Tres* (Leiden: Elzevir, 1616), f GC6
C6275 616g, Houghton Library, Harvard University.

215

gives a specific example of savage ancestors as living in the state of nature, he names "the old inhabitants of Germany."[38]

The addition of a Tacitean garb to De Bry's iconography was an apt reminder that things on the other side of the ocean were not quite as felicitous as the explorers' propaganda would have it. One year after the publication of Hariot's *A Briefe and True Report of the New Found Land of Virginia*, De Bry issued Le Moyne's account of the French discovery of Florida, which contained significant evidence of industry and society as well, but also scenes of savagery and warfare.[39] Even those accounts favorable to the Indians made it quite clear that these were very different people, an impression that could only have been reinforced by the rare but noteworthy and memorable appearances of Indians in London, as well as the occasional propagandistic iconography (Figure 13).[40]

The first attempts at English colonization, in the opening years of the seventeenth century, altered this picture for the worse, with stories of hardship and death. Of at least 6,000 people who went to Virginia between 1607 and 1624, 1,200 remained in 1625.[41] Even though it accounted for only a

[38] *The Elements of Law*, I.14.12. In *A Dialogue between a Philosopher and a Student, of the Common Laws of England*, the philosopher argues,

> The *Saxons*, as also all the rest of *Germany* not Conquer'd by the *Roman* Emperors, nor compelled to use the imperial Laws, were a Savage and Heathen People, living only by War and Rapine; and as some learned Men in the *Roman* Antiquities affirm, had their name of *Germans* from that their ancient trade of life, as if *Germans* and *Hommes de guerre* were all one. Their rule over their Family, Servants and Subjects was absolute, their Laws no other than natural Equity; written Law they had little, or none, and very few there were in the time of the *Caesars* that could write, or read. The right to the Government was either Paternal, or by Conquest, or by Marriages (139–40; see also *Behemoth*, 206–08).

[39] Le Moyne, *Brevis Narratio Eorum Qvæ in Florida Americæ Provīcia Gallis Acciderunt*. On the connection between Tacitism and English views of America, see Kupperman, *Indians & English*, 27–29, but cf. Fitzmaurice, *Humanism and America*, 160–66.

[40] See Vaughan, *Transatlantic Encounters*, Chapters 2 and 3. See the portraits of Eiakintomino and Matahan (Figure 13), who may have been the Algonquians who visited London and were displayed in St. James's Park in 1615 or 1616 (Vaughan, *ibid.*, 53–54). The broad similarity between their portraits in the lottery declaration, on the one hand, and White's depictions and the 1642 *De Cive*, on the other, is readily apparent. On the popularity of the lotteries, see Johnson, "The Lotteries of the Virginia Company." Even in the context of an attempt to capture the nuances in these accounts, Kupperman notes that

> Suspicion, hostility, and armed clashes suffuse the record from first to last. No author wrote in a humane way as we would define humaneness; even the most sympathetic writers easily moved into chilling denigration or worse. Some of the most intricate and sensitive accounts of native life were written by men on military expeditions, men who would carry out the most barbaric campaigns if they felt threatened or challenged. Those who saw the Indians as hostile opponents often took the most care to try to understand them. People who remained in England and wrote at second hand could pen dismissive accounts of pathetically primitive savages, but those on the front lines in America, whose lives depended on their knowledge, knew better (*Indians & English*, 15).

[41] Kupperman, "Apathy and Death in Early Jamestown," 24. Kupperman notes that "[v]irtually every letter from Virginia during this period speaks of the helplessness the colonists felt before the phenomenon of widespread deaths" (*ibid.*).

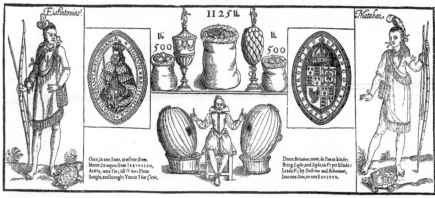

Once, in one State, as of one Stem,
Meete Strangers from I E R V S A L E M,
As Wee, were Tee; till O hers Pitte
Sought, and brought You to That Cittie.

Deere Britaines, now, do Tou as kinde:
Bring Light, and Sight, to Vs yet blinde:
Leade Vs, by Doctrine and Behauiour,
Into one Sion, to one S A V I O V R.

IT is apparent to the world, by how many former Publications we manifested our intents to haue drawne out the great ftanding Lotterie long before this day: which not failing out as our feluce defired, and others expected, whofe moneyes are already aduentured therein. We thought good therefore for auoiding al vniuft and finifter conftructions, to refolue the doubts of al indifferent minded, in three fpeciall points for their better fatisfaction.

The firft is, for as much as the aduenturers came in fo flackly with fuch poore and barren receits of moneys at the Lottery houfe for this twelue moneth paft, that without too much preiudice to our felues and the aduenturers in leffening the blankes & prizes. We found no meanes nor ability to proceed in any competent proportion, but of neceffity are driuen to the honourable Lords by petition, who out of their Noble care and difpofition to further that publike plantation of Virginia, haue recommended their letters to the Counties, Cities and good Townes in England, which we hope by fending in their voluntarie Aduentures, will fufficiently make that fupply of helpe, which otherwife we fhould not in any reafonable time haue effected.

The fecond poynt for fatiffaction to all honeft and wel affected minds, is, that notwithftanding this our meanes of Lottery anfwered not our hopes, yet haue we not failed in that Chriftian care of the Colony in Virginia, to whom we haue lately made two fundry fupplies of men and prouifions, where wee doubt not but they are all in health and in fo good a way with come and cattell to fubfift of themfelues, that were they now but a while fupplied with more hands and materials, we fhould the fooner refolue vpon a diuifion of the Countrey by lot, and fo fettle the generall charge, by leauing each feuerall tribe or family to hufband and manure his owne.

The third and laft is our conftant refolution, that feeing our credits are now fo farre engaged to the honourable Lords, & to the whole State for the drawing and accomplifhment of this great ftanding Lotterie. Which we intend fhall be our laft of all ftanding Lotteries for this plantation, that our time fixed and determined for accomplifhing thereof, fhall be if God permit, without longer delay, the 26. of June next being in Trinity tearme, defiring all fuch as haue vndertaken with bookes to folicite their friends, and all fuch as intend the profperity of that Worthie plantation, that they will not withhold their monies till the laft weeke or moneth be expired, left the be vnwillingly forced to proportion a leffe value and number of our blankes and prizes which hereafter follow.

And whofoeuer vnder one name or pofte fhall ad-

VVelcomes.

To him that firft fhall bee drawne out with a Blanke	100. Crownes.
To the fecond	50. Crownes.
To the third	25. Crownes.
To him that euery day during the drawing of this Lottery fhall bee firft drawne out with a Blanke	20. Crownes.

Prizes.

1. Great Prize of	4500 Crownes.
2. Great Prizes, each of	2000. Crownes.
4. Great Prizes, each of	1000. Crownes.
6. Great Prizes, each of	500. Crownes.
10. Prizes, each of	200. Crownes.
20. Prizes, each of	100. Crownes.
100. Prizes, each of	100. Crownes.
200. Prizes, each of	50. Crownes.
400. Prizes, each of	30. Crownes.
1000. Prizes, each of	10. Crownes.
1000. Prizes, each of	8. Crownes.
1000. Prizes, each of	6. Crownes.
4000. Prizes, each of	4. Crownes.
1000. Prizes, each of	3. Crownes.
1000. Prizes, each of	2. Crownes.

Rewards.

To him that fhall bee laft drawne out with a Blanke	25. Crownes.
To him that putteth in the greateft number of Lots vnder one name or Pofte	400. Crownes.
To him that putteth in the fecond greateft number	300. Crownes.
To him that putteth in the third greateft number	200. Crownes.
To him that putteth in the fourth greateft number	100. Crownes.

If diuers bee of equall number, then thefe Rewards are to be diuided proportionably.

Addition of new Rewards.

The Blanke that fhall bee drawne out next before the Greateft Prize, fhall haue	25. Crownes.
The Blanke that fhall bee drawne out next after the faid Great Prize, fhall haue	25. Crownes.
The Blankes that fhall be drawne out immediately before the 2. next Greateft Prizes, fhall haue each of them	10. Crownes.
The feuerall Blankes next after them fhall haue alfo each of them	10. Crownes.
The feuerall blankes next before the foure Great Prizes, fhall haue each of them	15. Crownes.
The feuerall Blankes next after them fhall haue alfo each of them	15. Crownes.
The feuerall Blankes next before the fix Great Prizes, fhall haue each of them	10. Crownes.
The feuerall Blankes next after them fhall haue alfo each of them	10. Crownes.

uenture twelue pounds ten fhillings or vpward. if he pleafe to leaue & remit his Prizes and Rewards, bee they more or leffe. the Lottery being drawne out, hee fhall haue a bill of Aduenture to Virginia, for the like fum he aduentured, & fhall be free of that Company, & haue his part in Lands, & all other profits hereafter arifing thence, according to his aduenture of twelue pounds ten fhillings or vpwards.

Whofoeuer is behinde with the payment of any fum of money, promifed heretofore to be aduentured to Virginia, if hee aduenture in this Lotterie the double of that fum. & make payment thereof in ready money to Sir Thomas Smith Knight, Treafurer for Virginia, he fhall be difcharged of the forefaid fumme fo promifed to haue been aduentured to Virginia, and of all actions and damages therefrom arifing, and haue alfo the benefit of all Prizes and Rewards whatfoeuer in this Lottery, due by reafon of the like fum which he fhall bring in and yet notwithftanding, if after the Lottery drawne, he lift to remit at his faid Prizes and Rewards, he fhall haue a bill of aduenture to Virginia for the faid entire fumme according to the laft preceding Article.

And if vpon too much delay of the Aduenturers to furnifh this Lottery. We bee driuen to draw the fame before it be full. the we purpofe to fhorten both blanks and Prizes in an equall proportion, according to that wherein we fhall come fhort. bee it more or leffe, that neither the Aduenturers may bee defrauded, nor our felues, as in the former, any way wronged.

The Prizes. Welcomes, & Rewards fhall be paid in ready money, plate, or other goods reafonably rated. If any diflike of the faid Plate or other goods, he fhall haue ready money for the fame, abating onely a tenth part: Except in fmall prizes of tenne Crownes or vnder, wherein nothing fhall be abated there.

The money for Aduentures is to be paid to Sir Thomas Smith Knight, Treafurer for Virginia, at his houfe in Philpot lane: or to fuch officers as fhall be appointed to attend for that purpofe at the Lottery houfe: or to fuch other as fhall elfewhere, for the eafe of the Countrey be authorized. vnder the Seale of the Company, for receipt thereof.

The Prizes, welcomes & Rewards being drawne, they fhall be paid by the Treafurer for Virginia, without delay, whenfoeuer they fhall be demanded.

And for the better expedition to make out fum compleat, as we wifh to haften the drawing of our Lottery as chiefly to inable vs the fooner to make good fupplies to the Colonie in Virginia. Whofoeuer vnder one name or pofte fhall bring in ready money for euery three pounds, either to the Lottery hou.e, or to any Colledge, the fame party receiuing their money. for euery three pounds fo receiued, fhall tender them prefently a filuer fpoone of 6. fhillings 8. pece price, or 6. fhillings 8. pece in money.

Imprinted at London by *Felix Kyngfton*, for *VVilliam VVelby*, the 12. of Februarie. 1615.

FIGURE 13. *A Declaration for the Certaine Time of Dravving the Great Standing Lottery* (London: By Felix Kyngston, for William Welby, 1615). Courtesy of the Society of Antiquaries of London.

fraction of those deaths, the massacre of 1622 seemed to encapsulate the
dangers of life in America and contributed to a wave of anti-Indian invective
in England (Figure 14).[42]

No longer simply the stuff of legend, in Hobbes's time the European
conception of America remained evolving and problematic. The paucity of Hobbes's references to America in his writings makes it tempting
to conclude that he took little interest in it, but the scant evidence available points in another direction. Aubrey tells us that Hobbes spent his time
"gaping on mappes, of which he takes notice in his life written by himselfe
in verse."[43] Hobbes's most significant and well-documented connection to
America, however, came in the form of his master's "most important and
time-consuming business interest" for several years, namely, his involvement
in the Virginia Company.[44] The company's records in the early 1620s show
that Hobbes attended meetings along with Cavendish, and that the latter
gave Hobbes one of his shares only a few months after the 1622 massacre,
thereby making him a member.[45] Hobbes's interests and involvement in the
company mean that he must have followed the developments in America

---

[42] See Kupperman, "English Perceptions of Treachery, 1583–1640," 265–66. Kupperman notes
that the extreme language used in the aftermath of the massacre was short-lived, but Malcolm
argues that in the context of the Virginia Company, at least, and despite opposition, the massacre made it "possible to regard any subsequent action against the Indians as self-defence
or justifiable retaliation" (*Aspects of Hobbes*, 61). Powell offers a sense of the colonists' lives
in the decade after the massacre, as well as samples of their letters to relatives in England, in
which they describe their difficulties ("Aftermath of the Massacre"). Vaughan argues that the
massacre put an end to arguments in favor of peace and cooperation with the Indians, and
transformed English policy to one of "unrestrained enmity and almost total separation that
reflected a persistent but often repressed contempt for the American natives" ("'Expulsion of
the Savages,'" 57–58). Vaughan notes that in some sense the shift was slight, since it "reflected
the profound prejudice that had clouded Indian-English contact from the beginning," but
adds that 1622 marked a turning point (*ibid.*, 81–82). On the significance of this event and its
use in English propaganda, see also Fausz, "The 'Barbarous Massacre' Reconsidered."

[43] Aubrey, *'Brief Lives,'* I: 329. Aubrey quotes from the poem:

> Ergo ad amoena magis me verto, librosque revolvo,
> Quos prius edoctus, non bene doctus eram.
> Pascebamque animum chartis imitantibus orbem,
> Telluris faciem, et sydera picta videns,
> Gaudebam soli comes ire, et cernere cunctis
> Terricolis justos qua facit arte dies (*ibid.*, 330).

[44] Malcolm, *Aspects of Hobbes*, 54.

[45] Kingsbury, ed., *The Records of the Virginia Company of London*, II: 40. The meeting in question took place on June 19, 1622. The Council in Virginia notified the company of the attack
in a letter which Kingsbury dates to the end of April (*ibid.*, III: 611–15). Malcolm finds Hobbes
listed as in attendance "at no fewer than thirty-seven meetings" in the two years after his accession to membership (*Aspects of Hobbes*, 54). It should be noted that the lists of attendees are
often followed by "with diuers others," so it is likely that Hobbes was present on other occasions as well. As Malcolm notes, on certain occasions Hobbes's presence coincided with that
of Purchas, whose collection, evidence suggests, Hobbes had read (*ibid.*, 61, n. 34).

CAPVT NONVM.

De magna clade, quam Angli anno 1622. 22. Martij in virginia acceperunt.

B eo tempore, quo Angli primùm in Virginiam venerũt, multas curas, moleftias, labores & pericula exantlarunt. Nam Diabolus per fua organa, nempe facerdotes, barbaros contra eos incitauit, ita, vt multos, quoties facultas fuit, obtruncarint. Tandem res eò deducta fuit, vt firma pax inter Anglos & barbaros ad aliquot annos contraheretur, & vtrinq; iurciurã do fanciretur. Rex quoq; Povvhatan promifit, fe regi Angliæ fubiectum ac tri butarium fore, pacemq; factam in æs incidi, & tabulam maximæ quercui ad fuum palatium affigi curauit: quam pacem vtraq; pars magno cum gaudio amplexa eft. Ad eam rem barbaros neceffitas impulit, vt fe Anglorum ope contra hoftes tuerentur. Angli verò eò fpe ctabant, vt per hanc pacem res fuas tanto melius in ea regione ftabilirent. Hæc pax longo tempo re inuiolata perftitit, adeò vt Angli paffim fine gladiis & fcloppetis incederent : & barbari eos crebrò inuifere, cum iis cibum capere, ac familiariter conuerfari cæperunt. Viciffim Angli in foli tudines ad ipfos fe contulerunt, & fpem conceperunt, fore, vt barbari tanto citiùs ac faciliusad Chriftianam fidem conuerterentur. Nam omnia inter ipfos tranquilla ac pacata erant.

Atq; vt pax hæc tantò firmiùs feruaretur , Angli Povvhatan, cum quo ipfis aliquid negotij erat, menfe Martio pacis memoriam refricarunt: quibus ille inter alia refpondit, fe pacem cũ ipfis optima fide culturum, futurumq; vt cælum potius diffoluatur, quàm illa rumpatur. Sed hæc me ra fuit fraus, fimulatio & hypocrifis. Nam barbari clam confilium iniuerant, Anglos omnes truci dandi. Biduo antequàm hoc facinus exequi decreuerat, quofdam Anglos per periculofas folitudi nes, incolumes deduxerant, & eos, qui linguæ addifcendæ caufsâ aliquandiu apud ipfos comorati fuerant, amicè dimiferant: præterea alios Anglos, qui cum fuis nauibus appulerant, benignè exce

FIGURE 14. De magna clade, quam Angli anno 1622. 22. Martiij in virginia acceperunt.

Source: Theodor De Bry, *Decima Tertia Pars "Historiæ Americanæ,"* ... (Frankfurt am Main: Mattæus Merian, 1634). Courtesy of the John Carter Brown Library at Brown University.

with considerable interest. Yet, the few, if prominent, references to America and its inhabitants in his writings raise more problems than they resolve about the status of the state of nature.[46]

For instance, it is hard to know what to make of the trajectory of Hobbes's references to the Indians, which one might sum up as an arc, beginning with their relatively important role in the *Elements*, reaching its peak in *De Cive*, and ending with their demotion to one of several examples mentioned briefly in *Leviathan* and other works published in the 1650s. Moreover, Hobbes's most notorious statement regarding the Indians is disappointing. That statement, in *Leviathan*, is offered as one possible piece of evidence in favor of his contention that there are people, even in his time, who live in the state of nature. His reason is that "the savage people in many places of *America*, except the government of small Families, the concord whereof dependeth on naturall lust, have no government at all; and live at this day in that brutish manner, as I said before."[47] Critics have seized on this claim as a sign of ignorance or even desperation. Pressed to offer an example of the kind of anarchy that characterizes his condition of war, Hobbes reached for one that was transparently problematic.[48]

As we have seen, accounts of American societies varied, but there was plenty of evidence, both in explorers' narratives and in visual representations, of social hierarchies, government, and even of commodious living on the other side of the Atlantic. Thus, Cowley mocked Hobbes's contention and Clarendon noted,

---

[46] See, for example, Malcolm, *Aspects of Hobbes*, 75–76. According to Malcolm, "[t]he four references to American Indians, the brief discussion of colonies in chapter 24 of *Leviathan*, and the single mention of the early administration of Virginia exhaust the direct echoes, in Hobbes's works, of his involvement in the Virginia Company" (*Aspects of Hobbes*, 76; cf. note 104). Malcolm is referring to *The Elements of Law*, I.13.3, *De Cive*, I.13, *Leviathan*, XIII: 63, and *Leviathan*, XLVI: 367. Landucci counts eight references, but does not list them (*I filosofi e i selvaggi*, 116, n. 59). In addition to the references listed by Malcolm, Hobbes also mentions the Indians twice more in *Leviathan* (XXX : 176; XLVI: 378), once in *De Corpore* (I.i.7), and once in the *Answer to the Preface to Gondibert* (143). He also alludes to them in *The Elements of Law* (I.14.12). In *Leviathan* XII, Hobbes refers to the King and founder of Peru, who "pretended himselfe and his wife to be the children of the Sunne" (57).

[47] *Leviathan*, XIII: 63. The "before" refers to the paragraph which describes the incommodities of the war of all against all. Landucci takes "in many places of America" as a conscious limitation that excepts certain politically advanced societies, such as those found in Peru and Mexico (*I filosofi e i selvaggi*, 117).

[48] Malcolm argues that Hobbes:

> must have been aware, if he had read accounts such as that of Purchas, that some Indian tribes did conform to his model of a commonwealth. This must have been embarrassing for his subsidiary theory that all the benefits of civilization sprang directly from the leisure provided by secure government; if Indians could have a sovereign and remain savages, then the political explanation of civilization supplied at best a necessary, not a sufficient, cause (*Aspects of Hobbes*, 75–76).

Nor will the instance he gives of the Inhabitants in *America*, be more to his purpose then the rest, since as far as we have any knowledg of them, the savage People there live under a most intire subjection and slavery to their several Princes; who indeed for the most part live in hostility towards each other, upon those contentions which engage all Princes in War, and which Mr. *Hobbes* allows to be a just cause of War, jealousie of each others Power to do them harm.[49]

For his part, Hobbes's bitter enemy, Bramhall, closed his critique of *Leviathan* with the proposal that

T. H. should have the sole privilege of setting up his form of government in America, as being calculated and fitted for that Meridian. And if it prosper there, then to have the liberty to transplant it hither: who knoweth (if there could but be some means devised to make them understand his language) whether the Americans might

---

[49] Clarendon, *A Brief View and Survey*, 30. Clarendon's judgment was not without foundation. Landucci cites Captain John Smith's account from 1612, according to which,

> Although the countrie people be very barbarous, yet have they amongst them such governement as that their Magistrats for good commanding and their people for due subiection and obeying excell many places that would be counted very civil. The forme of their Commonwealth is a monarchical governement. One as Emperor ruleth over many Kings or governours (*I filosofi e i selvaggi*, 103).

Landucci adds that Smith's example was not an isolated one, but part of a widespread tendency (*ibid.*, 104; cf. 105–07, but see also Mason, "Classical Ethnography and Its Influence on the European Perception of the Peoples of the New World," 149). A few years later, commenting on Shaftesbury's *Characteristics of Men, Manners, Opinions, Times*, Leibniz observed,

> Les Iroquois et les Hurons, Sauvages voisins de la Nouvelle France et de la Nouvelle Angleterre, ont renversé les Maximes politiques trop universelles d'Aristote et de Hobbes; ils ont montré par une conduite surprenante que des Peuples entiers peuvent etre sans Magistrats et sans querelles, et que par consequent les hommes ne sont ny assés portés par leur bon naturel, ny assés forcés par leur mechanceté à se pourvoir d'un gouvernement et à renoncer à leur liberté (Addendum to his letter to Coste, Hannover, May 30, 1712, in *Die Philosophischen Schriften*, III: 424).

Cowley writes,

> *Thou great* Columbus *of the* Golden Lands *of New Philosophies,*
> *Thy Task was harder much than his;*
> *For thy learn'd* America *is*
> *Not only found out first by thee,*
> *And rudely left to* future Industry;
> *But thy Eloquence, and thy Wit*
> *Has* planted, peopled, built, and civilized *it*
> (*The True Effigies of the Monster of Malmesbury*, 7–8).

Lucy criticizes Hobbes along lines similar to Clarendon's. He claims that anyone who reads the Indians' stories will see that they "had divers *Kings* and *Kingdomes*, and have Justice executed amongst them for misdemeanours" (*Observations, Censures and Confutations of Notorious Errours in Mr. Hobbes His Leviathan and Other His Bookes*, 156). Lucy accepts the contention regarding families, but cites Biblical examples to show that families can be at peace with neighboring kingdoms.

not chuse him to be their Soveraign? But all the fear is, that if he should put his principles in practise, as magistrally as he doth dictate them, his supposed subjects might chance to tear their *mortal God* in pieces with their teeth, and entomb his Soveraignty their bowels.[50]

This sample of reactions is telling, for not many of his critics took exception to Hobbes's contention regarding the Indians, and Bramhall's conclusion, which falls back on the far worse stereotype of the Americans as cannibals, reveals why.

In mid-seventeenth century England, and despite Clarendon's sober and fair observation, there was abundant testimony that for the most part, the Indians of America lacked sophisticated institutions of the kind that one found in Europe, and that even where their society displayed signs of organization, their way of life was largely primitive and their existence precarious. Traces of the inhuman traits that European lore had placed on terræ incognitæ for centuries remained in accounts of or ideas about America, and even the Bishop of Derry, as late as 1657, could not resist associating the Indians with cannibalism, despite having praised their several virtues.[51] Even the most up-to-date information did not disprove Hobbes's claim entirely, for there were many tribes whose political structure was based on familial ties and clans, and which were therefore more akin to the large families of *De Cive* than to its large and lasting societies.[52]

---

[50] Bramhall, *Castigations of Mr. Hobbes*, 572–73. Earlier, Bramhall invokes the example of the "most barbarous Americans" as evidence against Hobbes's state of nature, claiming that they "have more principles of naturall piety, and honesty, and morality, then are readily to be found in his writings" (*ibid.*, 531–32).

[51] In the commentary to his translation of Ovid's *Metamorphoses*, another member of the Virginia Company and likely acquaintance of Hobbes's, George Sandys, invokes the example of the Indians to show how savage the Cyclops Polyphemus was, "*who feasts himselfe with the flesh of his guests; more saluage then are the* West-Indians *at this day, who onely eate their enemies, whom they haue taken in the warres*" (*Ovid's Metamorphosis*, 478). On Sandys, see Malcolm, *Aspects of Hobbes*, 74–75. The persistence of this view is evident in Simmel's claim that the "relation of primitive groups is almost always one of hostility," of which "[p]erhaps the most devicive example comes from the American Indians, among whom every tribe was on principle considered in a state of war with every other tribe with which it had not concluded an explicit peace treaty" ("Conflict," 32).

[52] *De Cive*, I.2. Hulton describes the villages that White depicted and notes that they would have had between 100 and 200 inhabitants each (*America 1585*, 27–28). Citing the Indians, among other examples, in *The Wealth of Nations*, Smith argues for the precariousness of relatively small hunting bands and declares, "[n]othing can be more contemptible than an Indian war in North America" (V.i.a.5), although Marouby claims that Smith misrepresents the evidence on which he bases these claims ("Adam Smith and the Anthropology of the Enlightenment," 88–89). As Landucci points out, several others, some of whom Hobbes had read, consider families political units in this context (*I filosofi e i selvaggi*, 118–19; cf. 124, 136, 141). Examples include Tacitus (*Germania*, 7), Grotius (*De iure belli ac pacis*, II.xx. xlvi.4; *On the Origin of the Native Races of America*, 17), and Bodin (*De Republica Libri Sex*, I.vi).

Not long after Hobbes's accession to membership, the Virginia Company published Edward Waterhouse's report on the colony, together with "*A Relation of the Barbarous Massacre.*"[53] Therein, Waterhouse recounts how

that fatall Friday morning, there fell vnder the bloudy and barbarous hands of that perfidious and inhumane people, contrary to all lawes of God and men, of Nature & Nations, three hundred forty seuen men, women, and children, most by their owne weapons; and not being content with taking away life alone, they fell after againe vpon the dead, making as well as they could, a fresh murder, defacing, dragging, and mangling the dead carkasses into many pieces, and carrying some parts away in derision, with base and brutish triumph.[54]

At the conclusion of another report published by the authority of the Virginia Company that year, Bonoeil made a similar case, but in terms strikingly reminiscent of Hobbes's. As lawless and "most vnnaturall," the Indians "know no industry, no Arts, no culture, nor no good vse of this blessed Country heere, but are meere ignorance, sloth, and brutishnesse, and an vnprofitable burthen onely of the earth."[55]

The contrast between the Waterhouse and Bonoeil reports of 1622 and Whitaker's *Good Newes from Virginia* of just ten years before could not have been starker. Whitaker had described the Indians as "naked slaues of the diuell," but had urged the reader to let their miserable condition engender "compassion towards them."[56] For Whitaker, their condition was a result of their ignorance of the true God, and was no different than that of the Britons before the advent of Christianity. Both were children of Adam, their "common parent."[57] Wishing to portray Virginia as "a place of so great plentie," Whitaker described its riches and promise and the several virtues of the Indians.[58] They might have a "rude kinde of Common-wealth, and

---

Kupperman cites the example of the poet Michael Drayton, who "assumed that the Indians would all be like the 'meaner sort' of English people," and notes that this expectation was widespread in England itself, but complicated for Englishmen who found themselves on the other side of the ocean (*Indians & English*, 19). As Kupperman notes rightly, the dynamics of social relations in England need to be considered in attempting to make sense of these representations.

[53] The report was published in London in August 1622 (McCartney, "*A Declaration of the State of the Colony and Affaires in Virginia* (1622)").

[54] Waterhouse, *A Declaration of the State of the Colony and Affaires in Virginia*, 14. To demonstrate the "vnpartiall ingenuity" of the report, Waterhouse "freely confesse[d], that the Country is not so Good, as the *Natiues* are bad, whose barbarous Sauagenesse needs more cultiuation then the ground it selfe, being more ouerspread with inciuilitie and treachery, then that with Bryers" (11). The *Declaration* is replete with descriptions of the Indians as barbarous savages, and uses such terms as "miscreants" whose cruelty surpasses even that of the animals, whose brutishness is unnatural, and who are treacherous, false-hearted friends (15) and "miserable wretches" (17).

[55] Bonoeil, *His Maiesties Gracious Letter to the Earle of South-Hampton*, 85–86.

[56] Whitaker, *Good Newes from Virginia*, 23–24.

[57] Whitaker, *Good Newes from Virginia*, 24.

[58] Whitaker, *Good Newes from Virginia*, 42; cf. 41–44.

rough gouernement," but they have rules and boundaries that they respect, and punish crimes severely.[59]

Intended to harmonize the Indians with the image of America as a hospitable place, accounts such as Whitaker's deemphasized a threat that Hobbes's description of the state of nature would eventually expose: the danger inherent in effective equality among men. If the Indians were not helpless savages, but rather capable human beings with the potential to develop into something like the civilized Europeans, then perhaps they were also equally dangerous. As we have seen, however, even the most optimistic of accounts made it abundantly clear that life in America was unsafe, especially so for the colonists. Hobbes's term is thus fitting: life in America was marked by diffidence.[60]

Hobbes's successive statements regarding the Indians focused on their lack of commodious living, but it is a mistake to suppose that this is all he wanted his reader to conclude from them. Although important, the readers' desire for commodious living was not the whole story. His description of their savage life in *Leviathan* could fool one into believing that this was all about the Indians, but the frontispiece that Hobbes chose and insisted on for *De Cive* confirms that Hobbes was not interested in accurate ethnography, but in a persuasive, plausible illustration of the conditions that obtain when there is no reliable security. If we were to associate this condition exclusively with the Indians, we would be forgetting what it was like to try to settle America in the early years of the seventeenth century. Jamestown is, once again, an apt example: at the time, it lay in the "domain of the 'Great Emperor Powhatan,' whose overlordship of more than thirty tribes enabled him to evolve and carry out a policy designed to prevent the English from establishing themselves as the greatest power in tidewater Virginia"; on the other side was a small colony that lacked "proper discipline and good government."[61] The image that Hobbes had chosen for the frontispiece of *De Cive* serves as a reminder of that fact. The reader looking at the Algonquian chief on the right-hand side is in the position of the colonists. The Indian's menacing expression and the scenes that are unfolding behind him, however, show that from the mass of information coming from the other side of the ocean, it was possible to extract a simple, yet persuasive, reminder that the state of nature was very much real.

[59] Whitaker, *Good Newes from Virginia*, 26–27.
[60] See Landucci, *I filosofi e i selvaggi*, 125–27; Kupperman, "Apathy and Death in Early Jamestown"; Kupperman, "English Perceptions of Treachery." The extent of the misery facing the settlers has been highlighted by recent discoveries corroborating the literary evidence of cannibalism among the settlers as well (see Stromberg, "Starving Settlers in Jamestown Colony Resorted to Cannibalism." Josephus, whose works Hobbes knew (see, e.g., *Leviathan*, XXXIII: 204; Devonshire Mss., Chatsworth HS/E/1A), relates the paradigmatic episode of Mary of Bethezuba, in his history of the Jewish war against the Romans (VI.199–219), whom famine caused to kill and eat her son.
[61] Kupperman, "Apathy and Death in Early Jamestown," 38.

PART IV

A SCIENCE OF RHETORIC

forraine Words are unpleasant, because *Obscure*; and *Plaine Words*, because *too Manifest*, making us learne nothing new: but *Metaphors* please; for they beget in us by the *Genus* or by some *common thing* to that with another, a kind of *Science*

    – Hobbes, *A Briefe of the Art of Rhetorique*

9

All Things to All People

That which may perhaps make ... equality incredible, is but a vain concept of ones owne wisdome, which almost all men think they have in greater degree, than the Vulgar; that is, than all men but themselves, and a few others, whom by Fame, or for concurring with themselves, they approve. For such is the nature of men, that howsoever they may acknowledge many others to be more witty, or more eloquent, or more learned; Yet they will hardly believe there be many so wise as themselves: For they see their own wit at hand, and other mens at a distance.

– Hobbes, *Leviathan*

ELITISM FOR ALL: DISSIMULATION AND THE
FOOLISHNESS OF THE WISE

The publication of *De Corpore* in 1655 fulfilled part of Hobbes's promise to construct a philosophical system.[1] This work, which comprised the first part of that system, begins at the very beginning by considering the nature, scope, and purpose of philosophy. Hobbes had already signaled his intention to pick a fight with the intellectual powers that be in the Epistle Dedicatory to *The Elements of Law*, wherein he had accused those who had taken up questions of "justice and policy in general" of quarreling among themselves and contradicting one another.[2] Fifteen years later, with *De Cive* and *Leviathan* in print, he would begin the work that would provide the proper

---

[1] *Elementorum Philosophiæ Sectio Prima, De Corpore* (London: Andrew Crooke, 1655). The English edition was published the following year: *Elements of Philosophy, The First Section, concerning Body* (London: R. & W. Leybourn for Andrew Crooke, 1656); cf. Macdonald and Hargreaves, *Thomas Hobbes: A Bibliography*, nos. 55–56. For Hobbes's account of the sequence, see *De Cive*, Pref., §§ 18–19.

[2] *The Elements of Law*, Ep. Ded., xv.

foundation for philosophy with an appropriately ambitious statement: Natural philosophy was young, having received its first beginnings from Copernicus, Galileo, and Harvey, "but Civil Philosophy yet much younger, as being no older ... than my book *De Cive.*"[3] As we have seen, Hobbes couched his polemic in scientific language, and promised proper philosophy as the remedy for the ills wrought by eloquent rhetoricians.[4]

To demonstrate the inadequacy of extant political philosophy, Hobbes contrasted its incessant quarrels to the benefits flowing from the work of the mathematicians. In its positive or negative form, that list became for Hobbes the basis of the distinction between the chaos of the state of nature and the commodious living possible in civil society. Offered mainly in the context of political treatises, that device seemed itself a political one, a means, that is, of seeking a solution to a specifically political problem. Yet the distinction is perhaps inapposite for Hobbes, for whom politics is primary in the sense articulated by Aristotle: Philosophy, argues Hobbes in *Leviathan*, was only possible once "great Common-wealths" emerged, for "*Leasure* is the mother of *Philosophy*; and *Common-wealth*, the mother of *Peace*, and *Leasure.*"[5] In *De Corpore*, Hobbes makes it clear that the question of order leaves no area of human activity untouched, and that the purpose of philosophy is not simply the acquisition of knowledge, but the use of that knowledge for "the performing of some action, or thing to be done."[6] Hobbes argues that

what the *utility* of philosophy is, especially of natural philosophy and geometry, will be best understood by reckoning up the chief commodities of which mankind is capable, and by comparing the manner of life of such as enjoy them, with that of others which want the same. Now, the greatest commodities of mankind are the arts; namely, of measuring matter and motion; of moving ponderous bodies; of architecture; of navigation; of making instruments for all uses; of calculating the celestial motions, the aspects of the stars, and the parts of time, of geography, &c. By which sciences, how great benefits men receive is more easily understood than expressed.[7]

---

[3] *De Corpore*, Ep. Ded., I: ix.
[4] See esp. *The Elements of Law*, II.8.12–14.
[5] *Leviathan*, XLVI: 368. Despite Hobbes's dismissal of these works in the same chapter (370), his point here is in essence the same as Aristotle's, in the *Nicomachean Ethics* (1094a26-b11) and *Politics* (1253a25–26). In the *Historia Ecclesiastica*, Hobbes describes the origin of the commonwealth as follows:

> Therefore, for the sake of their own safety, many small men united so
> there could be one great man;
> And so that he could rout the common enemy with all of their resources,
> conserve peace and maintain justice at home.
> From this source originated power for kings and leisure for the people; and
> leisure was the wellspring of the liberal arts (115–20).

[6] *De Corpore*, I.i.6. The reason is that neither the "inward glory or triumph of mind a man may have for the mastering of some difficult and doubtful matter, or for the discovery of some hidden truth," nor teaching for teaching's sake, are worth the trouble involved (*ibid.*).
[7] *De Corpore*, I.i.7. Cf. *De Homine*, X.3.

Almost all the people of Europe, most in Asia, and some in Africa enjoy these benefits, but none in America or near the Poles, argues Hobbes; not because there is any difference in men's abilities, but because in those places there is less philosophy or none at all. Men everywhere have the same soul and the same faculties of mind, and the only thing standing between them and commodious living is a commonwealth large and lasting enough to allow for the emergence of philosophy.

As with all philosophy, so it is with civil philosophy: it is the absence of benefits rather than their presence that enables us to understand its value, and nothing encapsulates this privation in the way that war does.[8] The calamities that can render human life miserable, and which can be alleviated by human industry, argues Hobbes, "arise from war, but chiefly from civil war; for from this proceed slaughter, solitude, and the want of all things."[9] For Hobbes, the emergence of war is a paradox of sorts, since everyone knows its terrible consequences, yet no one can will something that does not seem good to him. War must therefore be the result of ignorance of "those duties which unite and keep men in peace."[10] It is no accident that Hobbes describes the state of nature as a state of war, despite the fact that his definition of war might strike many readers as overly broad.[11]

Hobbes's goal, already implicit in the material that accompanied his translation of Thucydides, but certainly explicit from the *Elements* to *De Corpore*, was to diminish the extent of this state of war as much as possible.[12] This formulation is not accidental, since no human condition can ever be entirely devoid of vestiges of the state of nature; the state of war can never be eradicated completely. On the scale from perfect order to perfect disorder, the extremes are there only as signposts because no actual condition corresponds fully to either. Human beings travel along this continuum, but never inhabit its poles. The most ordered condition contains discord on some level, and even amid what appears as complete chaos, one will

---

[8] See, for example, "Of the Life and History of Thucydides" (*EW*, VIII: xxiv); *De Cive*, Pref., § 4; *De Corpore*, I.i.7; *Leviathan*, XIII: 63, XXX: 175.

[9] *De Corpore*, I.i.7.

[10] These duties are the rules of civil life, the knowledge of which is moral philosophy (*De Corpore*, I.i.7).

[11] See *Leviathan*, XIII: 62; cf. *The Elements of Law*, I.14.11; *De Cive*, I.12; *Leviathan*, XVIII: 91.

[12] Recall Hobbes's view that "it would be an incomparable benefit to commonwealth, if every man held the opinions concerning law and policy here delivered" (*The Elements of Law*, Ep. Ded., xvi). In *De Cive*, Hobbes requests from the readers attention befitting the subject matter's "dignity or profit" (Pref., § 1), and promises that once he has shown the bright road to peace and dark paths of sedition, he will have offered them the most profitable knowledge (Pref., § 8). Hobbes's assessment of *Leviathan*, both in the work's Review and Conclusion and in his prose life, emphasizes its contributions toward peace (see, for example, *Leviathan*, Review and Conclusion: 395; *OL*, I: xv-xvi; *Considerations upon the Reputation, Loyalty, Manners, and Religion of Thomas Hobbes of Malmesbury*, 6–9; *EW*, VII: 335–36).

always be able to discern a certain amount of concerted action. Hobbes's examples of the natural condition make this abundantly clear. Perfect order did not exist even in the Garden of Eden, and even the bleakest state of war contains armies and bands, if only temporary. For Hobbes, this is part and parcel of human affairs more generally, which can never be without some inconvenience.[13] As he puts it in *Leviathan*, "man by nature chooseth the lesser evil."[14] The utility of civil philosophy in this case is the realization that the inconveniences of civil society are preferable to those of the state of nature. In such a scheme, a state of nature will always be a necessary reminder of what is required for peace.[15]

One might object to this description by pointing to Hobbes's focus on such concepts as philosophy, science, and truth, which occasionally approximates the promise of a radical transformation of politics. Thus, it has been suggested that Hobbes predicted the advent of universal peace, "and not because some political mechanism will ensure it but because deep features of human nature will have been transformed."[16] Similarly, it has been argued that Hobbes's "'principle of publicity' implied that, as a population became more enlightened and therefore more able to accept the true reasons for government policies, the degree of concealment and misdirection should gradually decline."[17] What might such an enlightenment look like? Imagine a people who understood that a preemptive war "was justified by true political principles" and would therefore "not need to have that war presented to them under a simulated pretext."[18] Although in the first instance the term "true" appears to refer to the fact that the government is not concealing the

---

[13] *De Cive*, Pref., § 20. Lloyd proposes a reading of the state of nature as a continuum of judgment from the extreme of absolute private judgment to political society, but points out that even among instances of the latter, "a state of nature may continue to obtain, just to the degree that those forms invite the use of private judgment" (*Morality in the Philosophy of Thomas Hobbes*, 20; cf. *ibid.*, 19–25).

[14] *Leviathan*, XIV: 70; cf. *ibid.*, XX: 107; *The Elements of Law*, I.7.8: "There are few things in this world, but either have a mixture of good and evil, or there is a chain of them so necessarily linked together, that the one cannot be taken without the other....Now when in the whole chain, the greater part is good, the whole is called good; and when the evil overweigheth, the whole is called evil." In discussing the condition of subjects under a sovereign, Hobbes entertains the objection that unlimited power is likely to become obnoxious to the former. He replies that those who so object tend to forget

> that the estate of Man can never be without some incommodity or other; and that the greatest, that in any forme of Government can possibly happen to the people in generall, is scarce sensible, in respect of the miseries, horrible calamities, that accompany a Civill Warre; or that dissolute condition of masterlesse men, without subjection to Lawes, and a coërcive Power to tye their hands from rapine and revenge (*Leviathan*, XVIII: 94).

[15] *Leviathan*, XVIII: 94.

[16] Tuck, "The Utopianism of *Leviathan*," 126. Cf. Lund, "The Historical and 'Political' Origins of Civil Society;" Johnson, "Hobbes and the Wolf-Man."

[17] Malcolm, *Reason of State, Propaganda, and the Thirty Years' War*, 123.

[18] Malcolm, *Reason of State, Propaganda, and the Thirty Years' War*, 123.

real reasons for its policy, it is hard to know what, for Hobbes, "true political principles" might be with which no one would disagree, and how these could be disseminated to an entire population without any "simulated pretext." No less telling is the appearance, here, of the term "enlightened." Once again, its use is not entirely unwarranted, since Hobbes himself uses the metaphor of light twice in the prefatory material of *De Cive*, but our post-Enlightenment prism is liable to distort what it meant for him.[19] There is no doubt that Hobbes aimed at some sort of transformation, but to transform politics to the extent described by some recent commentators, one would have to find a way to overcome the hurdles imposed by its very constitutive elements, namely human nature. Hobbes shows no sign of expecting anything this radical.[20]

It is tempting to think that Hobbes's radical transformation of man into an enlightened being of this sort has already begun with his insistence on effective equality by nature. After all, to be able to evaluate and accept the same set of political principles without the need for dissimulation, the citizens of this commonwealth would have to have achieved a common level of enlightenment. Yet, Hobbes's particular argument is problematic for enlightenment and radical transformation because it establishes equality by demonstrating that human beings are equally susceptible to poor judgment and vanity, and equally unlikely to escape them. A first set of reasons is discovered by observing the mechanics of perception and cognition. Here, the prospects of enlightenment are hampered by the mind's susceptibility to the deceptions of sense as well as to a host of other limitations and barriers to good judgment.[21] The same is true of self-interest and, therefore, of conflicts of interest. Hobbes points out repeatedly that human beings are very bad judges of their long-term interests, opting frequently for short-term gain, and merely postponing the reckoning until later. Once again, the cause is essential,

[f]or all men are by nature provided with notable multiplying glasses, (that is their Passions and Selfe-love,) through which, every little payment appeareth a great grievance; but are destitute of those prospective glasses, (namely Morall and Civill Science,) to see a farre off the miseries that hang over them, and cannot without such payments be avoyded.[22]

As with several other passages in Hobbes's writings, this could be read as the promise of a civil science that will correct excessive self-love and reveal

---

[19] *De Cive*, Ep. Ded., § 8; Pref., § 8.
[20] The notion of a cultural transformation is suggested by Johnston, who is surely correct in this, but too optimistic in claiming that the result of Hobbes's efforts would be a commonwealth based on "the firmer, more permanent basis of enlightened, rational self-interest" (*The Rhetoric of Leviathan*, 127).
[21] See, for example, *The Elements of Law*, I.2.10, I.5.14., I.7.8; *De Cive*, III.32; XIII.8; *Leviathan*, VI: 57, XVIII: 94; *De Homine*, X.3.
[22] *Leviathan*, XVIII: 94.

true political principles, but the limitations that Hobbes has identified in human beings stand in the way of such a radical transformation. Left to his own devices, even an individual who has been enlightened by Hobbes's diagnosis and has chosen to wipe the slate clean and begin anew will face the same hurdles as before. Nor could one rely on someone else to step in and aid the individual in question for, at the very least, such a guide would face the same obstacles himself, and would in any case be suspect, since his own self-interest ought to be expected to interfere with his impartiality.[23] These were the difficulties that Hobbes's rhetoric of science and direct appeal to the reader were meant to overcome.

The real problem with this account of equality, however, is that having argued for it, Hobbes also does so much to undermine it.[24] Already in the prefatory material to the translation of Thucydides, Hobbes dismisses the judgment of the multitude, however terrible it may be, because he has received the approval of those whose opinion he values, and notes that most people look to history for entertainment, rather than for its lessons. He adds that his edition is intended for "men of good judgment and education, (for whom it also was intended from the beginning by Thucydides)."[25] Statements of this kind are by no means confined to this early work. In *De Cive*, Hobbes declares his longstanding opinion: "That there was never yet any more-then-vulgar-prudence that had the luck of being acceptable to the Giddy People; but either it hath not been understood, or else having been so, hath been levell'd and cryed downe."[26] We have noted that Hobbes begins the Preface to the same work by describing the practice of the sages of antiquity of presenting their teachings about politics in the form of poetry or "*clouded with Allegories, … lest by the disputations of private men, it might be defiled.*"[27] Someone who is about to demonstrate the power of science and its ability to enlighten everyone should be expected to denounce this practice. There is even more reason to expect such a denunciation from Hobbes in particular, who frequently disparages ancient authors both for their erroneous views and for the unwarranted influence they have had on posterity only because of their antiquity. But as we have seen, Hobbes does the opposite. He concurs that politics is indeed a matter of the highest importance and concludes that the caution of the ancient sages was justified, given the dangers inherent in seditious doctrines. To demonstrate that he means what he says, he completes his assessment of this practice by offering his own twist on one of their allegories, through his retelling of the story of the presumptuous Ixion, who trespassed into realms in which he did not belong.

---

[23] In *Behemoth*, Hobbes writes, "[i]t is a hard matter, or rather … impossible, to know what other men mean, especially if they be crafty" (156); cf. *ibid.*, 158; *Leviathan*, XXX: 180.

[24] See Whelan, "Language and Its Abuses in Hobbes's *Leviathan*," 71.

[25] *EW*, VIII: vii-xi.

[26] *De Cive*, Ep. Ded., § 3.

[27] *De Cive*, Pref., § 2.

Perhaps most importantly for the project of alleged enlightenment, reason is not equally available to all, even though vanity is. In a note added to one of the most important passages of *De Cive*, wherein Hobbes explains what sort of sin atheism is, he writes,

As for my contention that God's existence *can be known by natural reason, this must be taken not as if I thought that all men can know it – unless they think it follows that because Archimedes discovered by natural reason the proportion of a sphere to a cylinder, any Tom, Dick or Harry could have done the same. I say therefore that although God's existence can be known by some men by the light of reason, it cannot be known by men who are constantly in pursuit of pleasure, wealth or honour, nor by those who do not have the habit, the ability or the concern to reason correctly, nor, finally, by fools – which is where the Atheist belongs.*[28]

This trend continues in the later works. Thus, in *Leviathan*, Hobbes notes how easy it is for men to come to believe anything from those who "have gotten credit with them; and can with gentlenesse, and dexterity, take hold of their fear, and ignorance," and worries throughout about those who are susceptible to manipulation and to the charms of seditious opinions based on false promises or disguised as the word of God.[29] Who are these people, and how many of them are there? For Hobbes,

They whom necessity, or covetousnesse keepeth attent on their trades, and labour; and they, on the other side, whom superfluity, or sloth carrieth after their sensuall pleasures, (which two sorts of men make up the greatest part of Man-kind,) being diverted from the deep meditation, which the learning of truth, not onely in the matter of Naturall Justice, but also of all other Sciences necessarily requireth, receive the Notions of their duty, chiefly from Divines in the Pulpit, and partly from such of their Neighbours, or familiar acquaintance, as having the Faculty of discoursing readily, and plausibly, seem wiser and better learned in cases of Law, and Conscience, than themselves.[30]

Contemplating the likelihood that an event such as the English Civil War might change this state of affairs, one of the interlocutors in *Behemoth* concludes, "that will be quickly forgot, and then we shall be no wiser than we were."[31]

[28] *De Cive*, XIV.19, note to "Should be classed among the sins of imprudence" (Silverthorne, trans). Cf. *The Elements of Law*, I.10.3, on dullness.
[29] *Leviathan*, XII: 56; cf. *De Cive*, Pref., § 21.
[30] *Leviathan*, XXX: 179. Cf. *Behemoth*, 158: "For the common people alwaies haue been and always will be ignorant of their duty to the publick; as neuer meditating any thing but their particular interest, in other things following their immediate leaders, which are either the Preachers, or the most potent of the Gentlemen that dwell amongst them, as common soldiers for the most part follow their immediate Captains, if they like them."
[31] *Behemoth*, 158. In light of this and similar statements in *Behemoth*, Skinner's claim that "Hobbes treats the period between 1640 and 1660 as little more than a demented interruption of England's natural and civilised line of intellectual development" (*Reason and Rhetoric in the Philosophy of Hobbes*, 435) is puzzling. Cf. *Leviathan*, XVIII: 93.

All this appears to cast doubt on the sincerity of Hobbes's insistence on effective equality, but we would do well to remember that Hobbes is offering these thoughts to the reader, in what Hobbes intends to be a one-on-one encounter. It is, more importantly, addressed to beings whose chief characteristic is an abiding concern with *bonum sibi*, and whom Hobbes identifies principally as the children of pride. The task of Leviathan is to reign over these beings, not by eliminating their vainglory, but by harnessing it. Hobbes paves the ground for this process by laying "such principles down for a foundation, as passion not mistrusting, may not seek to displace."[32] As this statement of purpose suggests, the solution to the problem of conflict lies not in the eradication of some challenging aspect of human nature, but in its neutralization, by means of deception: passion will not seek to displace Hobbes's foundation because it will not mistrust it. Hobbes insisted from the start that to succeed where everyone else had failed, it was necessary to proceed by means of the right method. He was also surely aware that the root of the Greek word μέθοδος, from which English gets "method," also yields "ruse."[33] In the only other instance, in the *Elements*, in which Hobbes writes of method, he notes how difficult it is to change the minds of men who have come to accept erroneous opinions. Those who possess them, namely the majority of men, are difficult to teach anew because of the prejudices they have come to hold as a result of their false estimation of their "knowledge."[34]

Yet, these are the very individuals whom Hobbes must "appease," which is why his attempt must begin by taking their vanity as seriously as they take its illusions.[35] Seeing themselves through its distorting prism, they fancy themselves superior to everyone else and hence doubt that men are effectively equal. Recall that what "may perhaps make ... equality incredible, is but a vain conceipt of ones owne wisdome, which almost all men think they have in greater degree, than the Vulgar; that is, than all men but themselves, and a few others, whom by Fame, or for concurring with themselves, they approve."[36] The consequences of this vanity are, of course, not confined to epistemology, but extend to the political realm as well. Even if *Leviathan* were written specifically for Charles II, it was certainly written for more than one prince, "[f]or there are very few so foolish, that had not rather governe themselves, than be goverened by others."[37] Those who think of themselves in this way, however, need to be flattered accordingly, and Hobbes treats

---

[32] *The Elements of Law*, Ep. Ded., xv.
[33] *The Elements of Law*, Ep. Ded., xv–xvi. Cf. *Leviathan*, V: 20, where the first cause of absurdities is the want of method.
[34] *The Elements of Law*, I.10.8.
[35] *The Elements of Law*, I.13.7.
[36] *Leviathan*, XIII: 61. This view is reproduced in *Behemoth* (321–22).
[37] *Leviathan*, XV: 77.

them as privy to the highest secrets of state, as interlocutors of the sages, as founders of civil society, and as princes.[38]

The road to equality begins with *captatio benevolentiæ*: Hobbes's insight that each reader thinks of himself as best equipped to judge his own circumstances and determine what he needs is central to his novel approach to civil philosophy. The first sign is the name of its most mature and prominent instantiation, which along with the unfinished epigraph from the Book of Job, refers the reader unmistakably to the importance of pride. A second sign is Hobbes's insistence on the importance of judgment throughout his political theory.[39] Individual judgment is simultaneously a central element of natural right and a sure path toward conflict, and its surrender in favor of a single judgment the only possible path to peace.[40] A third sign is Hobbes's sustained and vehement attack on arguments from authority, and related invitation to each reader to accept or reject his argument without relying on anyone else; a position that is stated repeatedly in all of Hobbes's political treatises, but is given with particular clarity in two of his later works. In the much later Latin *Leviathan* and the *Historia Ecclesiastica*, Hobbes writes of men – such as Epicurus, Plato, and Aristotle – who "read the world, not books, and each undertook to investigate / causes by means of his own natural intelligence."[41] Hobbes's solution to these problems begins with the recognition that pride cannot be eliminated or overcome, but must be appeased if it is to be neutralized. His invitation was doubly bold, for it considers the reader's judgment preferable to the received opinions of the age, and, through his acquiescence to Hobbes's propositions, renders the reader a founder and preserver of the commonwealth.

If human beings are liable to value their own judgment, Hobbes's contemporaries were especially so, and Hobbes was both well aware of the forces that were underpinning their estimation and conscious of the fact

---

[38] Tuck rests his case for Hobbes's utopianism in part on the expectation that vainglory can be eliminated because it is "*produced* by the false belief that one might enjoy 'precedency and superiority,'" rather than giving rise to such a belief ("The Utopianism of *Leviathan*," 132). For Hobbes, however, vanity is a direct result of mankind's "perpetuall desire of Power after power, that ceaseth onely in Death" (*Leviathan*, XI: 47), and hence cannot be eliminated. Rather, it must be approached in a way that will not render it suspicious and thus hostile.

[39] See Evrigenis, *Fear of Enemies and Collective Action*, 120–21.

[40] See *The Elements of Law*, II.10.8; *Leviathan*, XIV: 64–65.

[41] *Historia Ecclesiastica*, 405–10; cf. the Appendix to the Latin *Leviathan* (OL III: 540). Such individuals, for Hobbes, are "true philosophers," to be distinguished from their mindless disciples. In *De Homine*, Hobbes argues,

It ought to be understood, however, that not all men have the science whereunto they profess; for those that discuss the causes of things on the basis of others' writings, and those that make discoveries by copying others' sentences, are utterly worthless. For to do what hath been done, hath nothing good about it in itself; but on the contrary, this is sometimes evil, since by confirming ancient errors they obstruct the path of truth (XI.9; cf. *Leviathan*, A Review and Conclusion, 395).

that their effects would be irrevocable.[42] Foremost among them was the Reformation, with its invitation to believers everywhere to read the Bible and consider its teaching for themselves.[43] Hobbes was keenly aware of the far-reaching consequences of this shift. Toward the beginning of *Behemoth*, his history of the Civil War, Hobbes has one interlocutor ask another how the power of the Presbyterians came to be what it was. The exchange that follows is indicative:

A: This controuersy between the Papist and the Reformed Churches could not choose but make euery man to the best of his power examine by the Scriptures which of them was in the Right. And to that end they were translated into vulgar languages; whereas before the translation of them was not allowed, nor any man to read them but such as had expresse lycence so to doe. For the Pope did concerning the Scriptures, the same that Moses did concerning Mount Sinai, Moses suffered no man to go vp to it to hear God speake or gaze vpon him, but such as he himselfe tooke with him. And the Pope suffered none to speake with God in the Scriptures, that had not some part of the Popes spirit in him, for which he might be trusted.

B: Certainly Moses did therein very wisely and according to Gods owne commandement.

A: No doubt of it; and the euent it selfe hath made it since appear so. For after the Bible was translated into English, euery man, nay euery boy and wench that could read English, thought they spoke with God Almighty and vnderstood what he said, when by a certain number of chapters a day, they had read the Scriptures once or twice ouer. And so the reuerence and obedience due to the Reformed Church here, and to the Bishops and Pastors therin, was cast off; and euery man became a Judge of Religion, and an Interpreter of the Scriptures to himselfe.[44]

The reader familiar with Hobbes's political theory recognizes that a condition in which every man is a judge of religion and interpreter of Scripture is the antithesis of the well-ordered commonwealth, in which these powers belong only to the sovereign. In the first interlocutor's view, it was the license to interpret Scripture that gave rise to the sects that reared their heads "to the disturbance of the Commonwealth" – namely the state of nature that was the Civil War.[45]

Younger than the Reformation, but no less potent in the long term, a second and parallel process, the "Scientific Revolution," was well underway

---

[42] Hodgen argues that "[o]ne of the main differences between the thought of the Middle Ages and that of the Renaissance was the value attached to the trait of curiosity" (*Early Anthropology in the Sixteenth and Seventeenth Centuries*, 207).

[43] See Doyle, "The Contemporary Background of Hobbes' 'State of Nature'." Pacchi thus writes of the "restless melting pot of Protestantism, forever kept on the boil by the temptation of individual interpretation, [where] even quite heterodox stands find their place, and this is even more true of England in the Interregnum" ("Some Guidelines into Hobbes's Theology," 92). Cf. Funkenstein, *Theology and the Scientific Imagination from the Middle Ages to the Seventeenth Century*, 5.

[44] *Behemoth*, 134–35.

[45] *Behemoth*, 135.

by the time Hobbes addressed his audience.[46] By the end of the sixteenth
century, pursuits that had been previously confined to the universities and
monasteries began to interest a wide range of individuals who had hitherto
been considered outsiders, but who had now become participants in the
pursuit of natural philosophy, and users of its method and language in
ever-expanding areas of life.[47] When he surveyed these developments for
his history of the Royal Society in 1667, Sprat saw agreement between the
goals of the society and the church, both of which "may lay equal claim to
the word *Reformation*; the one having compas'd it in *Religion*, the other
purposing it in *Philosophy*."[48] Having worked for Bacon, whose role in
this transformation was crucial, and gone on to patrons whose interest in
natural philosophy was sustained and serious, Hobbes was acutely aware
of the shift that was taking place and of its rising significance. His own scientific activities attest to this fact.[49] The precise meaning of these new terms
and contents of the boundaries that were being redrawn were the subjects
of protracted and fundamental debates, but the challenge to established
authority was evident from the start, as was the expansion of the population whose judgment was deemed relevant.[50] Even where Hobbes disagreed
with his contemporaries as to what constituted proper science, he was
keenly aware of the extent to which scientific inquiry was already widespread and expanding, through a process that was irreversible.[51] Moreover,
as his theory of language shows, Hobbes was well aware of the importance

[46] This term has become controversial. Its appropriateness as a descriptor of the scientific
developments that took place during the sixteenth and seventeenth centuries is beyond the
present purpose, for which the term will suffice as a signpost of important shifts in method,
of the spreading interest in science, and of the increasing legitimacy attributed to science.
Cf. Park and Daston, Introduction to *Early Modern Science*, 8; Gaukroger, *The Emergence
of a Scientific Culture*, Chapter 1; Shapin, *The Scientific Revolution*; Dear, *Discipline and
Experience*, 1–2.

[47] Martin, for instance, argues that in the sixteenth century, natural philosophy "expanded
from the university and cloisters into the broader and more volatile public arena: not only
scholars, but a widening array of artisans and gentlemen were asserting a right to pursue
natural knowledge and make public pronouncements about its substance, proper methods
and uses" (*Francis Bacon, the State, and the Reform of Natural Philosophy*, 172–73).

[48] Sprat, *The History of the Royal-Society of London*, 369.

[49] Aubrey famously relates that Bacon "loved to converse with [Hobbes]," and that he pre-
ferred him to all other amanuenses, "because he understood what he wrote" ('*Brief Lives*,'
I: 331). On Hobbes's scientific activities more generally, see Jesseph, *Squaring the Circle*,
Chapter 1.

[50] These tendencies are already evident in Bacon (see, for example, *The Works of Francis Bacon*,
III: 321; IV: 8). In his lecture on Hobbes, Hegel would describe his significance as follows:

> Before this ideals were set before us, or Holy Scripture or positive law was quoted as
> authoritative. Hobbes, on the contrary, sought to derive the bond which holds the state
> together, that which gives the state its power, from principles which lie within us, which
> we recognize as our own (*Lectures on the History of Philosophy*, 316).

[51] See, for example, Hobbes, *Dialogus Physicus*.

A Science of Rhetoric

of ordinary usage as the starting point for reconsidering and establishing the meaning of terms.[52]

The scope of Hobbes's program, namely his desire to reform the political behavior of everyone through an individual and private appeal, attests to his awareness of the consequences of these transformations. That ambitious aim, however, also raises an important set of hurdles, for Hobbes recognizes that despite sharing certain fundamental formal characteristics, human beings are shaped by their environment and experiences, and hence come to desire different things.[53] Recognizing that this disparity of interests and desires means that no single set of positive goals will satisfy everyone equally, Hobbes opted for a focus on a hindrance that stands between all human beings and their individual goals, whatever those might be, for as he puts it in the very last sentence of *Leviathan*, "such Truth, as opposeth no mans profit, nor pleasure, is to all men welcome."[54]

It has been suggested that once transformed, Hobbes's enlightened citizens would operate on the basis of reason, rather than passion, and Hobbes's repeated contrast between reason and the passions would seem to lend credence to this interpretation. As it turns out, however, this distinction is meaningless for Hobbes, since passion sets the human agenda, and reason devises the means of acting on it. Neither part of the process can be ignored. The cooperation between reason and the passions in getting man out of the state of nature and into civil society shows that Hobbes's chasm was never as unbridgeable as he had suggested initially.[55] Rather, fully aware of the fact that it is impossible to eliminate the passions from this equation, Hobbes seeks to appeal to them in ways that will not cause them to oppose what is being proposed.[56] Those passions – the fear of violent death, the desire of the things necessary for commodious living, and the hope of attaining them – are the ones that Hobbes needs to prompt in his reader, but without causing him to suspect that the proposed course of action contravenes his self-interest.[57] As he notes, the best method for achieving this involves a contrast between an uncertain condition in which the fear of violent death interferes with one's ability to pursue the things necessary for commodious living, and one in which industry is possible because someone else is keeping watch.[58]

<hr />

[52] See Struever, "Dilthey's Hobbes and Cicero's Rhetoric," 253.

[53] See, for example, *The Elements of Law*, I.14.3; *Leviathan*, Introduction: 2; XI. Cf. Biletzki, "Thomas Hobbes," 63–64.

[54] *Leviathan*, A Review and Conclusion, 396.

[55] See Hoekstra, *Thomas Hobbes and the Creation of Order*.

[56] As Hobbes puts it in the fullest and most mature account of the state of nature, it is the passions that "encline men to Peace," and reason that suggests the means by which this peace may come about (*Leviathan*, XIII: 63).

[57] *Leviathan*, XIII: 63; *The Elements of Law*, Ep. Ded., xv.

[58] At the beginning of Part IV of *Leviathan*, Hobbes revisits the issue of comparisons from a different point of view, noting that signposts are necessary correctives to our native ignorance,

Far from relying on a civil philosophy pretending to the certainty of geometry to persuade his readers of the benefits of order, Hobbes makes it clear already in the *Elements* that in appeasing, "by which we increase or diminish one another's passions," one begins with an opinion, "no matter whether ... true or false, or the narration historical or fabulous," because "not truth, but image, maketh passion."[59] Hobbes conforms to this method to the letter. The starting point of his own attempt to appease is his doctrine, which he describes as his "opinions concerning law and policy."[60] His own image is that of the state of nature.

The diversity of experiences and circumstances, and, hence, of the objects of men's passions, means that Hobbes's image would have to be simultaneously one and many. It would need to be such as to allow every reader to find within it his own rationale for agreeing with Hobbes that the incommodities of civil society are preferable to those of the state of nature. This presupposes, however, that the reader would be convinced that the state of nature is both possible and probable, for he would otherwise have no reason to take it seriously.[61] Yet, at the same time, the conclusion should not be too closely associated with any single story or argument, and this for two reasons. First, because privileging any one rationale would win over some readers, but risk losing all those who would judge it irrelevant to their own concerns. Second, because making the conclusion too dependent on any single part of the story would render the entire argument as vulnerable as that part, so that the refutation of that part would risk bringing down the whole as well.[62] Hobbes's ambitious aim, however, imposes a further requirement on his image, for to bring about the transformation of his readers' political behavior, it would also have to be memorable and easily accessible. Being persuaded once, in the comfort of one's armchair, at the first – and possibly the last – reading of *Leviathan* would not suffice. To work, the deterrent would have to kick in every time one contemplated an action that might

---

providing us with a sense of perspective, and thus protecting us from those who seek to deceive us with erroneous doctrines (XLIV: 333–34); cf. Plato, *Republic*, 583b2–585a5.

[59] *The Elements of Law*, I.13.3. On the degree to which Hobbes's contemporaries would have seen various aspects of his state of nature as accurate reflections of reality, see Ashcraft, "Political Theory and Political Action."

[60] *The Elements of Law*, Ep. Ded., xvi.

[61] This was precisely the basis of Lowde's critique of Hobbes's state of nature (*A Discourse concerning the Nature of Man*, 170). As Tuck points out, persuading readers that the state of nature was possible was a central task of those who used the concept (*The Rights of War and Peace*, 7–8; Introduction to *On the Citizen*, xxv-xxvi). On the other hand, Biletzki argues that in Hobbes's case, "[i]f we emphasize the story, we can stop being bothered, for instance, about its status as real or imaginary, as fictional, or historical" ("Thomas Hobbes," 68). It is clear, however, that if it were to act as a deterrent, the state of nature must be both possible *and* likely.

[62] Recall, for instance, that Clarendon attacked Hobbes on precisely these grounds (*A Brief View and Survey*, 30).

jeopardize order, and do so automatically, rather than as the result of complicated ratiocinations.

But how does one create the impression of a custom-made approach in the midst of mass production? We have ample evidence to conclude that Hobbes was very interested in his readers' reactions and that he took account of their feedback in revising and preparing his works for publication.[63] The gradual transformation of the state of nature along principles already laid out in the *Elements* reinforces the sense that the changes reflect Hobbes's successive attempts to render his image more powerful and persuasive to his readers. The first three accounts of the state of nature – in the *Elements of Law* and the two versions of *De Cive* – fall short of these requirements. If their purpose was to persuade the reader that the state of nature is an undesirable condition that every sensible individual would seek to avoid, they fail to give any real reason why the reader should consider it a condition that he would be likely to encounter. In those first attempts, Hobbes does not ask explicitly whether the state of nature ever existed, and the examples that he offers to prove that it might have are rather anodyne. The American scene on the frontispiece of the first version of *De Cive*, the most vivid and frightening of Hobbes's examples, was seen only by very few readers and was, in any event, an unlikely prospect for most of them. Even if life among the Indians were as uncertain and undesirable as Hobbes had claimed – a proposition already dubious, as we have seen – it was not sufficiently threatening to enough of his readers to bring about the sweeping transformation of political behavior that he sought. The second example was even worse, for by invoking the savage ancestors of the civilized nations of his day, Hobbes proved that the state of nature had existed at one point, but also inadvertently confirmed those who were inclined to dismiss its threat as irrelevant, since it had been left behind for good.[64]

With four versions of a comprehensive political theory released in a span of eleven years and a fifth seventeen years later, Hobbes is something of a rarity. This wealth of material presents many problems for interpreters, who must find a way to make sense of it. A wide array of interpretations has emerged around this issue, ranging from those who see the various political treatises as attempts to develop a consistent theme, to those who read them as works occasioned by different motives or events.[65] Some commentators

---

[63] See, for example, the preface to the translation of Thucydides (*EW*, VIII: vii, ix); *De Cive*, Pref., §§ 23–24.

[64] Lund claims that "Hobbes is well known for his attack on the epistemological status of normative conclusions drawn from historical facts" ("The Historical and 'Politicall' Origins of Civil Society," 231). Hobbes is quite clear, however, that where politics and history are concerned, the best that can be hoped for is prudence (see, for example, *EW*, VIII: vii; *The Elements of Law*, II.8.13).

[65] Among those who read Hobbes as largely consistent, see Nauta, "Hobbes the Pessimist?" and Hoekstra, "The *de facto* Turn in Hobbes's Political Philosophy."

have argued that the differences reflect Hobbes's intellectual interests and even his work habits.[66] Although there is widespread agreement that *Leviathan* represents the mature version of Hobbes's political theory, it has also been suggested that the work "reflects a remarkable change of mind on Hobbes's part about the proper relations between *ratio* and *oratio*."[67] This judgment is based mainly on the contrast between Hobbes's hostility to rhetoric during his scientific phase and his concession to it in *Leviathan*.[68]

As we have seen, however, Hobbes knew from the outset that perhaps the most important barrier to the transition from the state of liberty to the commonwealth is the surrender of one's right to judge for oneself. His artificially neat division of the world into domains of reason and the passions, and his insistence that his own method belongs in the former, conceal the ways in which he brings the reader to the point at which he is willing to grant Hobbes's assumptions and validate his propositions. As we have seen, the history of the publication of *The Elements of Law* sheds some light on this matter and confirms this conclusion, for the unauthorized gap introduced between I.13 and I.14 made it that much more difficult to see how Hobbes's theory of instigation and appeasing was in practice followed by his own attempt, through his notorious image of the state of nature, "historical or fabulous."

What changed between the earlier political treatises and *Leviathan* was not Hobbes's view of rhetoric and its place in the transmission of truth, but rather his rhetorical approach. The rhetorical strategy surrounding the vision of a civil philosophy modeled after geometry was premised on the hypothesis that individuals accustomed to thinking that their opinion matters are likelier to agree with a proposition if they are made to feel as though they have validated its demonstration. In light of the momentous shifts that were underway during the first half of the seventeenth century, we might describe the combination of these observations as Hobbes's science of rhetoric. In the *Elements*, Hobbes put that idea to use by constructing artificially neat worlds of reason and passion, and inviting his readers to choose the order of the former over the disorder of the latter. That first account, however, focused too closely on the appeal of order, and as such bore too close a resemblance to the pursuit of the *summum bonum*. Hobbes's successive changes reveal a gradual shift from the relatively benign opposition between the mathematicians and the dogmatists to the grimmer antithesis between the state of nature and civil society. By 1647, all the elements that would eventually go into the state of nature were in place, if scattered.

---

[66] Baumgold, for instance, has suggested that the development of Hobbes's political treatises is the result of his method of composition (see Baumgold, "The Difficulties of Hobbes Interpretation;" cf. Springborg, "The Paradoxical Hobbes"; Baumgold, "The UnParadoxical Hobbes").

[67] Skinner, *Reason and Rhetoric in the Philosophy of Hobbes*, 334.

[68] See, for example, *Leviathan*, Review and Conclusion: 389–90.

Hobbes completed his image in *Leviathan*, whose Chapter XIII contains virtually nothing new. The method he employed was the one that he had laid out in I.13 of the *Elements*, and the makings of the image he was after were all pieces of a puzzle that he assembled from the different corners of his earlier works. The pattern of these changes reveals not a new strategy, but the gradual realization that the images he had been using up to that point had failed to persuade his readers. Without neglecting the appeal of commodious living, the new approach would instead emphasize the prior need to avoid the *summum malum*. Hobbes's hypothesis was that by postponing the question of what one desires, he would displace the attendant conflict between different ends.[69] This hypothesis was in turn based on the observation that the best way to make the case for something, especially something taken for granted, is to invite contemplation of what its absence might look like. The resulting picture was of a condition of anarchy, in which the effective equality of the parties made for pervasive uncertainty.

The psychological mechanism that Hobbes employs to evoke such uncertainty in his reader is the one he announces in the *Elements*, when he assesses the individual's capacity to comprehend the world: a proper sense of those abilities, both mental and physical, ought to lead to modesty, and modesty, in the absence of reliable protection, should lead to diffidence.[70] In *Leviathan*, this observation would become the tenth law of nature.[71] Yet, it is clear that Hobbes needs equality not simply because it instills a sense of modesty and diffidence in the reader, but also because it buttresses his method. We have seen that in the midst of his notorious demonstration of mental equality, in *Leviathan* XIII, Hobbes notes that all men think themselves wiser than anyone else, certainly wise enough to pronounce on matters of right and wrong, or of government.[72] Building on this tendency, Hobbes seeks to recreate for his reader, in political terms, his own experience with Euclid by bringing the reader to the point of accepting his propositions no matter how improbable they might seem, all the while feeling as though he had done so on his own. His private appeal to the reader to reconsider *nosce teipsum* is the first step of that process, in which *captatio benevolentiæ* is the result of flattery: every single reader ought to be capable, through introspection and experience, to judge whether Hobbes's argument is correct. Who could resist such an invitation? As Hobbes notes in *Leviathan*, "there is not ordinarily a

---

[69] As Sorell puts it, "[t]he idea behind the appeal to premature, painful death is not exactly that people are more likely to agree in their aversions than in their appetites, but rather that war imperils the satisfaction of all desires and so threatens the possession of all goods" ("Hobbes's UnAristotelian Political Rhetoric," 106). The same logic lies behind Hobbes's invitation to Christians to scale back their beliefs to the *Unum Necessarium* (see, for example, *De Cive*, XVIII; *Leviathan*, XLIII: 324).

[70] *The Elements of Law*, I.5.14. Cf. *Leviathan*, XIII: 60–61.

[71] *Leviathan*, XV: 77.

[72] *Leviathan*, XIII: 61; cf. *The Elements of Law*, II.8.13.

greater signe of the equall distribution of any thing, than that every man is contented with his share."⁷³ To complain about this would be to admit that one is stupid, and this, Hobbes wagers, no one will do.

Equally importantly, in political terms the equivalent of this validation is authorization. The reader who accepted Hobbes's premises and assented to every step of his demonstration could blame no one but himself for the conclusions he would face in the end. As subject, the reader thus becomes the author of the system that emerges with his approval, and thereby gives Hobbes an additional reason to address his readers as though they had all actually participated in the contract that founded civil society. The image of the state of nature is indispensable in this process.⁷⁴ The reader who encounters it and contemplates what his life would be like amid such uncertainty and chooses the preferable inconveniences of civil society over it, has thereby become one of the founders of civil society in this hypothetical original contract. The expression of his will is both tacit and explicit. It occurs not simply through inaction and silence – by abstaining from rebellious behavior – but also through such actions as will prevent others from destroying the commonwealth.⁷⁵ Thus, each reader who has been persuaded affirms and preserves civil society.

To provide the means whereby every reader could be convinced that his unwarranted confidence in himself should turn into modesty, Hobbes brought together in *Leviathan* XIII a series of images that, in a sufficiently vague form, are compatible with one another and with his overall aim, and yet also different enough to speak to individuals of very different interests and backgrounds. All around him, "in theology, philosophy, political history, anthropology, and mythology there were fragments of a counter-cosmology that were sufficiently compatible with Hobbesian ideas to guarantee them a serious consideration," and Hobbes reached to several such sources to ensure it.⁷⁶ One could add not only numerous other specific examples to this list, but also several other areas of knowledge and systems of belief.

The trajectory of these images in the overall account of the state of nature tells its own story regarding Hobbes's strategy. The first thing to note is the substantial increase in examples that occurred between 1642 and 1647, which reached its peak in 1651, and culminated in 1668. Between the private circulation of *De Cive* and its publication, it became clear to Hobbes that his examples of the savages of times past and of those of his day would not suffice. The revised version of that work thus saw the addition of an

---

⁷³ *Leviathan*, XIII: 61; cf. *The Elements of Law*, I.5.11.
⁷⁴ Biletzki thus argues, "[t]he only way to explain the civil state is to address man's situation in the state of nature" (*Talking Wolves*, 90–91).
⁷⁵ *De Cive*, Pref., §§ 20–21; *Leviathan*, Introduction: 2.
⁷⁶ Ashcraft, "Hobbes's Natural Man," 1085. Cf. Goldsmith, "Hobbes: Ancient and Modern," 317, 334; Landucci, *I filosofi e i selvaggi*, 115–16, n. 55, 139; Hoekstra, *Thomas Hobbes and the Creation of Order*.

important set of examples taken from the everyday experiences of his readers. In the Preface that he added for publication, Hobbes invited the readers to consider the extent to which their own most mundane actions bespeak a sense of insecurity. Contemplating the significance of those actions and the frame of mind that justifies them is the first step on the road toward a full appreciation of the state of nature. Their addition shows that the natural condition of mankind is not simply some far-off land, an irrelevant exercise in antiquarianism, or a thought experiment, but a condition that one may encounter daily, in one form or another. Recall that walk across an ill-lit park at night, or that journey through the woods unaccompanied, and you will see that the chasm between reliable security and insecurity is not as wide as you might think.

Yet, the reader who compares *De Cive* with *Leviathan* realizes that Hobbes has not yet taken advantage of some very powerful arguments at his disposal. The growing influx of information from America rendered the example of the Indians increasingly problematic for, as commentators noted, there was some evidence to support Hobbes's description, but plenty of evidence to challenge it as well. This perhaps accounts for the shift in Hobbes's language from the earlier accounts to the later ones, which betrays a transition from certainty toward hesitation.[77] In the English *Leviathan*, wherein Hobbes finally gave voice to a complaint he must have heard countless times, namely that "there was never such a time, nor condition of warre as this," he answered by naming the beast that had been lurking in the background for so long, informing his efforts. Anyone who wanted to know what a condition of anarchy looks like would do well to consider those places that have made the fateful journey from civil society toward civil war. If, despite their allure, the Indians and Picts were largely irrelevant or harmless, the Thirty Years War and the English Civil War offered vivid reminders of the perils of anarchy to any doubters.[78] This example, reinforced by the iconic Biblical

---

[77] The English *Leviathan* includes "in many places of *America*," (XIII: 63), and the Latin the further qualification of paternal rule in those families (*OL*, III: 101).

[78] Wilson notes that 5 million people died between 1618 and 1648 in the Holy Roman Empire, which accounted for 20 percent of the prewar population, whereas the nearly 34 million deaths that occurred in Europe between 1939 and 1945 accounted for only 6 percent of the prewar population (*The Thirty Years War*, 787). In discussing the ways in which the earlier war was experienced, Wilson draws the very useful distinction between *Erlebnis* and *Erfahrung*, noting that while the former is fleeting and perhaps hard to capture, the latter "is the accumulative knowledge an individual acquires from his or her transient experience, involving a process of selection and reflection on life," and adding that the latter "can be studied, because such reflections have been committed to paper and preserved" (*ibid.*, 822). Wilson notes that fear during the War was "debilitating," transforming an already dangerous early modern world into an environment rife with uncertainty:

> Even in peacetime, most people carried a knife or club if they went out after dark or any distance from home. The war heightened these anxieties. People were afraid to travel, send messages or goods in case they were robbed. The increased uncertainty violated

fratricide in the Latin edition, offered the unmistakable lesson that the state of nature is never far off.

According to the false promise of the enlightened commonwealth, the application of a successful deterrent and the avoidance of anarchy mark the starting point for the transformation of the citizens that will in turn bring about a condition in which conflict has been transcended. Such, it seems, is the landscape depicted on the frontispiece of *Leviathan*, but Hobbes's final example of the state of nature in that work, the condition in which sovereigns assume the posture of gladiators for lack of a superior authority on earth, serves as reminder of the limits of that transformation. Since human life can never be without some inconvenience, the best that one can hope for is an association of sufficient magnitude as to be able to allow those who live under its protection to lift themselves out of misery, through their industry. Their labors will in turn strengthen the commonwealth, thereby making this highest manifestation of the state of nature radically different than all the others, by eliminating effective equality from the equation. The posture that makes this way of life possible, with sword at the ready, is essential to this outcome. Equally telling, however, is the absence of a specific threat from Hobbes's frontispiece, which allows the reader to fill in the blank as he sees fit.[79]

Hobbes continued to build on the artificially neat contrasts drawn in *The Elements of Law* throughout his successive treatises in order to awaken his readers to the consequences of misjudging the options that lay before them. The history of their development from the *Elements* onward shows that despite Hobbes's insistence on precise definitions and strict boundaries between concepts and domains, the poles of his respective contrasts are first and foremost signposts of approbation and disapprobation. Hobbes confirms that this is the case once more in the final part of his system, *De Homine*. Therein, shortly after he challenges the boundaries between poetry and philosophy in his answer to *Gondibert* and offers his views regarding the relationship between geometry and civil philosophy in *De Corpore*, Hobbes returns to the reality facing anyone who wishes to persuade broadly. In the Epistle addressed to the Earl of Devonshire, he notes that one part of his task is difficult because it "consists of demonstrations, the other of experience; one can be understood by few, the other

the familiar. Routine activities ... might become dangerous or even impossible (*ibid.*, 841; for a more general account of how the war was perceived by contemporaries, see *ibid.*, Chapter 23).

[79] On the psychological basis of *Leviathan*'s sovereign, see Tarlton, "The Creation and Maintenance of Government," esp. 325–27. On the difficulties facing any attempt at radical transformation, see Whelan, "Language and Its Abuses in Hobbes's Political Philosophy," 73–74.

by all."[80] He who wishes to persuade all must do so through language.[81] Whereas in Athens and Rome that language was used mainly by speakers in assemblies, and despite the fact that pulpits remained dangerous in Hobbes's day, the authors of written works had emerged as the new potential destroyers or saviors of civil society. This was the ground on which the battle to form opinions began, the arena in which Hobbes fought with beasts.[82]

In enumerating the advantages of language, Hobbes notes that in addition to teaching and warning others, commanding and understanding commands is "truly the greatest," adding, "[f]or without this there would be no society among men, no peace, and consequently no disciplines; but first savagery, then solitude, and for dwellings, caves."[83] The familiar topos of the advantages of civil society is the result of the fact that "man errs more widely and dangerously than can other animals" because he can perpetuate teachings that he knows to be untrue, "render the minds of men hostile to the conditions of society and peace," and become the mindless imitator of philosophers and schoolmen.[84] The important lesson, therefore, is the one that Aristotle draws in the *Rhetoric*, namely that language is but the medium, which can be enlisted in the service of good or evil. Notwithstanding his insistence on likening politics and ethics to geometry because both involve maker's knowledge, Hobbes notes the difference between *scientia* and *sapientia*, but adds that there is utility in wisdom because it provides some protection.[85] If it were possible, one would of course wish to have access to the certainty of *scientia* rather than the probability of *sapientia*, but in all sorts of science one has to make due with the latter. Thus,

Letters are also good, especially languages and histories; for they are pleasing. They are useful, too, especially histories; for these supply in abundance the evidence on which rests the science of causes; in truth, natural history for physics and also civil

[80] *De Homine*, Ep. Ded. Cf. *Examinatio & Emendatio Mathematicæ Hodiernæ qualis Explicatur in Libris Johannis Wallisii Geometriæ Professoris Saviliani in Academia Oxoniensi*, Dialogue I (*OL*, IV, esp. pp. 38–40).
[81] *De Homine*, X.3. Gert, et al., translate Hobbes's "oratione" as "language," which given the medium in question is the more appropriate term. It should be noted, however, that the marginal note summarizes the content of X.3 as "Sermonis commoda et incommoda" (*OL*, III: 90).
[82] In the Epistle Dedicatory to *De Homine*, Hobbes explains to his patron that the missing part of his system took as long as it did because he was engaged in a θηριομαχία with his own Demetriuses and Alexanders, and expressed confidence in his ability to strike flies with his pen as Domitian had done (cf. Suetonius, *Lives of the Caesars: Domitian*, 3). Cf. *A Briefe of the Art of Rhetorique*, III.11.
[83] *De Homine*, X.3.
[84] *De Homine*, X.3. Cf. *Leviathan*, A Review and Conclusion, 395.
[85] *De Homine*, X.4–5, XI.8. On Hobbes's application of this concept to civil philosophy, see Funkenstein, *Theology and the Scientific Imagination*, 327–38; Hanson, "The Meaning of 'Demonstration' in Hobbes's Science," esp. 619–26.

history for civil and moral science; and this is so *whether they be true or false, provided that they are not impossible.* For in the sciences causes are sought not only of those things that were, but also of those things that *can* be.[86]

The similarity of this mature formulation to the much earlier statement of method outlined in *Elements* I.13 is striking and reinforces the sense that Hobbes's attention to images as mnemonic devices was a central component of his political theory, whose development is captured by the evolution of his state of nature.

---

[86] *De Homine*, XI.10, emphasis added. Cf. *A Briefe of the Art of Rhetorique*, III.10.

Epilogue

Those who see a radical change in Hobbes's attitude toward rhetoric some-times point to *Leviathan*'s Review and Conclusion, wherein Hobbes declares that "Reason, and Eloquence, (though not perhaps in the Naturall Sciences, yet in the Morall) may stand very well together," because "wheresoever there is place for adorning and preferring of Errour, there is much more place for adorning and preferring of Truth, if they have it to adorn."[1] This statement is supposed to mark the culmination of a dramatic shift away from complete faith in the power of reason to convey truth and a complete repudiation of rhetoric as a tool of manipulation, purportedly the hallmarks of Hobbes's scientific phase. To constitute a radical break with the past, however, one would have to see the earlier Hobbes as clinging to the naive expectation that all readers can indeed bring the attention that the demonstration of the truth demands of them, so that no recourse to a shorter road would be necessary.[2] Yet Hobbes had already noted the difference between the natu-ral and moral sciences in the *Elements*, where, in discussing the connection between eloquence and wisdom, he observed that "not he that hath skill in geometry, or any other science speculative, but only he that understand-eth what conduceth to the good and government of the people, is called a wise man."[3]

Hobbes's choice of words in both passages betrays his indebtedness to Cicero's *De inventione*, a work occasioned by the question "whether men and communities have received more good or evil from oratory and a

---

[1] *Leviathan*, Review and Conclusion: 389–90. See, for example, Skinner, *Reason and Rhetoric in the Philosophy of Hobbes*, 5, but cf. Vickers, "'Tis the Goddesse of Rhetorick."

[2] *The Elements of Law*, I.1.3: "On the other side, if reasoning aright I win not consent (which may very easily happen) from them that being confident of their own knowledge weigh not what is said, the fault is not mine, but theirs. For as it is my part to show my reasons, so it is theirs to bring attention."

[3] *The Elements of Law*, II.8.13. Cf. *De Cive*, Pref., § 3; *Leviathan*, XXV: 135.

consuming devotion to eloquence."[4] Cicero's considered conclusion is that "wisdom without eloquence does too little for the good of states, but that eloquence without wisdom is generally highly disadvantageous and is never helpful."[5] Cicero's language and imagery are doubly important in the present context, for he traces the utility of eloquence back to the state of nature, to a time when men wandered the fields like animals, knowing no reason or religion, nor social duties or familial ties, but followed only passion and used only force.[6] It was then that a great and wise man realized the potential inherent in human beings, gathered them, and taught them everything useful. At first they resisted, because all this was too new, but his reason and eloquence taught them to listen, and "transformed them from wild savages into a kind and gentle folk."[7] Cicero considers it impossible that this transformation could have been accomplished by reason alone, without the aid of eloquence. The suspicion that it played a crucial part in the establishment of civil society is reinforced when one considers its equally important role in its preservation, for,

> how could it have been brought to pass that men should learn to keep faith and observe justice and become accustomed to obey others voluntarily and believe not only that they must work for the common good but even sacrifice life itself, unless men had been able by eloquence to persuade their fellows of the truth of what they had discovered by reason?[8]

Although in the *Elements* Hobbes focuses on the vicious consequences of eloquence coupled with a lack of wisdom, there is nothing in his account that precludes the constructive scenario envisioned by Cicero. Hobbes's attack in his first political treatise was not one on eloquence *simply*, but rather an attack on eloquence devoid of wisdom.[9] Hobbes notes that eloquence by itself is not sufficient; it is but one of the three characteristics of seditious men, alongside discontent and poor judgment.[10] On its own, eloquence is "nothing else but the power of winning belief of what we say; and to that end we must have aid from the passions of the hearer."[11]

Given his own aim, as stated in the Epistle Dedicatory of the *Elements of Law*, it is clear that Hobbes and indeed anyone else wishing to convince others of anything, including the truth, must do so with a certain amount of eloquence. Hobbes names one reason why this is the case, namely that

---

[4] Cicero, *De inventione*, I.i.i.
[5] Cicero, *De inventione*, I.i.1.
[6] Cicero, *De inventione*, I.ii.2.
[7] Cicero, *De inventione*, I.ii.2.
[8] Cicero, *De inventione*, I.ii.3.
[9] *The Elements of Law*, II.8.13. As Hobbes notes, his exemplar, Catiline, "author of the greatest sedition that ever was in Rome," was rendered seditious by the conjunction of these attributes.
[10] *The Elements of Law*, II.8.12.
[11] *The Elements of Law*, II.8.14. Cf. *A Briefe of the Art of Rhetorique*.

to demonstration and teaching of the truth, there are required long deductions, and great attention, which is unpleasant to the hearer; therefore they which seek not truth, but belief, must take another way, and not only derive what they would have to be believed, from somewhat believed already, but also by aggravations and extenuations make good and bad, right and wrong, appear great or less, according as it shall serve their turns.[12]

The distinction between truth and belief in this passage might give the false impression of a radical chasm between truth and falsehood. This, however, would be a serious misunderstanding, for it would be disregarding Hobbes's emphasis on utility. One can be aware of the truth, as well as of the need to persuade others of its essence, while also being aware of the fact that not everyone can come to accept it for the same reasons and in the same manner. To begin with, a diversity of interests means that not everyone will find a single argument appealing. Thus, distinguishing between a philosopher's practical goal and what that philosopher sees as the truth, Hoekstra has suggested that Hobbes engages in "eirenic deceit," and likens the presentation of different arguments to "a company that produces different products for different markets in order to boost overall sales."[13]

Equally importantly, however, readers bring widely divergent capacities to an argument. For instance, different circumstances will mean that some individuals will be better able to follow long and complicated demonstrations than others because they will have a greater store of experience to draw from or because they are less distracted.[14] If we were to agree, therefore, that Hobbes thought it true that peace is preferable to war, we would have to ask ourselves what it would take to get others to believe that truth.[15] It is clear that there are several possibilities. The best of these – a world in which a demonstration of the benefits of peace would suffice to convince everyone once and for all of its truth, so that not only would they refrain from violence, but would also know the real reasons why – seems beyond reach. If, rather, the goal were not an academic demonstration, but utility, as it is for Hobbes, then acceptance of peace over war would suffice, regardless of the means by which it had come about. For all sorts of reasons, several of which Hobbes enumerates, human beings come to accept useful

---

[12] *The Elements of Law*, II.8.14.

[13] Hoekstra, "The End of Philosophy," 41, 59.

[14] Thus, Weinberger argues that "Hobbes's intention was to persuade those who think as well as those who do not," adding that "[h]is persuasion reveals his distrust of most men who think as well as his distrust of those who do not" ("Hobbes's Doctrine of Method," 1353). Harwood argues that "Hobbes's general distrust of his audience's skill in reasoning helps explain ... his great fear of rhetoric in human society" (Introduction to *The Rhetorics of Thomas Hobbes and Bernard Lamy*, 15). Cf. Kahn, *Rhetoric, Prudence, and Skepticism in the Renaissance*, 180–81; Sorell, "Hobbes's UnAristotelian Political Rhetoric," 99–100; Struever, "Dilthey's Hobbes and Cicero's Rhetoric," 242.

[15] See, for example, *Leviathan*, XVIII: 91: "For Doctrine repugnant to Peace, can no more be True, than Peace and Concord can be against the Law of Nature."

doctrines by means far short of infallible demonstration. For instance, many people nowadays accept that microwaves exist and can describe one or two of their functions, even though they are incapable of demonstrating their existence to anyone without the assistance of a microwave oven.[16] Similarly, small children know that under certain circumstances, it is necessary to take medicine in order to feel better and they may be able to give a rudimentary explanation of why that is the case, but they cannot approximate the sophistication of a professor of medicine, let alone demonstrate the truth of their explanation. Thus, amending Hoekstra's example slightly, we could argue that Hobbes's commitment to peace would be consistent with a strategy that varies depending on the reader's capacity, just as an environmental group's campaign to explain the effects of global warming may include children's books and cartoons, pamphlets, videos, and fact-filled scientific studies, all aimed at getting the same essential message across. Hobbes knew well how unlikely it was that the same material and method would appeal equally to the scientifically minded few who read the *Elements* and first version of *De Cive*, the many more who read the second version of it, and the even greater number who read *Leviathan*.[17]

But the gulf separating Hobbes's method from Catiline's is, in fact, much narrower, for, as Hobbes notes in the *Elements*, appeasing and instigation are based on the same mechanism: an appeal to the audience's passions or opinions.[18] When, in the context of his attack on foolish eloquence, Hobbes is describing that effect, he might as well be describing the effect he intended to achieve through the state of nature. The power of eloquence, he argues, is such that it can sometimes cause one to believe that he is experiencing pain and suffering when he is not. In this manner, the instigator would produce the discontent necessary to incite rebellion. In *De Cive*, Hobbes adds that they do this by making a good condition seem bad and a bad condition seem worse by diminishing danger and increasing hope. Recall, however, that Hobbes's own goal was to put the reader in mind of the uncertainty and misery of a condition that would render his own acceptable by comparison. These, it seems, are two sides of the same coin.

Hobbes sought to persuade as many people as possible that no matter how attractive the false promise of greater liberty might appear, it always entailed violent disorder.[19] His earlier attempts contain numerous signs of hostility to rhetoric and appreciation for science, but Hobbes's own diagnosis of the

---

[16] A demonstration that, of course, would still not prove what in particular caused the outcome in question, and how.

[17] See, for instance, the Epistle Dedicatory to Hobbes's translation of Thucydides; *A Briefe of the Art of Rhetorique*, I.1; *The Elements of Law*, II.8.14; *De Cive*, XIII.9; *The Questions concerning Liberty, Necessity, and Chance*, EW, V: 267; *Behemoth*, 322.

[18] *The Elements of Law*, I.13.7; cf. II.8.14.

[19] See the prefatory remarks to his edition of Thucydides and to his political treatises, as well as his autobiographical works.

causes of conflict give ample reasons to challenge the status of those claims. The apparently fundamental divide that he establishes, from the *Elements* onward, between reason and the passions is one that he does not accept in practice. Regardless of its philosophical value, however, that divide has considerable rhetorical value, for it takes advantage of a set of terms which, in addition to their proper designations, also operate as terms of approbation and disapprobation. This is especially true of Hobbes's principal terms. Faced with the choice between autonomy and authority, what reader would not rather be on the side of autonomy? Similarly, speakers and audiences alike know that even though it also refers to a subject of the humanist curriculum, the term "rhetoric" is never attached to someone's utterances as a compliment.[20] Despite Hobbes's overly rigid and neat dichotomies, knowledge of the ways in which the human mind forms conceptions of the world and is affected by words can lay as much of a claim to the status of science as civil philosophy, with all its uncertainties.[21] One might suggest, therefore, that Hobbes puts his rhetoric of science in the service of his science of rhetoric.[22]

Hobbes's first contrast – between reason and the passions, which went on to become the basis of the opposition between the mathematicians and the dogmatists – shows that this science of rhetoric was at work from the start. Through it, Hobbes sought to apply the fundamental principle of philosophy, which must begin with an exercise in privation. In combining thus the power of eloquence with the potential to reason, Hobbes himself became one of those great men who, according to Cicero, sought to transform those around him "from wild savages into a kind and gentle folk."[23] Hobbes knew

---

[20] In the course of an examination of the territorial dispute between philosophy and rhetoric, Vickers notes the degree to which "'rhetoric' or 'rhetorical' persist as pejorative terms" ("Territorial Disputes," 247). Several commentators have identified this strategy in *Leviathan*. Thus, for example, Stillman notes Hobbes's "anti-rhetorical rhetoric" ("Hobbes's *Leviathan*," 801), Harwood writes of Hobbes's "famous anti-rhetoric rhetoric," (introduction to *The Rhetorics of Thomas Hobbes and Bernard Lamy*, 31), Springborg of the "rhetor who deplores all rhetoricians," ("Hobbes's Biblical Beasts," 368), and Garsten of Hobbes's "rhetoric against rhetoric" (*Saving Persuasion*, 25); cf. Kahn, *Rhetoric, Prudence, and Skepticism in the Renaissance*, 157–58. As we have seen, however, there is evidence of this strategy all along. With regard to the *Elements*, for example, Martinich notes that "it does not follow that if an author professes to eschew rhetoric, he does eschew it," and adds, "denying that someone will do something as a preface to doing it is one of the grandest rhetorical devices: pretermission" (*Hobbes: A Biography*, 125–26). On the other side of the divide, Hobbes's use of science, see Keller, "In the Service of 'Truth' and 'Victory,'" 147.
[21] *Pace* Johnston, *The Rhetoric of Leviathan*, 61–62. See, *The Elements of Law*, II.8.13; *Leviathan*, V: 22; *Behemoth*, 318; cf. Jesseph, "*Scientia* in Hobbes."
[22] According to Weinberger, "just as the doctrine of method requires the use of philosophic rhetoric in the presentation of a necessary political science, so too the doctrine of method itself must be veiled by a subtle rhetoric" ("Hobbes's Doctrine of Method," 1353).
[23] *De inventione*, I.ii.2; cf. Seneca, Epistle XC. Cf. Nederman, "Nature, Sin and the Origins of Society"; Nederman, "The Union of Wisdom and Eloquence before the Renaissance"; Kahn,

well, however, that important though that first transformation might be, to have a lasting effect it would have to be renewed constantly. In scientific terms, one could describe this as a periodic exercise in privation that would remind each human being what the alternative looks like, so as to instill a proper sense of perspective. In political terms, this exercise is in accordance with Aristotle's cautionary remark to those interested in preserving the constitution – to not simply keep dangers far, but to occasionally let them get close so as to keep citizens vigilant – or with Machiavelli's suggestion that to preserve the state, one should periodically refound it.[24] Hobbes's implementation of this advice through the state of nature constitutes an important innovation because it allows him to recreate the frame of mind that characterizes the founding, without risking the state itself.[25] By inviting the reader to suppose away all the trappings of commodious living, Hobbes provides the framework for an exercise in privation.[26] By grounding the state of nature in a multitude of possible, probable, and memorable examples, he makes it clear that that exercise is no mere philosophical dispute, but a matter of commodious life or death.

To the reader who wondered whether the state of nature had ever existed, Hobbes responded that there was never a universal war of all against all, but that such a condition had existed and continued to exist. To prove that this was the case, he offered a series of suggestive examples of conditions in which life was uncertain and precarious. Brief and elusive, some of these examples were also prima facie problematic and open to obvious challenges. As we have seen, however, even the least questionable among them was open to interpretation, and there were many readers who were willing to accept Hobbes's contention that they constituted accurate descriptions of a condition very much like his state of nature. This multitude of images and languages of anarchy points to a further important feature of Hobbes's method. It is often thought that the state of nature represents nothing other than the counterpart to civil society. This view, which owes much to Hobbes's exaggerated antitheses, obscures the fact that the contrast between the two conditions can manifest itself at any point along the continuum between complete chaos and absolute order. As the example of Adam's disobedience makes clear, there is no domain so well ordered that it is entirely immune to disorder. This should come as no surprise, given that the author of this system believes that the human condition consists of a series of compromises.

Rhetoric, Prudence, and Skepticism in the Renaissance, 177; Struever, "Dilthey's Hobbes and Cicero's Rhetoric," 240; Syros, "Founders and Kings Versus Orators."

[24] On the Aristotelian element in Hobbes's project, see Evrigenis, *Fear of Enemies and Collective Action*; Hoekstra, "Hobbes on the Natural Condition of Mankind." On Aristotelian and Machiavellian elements, see Evrigenis, "Hobbes's Clockwork."

[25] Machiavelli warns of this risk in the *Discourses on Livy* (III.i § 6).

[26] Not the radical privation of *De Corpore* often invoked by commentators, but rather one rooted in uncertainty. See, for example, Biletzki, "Thomas Hobbes," 65–66.

It also explains why Hobbes's notorious description of life in the state of nature as "solitary, poore, nasty, brutish, and short," is less a literal description of the state of nature and more a key to the frame of mind that any condition of uncertainty entails.

The force of these examples is evident in the reception of the state of nature. From the publication of *Leviathan* onward, Hobbes's concept of the natural condition of mankind became an inescapable point of reference for pamphleteers and philosophers. As the octogenarian Hobbes was turning his attention to Homer, Bishop Parker attacked the state of nature as a "lamentable Foundation," yet he noted that "as odd as it is," Hobbes's concept "is become the Standard of our Modern Politicks; by which men that pretend to understand the real Laws of Wisdom and Subtility must square their Actions, and therefore is swallowed down, with as much greediness as an Article of Faith by the Wild and Giddy People of the Age."[27] If anything, Parker's assessment underestimated the force of Hobbes's state of nature, which quickly became all things to all people and has appeared in contexts as dissimilar as seventeenth-century sermons and twenty-first-century textbooks of international relations.[28]

The diversity of the settings in which the state of nature played an important role during this period is but one sign of the considerable success of Hobbes's method. A clearer sign, perhaps, is the fact that it became the focus not simply of those who agreed with Hobbes, but also of those who disagreed with him. Thinkers whose accounts of man's natural sociability diverged from Hobbes's nevertheless used the state of nature as a necessary starting point, taking exception not to the proposition that it existed, but to Hobbes's description of it. For Hobbes, the absence of a common power made the state of nature a condition of anarchy and equality; that is, one of uncertainty sufficient to cause any sensible individual to wish to abandon it at more or less any cost. Writing under different circumstances and with different motives, some of Hobbes's emulators and critics found certain costs too high. By rearranging the characteristics of Hobbes's state of nature and placing emphasis on one or another, they reached conclusions that seem unexpected given their Hobbist origins.[29]

---

[27] [Parker], *A Discourse of Ecclesiastical Politie*, 116, 118.

[28] See, for example, Allestree, *A Sermon Preached before the King at White Hall on Sunday Nov. 17, 1667*, 7; Nye, *Understanding International Conflicts*, 3.

[29] For instance, Hobbes's attention to the need to accommodate a diverse audience helps explain his insistence on grounding the social contract in universal individual agency. This objective and method help account for the fact that interpretations of Hobbes range from a majority that has seen his thought as authoritarian to a recent few who see him as something of a democrat (for example, Tuck, "Hobbes and Democracy" and Martel, *Subverting the Leviathan*, but cf. Hoekstra, "A Lion in the House") and even as a theorist of resistance (for example, Sreedhar, *Hobbes on Resistance*).

For those who focus on anarchy as its principal characteristic, the state of nature is the condition in which sovereigns assume the posture of gladiators. Here, one encounters such thinkers as Pufendorf, Vattel, Kant, and Hegel, treating sovereignty, war, and international law. In this domain, it is not just Hobbes's conception and imagery, but also his vocabulary that remains alive and well.[30] Those, on the other hand, whose interest lies primarily in rights and obligation, tend to focus on equality. The dominance of Locke, Rousseau, and Kant in this area and the transformation of the vocabulary of rights and institutions perhaps give the impression that Hobbes's influence has been limited to the social contract tradition – yet it is here that the state of nature has had its biggest impact. Long after critics such as Hume and Mill had contested the notion that individuals were bound by a social contract, thinkers from Montesquieu to Rawls – concerned with fixing the boundaries of individual rights, demarcating the proper sphere for state intervention, and determining the marks of sovereignty – continued to utilize the state of nature as their point of reference.[31]

Hobbes's strategy of oppositions is largely responsible for the fact that the state of nature tends to be contrasted to life under government. Its manifestations, therefore, are as many as the visions of government that animate those contrasts. Throughout his successive political treatises, Hobbes improved its versatility by offering a multitude of examples, allusions, and cues as to the status of the state of nature, so as to conjure the image that would permit him to persuade individuals who might otherwise disagree widely, that obedience to a single authority was the only way to end conflict. When he surveyed the attempts of previous writers on politics, Hobbes saw a series of failures stemming from the fact that each one put forth his own views and tried to back them up with the "opinions of Philosophers," which made for a perpetual war of the pens.[32] Hobbes realized that the only way to move forward from this impasse was to treat individual opinions with the same respect that their holders accorded them.[33] Rather than enlisting the authority of Aristotle or Cicero, he would persuade his reader that he could judge the merits of his argument for himself. Hobbes suggested that this invitation removed his effort from the realm of dogma and made it civil philosophy. In his multifaceted portrayal of disorder, each reader would find reasons for agreeing that something called the state of nature exists and

---

[30] For an overview, see Williams, "The Hobbesian Theory of International Relations." Cf. Evrigenis, *Fear of Enemies and Collective Action*; Moloney, "Hobbes, Savagery, and International Anarchy."

[31] The most obvious examples of this tendency are Rawls's description of the original position as an initial situation in which individuals are stripped of advantages and disadvantages caused by "natural fortune or social circumstances" (*A Theory of Justice*, § 4, p. 18) and Nozick's response in Part I of *Anarchy, State, and Utopia*.

[32] *De Cive*, Ep. Ded., § 6.

[33] *Leviathan*, XIII: 92.

needs to be avoided. So appealing was the method by which the reader was brought to this agreement that it rendered believable the outlandish notion that civil society was based on a contract. Yet, by authorizing Hobbes's account, individual readers stamped his founding myth with their approval and made it seem less implausible, showing that behind Hobbes's rhetoric of science lay something of a science of rhetoric.[34]

[34] *A Briefe of the Art of Rhetorique*, III.9.

List of Manuscripts

Devonshire Mss., Chatsworth HS/A/2A [The Elements of Law, Natural and Politic]
Devonshire Mss., Chatsworth HS/A/2B The Elementes of Law, Naturall, and Politique
Devonshire Mss., Chatsworth HS/A/2C [The Elements of Law, Natural and Politic]
Devonshire Mss., Chatsworth HS/D/1 [Cavendish notebook]
Devonshire Mss., Chatsworth HS/E/1A Old Catalogue [Hardwick Library Catalogue in Hobbes's Hand]
London Mss., British Library Add. 4294 [Leibniz to Hobbes, Mainz, 13/23 July 1670]
London Mss., British Library Egerton 1910 Thomas Hobbes, *Leviathan*
London Mss., British Library Egerton 2005 The Elements of Law, Natural and Politic
London Mss., British Library Harl. 1325 The Elements of Law, Natural and Politic
London Mss., British Library Harl. 4235 The Elements of Law, Natural and Politic
London Mss., British Library Harl. 4236 The Elements of Law, Natural and Politic
London Mss., British Library Harl. 6858 [Humane Nature, Chapters 1–13 only]

Bibliography

Ahrensdorf, Peter J. "The Fear of Death and the Longing for Immortality: Hobbes and Thucydides on Human Nature and the Problem of Anarchy." *American Political Science Review* 94, no. 3 (2000): 579–93.

Ainsworth, Henry. *Annotations vpon the Five Bookes of Moses; the Booke of the Psalmes, and the Song of Songs, or, Canticles.* London: John Bellamie, 1627.

Allestree, Richard. *A Sermon Preached before the King at White Hall on Sunday Nov. 17, 1667.* London: n.p., 1667.

Almond, Philip C. *Adam and Eve in Seventeenth-Century Thought.* Cambridge: Cambridge University Press, 1999.

Andrewes, Lancelot. Ἀποσπασμάτια *Sacra: Or a Collection of Posthumous and Orphan Lectures: Delivered at St. Pauls and St. Giles his Church, etc.* London: R. Hodgkinsonne, 1657.

Lancelot Andrewes: Selected Sermons and Lectures. Edited by Peter E. McCullough. Oxford: Oxford University Press, 2005.

A Paterne of Catechisticall Doctrine, etc. London: William Garrett, 1630.

XCVI. Sermons by the Right Honorable and Reverend Father in God, Lancelot Andrevves, etc. London: George Miller for Richard Badger, 1629.

Anghiera, Pietro Martire d'. *The Decades of the Newe Worlde or West India, etc.* Translated by Richard Eden. London: William Powell, 1555.

Apollodorus. *Library.* Edited by James George Frazer. 2 volumes. Cambridge, MA: Harvard University Press, 1921.

Aquinas, Saint Thomas. *On Kingship, to the King of Cyprus.* Translated by Gerald B. Phelan. Revised with introduction and notes by I. Th. Eschmann, O. P. Toronto: Pontifical Institute of Mediaeval Studies, 2000.

Sententia libri politicorum, tabula libri ethicorum. Volume XLVIII of *Opera Omnia.* Edited by the Leonine Commission. Rome: Santa Sabina, 1971.

Aratus. *Phaenomena.* In *Callimachus, Lycophron, Aratus,* edited by G. R. Mair, 183–299. Cambridge, MA: Harvard University Press, 1960.

Arber, Edward, ed. *A Transcript of the Registers of the Company of Stationers of London, 1554–1640 A.D.* 5 volumes. London: privately printed, 1875–1894.

Aristotle. Ἀριστοτέλους τέχνης ῥητορικῆς βιβλία τρία. *Aristotelis de Rhetorica Seu Arte Dicendi Libri Tres, Græcolat., etc.* Edited and translated by Theodore Goulston. London: Edward Griffin, 1619.
"*Art*" *of Rhetoric.* Translated by John Henry Freese. Cambridge, MA: Harvard University Press, [1926] 2000.
Ethica Nicomachea. Edited by I. Bywater. Oxford: The Clarendon Press, 1991.
Historia animalium. Translated by A. L. Peck. 3 volumes. Cambridge, MA: Harvard University Press, 1965.
Metaphysics. Translated by Hippocrates G. Apostle. Grinnell, IA: The Peripatetic Press, 1979.
Physics. Translated by Hippocrates G. Apostle. Grinnell, IA: The Peripatetic Press, 1980.
Politica. Edited by W. D. Ross. Oxford: The Clarendon Press, 1957.
Prior Analytics. Edited by A. J. Jenkinson. In *The Complete Works of Aristotle,* 2 volumes, edited by Jonathan Barnes. Princeton, NJ: Princeton University Press, 1984.
Rhetoric. Translated by W. Rhys Roberts. In *The Complete Works of Aristotle,* 2 volumes, edited by Jonathan Barnes. Princeton, NJ: Princeton University Press, 1984.
Topics. Translated by W. A. Pickard. In *The Complete Works of Aristotle,* 2 volumes, edited by Jonathan Barnes. Princeton, NJ: Princeton University Press, 1984.
Armitage, David. "The New World and British Political Thought: From Richard Hakluyt to William Robertson." In *America in European Consciousness, 1493–1750,* edited by Karen Ordahl Kupperman, 52–75. Chapel Hill: The University of North Carolina Press for the Institute of Early American History and Culture, 1995.
Asconius Pedianus, Quintus. Commentary on Cicero's *Pro T. Annio Milone oratio.* In *Cicero XIV.* Edited by N. H. Watts, 124–36. Cambridge, MA: Harvard University Press, 1931.
Ashcraft, Richard. "Hobbes's Natural Man: A Study in Ideology Formation." *The Journal of Politics* 33, no. 4 (1971): 1076–1117.
"*Leviathan* Triumphant: Thomas Hobbes and the Politics of Wild Men." In *The Wild Man within: An Image in Western Thought from the Renaissance to Romanticism,* edited by Edward Dudley and Maximillian E. Novak, 141–81. Pittsburgh: University of Pittsburgh Press, 1972.
"Political Theory and Political Action: A Reconsideration of Hobbes's State of Nature." *Hobbes Studies* 1 (1988): 63–88.
Aubrey, John. '*Brief Lives,*' *Chiefly of Contemporaries, Set Down by John Aubrey, between the Years 1669 & 1696.* Edited by Andrew Clark. 2 volumes. Oxford: The Clarendon Press, 1898.
Augustine of Hippo, Saint. *Concerning the City of God against the Pagans.* Translated by Henry Bettenson. London: Penguin, 2003.
The Literal Meaning of Genesis. Translated by John Hammond Taylor, S.J. 2 volumes. New York: Newman Press, 1982.
Babington, Gervase. *Certaine Plaine, Briefe, and Comfortable Notes upon Euerie Chapter of Genesis, etc.* London: Thomas Charde, 1592.
Bacon, Francis. *The Elements of the Common Lawes of England, Branched into a Double Tract, etc.* London: I. More, 1630.

The Works of Francis Bacon, edited by J. Spedding, R. L. Ellis, and D. D. Heath. 14 volumes. Cambridge: Cambridge University Press, 2011.

Badian, Ernst. "Annius Milo, Titus." In *The Oxford Classical Dictionary*, edited by Simon Hornblower and Antony Spawforth, 99–100. Third edition. Oxford: Oxford University Press, 1996.

Baldry, H. C. "Hesiod's Five Ages." *Journal of the History of Ideas* 17, no. 4 (1956): 553–54.

"Who Invented the Golden Age?" *The Classical Quarterly* NS 2, no. 1/2 (1952): 83–92.

Barbour, Reid. *English Epicures and Stoics: Ancient Legacies in Early Stuart Culture.* Amherst: The University of Massachusetts Press, 1998.

Baumgold, Deborah. "The Difficulties of Hobbes Interpretation." *Political Theory* 36, no. 6 (2008): 827–55.

"UnParadoxical Hobbes: In Reply to Springborg." *Political Theory* 37, no. 5 (2009): 689–93.

Bede. *On Genesis.* Translated by Calvin B. Kendall. Liverpool: Liverpool University Press, 2008.

Beer, E.S. de, ed. *The Correspondence of John Locke.* 8 volumes. Oxford: The Clarendon Press, 1976–89.

Bentley, Richard. *The Folly and Unreasonableness of Atheism Demonstrated, etc.* 4th edition. London: J. H. for H. Mortlock, 1669.

Bignone, Ettore. *Studi sul pensiero antico.* Rome: "L'Erma" di Bretschneider, 1965.

Biletzki, Anat. *Talking Wolves: Thomas Hobbes on the Language of Politics and the Politics of Language.* Dordrecht: Kluwer Academic Publishers, 1997.

"Thomas Hobbes: Telling the Story of the Science of Politics." *Philosophy & Rhetoric* 33, no. 1 (2000): 59–73.

Black, Anthony. *Political Thought in Europe, 1250–1450.* Cambridge: Cambridge University Press, 1992.

Blickman, Daniel R. "Lucretius, Epicurus, and Prehistory." *Harvard Studies in Classical Philology* 92 (1989): 157–91.

Blum, Paul Richard. *Studies on Early Modern Aristotelianism.* Leiden: Brill, 2012.

Bobbio, Norberto. *Thomas Hobbes and the Natural Law Tradition.* Translated by Daniella Gobetti. Chicago: The University of Chicago Press, 1993.

Bodin, Jean. *Colloquium of the Seven about Secrets of the Sublime.* Translated by Marion Leathers Daniels Kuntz. Princeton, NJ: Princeton University Press, 1975.

De la Demonomanie des Sorciers. Paris: Jacques du Puys, 1581.

De Republica Libri Sex. Paris: Jacques du Puys, 1586.

De Republica Libri Sex. Frankfurt: N. Hoffmann for P. Fischer, 1609.

Les six livres de la republique. Paris: Jacques du Puys, 1583.

Method for the Easy Comprehension of History. Translated by Beatrice Reynolds. New York: Columbia University Press, 1945.

On the Demon-Mania of Witches. Translated by Randy A. Scott. Toronto: Centre for Reformation and Renaissance Studies, 2001.

The Six Bookes of a Commonweale. Translated by Richard Knolles. London: G. Bishop, 1606.

The Six Bookes of a Commonweale. Translated by Richard Knolles. Edited by Kenneth Douglas McRae. Cambridge, MA: Harvard University Press, 1962.

Bonoeil, John. *His Maiesties Graciovs Letter to the Earle of Sovth-Hampton, etc.* London: Felix Kyngston, 1622.

Botero, Giovanni. *Relations of the Most Famous Kingdomes and Common-wealths thorowout the World Discoursing of their Situations, Religions, Languages, Manners, Customes, Strengths, Greatnesse, and Policies.* Translated by Robert Johnson. London: John Haviland for John Partridge, 1630.

Bramhall, John. *Castigations of Mr. Hobbes, etc.* London: J. Crook, 1657.

The Works of the Most Reverend Father in God, John Bramhall D. D., etc. Dublin: His Majestie's Printing House, 1676.

Brandt, Frithiof. *Thomas Hobbes' Mechanical Conception of Nature.* Copenhagen: Levin & Munsgaard, 1928.

Bredekamp, Horst. *Thomas Hobbes Der Leviathan: Das Urbild des modernen Staates und seine Gegenbilder, 1651–2001.* Third, corrected edition. Berlin: Akademie Verlag, 2006.

"Thomas Hobbes's Visual Strategies." In *The Cambridge Companion to Hobbes's Leviathan*, edited by Patricia Springborg, 29–60. Cambridge: Cambridge University Press, 2007.

Brett, Annabel. *Liberty, Right and Nature: Individual Rights in Later Scholastic Thought.* Cambridge: Cambridge University Press, 1997.

Brown, Clifford W., Jr. "Thucydides, Hobbes, and the Derivation of Anarchy." *History of Political Thought* 8, no. 1 (Spring 1987): 33–62.

Brown, Keith. "The Artist of the *Leviathan* Title-Page." *The British Library Journal* 4 (1978): 24–36.

Burckhardt, Jacob. *The Civilization of the Renaissance in Italy.* Translated by S. G. C. Middlemore. 2 volumes. New York: Harper Torchbooks, 1958.

Burke, Peter. "America and the Rewriting of World History." In *America in European Consciousness, 1493–1750*, edited by Karen Ordahl Kupperman, 33–51. Chapel Hill: The University of North Carolina Press for the Institute of Early American History and Culture, 1995.

"The Spread of Italian Humanism." In *The Impact of Humanism on Western Europe*, edited by Anthony Goodman and Angus MacKay, 1–22. London: Longman, 1990.

Calvin, Jean. *A Commentarie of John Caluine, upon the First Booke of Moses Called Genesis.* Translated by Thomas Tymme. London: John Harison and George Bishop, 1578.

Campanella, Tommaso. *La città del sole: dialogo poetico.* Translated by Daniel J. Donno. Berkeley: The University of California Press, 1981.

Campbell, Gordon. *Lucretius on Creation and Evolution: A Commentary on De Rerum Natura, Book V, Lines 772–1104.* Oxford: Oxford University Press, 2003.

Canning, Joseph. *A History of Medieval Political Thought, 300–1450.* London: Routledge, 1996.

Cary, M. and H. H. Scullard. *A History of Rome down to the Reign of Constantine.* Third edition. Basingstoke: Macmillan, 1979.

Chalk, Alfred F. "Natural Law and the Rise of Economic Individualism in England." *Journal of Political Economy* 59, no. 4 (1951): 332–47.

Charron, Pierre. *Of Wisdome Three Bookes Written in French by Peter Charrō Doctr of Lawe in Paris.* Translated by Samson Lennard. London: Edward Blount and William Aspley, [1608].

Cicero, Marcus Tullius. *De finibus.* Edited by H. Rackham. Cambridge, MA: Harvard University Press, 1914.
  De inventione. In *Cicero II.* Edited by H. M. Hubbell. Cambridge, MA: Harvard University Press, 2000.
  De officiis. In *Cicero XXI.* Edited by Walter Miller. Cambridge, MA: Harvard University Press, 1913.
  Pro T. Annio Milone oratio. In *Cicero XIV.* Edited by N. H. Watts. Cambridge, MA: Harvard University Press, 1931.
Clarendon, Edward Hyde, Earl of. *A Brief View and Survey of the Dangerous and Pernicious Errors to Church and State in Mr. Hobbes's Book, Entitled Leviathan.* Oxford: n.p., 1676.
  The Miscellaneous Works of the Right Honourable Edward, Earl of Clarendon, etc. Second edition. London: Printed for Samuel Patterson, 1751.
Clark, W. Malcolm. "A Legal Background to the Yahwist's Use of 'Good and Evil' in Genesis 2–3." *Journal of Biblical Literature* 88, no. 3 (September 1969): 266–78.
Clüver, Philipp. *Germaniæ Antiquæ Libri Tres.* Leiden: Ludwig Elsevier, 1616.
  Sicilia Antiqva; Cum Minoribus Insulis Ei Adjacentibus. Item Sardinia et Corsica, etc. Leiden: Elsevier, 1619.
Cogan, Marc. *The Human Thing: The Speeches and Principles of Thucydides' History.* Chicago: The University of Chicago Press, 1981.
Cohen, Ted. "Metaphor and the Cultivation of Intimacy." *Critical Inquiry* 5, no. 1, Special Issue on Metaphor (Autumn 1978): 3–12.
Coke, Roger. *A Survey of the Politicks of Mr. Thomas White, Thomas Hobbes, and Hugo Grotius, etc.* London: G. Bedell and T. Collins, 1662.
Coke, Sir Edward. *The Selected Writings and Speeches of Sir Edward Coke.* Edited by Steve Sheppard. 3 volumes. Indianapolis, IN: Liberty Fund, 2003.
Cole, Thomas. *Democritus and the Sources of Greek Anthropology.* n.p.: Western Reserve University Press for the American Philological Association, 1967.
Coles, Elisha. *An English Dictionary, etc.* London: Printed for Peter Parker, 1677.
Collins, Jeffrey R. *The Allegiance of Thomas Hobbes.* Oxford: Oxford University Press, 2005.
Commager, H. S., Jr. "Lucretius' Interpretation of the Plague." *Harvard Studies in Classical Philology* 62 (1957): 105–18.
Condren, Conal. *Thomas Hobbes.* New York: Twayne Publishers, 2000.
Connor, W. Robert. *Thucydides.* Princeton, NJ: Princeton University Press, 1984.
Cook, Paul D. *Hobbes and Christianity: Reassessing the Bible in Leviathan.* Lanham, MD: Rowman and Littlefield, 1996.
Corbett, Margery & R. W. Lightbown. *The Comely Frontispiece: The Emblematic Title-page in England 1550–1660.* London: Routledge and Kegan Paul, 1979.
Cowley, Abraham. *The True Effigies of the Monster of Malmesbury: or, Thomas Hobbes in His Proper Colours.* London: n.p., 1680.
Cro, Stelio. *The Noble Savage: Allegory of Freedom.* Waterloo, ON: Wilfrid Laurier University Press, 1990.
Cromartie, Alan. "*The Elements* and Hobbesian Moral Thinking." *History of Political Thought* 32, no. 1 (Spring 2011): 21–47.
Cudworth, Ralph. *The True Intellectual System of the Universe: The First Part; wherein, All the Reason and Philosophy of Atheism is Confuted; and Its Impossibility Demonstrated.* London: Richard Royston, 1678.

Cumberland, Richard. *A Treatise of the Laws of Nature*. Translated by John Maxwell. Edited by Jon Parkin. Indianapolis, IN: Liberty Fund, 2005.

Curley, Edwin. "The Covenant with God in Hobbes's *Leviathan*." In *Leviathan after 350 Years*, edited by Tom Sorell and Luc Foisneau, 199–216. Oxford: The Clarendon Press, 2004.

Dante. *Monarchy*. Edited by Prue Shaw. Cambridge: Cambridge University Press, 2005.

Davenant, Sir William. *The Preface to Gondibert, an Heroick Poem, etc.* Paris: Matthieu Guillemot, 1650.

Davidson, R. *The Cambridge Bible Commentary: Genesis 1–11*. Cambridge: Cambridge University Press, 1973.

Davies, J. K. "Cultural, Social and Economic Features of the Hellenistic World." In *The Cambridge Ancient History*. Volume VII, part I, *The Hellenistic World*, edited by F. W. Walbank et al., 257–320. Second edition. Cambridge: Cambridge University Press, 1984.

Davies, Sir John. *The Original, Nature, and Immortality of the Soul. A Poem. With an Introduction concerning Human Knowledge*. London: W. Rogers, 1697.

Demosthenes. Περὶ τῆς Παραπρεσβείας. In *Demosthenes II*, edited by C. A. Vince and J. H. Vince. Cambridge, MA: Harvard University Press, 1926.

Descartes, René. *Meditations, Objections, and Replies*. Edited by R. Ariew and D. Cress. Indianapolis, IN: Hackett Publishing Company, 2006.

Dienstag, Joshua Foa. "Man of Peace: Hobbes between Politics and Science." *Political Theory* 37, no. 5 (2009): 694–705.

Diodorus Siculus. *Library of History*, Books I–XV.19. 6 volumes. Edited by C. H. Oldfather. Cambridge, MA: Harvard University Press, 1933–54.

Diogenes Laertius. *Lives of the Eminent Philosophers*. 2 volumes. Edited by R. D. Hicks. Cambridge, MA: Harvard University Press, 2000.

Dodd, Mary C. "The Rhetorics in Molesworth's Edition of Hobbes." *Modern Philology* 50, no. 1 (August 1952): 36–42.

Dowdall, H. C. "The Word 'State.'" *Law Quarterly Review* 39 (1923): 98–125.

Doyle, Phyllis. "The Contemporary Background of Hobbes' 'State of Nature.'" *Economica* 21 (1927): 336–55.

Duncan, Joseph E. "Paradise as the Whole Earth." *Journal of the History of Ideas* 30, no. 2 (April 1969): 171–86.

Dunn, Richard S. "Seventeenth-Century English Historians of America." In *Seventeenth-Century America: Essays in Colonial History*, edited by James Morton Smith, 195–225. Chapel Hill: The University of North Carolina Press, 1959.

Dzelzainis, Martin. "Edward Hyde and Thomas Hobbes's *Elements of Law, Natural and Politic*." *The Historical Journal* 32, no. 2 (1989): 303–17.

[Eachard, John]. *Mr. Hobbs's State of Nature Considered, In a Dialogue between Philautus and Timothy, etc.* London: E. T. and R. H. for Nath. Brooke, 1672.

Edmunds, Lowell. "Thucydides' Ethics as Reflected in the Description of Stasis (3.82–83)." *Harvard Studies in Classical Philology* 79 (1975): 73–92.

Edwards, John. *The Eternal and Intrinsick Reasons of Good and Evil. A Sermon Preach'd at the Commencement at Cambridge, on Sunday the 2d Day of July, 1699*. Cambridge: Cambridge University Press, for Edmund Jeffery, 1699.

Eggers, Daniel. *Die Naturzustandstheorie des Thomas Hobbes: Eine vergleichende Analyse von The Elements of Law, De Cive, und den englischen und lateinischen Fassungen des Leviathan.* Berlin: Walter de Gruyter, 2008.

"Hobbes and Game Theory Revisited: Zero-Sum Games in the State of Nature." *The Southern Journal of Philosophy* 49, no. 3 (September 2011): 193–226.

Egmond, Florike and Peter Mason. *The Mammoth and the Mouse: Microhistory and Morphology.* Baltimore, MD: The Johns Hopkins University Press, 1997.

Elliott, John Huxtable. *The Old World and the New 1492–1650.* Cambridge: Cambridge University Press, 1992.

Elyot, Sir Thomas. *The Dictionary of Syr Thomas Eliot Knyght.* London: Thomas Bartlett, [1538].

Euclid. *The Elements of Geometrie of the Most Auncient Philosopher Evclide of Megara.* Translated by H. Billingsley. London: John Daye, [1570].

Evelyn, John. *An Essay on the First Book of T. Lucretius Carus De Rerum Natura.* London: For Gabriel Bedle and Thomas Collins, 1656.

Evrigenis, Ioannis D. *Fear of Enemies and Collective Action.* Cambridge: Cambridge University Press, 2008.

"Hobbes's Clockwork: The State of Nature and Machiavelli's Return to the Beginnings of Cities." In *The Arts of Rule: Essays in Honor of Harvey Mansfield,* edited by Sharon Krause and Mary Ann McGrail, 185–99. Lanham, MD: Lexington Books, 2009.

Farr, James. "Atomes of Scripture: Hobbes and the Politics of Biblical Interpretation." In *Thomas Hobbes and Political Theory,* edited by Mary Dietz, 172–96. Lawrence: The University Press of Kansas, 1990.

Fausz, J. Frederick. "The 'Barbarous Massacre' Reconsidered: The Powhatan Uprising of 1622 and the Historians." *Explorations in Ethnic Studies* 1 (1978): 16–36.

Fawne, Luke, Samuel Gellibrand, Joshua Kirton, John Rothwell, Thomas Underhill, and Nathaniel Webb. *A Beacon Set on Fire, or, The Humble Information of Certain Stationers, Citizens of London, to the Parliament and Commonwealth of England, etc.* London: n.p., 1652.

Feldman, Karen S. "Conscience and the Concealments of Metaphor in Hobbes's *Leviathan.*" *Philosophy & Rhetoric* 34, no. 1 (2001): 21–37.

Ferguson, Arthur B. *The Articulate Citizen and the English Renaissance.* Durham, NC: Duke University Press, 1965.

Ferlauto, Filippo. *Il testo di Tucidide e la traduzione latina di Lorenzo Valla.* Palermo: Università di Palermo, Istituto di Filologia Greca, 1979.

[Filmer, Robert]. *Observations Concerning the Originall of Government, etc.* London: R. Royston, 1652.

Finnis, John. *Aquinas: Moral, Political, and Legal Theory.* Oxford: Oxford University Press, 1998.

Fitzmaurice, Andrew. *Humanism and America: An Intellectual History of English Colonization, 1500–1625.* Cambridge: Cambridge University Press, 2003.

Fletcher, J. M. "The Faculty of Arts." In *The History of the University of Oxford, Volume III: The Collegiate University,* edited by James McConica, 157–99. Oxford: The Clarendon Press, 1986.

Forbes, W. H., ed. *Thucydides Book I.* Oxford: The Clarendon Press, 1895.

Forsett, Edward. *A Comparative Discovrse of the Bodies Natvral and Politiqve.* London: John Bill, 1606.

Foster, Edith. "The Rhetoric of Materials: Thucydides and Lucretius." *American Journal of Philology* 130 (2009): 367–99.

Fowler, D. P. "Lucretius and Politics." In *Lucretius*, edited by Monica R. Gale, 397–431. Oxford: Oxford University Press, 2007.

Fowler, Peta. "Lucretian Conclusions." In *Classical Closure: Reading the End in Greek and Latin Literature*, edited by Deborah H. Roberts, Francis M. Dunn, and Don Fowler, 112–38. Princeton, NJ: Princeton University Press, 1997.

Freund, Julien. "Le dieu mortel." In *Hobbes Forschungen*, edited by Reinhart Koselleck and Roman Schnur, 33–52. Berlin: Duncker and Humblot, 1969.

Friedman, John Block. *The Monstrous Races in Medieval Art and Thought.* Cambridge, MA: Harvard University Press, 1981.

Funkenstein, Amos. *Theology and the Scientific Imagination from the Middle Ages to the Seventeenth Century.* Princeton, NJ: Princeton University Press, 1986.

Gale, Monica. *Myth and Poetry in Lucretius.* Cambridge: Cambridge University Press, 1994.

Gaukroger, Stephen. *The Emergence of a Scientific Culture: Science and the Shaping of Modernity 1210–1685.* Oxford: Oxford University Press, 2006.

Francis Bacon and the Transformation of Early-Modern Philosophy. Cambridge: Cambridge University Press, 2001.

Giamatti, A. Bartlett. *The Earthly Paradise and the Renaissance Epic.* Princeton, NJ: Princeton University Press, 1966.

Gibson, Strickland, ed. *Statvta Antiqva Vniversitatis Oxoniensis.* Oxford: The Clarendon Press, 1931.

Gliozzi, Giuliano. *Adamo e il nuovo mondo: La nascita dell'antropologia come ideologia coloniale: dalle genealogie bibliche alle teorie razziali (1500–1700).* Florence: La Nuova Italia Editrice, 1977.

Glover, Willis B. "God and Thomas Hobbes." In *Hobbes Studies*, edited by K. C. Brown, 141–68. Cambridge, MA: Harvard University Press, 1965.

Goldie, Mark. "The Reception of Hobbes." In *The Cambridge History of Political Thought, 1450–1700*, edited by J. H. Burns with the assistance of Mark Goldie, 589–615. Cambridge: Cambridge University Press, 1991.

Goldschmidt, Victor. *La doctrine d'Épicure et le droit.* Paris: J. Vrin, 1977.

Goldsmith, Maurice M. "Hobbes: Ancient and Modern." In *The Rise of Modern Philosophy: The Tension between the New and Traditional Philosophies from Machiavelli to Leibniz*, edited by Tom Sorell, 317–36. Oxford: The Clarendon Press, 1993.

"Hobbes's Ambiguous Politics." *History of Political Thought* 11, no. 4 (Winter 1990): 639–73.

Hobbes's Science of Politics. New York: Columbia University Press, 1966.

"Picturing Hobbes's Politics? The Illustrations to *Philosophicall Rudiments.*" *Journal of the Warburg and Courtauld Institutes* 44 (1981): 232–37.

Gomme, A. W., et al. *A Historical Commentary on Thucydides.* 4 volumes. Oxford: The Clarendon Press, 1945–70.

Goodrum, Matthew R. "Atomism, Atheism, and the Spontaneous Generation of Human Beings: The Debate over a Natural Origin of the First Humans in Seventeenth-Century Britain." *Journal of the History of Ideas* 63, no. 2 (2002): 207–24.

Grafton, Anthony. "Humanism and Political Theory." In *The Cambridge History of Political Thought, 1450–1700*, edited by J. H. Burns with the assistance of Mark Goldie, 9–29. Cambridge: Cambridge University Press, 1991.

Green, Lawrence D. "Aristotle's *Rhetoric* and Renaissance Views of the Emotions." In *Renaissance Rhetoric*, edited by Peter Mack, 1–26. London: The Macmillan Press, 1994.

"The Reception of Aristotle's *Rhetoric* in the Renaissance." In *Peripatetic Rhetoric after Aristotle*, edited by William W. Fortenbaugh & David C. Mirhady, 320–48. New Brunswick, NJ: Transaction Publishers, 1994.

Green, Lawrence D., ed. *John Rainolds's Oxford Lectures on Aristotle's Rhetoric.* Newark: The University of Delaware Press, 1986.

Green, Lawrence D. and James J. Murphy. *Renaissance Rhetoric Short-Title Catalogue 1460–1700.* Second edition. Aldershot: Ashgate, 2006.

Greenleaf, W. H. "A Note on Hobbes and the Book of Job." *Anales de la Cátedra Francisco Suárez* 14 (1974): 10–34.

Greenslade, B. D. "Clarendon's and Hobbes's 'Elements of Law.'" *Notes and Queries* 202 (1957): 150.

Griffiths, J. Gwyn. "Archaeology and Hesiod's Five Ages." *Journal of the History of Ideas* 17, no. 1 (1956): 109–19.

"Did Hesiod Invent the 'Golden Age?'" *Journal of the History of Ideas* 19, no. 1 (1958): 91–93.

Groesen, Michiel van. *The Representations of the Overseas World in the De Bry Collection of Voyages (1590–1634).* Leiden: Brill, 2008.

Grotius, Hugo. *De Jure Belli ac Pacis Libri Tres, etc.* Paris: Nicolaus Buon, 1625.

De Jure Belli ac Pacis Libri Tres, etc. Second edition. Amsterdam: W. Blaev, 1631.

On the Origin of the Native Races of America. A Dissertation. Translated by Edmund Goldsmid. Edinburgh: Privately printed, 1884.

Hakluyt, Richard. *The Principal Navigations, Voyages, Traffiqves and Disoveries of the English Nation, etc.* London: George Bishop, Ralph Newberie, and Robert Barker, 1599.

Hamlin, William M. "Florio's Montaigne and the Tyranny of 'Custome'." *Renaissance Quarterly* 63, no. 2 (2010): 491–544.

The Image of America in Montaigne, Spencer, and Shakespeare: Renaissance Ethnography and Literary Reflection. New York: St. Martin's Press, 1995.

Hanson, Donald W. "The Meaning of 'Demonstration' in Hobbes's Science. *History of Political Thought* XI, no. 4 (1990): 587–626.

Harden, J. David. "Liberty Caps and Liberty Trees." *Past & Present* 146 (1995): 66–102.

Hariot, Thomas. *A Briefe and True Report of the New Found Land of Virginia, etc.* London: n.p., 1588.

A Briefe and True Report of the New Found Land of Virginia, etc. Frankfurt am Main: Johann Wechel for Theodor De Bry, 1590.

Harrington, James. *The Common-Wealth of Oceana.* London: J. Streater for Livewell Chapman, 1656.

Politicaster: or, A Comical Discourse, in Answer to Mr. Wren's Book, Intituled, Monarchy Asserted, against Mr. Harrington's Oceana. London: J. C. for Henry Fletcher, 1659.

The Prerogative of Popular Government. London: Thomas Brewster, 1657.

Harrison, Charles T. "The Ancient Atomists and English Literature of the Seventeenth Century." *Harvard Studies in Classical Philology* 45 (1934): 1–79.

"Bacon, Hobbes, Boyle, and the Ancient Atomists." *Harvard Studies and Notes in Philology and Literature* 15 (1933): 191–218.

Harrison, Peter. *The Fall of Man and the Foundations of Modern Science.* Cambridge: Cambridge University Press, 2007.

Hartog, François. *The Mirror of Herodotus: The Representation of the Other in the Writing of History.* Translated by Janet Lloyd. Berkeley: University of California Press, 1988.

Harvey, Warren Zev. "The Israelite Kingdom of God in Hobbes' Political Thought." *Hebraic Political Studies* I, no. 3 (Spring 2006): 310–27.

Harwood, John T., ed. *The Rhetorics of Thomas Hobbes and Bernard Lamy.* Carbondale: Southern Illinois University Press, 1986.

Hatcher, Thomas, ed. *G. Haddoni Legum Doctoris, Reginæ Elisabethæ à Supplicum Libellis, Lucubrationes Passim Collectæ, & Editæ.* London: William Seres, 1567.

Hegel, Georg Wilhelm Friedrich. *Lectures on the History of Philosophy.* 3 volumes. Translated by E. S. Haldane and Frances H. Simon. Lincoln: University of Nebraska Press, 1995.

Hendel, Ronald S. "'The Flame of the Whirling Sword': A Note on Genesis 3:24." *Journal of Biblical Literature* 104, no. 4 (December 1985): 671–74.

Herrick, Mervin T. "The Early History of Aristotle's *Rhetoric* in England." *Philological Quarterly* 5, no. 4 (1926): 242–57.

Hesiod. *Works and Days.* Edited with prolegomena and commentary by M. L. West. Oxford: The Clarendon Press, 1978.

Works and Days. In *Hesiod I,* edited by Glenn W. Most. Cambridge, MA: Harvard University Press, 2006.

Hill, Christopher. *Change and Continuity in Seventeenth-Century England.* Cambridge, MA: Harvard University Press, 1975.

The English Bible and the Seventeenth Century Revolution. Harmondsworth: Penguin, 1994.

Hobbes, Thomas. *Ad Nobilissimum Dominum Gulielmum Comitem Devoniæ, & c. De Mirabilibus Pecci, Carmen Thomæ Hobbes.* n.p.: n.p., n.d.

The Answer of Mr. Hobbes to Sir Will. Davenant's Preface before Gondibert. In *The Preface to Gondibert, an Heroick Poem, etc.,* by Sir William Davenant, 129–60. Paris: Matthieu Guillemot, 1650.

The Art of Rhetoric, with a Discourse of the Laws of England. London: William Crooke, 1681.

Behemoth or the Long Parliament. Edited by Paul Seaward. Oxford: The Clarendon Press, 2010.

A Briefe of the Art of Rhetorique, etc. London: Andrew Crook, [1637?].

A Briefe of the Art of Rhetorique. In *The Rhetorics of Thomas Hobbes and Bernard Lamy,* edited by John T. Harwood, 33–128. Carbondale: Southern Illinois University Press, 1986.

Critique du De Mundo de Thomas White. Edited by Jean Jacquot and Harold Whitmore Jones. Paris: J. Vrin-CNRS, 1973.

De Cive, The English Version. Edited by Howard Warrender. Oxford: The Clarendon Press, 1983.

De Cive, The Latin Version. Edited by Howard Warrender. Oxford: The Clarendon Press, 1983.

De Corpore Politico. Or the Elements of Lavv, Moral and Politick. With Discourses upon Several Heads; as of The Law of Nature. Oathes and Covenants. Severall Kind of Government. With the Changes and Revolutions of Them. London: J. Martin and J. Ridley, 1650.

A Dialogue between a Philosopher and a Student, of the Common Laws of England. In *Writings on Common Law and Hereditary Right,* edited by Alan Cromartie and Quentin Skinner. Oxford: The Clarendon Press, 2008.

Dialogus Physicus. Translated by Simon Schaffer. In *Leviathan and the Air-Pump: Hobbes, Boyle, and the Experimental Life,* by Steven Shapin and Simon Schaffer, 345–91. Princeton, NJ: Princeton University Press, 1985.

Elementorvm Philosophiæ Sectio Tertia De Cive. Paris: n.p., 1642.

The Elements of Law Natural and Politic. Edited by Ferdinand Tönnies. London: Simpkin and Marshall, 1889.

The Elements of Law Natural and Politic. Edited by Ferdinand Tönnies. Second edition with an introduction by M. M. Goldsmith. London: Frank Cass, 1969.

The English Works of Thomas Hobbes. Edited by William Molesworth. 11 volumes. London: John Bohn, 1839–45.

Historia Ecclesiastica. Edited by Patricia Springborg, Patricia Stablein, and Paul Wilson. Paris: Honoré Champion, 2008.

An Historical Narration Concerning Heresie and the Punishment Thereof. London: n.p., 1680.

Hobbs's Tripos in Three Discourses, etc. London: n.p., 1684.

Humane Nature: Or, the Fundamental Elements of Policie. Being a Discoverie of the Faculties, Arts, and Passions of the Soul of Man, from Their Original Causes, according to Such Philosophical Principles as Are Not Commonly Known or Affected. London: T. Newcomb, 1650.

Leviathan, or the Matter, Forme and Power of a Commonwealth Ecclesiasticall and Civil. London: printed for Andrew Crooke, 1651.

Leviathan, sive De Materia, Forma, & Potestate Civitatis Ecclesiasticæ et Civilis. London: J. Thomson, 1678.

Leviathan with Selected Variants from the Latin Edition of 1668. Edited by Edwin Curley. Indianapolis: Hackett Publishing Company, 1994.

Leviathan. Edited by Richard Tuck. Cambridge: Cambridge University Press, 1996.

Leviathan. Edited by Noel Malcolm. 3 volumes. Oxford: The Clarendon Press, 2012.

Man and Citizen (De Homine and De Cive). Edited by Bernard Gert. Indianapolis, IN: Hackett Publishing Company, 1991.

Mr. Hobbes Considered in His Loyalty, Religion, Reputation, and Manners. By Way of a Letter to Dr. Wallis. London: A. Crooke, 1662.

Of Liberty and Necessity, etc. In *The English Works of Thomas Hobbes.* Edited by William Molesworth. 11 volumes, volume IV, 229–78. London: John Bohn, 1840.

Of Liberty and Necessity. In *Hobbes and Bramhall on Liberty and Necessity*, edited by Vere Chappell, 15–42. Cambridge: Cambridge University Press, 1999.
On the Citizen. Edited by Richard Tuck and Michael Silverthorne. Cambridge: Cambridge University Press, 1998.
Philosophicall Rudiments concerning Government and Society, etc. [Translated by Charles Cotton]. London: J. G. for R. Royston, 1650.
Quadratura Circuli, Cubatio Sphæræ, Duplicatio Cubi, Breviter Demonstrata. London: Andrew Crooke, 1669.
The Questions concerning Liberty, Necessity, and Chance, Clearly Stated and Debated between Dr. Bramhall, Bishop of Derry, and Thomas Hobbes of Malmesbury. In *The English Works of Thomas Hobbes*. Edited by William Molesworth. 11 volumes, volume V. London: John Bohn, 1841.
Six Lessons to the Professors of the Mathematiques, One of Geometry, the Other of Astronomy, etc. London: J. M. for Andrew Crook, [1656].
Thomæ Hobbes Malmesburiensis Opera Philosophica quæ Latine Scripsit Omnia in Unum Corpus Nunc Primum Collecta. Edited by William Molesworth. 5 volumes. London: John Bohn, 1839–45.
Thomæ Hobbesii Malmesburiensis Vita. London: n.p., 1679.
Thomas White's De Mundo Examined. Edited by Harold Whitmore Jones. London: Bradford University Press in association with Crosby, Lockwood, Staples, 1976.
Hodgen, Margaret T. *Early Anthropology in the Sixteenth and Seventeenth Centuries*. Philadelphia: The University of Pennsylvania Press, 1964.
Hoekstra, Kinch. "The *de facto* Turn in Hobbes's Political Philosophy." In *Leviathan after 350 Years*, edited by Tom Sorell and Luc Foisneau, 33–73. Oxford: The Clarendon Press, 2004.
"The End of Philosophy (The Case of Hobbes)." *Proceedings of the Aristotelian Society* New Series 106 (2006): 25–62.
"Hobbes on the Natural Condition of Mankind." In *The Cambridge Companion to Hobbes's Leviathan*, edited by Patricia Springborg, 109–27. Cambridge: Cambridge University Press, 2007.
"Hobbesian Equality." In *Hobbes Today*, edited by S. A. Lloyd, 76–112. Cambridge: Cambridge University Press, 2012.
"A Lion in the House: Hobbes and Democracy." In *Rethinking the Foundations of Modern Political Thought*, edited by Annabel Brett and James Tully with Holly Hamilton-Bleakley, 191–218. Cambridge: Cambridge University Press, 2006.
Thomas Hobbes and the Creation of Order. Oxford: Oxford University Press, forthcoming.
Hoffmann, George. "Anatomy of the Mass: Montaigne's 'Cannibals.'" *PMLA* 117, no. 2 (2002): 207–21.
Homer. *Homer's Iliads in English, etc.* Translated by Thomas Hobbes. London: William Crook, 1676.
Homer's Odysses. Translated by Thomas Hobbes. London: William Crook, 1675.
Hood, F. C. *The Divine Politics of Thomas Hobbes: An Interpretation of Leviathan*. Oxford: The Clarendon Press, 1964.
Hooker, Richard. *Of the Laws of Ecclesiastical Polity*. Edited by Christopher Morris. 2 volumes. London: J. M. Dent and Sons, 1963.

Horn, Georg. *Arca Noæ, sive Historia Imperiorum et Regnorum à Condito Orbe ad Nostra Tempora*. Leiden and Rotterdam: Officina Hackiana, 1666.
Hornblower, Simon. *A Commentary on Thucydides*. 3 volumes. Oxford: Oxford University Press, 1991–2008.
Hull, Gordon. "'Against this *Empusa:*' Hobbes's *Leviathan* and the *Book of Job*." *British Journal for the History of Philosophy* 10, no. 1 (2002): 3–29.
Hulton, Paul. *America 1585: The Complete Drawings of John White*. Chapel Hill: The University of North Carolina Press, 1984.
Hyginus. *Hygini fabvlae*. Edited H. J. Rose. Leiden: A. W. Sijthoff, [1934].
Jackson, Arthur. *A Help for the Understanding of the Holy Scripture, etc.* Cambridge: Roger Daniel, 1643.
Jesseph, Douglas M. "*Scientia* in Hobbes." In *Scientia in Early Modern Philosophy: Seventeenth-Century Thinkers on Demonstrative Knowledge from First Principles*, edited by Tom Sorell, G. A. J. Rogers, and Jill Kraye, 117–27. Dordrecht: Springer, 2010.
Squaring the Circle: The War between Hobbes and Wallis. Chicago: The University of Chicago Press, 1999.
Johnson, Paul J. "Hobbes and the Wolf-Man." In *Hobbes's 'Science of Natural Justice,'* edited by C. Walton and P. J. Johnson, 139–51. Dordrecht: Martinus Nijhoff Publishers, 1987.
Johnson, Robert. *Nova Britannia. Offring Most Excellent Fruites by Planting in Virginia, etc.* London: Samuel Macham, 1609.
Johnson, Robert C. "The Lotteries of the Virginia Company." *The Virginia Magazine of History and Biography* 74, no. 3 (1966): 259–92.
Johnston, David. *The Rhetoric of Leviathan: Thomas Hobbes and the Politics of Cultural Transformation*. Princeton, NJ: Princeton University Press, 1986.
Johnston, Patricia A. *Vergil's Agricultural Golden Age: A Study of the Georgics*. Leiden: E. J. Brill, 1980.
Jolley, Nicholas. "The Relation between Philosophy and Theology." In *The Cambridge History of Seventeenth-Century Philosophy*, 2 volumes, edited by Daniel Garber and Michael Ayers, 363–92. Cambridge: Cambridge University Press, 1998.
Jones, Howard. *Pierre Gassendi 1592–1655: An Intellectual Biography*. Nieuwkoop: B. De Graaf, 1981.
Josephus. *History of the Jewish War against the Romans*. Volumes 2 and 3 of *Josephus*. Translated by H. St. J. Thackeray. Cambridge, MA: Harvard University Press, 1956–57.
Kahn, Victoria. "Hobbes, Romance, and the Contract of Mimesis." *Political Theory* 29, no. 1 (2001): 4–29.
Rhetoric, Prudence, and Skepticism in the Renaissance. Ithaca, NY: Cornell University Press, 1985.
Kantorowitz, Ernst H. *The King's Two Bodies: A Study in Mediaeval Political Theology*. With a new preface by William Chester Jordan. Princeton, NJ: Princeton University Press, 1997.
Kargon, Robert Hugh. *Atomism in England from Hariot to Newton*. Oxford: The Clarendon Press, 1966.
Keller, Eve. "In the Service of 'Truth' and 'Victory': Geometry and Rhetoric in the Political Works of Thomas Hobbes." *Prose Studies* 15, no. 2 (August 1992): 129–52.

Kendrick, T. D. *British Antiquity*. London: Methuen and Co., 1950.

King, Preston. *The Ideology of Order: A Comparative Analysis of Jean Bodin and Thomas Hobbes*. New York: Barnes and Noble, 1974.

Kingsbury, Susan Myra, ed. *The Records of the Virginia Company of London*. 4 volumes. Washington, DC: Government Printing Office, 1906–35.

Klosko, George and Daryl Rice. "Thucydides and Hobbes's State of Nature." *History of Political Thought* 6, no. 3 (1985): 405–09.

Kluger, Rivkah Schärf. *Satan in the Old Testament*. Translated by Hildegard Nagel. Evanston, IL: Northwestern University Press, 1967.

Krause, Joachim J. "Der Bund im Alten Testament und bei Hobbes: Eine Perspective auf den *Leviathan*." *Politisches Denken Jahrbuch* (2005): 9–39.

Kraynak, Robert P. *History and Modernity in the Thought of Thomas Hobbes*. Ithaca, NY: Cornell University Press, 1990.

Kristeller, Paul Oskar. *The Classics and Renaissance Thought*. Cambridge, MA: Harvard University Press for Oberlin College, 1955.

"Humanism." In *The Cambridge History of Renaissance Philosophy*, edited by Charles B. Schmitt, et al., 113–37. Cambridge: Cambridge University Press, 1988.

Renaissance Thought: The Classic, Scholastic, and Humanist Strains. New York: Harper Torchbooks, 1961.

Kuhlemann, Ute. "Between Reproduction, Invention and Propaganda: Theodor De Bry's Engravings after John White's Watercolours." In *A New World: England's First View of America*, edited by Kim Sloan, 79–92. London: The British Museum Press, 2007.

Kupperman, Karen Ordahl. "Apathy and Death in Early Jamestown." *The Journal of American History* 66, no. 1 (1979): 24–40.

"English Perceptions of Treachery, 1583–1640: The Case of the American 'Savages.'" *The Historical Journal* 20, no. 2 (1977): 263–87.

Indians and English: Facing Off in Early America. Ithaca, NY: Cornell University Press, 2000.

"Roanoke's Achievement." In *European Visions: American Voices*, edited by Kim Sloan, 3–12. London: The British Museum, 2009.

Lactantius. *Divine Institutes*. Translated by Anthony Bowen and Peter Garnsey. Liverpool: Liverpool University Press, 2003.

Laird, John. *Hobbes*. London: Ernest Benn Limited, 1934.

Landucci, Sergio. *I filosofi e i selvaggi, 1580–1780*. Bari: Editori Laterza, 1972.

Leibniz, Gottfried Willhelm. *Die Philosophischen Schriften von Gottfried Wilhelm Leibniz*, Volume 3. Edited by C. J. Gerhardt. Berlin: Weidmannsche Buchhandlung, 1887.

Leijenhorst, Cees. "'Insignificant Speech:' Thomas Hobbes and Late Aristotelianism on Words, Concepts, and Things." In *Res et Verba in der Renaissance*, edited by Eckhard Kessler and Ian Maclean, 337–67. Wiesbaden: Harrassowitz im Kommission, 2002.

The Mechanisation of Aristotelianism: The Late Aristotelian Setting of Thomas Hobbes's Natural Philosophy. Leiden: Brill, 2002.

Lemetti, Juhana. "The Most Natural and the Most Artificial: Hobbes on Imagination." *Hobbes Studies* 17 (2005): 46–71.

Le Moyne de Morgues, Jacques. *Brevis Narratio Eorum Qvæ in Florida Americæ Provīcia Gallis Acciderunt, etc.* Frankfurt a. m.: Johann Wechel, 1591.

Lescarbot, Marc. *Nova Francia: Or the Description of that Part of Nevv France, which Is One Continent with Virginia, etc.* Translated by P. E [rondelle]. London: G. Bishop, 1609.

Lessay, Franck. "Hobbes's Covenant Theology and Its Political Implications." In *The Cambridge Companion to Hobbes's Leviathan*, edited by Patricia Springborg, 243–70. Cambridge: Cambridge University Press, 2007.

Levin, Harry. *The Myth of the Golden Age in the Renaissance*. Bloomington: Indiana University Press, 1969.

Levine, Alan. *Sensual Philosophy: Toleration, Skepticism, and Montaigne's Politics of the Self*. Lanham, MD: Lexington Books, 2001.

Lloyd, S. A. *Ideals as Interests in Hobbes's Leviathan: The Power of Mind over Matter*. Cambridge: Cambridge University Press, 1992.

Morality in the Philosophy of Thomas Hobbes: Cases in the Law of Nature. Cambridge: Cambridge University Press, 2009.

Lovejoy, Arthur O. *Essays in the History of Ideas*. Baltimore, MD: The Johns Hopkins Press, 1948.

Lovejoy, Arthur O. and George Boas. *Primitivism and Related Ideas in Antiquity.* With supplementary essays by W. F. Albright and P. E. Dumont. Baltimore, MD: The Johns Hopkins University Press, 1997.

Lowde, James. *A Discourse concerning the Nature of Man, Both in His Natural and Political Capacity, etc.* London, 1694.

Lucretius Carus, Titus. *De rerum natura.* Edited by Cyril Bailey. 3 volumes. Oxford: The Clarendon Press, 1947.

De rerum natura. Translated by Lucy Hutchinson. Edited by Hugh de Quehen. Ann Arbor: The University of Michigan Press, 1996.

De rerum natura. Translated by W. H. D. Rouse and revised by Martin F. Smith. Cambridge, MA: Harvard University Press, 1992.

T. Lucreti Cari De rerum natura libri sex: revisione del testo, commento e studi introdutivi. Edited by Carlo Giussani. 4 volumes. Turin: Ermann Loescher, 1896–98.

T. Lucretius Carus the Epicurean Philosopher, His Six Books De Natura Rerum, etc. Translated by Thomas Creech. Oxford: L. Lichfield for Anthony Stephens, 1682.

Titi Lucretii Cari De Rerum Natura Libri Sex., etc. Edited by Tan[aquil] Lefebvre. Cambridge: John Hayes for W. Morden, 1675.

Lucy, William. *Observations, Censures and Confutations of Notorious Errours in Mr. Hobbes His Leviathan and Other His Bookes, etc.* London: J. G. for Nath. Brooke, 1663.

Ludwig, Bernd. "Cicero oder Epikur? Über einen 'Paradigmenwechsel' in Hobbes' politischer Philosophie." In *Der Einfluß des Hellenismus auf die Philosophie der Frühen Neuzeit*, edited by Gábor Boros, 159–79. Wiesbaden: Harrassowitz Verlag, 2005.

Die Wiederentdeckung des epikureischen Naturrechts: Zu Thomas Hobbes' philosophischer Entwicklung von De Cive zum Leviathan in Pariser Exil 1640–1651. Frankfurt a. M.: Vittorio Klostermann, 1998.

Lund, William R. "The Historical and 'Politicall' Origins of Civil Society: Hobbes on Presumption and Certainty." *History of Political Thought* 9, no. 2 (1988): 223–35.

"Hobbes on Opinion, Private Judgment and Civil War." *History of Political Thought* 13, no. 1 (1992): 51–72.

Luscombe, David E. "The State of Nature and the Origin of the State." In *The Cambridge History of Later Medieval Philosophy: From the Rediscovery of Aristotle to the Disintegration of Scholasticism, 1100–1600*, edited by Norman Kretzmann, Anthony Kenny, Jan Pinborg, and Eleonore Stump, 757–70. Cambridge: Cambridge University Press, 1982.

Lutri, Joseph R. de. "Montaigne's 'Des Cannibales': Invention/Experience." *Bibliothèque d'Humanisme et Renaissance* 38, no. 1 (1976): 77–82.

Macdonald, Hugh and Mary Hargreaves. *Thomas Hobbes: A Bibliography*. London: The Bibliographical Society, 1952.

Machiavelli, Niccolò. *Discourses on Livy*. Translated by Harvey C. Mansfield and Nathan Tarcov. Chicago: The University of Chicago Press, 1996.

The Prince. Translated by Harvey C. Mansfield. Second edition. Chicago: The University of Chicago Press, 1998.

Mack, Peter. *A History of Renaissance Rhetoric 1380–1620*. Oxford: Oxford University Press, 2011.

Macleod, C. W. "Thucydides on Faction (3.82–83)." *Proceedings of the Cambridge Philological Society* 205 (1979): 52–69.

Macpherson, C. B. *The Political Theory of Possessive Individualism: Hobbes to Locke*. Oxford: Oxford University Press, 1962.

Malcolm, Noel. *Aspects of Hobbes*. Oxford: Oxford University Press, 2002.

"The Name and Nature of Leviathan: Political Symbolism and Biblical Exegesis." *Intellectual History Review* 17, no. 1 (2007): 21–39.

ed. *The Correspondence of Thomas Hobbes*. 2 volumes. Oxford: The Clarendon Press, 1994.

ed. *Reason of State, Propaganda, and the Thirty Years' War: An Unknown Translation by Thomas Hobbes*. Oxford: The Clarendon Press, 2007.

Marouby, Christian. "Adam Smith and the Anthropology of the Enlightenment: The 'Ethnographic' Sources of Economic Progress." In *The Anthropology of the Enlightenment*, edited by Larry Wolff and Marco Cipolloni, 85–102. Stanford, CA: Stanford University Press, 2007.

Marsilius of Padua. *The Defender of the Peace*. Translated by Annabel Brett. Cambridge: Cambridge University Press, 2005.

Martel, James. *Subverting the Leviathan: Reading Thomas Hobbes as a Radical Democrat*. New York: Columbia University Press, 2007.

Martin, Julian. *Francis Bacon, the State, and the Reform of Natural Philosophy*. Cambridge: Cambridge University Press, 1992.

Martinich, A. P. *Hobbes: A Biography*. Cambridge: Cambridge University Press, 1999.

"The Interpretation of Covenants in *Leviathan*." In *Leviathan after 350 Years*, edited by Tom Sorell and Luc Foisneau, 217–40. Oxford: The Clarendon Press, 2004.

Review of *Reason and Rhetoric in the Philosophy of Hobbes*, by Quentin Skinner. *The Journal of Modern History* 70, no. 1 (1998): 149–51.

The Two Gods of Leviathan: Thomas Hobbes on Religion and Politics. Cambridge: Cambridge University Press, 1992.

Mason, Peter. "Classical Ethnography and Its Influence on the European Perception of the Peoples of the New World." In *European Images of the Americas and the Classical Tradition,* Part I, Volume I of *The Classical Tradition and the Americas,* edited by Wolfgang Haase and Meyer Reinhold, 135–72. Berlin: Walter De Gruyter, 1994.

Deconstructing America: Representations of the Other. London: Routledge, 1990.

Mayo, Thomas Franklin. *Epicurus in England (1650–1725).* Dallas, TX: The Southwest Press, 1934.

McCartney, Martha. "*A Declaration of the State of the Colony and Affaires in Virginia* (1622)." In *Encyclopedia Virginia,* edited by Brendan Wolfe. Virginia Foundation for the Humanities. Retrieved from http://www.EncyclopediaVirginia.org/_Declaration_Edward_Waterhouse_s (last accessed April 6, 2012).

McConica, James. "Elizabethan Oxford: The Collegiate Society." In *The History of the University of Oxford, Volume III: The Collegiate University,* edited by James McConica, 645–732. Oxford: The Clarendon Press, 1986.

"Humanism and Aristotle in Tudor Oxford." *The English Historical Review* 94, no. 371 (April 1979): 291–317.

McCullough, Peter E. "Andrewes, Lancelot (1555–1626)." *Oxford Dictionary of National Biography,* edited by H. C. G. Matthew and Brian Harrison. Oxford: Oxford University Press, 2004. Online ed. Edited by Lawrence Goldman, January 2008. Retrieved from http://www.oxforddnb.com/view/article/520 (last accessed August 2, 2011).

McGiffert, Michael. "From Moses to Adam: The Making of the Covenant of Works." *The Sixteenth Century Journal* 19, no. 2 (Summer 1988): 131–55.

McNeilly, F. S. "Egoism in Hobbes." *The Philosophical Quarterly* 16, no. 64 (1966): 193–206.

Medick, Hans. *Naturzustand und Naturgeschichte der bürgerlichen Gesellschaft.* Göttingen: Vandenhoeck and Ruprecht, 1973.

Mercator, Gerhard. *Historia Mundi: or Mercator's Atlas Containing his Cosmographicall Description of the Fabricke and Figure of the World, etc.* Translated by Wye Saltonstall. London: T. Cotes for Michael Sparke and Samuel Cartwright, 1635.

Mercer, Christia. "The Vitality and Importance of Early Modern Aristotelianism." In *The Rise of Modern Philosophy: The Tension between the New and Traditional Philosophies from Machiavelli to Leibniz,* edited by Tom Sorell, 33–67. Oxford: The Clarendon Press, 1993.

Migne, Jacques-Paul. *Patrologia Cursus Completus. Series Latina.* Paris: Migne, 1844–90.

Miller, Ted H. "The Uniqueness of *Leviathan*: Authorizing Poets, Philosophers, and Sovereigns." In Leviathan after 350 Years, edited by Tom Sorell, 75–103. Oxford: The Clarendon Press, 2004.

Milner, Benjamin. "Hobbes on Religion." *Political Theory* 16, no. 3 (August 1988): 400–425.

Mintz, Samuel I. *The Hunting of Leviathan: Seventeenth-Century Reactions to the Materialism and Moral Philosophy of Thomas Hobbes.* Bristol: Thoemmes Press, 1996.

"Leviathan as Metaphor." *Hobbes Studies* 2 (1989): 3–9.

Moloney, Pat. "Hobbes, Savagery, and International Anarchy." *American Political Science Review* 105, no. 1 (2011): 189–204.

"Leaving the Garden of Eden: Linguistic and Political Authority in Thomas Hobbes." *History of Political Thought* 18, no. 2 (Summer 1997): 242–66.

Montaigne, Michel de. *The Complete Essays of Montaigne.* Translated by Donald M. Frame. Stanford, CA: Stanford University Press, 2000.

The Essayes, or Morall, Politike and Millitarie Discourses, etc. Translated by John Florio. London: Val. Sims for Edward Blount and William Barret, 1603.

Morison, Samuel Eliot, trans. and ed. *Journals and Other Documents on the Life and Voyages of Christopher Columbus.* New York: The Heritage Press, 1963.

Müri, Walter. "Politische Metonomasie (zu Thukydides 3, 82, 4–5). *Museum Helveticum* 26, no. 2 (1969): 65–79.

Nauta, Lodi. "Hobbes the Pessimist? Continuity of Hobbes's Views on Reason and Eloquence between *The Elements of Law* and *Leviathan.*" *British Journal for the History of Philosophy* 10, no. 1 (2002): 31–54.

Nederman, Cary J. "Aristotelianism and the Origins of 'Political Science' in the Twelfth Century." *Journal of the History of Ideas* 52, no. 2 (1991): 179–94.

"Aristotle as Authority: Alternative Aristotelian Sources of Late Mediaeval Political Theory." *History of European Ideas* 8, no. 1 (1987): 31–44.

"The Meaning of 'Aristotelianism' in Medieval Moral and Political Thought." *Journal of the History of Ideas* 57, no. 4 (1996): 563–85.

"Nature, Sin and the Origins of Society: The Ciceronian Tradition in Medieval Political Thought." *Journal of the History of Ideas* 49, no. 1 (1988): 3–26.

"The Union of Wisdom and Eloquence before the Renaissance – The Ciceronian Orator in Medieval Thought." *Journal of Medieval History* 18, no. 1 (1992):75–95.

Norlin, George. "Ethnology and the Golden Age." *Classical Philology* 12, no. 4 (1917): 351–64.

Norton, David. *The King James Bible: A Short History from Tyndale to Today.* Cambridge: Cambridge University Press, 2011.

Nozick, Robert. *Anarchy, State, and Utopia.* New York: Basic Books, 1974.

Nye, Joseph S. *Understanding International Conflicts: An Introduction to Theory and History.* Fifth edition. New York: Pearson/Longman, 2005.

Oakeshott, Michael. Introduction to *Leviathan,* by Thomas Hobbes. Oxford: Basil Blackwell, 1950.

Ockham, William of. *The Dialogue.* Translated by Francis Oakley. In *Medieval Political Philosophy,* edited by Ralph Lerner and Muhsin Mahdi, 492–506. Ithaca, NY: Cornell University Press, 1989.

Offler, H. S. "The Three Modes of Natural Law in Ockham: A Revision of the Text." *Franciscan Studies* 37 (1977): 207–18.

Ong, Walter J., S. J. "Hobbes and Talon's Ramist Rhetoric in English." *Transactions of the Cambridge Bibliographical Society* (1951): 260–69.

Ormerod, Henry A. *Piracy in the Ancient World: An Essay in Mediterranean History.* Liverpool: The University Press of Liverpool, 1924.

Orwin, Clifford. *The Humanity of Thucydides.* Princeton, NJ: Princeton University Press, 1994.

"Stasis and Plague: Thucydides on the Dissolution of Society." *Journal of Politics* 50, no. 4 (1988): 831–47.

Osler, Margaret J. "Ancients, Moderns, and the History of Philosophy." In *The Rise of Modern Philosophy: The Tension between the New and Traditional Philosophies from Machiavelli to Leibniz*, edited by Tom Sorell, 129–43. Oxford: The Clarendon Press, 1993.

Ovid. [Publius Ovidius Naso]. *Metamorphoses*. Translated by Frank Justus Miller and revised by G. P. Goold. 2 volumes. Cambridge, MA: Harvard University Press, 1994.

Ovid's Metamorphosis Englished, Mythologiz'd, and Represented in Figures. An Essay to the Translation of Virgil's Æneid. By G. S. Translated by G[eorge] S[andys]. Oxford: John Lichfield, 1632.

Pacchi, Arrigo. *Scritti Hobbesiani (1978–1990)*. Edited by Agostino Lupoli with an introduction by François Tricaud. Milan: Franco Angeli, 1998.

"Some Guidelines into Hobbes's Theology." *Hobbes Studies* 2 (1989): 87–103.

"Una 'biblioteca ideale' di Thomas Hobbes: Il MS E2 dell' archivio di Chatsworth." *Acme* 21 (1968): 5–42.

Paganini, Gianni. "Hobbes, Gassendi and the Tradition of Political Epicureanism." *Hobbes Studies* 14 (2001): 3–24.

"Hobbes, Gassendi et le *De Cive*." In *Materia Actuosa. Antiquité, âge classique, Lumières. Mélanges en l'honneur d'Olivier Bloch*, edited by Miguel Benitez, et al., 183–206. Paris: Honoré Champion, 2000.

Pagden, Anthony. *The Fall of Natural Man: The American Indian and the Origins of Comparative Ethnology*. Cambridge: Cambridge University Press, 1990.

Pangle, Thomas L. "A Critique of Hobbes's Critique of Biblical and Natural Religion in *Leviathan*." *Jewish Political Studies Review* 4, no. 2 (Fall 1992): 25–57.

Park, Katharine and Lorraine Daston. Introduction to *Early Modern Science*. Volume 3 of *The Cambridge History of Science*, edited by Katharine Park and Lorraine Daston. Cambridge: Cambridge University Press, 2006.

Parker, Samuel. *A Demonstration of the Divine Authority of the Law of Nature, and of the Christian Religion*. London: M. Flesher for R. Royston and R. Chiswell, 1681.

A Discourse of Ecclesiastical Politie, etc. London: John Martyn, 1670.

Disputationes de Deo, et Providentia Divina. London: M. Clark for J. Martyn, 1678.

A Reproof to the Rehearsal Transposed, in a Discourse to Its Author, etc. London: James Collins, 1673.

Parkin, Jon. *Taming the Leviathan: The Reception of the Political and Religious Ideas of Thomas Hobbes in England 1640–1700*. Cambridge: Cambridge University Press, 2007.

[Pasquier, Etienne]. *The Iesuites Catechisme. Or Examination of Their Doctrine, etc.* [Translated by William Watson. London]: n.p., 1602.

Patapan, Haig. "'Lord over the Children of Pride:' The *Vaine-Glorious* Rhetoric of Hobbes's *Leviathan*." *Philosophy & Rhetoric* 33, no. 1 (2000): 74–93.

Peacham, Henry. *The Garden of Eloquence, etc.* London: H. Jackson, 1577.

The Garden of Eloquence, etc. Second edition. London: H. Jackson, 1593.

Peters, Richard. *Hobbes*. Baltimore, MD: Peregrine Books, 1967.

Pettit, Philip. *Made with Words: Hobbes on Language, Mind, and Politics.* Princeton, NJ: Princeton University Press, 2008.

Pindar. *Pythian Odes.* In *Pindar I: Olympian Odes, Pythian Odes.* Edited by William H. Race. Cambridge, MA: Harvard University Press, 1997.

Plato. *Platonis Opera,* volumes 2–4. Edited by John Burnet. Oxford: The Clarendon Press, 1901–07.

Plautus, Titus Maccius. *Assinaria.* In *Plautus I.* Edited by Wolfgang de Mello. Cambridge, MA: Harvard University Press, 2011.

Plutarch. *Marcus Cato.* In *Lives II.* Translated by Bernadotte Perrin. Cambridge, MA: Harvard University Press, 2006.

Pope, Peter. "*A True and Faithful Account:* Newfoundland in 1680." *Newfoundland Studies* 12 (1996): 32–49.

Powell, Anthony. *John Aubrey and His Friends.* New York: Barnes and Noble, 1963.

Powell, J. U. "The Papyri of Thucydides and the Translation of Laurentius Valla." *The Classical Quarterly* 23, no. 1 (1929): 11–14.

Powell, William S. "Aftermath of the Massacre: The First Indian War, 1622–32." *The Virginia Magazine of History and Biography* 66, no. 1 (1958): 44–75.

Pratt, Stephanie. "Truth and Artifice in the Visualization of Native Peoples: From the Time of John White to the Beginning of the 18th Century." In *European Visions: American Voices,* edited by Kim Sloan, 33–40. London: The British Museum, 2009.

Prior, Charles W. A. "Trismegistus 'His Great Giant.'" *Notes & Queries* 51, no. 4 (2004): 366–70.

Pufendorf, Samuel. *De Jure Naturæ et Gentium Libri Octo.* Translated by C. H. Oldfather and W. A. Oldfather. 2 volumes. New York: Oceana Publications, 1964.

Purchas, Samuel. *Purchas His Pilgrimes in Fiue Bookes, etc., The First Part.* London: William Stansby for Henrie Fetherstone, 1625.

Quillet, Jeannine. "Community, Counsel and Representation." In *The Cambridge History of Medieval Political Thought, c. 350–c. 1450,* edited by J. H. Burns, 520–72. Cambridge: Cambridge University Press, 1988.

Rad, Gerhard von. *Genesis: A Commentary.* Revised edition. Philadelphia, PA: The Westminster Press, 1972.

Raleigh, Sir Walter. *The Discovery of the Large, Rich, and Beautiful Empire of Guiana, etc.* Edited by Robert H. Schomburgk. Cambridge: Cambridge University Press, 2010.

Rawls, John. *A Theory of Justice.* Cambridge, MA: The Belknap Press of Harvard University Press, 1971.

Rawson, Elizabeth. *Cicero: A Portrait.* London: Bristol Classical Press for Gerald Duckworth and Co., 1983

Rayner, Jeremy. "Hobbes and the Rhetoricians." *Hobbes Studies* 5 (1991): 76–95.

Reik, Miriam M. *The Golden Lands of Thomas Hobbes.* Detroit: Wayne State University Press, 1977.

Relf, Frances Helen. *The Petition of Right.* Minneapolis: Bulletin of the University of Minnesotta, 1917.

Remer, Gary. "Hobbes, the Rhetorical Tradition, and Toleration." *The Review of Politics* 54, no. 1 (1992): 5–33.

Reventlow, Henning Graf. *The Authority of the Bible and the Rise of the Modern World*. Translated by John Bowden. Philadelphia: Fortress Press, 1985.

Ripa, Cesare. *Cesare Ripa's Iconologia of Uytbeeldinghen des Verstants*. Translated by Dirck Pietersz Pers. 1644. Reprint, Soest: Davaco Publishers, 1971. Retrieved from http://www.dbnl.org/tekst/persooicesaoi_oi/

Iconologia di Cesare Ripa Pervgino, etc. Venice: Cristoforo Tomasini, 1645.

Rives, James B. "*Germania*." In *A Companion to Tacitus*, edited by Victoria Emma Pagán, 45–61. Malden, MA: Wiley-Blackwell, 2012.

Robertson, George Croom. *Hobbes*. Edinburgh: William Blackwood and Sons, 1886.

Rogow, Arnold A. *Thomas Hobbes: Radical in the Service of Reaction*. New York: W. W. Norton and Co., 1986.

Romilly, Jacqueline de. *Histoire et raison chez Thucydide*. Paris: Les Belles Lettres, 1956.

Ross, Alexander. *The First Booke of Questions and Answers upon Genesis, etc*. London: Nicholas Okes, for Francis Constable, 1620.

Ross, George Macdonald. "Hobbes and the Authority of the Universities." *Hobbes Studies* 10 (1997): 68–80.

Rousseau, Jean-Jacques. *Discourse on the Origin and Foundations of Inequality among Men*. In *The Discourses and Other Early Political Writings*, edited by Victor Gourevitch, 111–222. Cambridge: Cambridge University Press, 1997.

Of the Social Contract. In *Of the Social Contract and Other Later Political Writings*, edited by Victor Gourevitch, 39–152. Cambridge: Cambridge University Press, 1997.

Rubiés, Joan-Pau. "Hugo Grotius's Dissertation on the Origin of the American Peoples and the Use of Comparative Methods." *Journal of the History of Ideas* 52, no. 2 (1991): 221–44.

"Texts, Images, and the Perception of 'Savages' in Early Modern Europe: What We Can Learn from White and Harriot." In *European Visions: American Voices*, edited by Kim Sloan, 120–30. London: The British Museum, 2009.

Rummel, Erika. *The Humanist-Scholastic Debate in the Renaissance and Reformation*. Cambridge, MA: Harvard University Press, 1995.

Rushworth, John. *Historical Collections of Private Passages of State, etc*. London: G. Thomason, 1659.

Sacksteder, William. "Hobbes: Man the Maker." In *Thomas Hobbes: His View of Man. Proceedings of the Hobbes Symposium at the International School of Philosophy in the Netherlands (Leusden, September 1979)*, edited by J. G. van der Bend, 77–88. Amsterdam: Rodopi B. V., 1982.

"Man the Artificer: Notes on Animals, Humans and Machines in Hobbes." *The Southern Journal of Philosophy* 22 (1984): 105–21.

Sarasohn, Lisa T. *Gassendi's Ethics: Freedom in a Mechanistic Universe*. Ithaca, NY: Cornell University Press, 1996.

"Motion and Morality: Pierre Gassendi, Thomas Hobbes and the Mechanical World-View." *Journal of the History of Ideas* 46, no. 3 (1985): 363–79.

Saxonhouse, Arlene W. "Nature & Convention in Thucydides' History." *Polity* 10, no. 4 (1978): 461–87.

Schama, Simon. *The Embarrassment of Riches: An Interpretation of Dutch Culture in the Golden Age.* New York: Alfred A. Knopf, 1987.

Schlatter, Richard. "Thomas Hobbes and Thucydides." *Journal of the History of Ideas* 6, no. 3 (1945): 350–62.

Schmitt, Carl. *The Leviathan in the State Theory of Thomas Hobbes: Meaning and Failure of a Political Symbol.* Translated by George Schwab and Erna Hilfstein. Westport, CT: Greenwood Press, 1996.

Schmitt, Charles B. *Aristotle and the Renaissance.* Cambridge, MA: Harvard University Press for Oberlin College, 1983.

"Philosophy and Science in Sixteenth-Century Universities: Some Preliminary Remarks." In *The Cultural Context of Medieval Learning: Proceedings of the First International Colloquium of Philosophy, Science, and Theology in the Middle Ages – September 1973,* edited by John Emery Murdoch and Edith Dudley Sylla, 485–537. Dordrecht: D. Reidel Publishing Company, 1975.

Schochet, Gordon J. "Thomas Hobbes on the Family and the State of Nature." *Political Science Quarterly* 82, no. 3 (September 1967): 427–45.

Schuhmann, Karl. "Hobbes and Renaissance Philosophy." In *Hobbes oggi,* edited by Andrea Napoli and Guido Canziani, 331–49. Milan: Franco Angeli, 1990.

"Hobbes und Gassendi." In *Veritas Filia Temporis? Philosophiehistorie zwischen Wahrheit und Geschichte: Festschrift für Rainer Specht zum 65. Geburtstag,* edited by Rolf W. Puster, 163–69. Berlin: De Gruyter, 1995.

Hobbes une chronique, cheminement de sa pensée et de sa vie. Paris: J. Vrin, 1998.

"Skinner's Hobbes." *British Journal for the History of Philosophy* 6, no. 1 (1998): 115–25.

Scott, Jonathan. "The Peace of Silence: Thucydides and the English Civil War." In *Hobbes and History,* edited by G. A. J. Rogers and Tom Sorell, 112–36. London: Routledge, 2000.

Segal, Charles. *Lucretius on Death and Anxiety: Poetry and Philosophy in De Rerum Natura.* Princeton, NJ: Princeton University Press, 1990.

Seneca [Lucius Annaeus Seneca]. *Seneca ad Lucilium epistulae morales.* 3 volumes. Translated by Richard M. Gummere. London: William Heinemann, 1930.

Sextus Empiricus. *Against the Professors.* Translated by R. G. Bury. Cambridge, MA: Harvard University Press, 1949.

Shapin, Steven. *The Scientific Revolution.* Chicago: The University of Chicago Press, 1996.

Shapiro, Barbara. *Probability and Certainty in Seventeenth-Century England: A Study of the Relationships between Natural Science, Religion, History, Law, and Literature.* Princeton, NJ: Princeton University Press, 1983.

Shapiro, Gary. "Reading and Writing in the Text of Hobbes's *Leviathan.*" *Journal of the History of Philosophy* 18, no. 2 (April 1980): 147–57.

Sigmund, Paul E. "Law and Politics." In *The Cambridge Companion to Aquinas,* edited by Norman Kretzmann and Eleonore Stump, 217–31. Cambridge: Cambridge University Press, 1993.

Silver, Victoria. "The Fiction of Self-Evidence in Hobbes's *Leviathan.*" *ELH* 55, no. 2 (1988): 351–79.

"A Matter of Interpretation." *Critical Inquiry* 20, no. 1 (Autumn 1993): 160–71.

Simmel, Georg. "Conflict." In *Conflict and the Web of Group Affiliations,* translated by Kurt H. Wolff and Reinhard Bendix. New York: The Free Press, 1964.

Simpson, Peter L. Phillips. *A Philosophical Commentary on the Politics of Aristotle.* Chapel Hill: The University of North Carolina Press, 1998.

Skinner, Quentin. *Hobbes and Civil Science,* volume III of *Visions of Politics.* Cambridge: Cambridge University Press, 2002.

Hobbes and Republican Liberty. Cambridge: Cambridge University Press, 2008.

"Meaning and Understanding in the History of Ideas." *History and Theory* 8, no. 1 (1969): 3–53.

Reason and Rhetoric in the Philosophy of Hobbes. Cambridge: Cambridge University Press, 1996.

Sloan, Kim. *A New World: England's First View of America.* London: The British Museum, 2007.

Slomp, Gabriella. "Hobbes, Thucydides, and the Three Greatest Things." *History of Political Thought* 11, no. 4 (Winter 1990): 565–86.

Thomas Hobbes and the Political Philosophy of Glory. New York: St. Martin's Press, Inc., 2000.

Smiles, Sam. "John White and British Antiquity: Savage Origins in the Context of Tudor Historiography." In *European Visions: American Voices,* edited by Kim Sloan, 106–12. London: The British Museum, 2009.

Smith, Adam. *An Inquiry into the Nature and Causes of the Wealth of Nations.* 2 volumes, edited by R. H. Campbell and A. S. Skinner. Textual editor, W. B. Todd. Indianapolis, IN: Liberty Fund, 1981.

Smith, Arthur Lionel. "English Political Philosophy in the Seventeenth and Eighteenth Centuries." *The Eighteenth Century,* Volume VI of *The Cambridge Modern History,* edited by A. W. Ward, G. W. Prothero, and Stanley Leathes, 785–821, 964–67. New York: The Macmillan Company, 1909.

Smith, Captain John. *The Generall Historie of Virginia, New-England, and the Summer Isles, etc.* London: Michael Sparkes, 1624.

Sommerville, Johann P. "John Selden, the Law of Nature, and the Origins of Government." *The Historical Journal* 27, no. 2 (1984): 437–47.

Politics and Ideology in England, 1603–1640. London: Longman, 1986.

Thomas Hobbes: Political Ideas in Historical Context. New York: St. Martin's Press, 1992.

Somos, Mark. "Hobbes's Use of the Authorised Version, the Geneva and Other Bibles in *Leviathan,* Part III." Ms., on file with the author.

Secularisation and the Leiden Circle. Leiden: Brill, 2011.

Sorell, Tom. *Hobbes.* London: Routledge and Kegan Paul, 1986.

"Hobbes and Aristotle." In *Philosophy in the Sixteenth and Seventeenth Centuries: Conversations with Aristotle,* edited by Constance Blackwell and Sachiko Kusukawa, 364–79. Aldershot: Ashgate, 1999.

"Hobbes and Gassendi." In *The Renaissance and Seventeenth-Century Rationalism,* edited by G. H. R. Parkinson, 235–72. London: Routledge, 1993.

"Hobbes Overcontextualized." *The Seventeenth Century* 16 (2001): 123–46.

"Hobbes's UnAristotelian Political Rhetoric." *Philosophy and Rhetoric* 23, no. 2 (1990): 96–108.

Speed, John. *The History of Great Britaine under the Conquests of ye Romans, Saxons, Danes, and Normans, etc.* London: [William Hall], 1611 [1612].

The Theatre of the Empire of Great Britaine, etc. London: [William Hall], 1611 [1612].

Spragens, Thomas A., Jr. *The Politics of Motion: The World of Thomas Hobbes.* Lexington: The University Press of Kentucky, 1973.

Sprat, Thomas. *The History of the Royal-Society of London, for the Improving of Natural Knowledge.* London: T. R. for J. Martyn and J. Allestry, 1667.

Springborg, Patricia. "Hobbes's Biblical Beasts: Leviathan and Behemoth." *Political Theory* 23, no. 2 (May 1995): 353–75.

"The Paradoxical Hobbes." *Political Theory* 37, no. 5 (2009): 676–88.

Sreedhar, Susanne. *Hobbes on Resistance: Defying the Leviathan.* Cambridge: Cambridge University Press, 2010.

Statius, Publius Papinius. *Silvae.* Translated by D. R. Shackleton Bailey. Cambridge, MA: Harvard University Press, 2003.

Steadman, John M. "Leviathan and Renaissance Etymology." *Journal of the History of Ideas* 28, no. 4 (October–December 1967): 575–76.

Stephen, Leslie. *Hobbes.* London: Macmillan and Co., 1904.

Stillman, Robert E. "Hobbes's *Leviathan*: Monsters, Metaphors, and Magic." *ELH* 62, no. 4 (Winter 1995): 791–819.

Strauss, Leo. *The Political Philosophy of Hobbes: Its Basis and Its Genesis.* Translated by Elsa M. Sinclair. Chicago: The University of Chicago Press, 1952.

Stromberg, Joseph. "Starving Settlers in Jamestown Colony Resorted to Cannibalism." *Smithsonian Magazine.* Retrieved from http://www.smithsonianmag.com/history-archaeology/Starving-Settlers-in-Jamestown-Colony-Resorted-to-Eating-A-Child-205472161.html (last accessed August 3, 2013).

Strong, Tracy B. "How to Write Scripture: Words, Authority, and Politics in Thomas Hobbes." *Critical Inquiry* 20, no. 1 (Autumn 1993): 128–59.

"When Is a Text Not a Pretext? A Rejoinder to Victoria Silver." *Critical Inquiry* 20, no. 1 (Autumn 1993): 172–78.

Struever, Nancy S. "Dilthey's Hobbes and Cicero's Rhetoric." In *Rhetorica Movet: Studies in Historical and Modern Rhetoric in Honour of Heinrich F. Plett,* edited by Peter L. Oesterreich and Thomas O. Sloane, 233–61. Leiden: Brill, 1999.

The Language of History in the Renaissance: Rhetoric and Historical Consciousness in Florentine Humanism. Princeton: Princeton University Press, 1970.

Rhetoric, Modality, Modernity. Chicago: The University of Chicago Press, 2009.

Suetonius Tranquillus, C. *Lives of the Caesars.* 2 volumes. Edited by J. C. Rolfe. Cambridge, MA: Harvard University Press, 2001.

Syme, Ronald. *Tacitus.* 2 volumes. Oxford: The Clarendon Press, 1958.

Syros, Vasileios. "Founders and Kings Versus Orators: Medieval and Early Modern Views on the Origins of Social Life." *Viator* 42, no. 1 (2011): 383–408.

Marsilius of Padua at the Intersection of Ancient and Medieval Traditions of Political Thought. Toronto: University of Toronto Press, 2012.

Die Rezeption der aristotelischen politischen Philosophie bei Marsilius von Padua: Eine Untersuchung zur ersten Diktion des Defensor Pacis. Leiden: Brill, 2007.

Tacitus, Cornelius. *Annals I-III.* In *Tacitus III,* edited by Clifford H. Moore and John Jackson. Cambridge, MA: Harvard University Press, 2005.

Tarlton, Charles D. "The Creation and Maintenance of Government: A Neglected Dimension of Hobbes's *Leviathan*." *Political Studies* 26, no. 3 (1978): 307–27.

Taylor, A. E. *Thomas Hobbes.* London: Archibald Constable and Co., 1908.

Templer, John. *Idea Theologiæ Leviathanis, etc.* London: E. Flesher for G. Morden, 1673.

Tenison, Thomas. *The Creed of Mr. Hobbes Examined; in a Feigned Conference between Him and a Student in Divinity.* Second edition. London: F. Tyton, 1671.

Theophrastus. *Theophrastus of Eresus: Sources for his Life, Writings, Thought, and Influence.* Edited by William W. Fortenbaugh, Pamela M. Huby, Robert W. Sharples, and Dimitri Gutas. 2 volumes. Leiden: Brill, 1992.

Thornton, Helen. *State of Nature or Eden? Thomas Hobbes and His Contemporaries on the Natural Condition of Human Beings.* Rochester, NY: The University of Rochester Press, 2005.

Thucydides. *Eight Bookes of the Peloponnesian Warre, etc.* Translated by Thomas Hobbes. London: Hen. Seile, 1629.

Eight Bookes of the Peloponnesian Warre. Translated by Thomas Hobbes. Edited by Richard Schlatter. New Brunswick, NJ: Rutgers University Press, 1975.

Historiae. Edited by Henry Stuart Jones. 2 volumes. Oxford: The Clarendon Press, 1900–02.

The Peloponnesian War: The Complete Hobbes Translation. Edited by David Grene. Chicago: The University of Chicago Press, 1989.

Tibullus, Albius. *Elegies.* Translated by A. M. Juster. Oxford: Oxford University Press, 2012.

Tierney, Brian. *The Idea of Natural Rights: Studies on Natural Rights, Natural Law, and Church Law 1150–1625.* Grand Rapids, MI: William B. Eerdmans Publishing Company, 1997.

Tilley, Morris Palmer. *A Dictionary of the Proverbs in England in the Sixteenth and Seventeenth Centuries.* Ann Arbor: University of Michigan Press, 1950.

Tricaud, François. "Hobbes's Conception of the State of Nature from 1640 to 1651." In *Perspectives on Thomas Hobbes*, edited by G. A. J. Rogers and A. Ryan, 107–23. Oxford: The Clarendon Press, 1988.

"'Homo homini Deus,' 'Homo homini Lupus': Recherche des sources des deux formules de Hobbes." In *Hobbes Forschungen*, edited by Reinhart Koselleck and Roman Schnur, 61–70. Berlin: Duncker and Humblot, 1969.

Tuck, Richard. *Hobbes.* Oxford: Oxford University Press, 1989.

"Hobbes and Democracy." In *Rethinking the Foundations of Modern Political Thought*, edited by Annabel Brett and James Tully with Holly Hamilton-Bleakley, 171–90. Cambridge: Cambridge University Press, 2006.

"Hobbes and Descartes." In *Perspectives on Thomas Hobbes*, edited by G. A. J. Rogers and A. Ryan, 11–41. Oxford: The Clarendon Press, 1988.

"Hobbes and Tacitus." In *Hobbes and History*, edited by G. A. J. Rogers and Tom Sorell, 99–111. London: Routledge, 2000.

"Optics and Sceptics." In *Conscience and Casuistry in Early Modern Europe*, edited by Edmund Leites, 235–63. Cambridge: Cambridge University Press, 1988.

Philosophy and Government, 1572–1651. Cambridge: Cambridge University Press, 1993.

The Rights of War and Peace: Political Thought and the International Order from Grotius to Kant. Oxford: Oxford University Press, 1999.

"The Utopianism of *Leviathan*." In *Leviathan after 350 Years*, edited by Tom Sorell and Luc Foisneau, 125–38. Oxford: The Clarendon Press, 2004.

Tyrrell, James. *A Brief Disquisition of the Law of Nature, etc.* London, 1692.

Ullman, Walter. *Principles of Government and Politics in the Middle Ages.* New York: Barnes and Noble, 1966.

Vaughan, Alden T. "'Expulsion of the Savages': English Policy and the Virginia Massacre of 1622." *The William and Mary Quarterly* 3rd series 35, no. 1 (1978): 57–84.

Transatlantic Encounters: American Indians in Britain, 1500–1776. Cambridge: Cambridge University Press, 2006.

Verdon, Michel. "Of the Laws of Physical and Human Nature: Hobbes' Physical and Social Cosmologies." *Journal of the History of Ideas* 43, no. 4 (1982): 653–63.

Vickers, Brian. "Territorial Disputes: Philosophy *versus* Rhetoric." In *Rhetoric Revalued: Papers from the International Society for the History of Rhetoric,* edited by Brian Vickers, 247–66. Binghamton, NY: Center for Medieval and Early Renaissance Studies, 1982.

"'Tis the Goddesse of Rhetorick," Review of *Reason and Rhetoric in the Philosophy of Hobbes,* by Quentin Skinner. *Times Literary Supplement,* 16 August 1996, 27–28.

Vindiciæ Contra Tyrannos, or, Concerning the Legitimate Power of a Prince over the People, and of the People over a Prince. Edited by George Garnett. Cambridge: Cambridge University Press, 2003.

Virgil [Publius Vergilius Maro]. *Eclogues, Georgics.* In *Virgil I,* edited by H. R. Fairclough and revised by G. P. Goold. Cambridge, MA: Harvard University Press, 1999.

Virginia Company of London. *A Declaration for the Certaine Time of Dravving the Great Standing Lottery.* London, 1616. *Early English Books Online.* Retrieved from http://gateway.proquest.com.ezproxy.library.tufts.edu/openurl?ctx_ver=Z 39.88-2003&res_id=xri:eebo&rft_id=xri:eebo:image:178646 (last accessed April 6, 2012).

Vitoria, Francisco de. *On the American Indians.* In *Political Writings,* edited by Anthony Pagden and Jeremy Lawrance, 231–92. Cambridge: Cambridge University Press, 1999.

Wallace, Malcolm William. *The Life of Sir Philip Sidney.* Cambridge: Cambridge University Press, 1915.

Wallis, John. *Hobbius Heauton-timorumenos. Or a Consideration of Mr. Hobbes His Dialogves, etc.* Oxford: A. and L. Lichfield for Samuel Thomson, 1662.

Ward, John O. "From Antiquity to the Renaissance: Glosses and Commentaries on Cicero's *Rhetorica.*" In *Medieval Eloquence: Studies in the Theory and Practice of Medieval Rhetoric,* edited by James J. Murphy, 25–67. Berkeley: University of California Press, 1978.

"The Medieval and Early Renaissance Study of Cicero's *De inventione* and the *Rhetorica ad Herennium*: Commentaries and Contexts." In *The Rhetoric of Cicero in Its Medieval and Early Renaissance Commentary Tradition,* edited by Virginia Cox and John O. Ward, 3–75. Leiden: Brill, 2006.

Ward, Seth. *In Thomæ Hobbii Philosophiam Exercitatio Epistolica, etc.* Oxford: H. Hall for Richard Davis, 1656.

Vindiciæ Academiarum Containing, Some Briefe Animadversions upon Mr Websters Book, Stiled The Examination of Academies. Oxford: Leonard Lichfield for Thomas Robinson. 1654.

Warrender, Howard. *The Political Philosophy of Hobbes: His Theory of Obligation.* Oxford: The Clarendon Press, 1957.

Waterhouse, Edward. *A Declaration of the State of the Colony and Affaires in Virginia, with Relation of the Barbarous Massacre in the Time of Peace and League, Treacherously executed by the Natiue Infidels vpon the English, the 22 of March Last, etc.* London: G. Eld for Robert Mylbourne, 1622.

Watkins, J. W. N. *Hobbes's System of Ideas: A Study in the Political Significance of Philosophical Theories.* London: Hutchinson University Library, 1965.

Weinberger, J. "Hobbes's Doctrine of Method." *The American Political Science Review* 69, no. 4 (1975): 1336–53.

West, James King. *Introduction to the Old Testament.* Second edition. New York: Macmillan Publishing Co., 1981.

Westfall, Richard S. *Science and Religion in Seventeenth-Century England.* New Haven, CT: Yale University Press, 1958.

Wey Gómez, Nicolás. *The Tropics of Empire: Why Columbus Sailed South to the Indies.* Cambridge: The Massachusetts Institute of Technology Press, 2008.

Whelan, Frederick. "Language and Its Abuses in Hobbes's Political Philosophy." *American Political Science Review* 75, no. 1 (1981): 59–75.

Whitaker, Alexander. *Good Newes from Virginia, etc.* London: Felix Kyngston for William Welby, 1613.

Wildermuth, Mark E. "Hobbes, Aristotle, and the Materialist Rhetor." *Rhetoric Society Quarterly* 27, no. 1 (1997): 69–80.

Willet, Andrew. *Hexapla in Genesin & Exodum: That is, a Sixfold Commentary upon the Two First Bookes of Moses, being Genesis and Exodus, etc.* London: John Haviland, 1633.

Willey, Basil. *The Seventeenth Century Background: Studies in the Thought of the Age in Relation to Poetry and Religion.* New York: Columbia University Press, 1950.

Williams, Garrath. "Normatively Demanding Creatures: Hobbes, the Fall and Individual Responsibility." *Res Publica* 6 (2000): 301–19.

Williams, Mark F. "Two Traditional Elements in Thucydides' Corcyrean Excursus." *The Classical World* 79, no. 1 (1985): 1–3.

Williams, Michael C. "The Hobbesian Theory of International Relations: Three Traditions." In *Classical Theory in International Relations*, edited by Beate Jahn, 253–76. Cambridge: Cambridge University Press, 2006.

Williams, Robert A. *The American Indian in Western Legal Thought: The Discourses of Conquest.* Oxford: Oxford University Press, 1990.

Wilson, Catherine. *Epicureanism at the Origins of Modernity.* Oxford: The Clarendon Press, 2008.

Wilson, John. "'The Customary Meanings of Words Were Changed' – Or Were They? A Note on Thucydides 3.82.4." *The Classical Quarterly* 32, no. 1 (1982): 18–20.

Wilson, Peter H. *The Thirty Years War: Europe's Tragedy.* Cambridge, MA: Harvard University Press, 2009.

Wittkower, Rudolf. "Monsters of the East: A Study in the History of Monsters." *Journal of the Warburg and Courtauld Institutes* 5 (1942): 159–97.

Wolin, Sheldon. *Hobbes and the Epic Tradition of Political Theory.* Los Angeles: William Andrews Clark Memorial Library, University of California, Los Angeles, 1970.

Politics and Vision: Continuity and Innovation in Western Political Thought. Expanded edition. Princeton, NJ: Princeton University Press, 2004.

Wolseley, Sir Charles. *The Unreasonablenesse of Atheism Made Manifest, etc.* Second edition. London: Nathaniel Ponder, 1669.

Wood, Anthony à. *Historia et Antiquitates Vniversitatis Oxoniensis.* Oxford: Sheldonian Theatre, 1674.

Wood, Neal. *Cicero's Social and Political Thought.* Berkeley: University of California Press, 1988.

Yack, Bernard. *The Problems of a Political Animal: Community, Justice, and Conflict in Aristotelian Political Thought.* Berkeley: University of California Press, 1993.

Zappen, James P. "Aristotelian and Ramist Rhetoric in Thomas Hobbes's *Leviathan*: Pathos versus Ethos and Logos." *Rhetorica: A Journal of the History of Rhetoric* 1, no. 1 (Spring 1983): 65–91.

Index

173n70, 180, 193, 194, 205, 231,
231n20, 232, 233n30, 238
Seneca. *see* Annaeus Seneca, Lucius
Sepúlveda, Juan Ginés de, 204n7
Sergius Catilina, Lucius, 249n9, 251
Settle, Dionise, 208n28
Sextus Empiricus, 67n23, 68n23
Shakespeare, William, 205n14
Shapin, Steven, 237n46
Shapiro, Barbara, 65n10, 96n60
Shapiro, Gary, 49n17, 135n47
Sidney, Sir Philip, 51n26, 52n26
Sigmund, Paul E., 100n86
Silver, Victoria, 15n60, 19n76, 19n81,
20n85, 133n39
Silverthorne, Michael, 88n21, 88n22,
89n26, 92n43, 94n53, 98n75,
100n87, 107n122, 107n122,
108n125, 168n42, 233n28
Simmel, Georg, 222n51
Simpson, Peter L. Phillips, 101n89
Skinner, Quentin, 5n12, 5n13, 5n14, 6n16,
6n18, 6n19, 7n23, 9, 9n31, 10n40,
10n41, 11, 11n47, 15n62, 16n66,
25n1, 25n2, 28n16, 28n17, 45n3,
45n5, 47n13, 48n13, 49n16, 51n23,
51n25, 51n26, 58n56, 78n73, 94n53,
96n60, 193n72, 193n73, 233n31,
241n67, 248n1
Sloan, Kim, 203n5
Slomp, Gabriella, 9n30, 16n63, 19n80,
143n93, 177n91, 192n69
Smiles, Sam, 209n30
Smith, Adam, 202n1, 222n52
Smith, Arthur Lionel, 126n2
Smith, Captain John, 147n108, 221n49
social contract, 1, 15, 112–15, 168, 243,
254n29, 255, 256
Socrates, 92
Solon, 192n69
Sommerville, Johann P., 28n16, 28n17,
29n21, 88n19, 118n171,
119n173, 160n4
Somos, Mark, 65n13, 163n19, 165n22,
165n25
Sophocles, 26
Sorbière, Samuel, 81n2, 82n7, 82n8, 85,
85n13, 86, 86n14
Sorell, Tom, 5n11, 45n3, 48n13, 49n17,
49n18, 78n73, 135n46, 135n47,
138n68, 148n110, 160n4, 178n94,
182n12, 242n69, 250n14
Speed, John, 211, 211n36, 213f10

Spragens, Thomas A., Jr., 160n4
Sprat, Thomas, 237, 237n48
Springborg, Patricia, 135n47, 241n66, 252n20
Sreedhar, Susanne, 254n29
Statius, Publius Papinius, 199n99
Steadman, John M., 127n7
Stephen, Leslie, 29n20
Stillman, Robert E., 127n7, 135n47, 252n20
Strauss, Leo, 5n11, 5n13, 6, 6n17, 6n19,
7n23, 10, 10n38, 10n40, 11, 11n45,
11n47, 16n65, 20n83, 28n17, 29n19,
45n3, 45n5, 47n13, 48n14, 49n16,
51n25, 59n57, 97n67, 99n75,
114n153, 116n156, 132n32, 164n21
Stromberg, Joseph, 224n60
Strong, Tracy, 7n21, 12n48, 50n20, 97n67,
127n6, 132n32, 133n39, 177n87
Struever, Nancy S., 7n21, 10n36, 11n42,
47n13, 57n53, 238n52, 250n14,
253n23
Suetonius. *see* Gaius Suetonius Tranquillus
summum bonum, 16, 20, 40n81, 78,
136–39, 145, 152n136, 154, 241
summum malum, 20–21, 40n81, 73, 102,
103, 136–39, 138n66, 144–47, 242
Syme, Ronald, 208n29
Syros, Vasileios, 100n84, 253n23

Tacitus. *see* Cornelius Tacitus
Talaska, Richard, 205n13
Tarlton, Charles, 245n79
Tate, Nahum, 183n17, 184n21
Taylor, A. E., 29n20
Templer, John, 161n7
Tenison, Thomas, 55n42, 82n6, 159, 159n3,
162n11
Theognis, 151
Theophrastus, 23
Thirty Years War, 27n14, 30n25, 160n4,
195, 244, 244n78
Thornton, Helen, 160n4, 162n8, 163n15,
165n24, 175n83, 177n91
thought experiment, 2, 68, 68n24, 111,
111n141, 115, 116, 121, 121n184,
134, 146, 244
Thucydides, 7, 7n23, 10, 11, 12, 13n52,
14, 14n58, 14n59, 15, 15n63, 16,
16n63, 18, 19, 21, 26–46, 28n16,
28n17, 29n18, 29n21, 30n26, 37n64,
37n65, 40n81, 48n13, 50, 50n20,
51, 56–58, 64, 73n47, 82n6, 86n15,
89–90, 92, 107, 107n121, 107n122,
108, 108n124, 112, 112n142, 119,